ROUTLEDGE LIBRARY EDITIONS:
INDUSTRIAL ECONOMICS

Volume 10

THE INDUSTRIAL DEVELOPMENT OF BIRMINGHAM AND THE BLACK COUNTRY 1860–1927

THE INDUSTRIAL DEVELOPMENT
OF BIRMINGHAM
AND THE BLACK COUNTRY
1860–1927

G. C. ALLEN

With an Introduction by
J. F. REES

Routledge
Taylor & Francis Group

LONDON AND NEW YORK

First published in 1929 by George Allen & Unwin Ltd

This edition first published in 2018
by Routledge
2 Park Square, Milton Park, Abingdon, Oxon OX14 4RN

and by Routledge
711 Third Avenue, New York, NY 10017

Routledge is an imprint of the Taylor & Francis Group, an informa business

British Library Cataloguing in Publication Data
A catalogue record for this book is available from the British Library

ISBN: 978-1-138-30830-5 (Set)
ISBN: 978-1-351-21102-4 (Set) (ebk)
ISBN: 978-0-8153-6929-5 (Volume 10) (hbk)
ISBN: 978-0-8153-6991-2 (Volume 10) (pbk)
ISBN: 978-1-351-25134-1 (Volume 10) (ebk)

Publisher's Note
The publisher has gone to great lengths to ensure the quality of this reprint but points out that some imperfections in the original copies may be apparent.

Disclaimer
The publisher has made every effort to trace copyright holders and would welcome correspondence from those they have been unable to trace.

THE INDUSTRIAL DEVELOPMENT

of BIRMINGHAM

AND THE BLACK COUNTRY

1860-1927

By G. C. ALLEN, M.Com., Ph.D.,

With an Introduction by
J. F. REES, M.A., M.Com.

ILLUSTRATED

LONDON
GEORGE ALLEN & UNWIN LTD
MUSEUM STREET

PRINTED IN GREAT BRITAIN
BY THE RIVERSIDE PRESS LIMITED
EDINBURGH

PREFACE

THE economic development of Birmingham and the Black Country during the eighteenth century has received a good deal of attention, for the part played by the area in the growth of the new iron and engineering trades has necessarily claimed the notice of those who are concerned with modern industrial history. But the development of the district during the nineteenth century has been almost entirely neglected, and nothing at all has been done to describe and to interpret the great changes which have occurred in the course of the last seventy or eighty years. Yet these changes are not only of great intrinsic interest, but they reflect very clearly the forces which of late have been modifying the industrial character of the country as a whole.

For many years before the present work was begun it had been obvious that the industrial life of Birmingham and District was undergoing a process of transformation, which during the war and the post-war depression was immensely accelerated. Many of the older trades, it was seen, were decaying; while at the same time a number of new manufactures were making a remarkably rapid advance. It was clear that, as a result of these developments, the industrial structure of the area during the third decade of the twentieth century was made up of very different constituents from those of which it was composed fifty or sixty years previously. It was thought desirable, therefore, to make an investigation of these changes with the object of discovering their magnitude, the period when they began, and the causes which brought them about. This contribution to regional economic history, which was made possible through a generous endowment,[1] has resulted.

Fortunately, a study of the leading West Midland industries had been made, under the editorship of Samuel Timmins, when the British Association visited Birmingham in 1866. The accounts of the trades which were included in *Birmingham and the Midland Hardware District* varied greatly in value from the standpoint of the economic historian; but they provided detailed information, which could be supplemented from numerous

---

[1] See note on p. xv.

other sources, concerning certain aspects of the local industrial structure. It was thus possible to obtain a more comprehensive and accurate conception of the character of the area during the sixties than at any subsequent or preceding date. The period when these studies were made, moreover, happened to correspond roughly to a point of time which immediately preceded an era of far-reaching industrial change. This fortunate coincidence, then, settled the point of departure in this investigation at somewhere during the early sixties. It was thought necessary, however, that the work should begin with a brief account of the development of the area up to that date, as this would serve to bring out clearly the changes in the direction of industrial growth and in the tendencies which were to be investigated. So the book begins with an outline of the district's early history. A detailed account is then given of the character, size and localization of the leading trades as they appeared in 1860; while the main subject-matter of the succeeding chapters consists of a description of the changes in the relative magnitude of the different trades, of the decay of the older manufactures and the rise of new ones, and of the general transformation in the area's industrial activities.

The scope of the work is, however, wider than this; for my second object has been to examine the forms of industrial organization which have existed in the area at different times. Along with the changes in the relative importance of the leading industries there has occurred during the last sixty years an equally significant transformation in the methods of manufacture and of marketing, in the scale of production, and in the relation between the individual business units. So, after describing the way in which the major trades were organized in 1860, I have tried to show how and when the new forms of organization began to displace the old, and what forces were responsible for the modifications which have taken place.

This book, then, resolves itself into two main parts: first, a history of the changes which have occurred since 1860 in the industrial interests of Birmingham and the Black Country; and, second, a history of certain aspects of industrial organization within the area. The multiplicity of the district's trades has made it impossible for me to describe any one of them in great detail; while certain minor manufactures have necessarily been ignored. Some important aspects of industrial organization, moreover, have been passed over, or have not received the attention which they merit, and which they could claim in a specialized study. My aim has been to give a picture of general industrial change, to record faithfully the outstanding characteristics of a great manufacturing area during the course of the last seventy years, and to indicate the main trends and influences to which it has been subjected.

Of the sources of the written materials which have been consulted the excellent Birmingham Collection in the Birmingham Public Reference Library has proved the most useful; while the Wolverhampton Public Library, the Coventry Public Library and private collections have also been found to contain valuable information. The earlier part of the work has naturally depended to a large extent on these written materials. Yet, since the history covers a period within the memory of men now living, it has been possible to gather the bulk of the data required for the work, and to check and to supplement printed authorities, by personal inquiries among those who are, or who have been, connected with local industries. I succeeded in discovering within each of the major trades a few representative firms who were willing to assist me, and it has been from interviews with their proprietors and officials that the most valuable part of the information has been obtained. This applies particularly to the sections of the book which deal with organization. In some industries trade associations and trade union officials have been consulted; while another important source of material has consisted of works histories and the private publications of certain old-established concerns.

I have not thought it desirable to give references to the sources of the information which has been gleaned from interviews or from works histories and souvenirs, for the majority of the firms, in providing information, expressed a wish that no mention should be made of them. This accounts for the paucity of references in the latter part of the book, which is based almost entirely on personal inquiries; but these omissions are not serious, as statements concerning recent developments can be easily checked by consultation with business men engaged in trades to which the statements refer. For similar reasons the names of existing concerns have not been mentioned, except when the context has made their identity clear to anyone in close touch with West Midland industrial life.

Since it is not possible for me to express my indebtedness to every member of the local business community who has generously given of his time in describing to me the growth of his industry, and in explaining the organization and the processes of manufacture, I should like to offer my thanks to all firms in the Midland area who have supplied me with data for this work. The secretiveness and lack of concern with matters of general interest with which the British business man is sometimes charged have certainly not been conspicuous (with a few notable exceptions) among local manufacturers. Indeed, the work could not have been carried out without their close co-operation. In particular I should like to record my obligations to the following, either because they supplied me with material of special value, or because they put me in touch with sources of information in connection with trades in which the data were scanty: Mr Dudley Evans, Secretary of the Iron Exchange, Birmingham; Mr Edwards, Secretary of the Birmingham Association of Gunmakers (for valuable information concerning the old gun trade); Mr R. E. Freeman, Secretary of the Brassfounders Employers' Federation; Colonel F. Goode (for a valuable account of the brush trade); Mr Gibbard, Secretary of the National Association of Amalgamated Brassworkers; Mr J. W. Hall (for much useful material concerning the Staffordshire iron trade); Mr F. Hickinbotham of Messrs Rabone Bros. & Co.; Mr G. Head of Tipton (for information about the local pig-iron industry); Mr Edgar Harcourt (for help in connection with the history of the brassfoundry industry); Mr Hoadley (for an account of the history of the bedstead trade); Messrs Joseph Gillott and Messrs Leonardt (for material concerning the pen trade); Mr G. W. Mullins of the Cold Rolled Brass and Copper Association; Messrs Legge and Chilton (for information concerning the lock trade); Mr C. E. Partridge of Rubery, Owen & Co., who went to great trouble to provide me with data in connection with the Darlaston industries; the Staffordshire Ironmasters' Association; Mr G. E. Wright, Secretary of the Birmingham Chamber of Commerce; Mr H. W. Ward (for a history of the machine-tool trade), and Mr H. Reece (for information concerning the chain industry). I have to record my special indebtedness to the Birmingham Small Arms Co. Ltd. for their kindness in lending me a detailed history (in manuscript) of their firm. I should also mention that I have made use of several theses which have been submitted for the degree of Master of Commerce at Birmingham University. The most valuable of these proved to be a *History of the Midland Glass Trade,* by G. N. Sandilands, and *The History, Development and Organization of the Birmingham Jewellery and Allied Trades,* by J. C. Roche. Mr Roche also did useful work in typing and indexing the notes which I had obtained from printed sources.

Several local firms supplied me with photographs, from which certain of the illustrations in this book have been prepared. The concerns which were good enough to help me in this way were the Austin Motor Co. Ltd., the Birmingham Small Arms Co. Ltd., British Pens Ltd., Messrs Cadbury Bros. Ltd., Messrs Earle, Bourne & Co. Ltd., Alfred Hickman Ltd., the Metropolitan-Cammell Carriage, Wagon and Finance Co. Ltd., and Messrs Taylor & Challen Ltd. My thanks are due to these firms, to Mr A. Fenn for lending me a photograph from his collection, and to Mr Hugo van Wadenoyen, F.R.P.S., for his two photographic studies of the Black Country.

I am very grateful to the staffs of the local reference libraries for their assistance during the period when I was consulting printed records, and I am particularly indebted to the officials of the Birmingham Public Reference Library, whom I put to great trouble. I have also to thank Miss E. C. M. Shanks for help in the preparation of the index.

Finally, I must record my deep obligations to Professor J. F. Rees, who supervised the research and gave me invaluable advice at every stage of the work.

G. C. ALLEN.

University of Birmingham,
June 1929.

b

MAP OF BIRMINGHAM AND THE BLACK COUNTRY
SHOWING CHIEF INDUSTRIAL TOWNS AND VILLAGES.

REFERENCES   SCALE: 2 MILES TO AN INCH.
BOUNDARY OF THE CITY OF BIRMINGHAM (1911) ....
AND OF THE BOROUGH OF WOLVERHAMPTON (1927) -------
BOUNDARY OF BIRMINGHAM & THE BLACK COUNTRY -----
(AS DEFINED IN PART I, CHAP. I)

CONTENTS

xi

CONTENTS

PART V

WAR AND POST-WAR, 1914–1927

APPENDICES

MAPS

INTRODUCTION

THE genesis of this book demands a word of explanation. Four years ago " A Birmingham Firm " put at the disposal of the University of Birmingham a sum of money with the request that the Faculty of Commerce should undertake a survey of the industrial development of Birmingham and District during the last half-century.[1] The main lines of the proposed inquiry were defined as an examination of the nature of the leading industries, their relative position, the scale of operations, the methods of organization and the distribution of the labour force. The endowment enabled the University to appoint a Research Fellow in Industrial History. Fortunately, Mr G. C. Allen, a graduate of the University and a native of the Midlands, returned from Japan at this juncture and was elected to the Fellowship. Those who have met him during the four years he has been engaged in collecting material will recognize that the confidence he has inspired has been an important factor in securing that co-operation with business men which was essential for his purpose.

The first problem we had to solve was that of the demarcation of the area within which the inquiry was to be confined. Close consideration of this was necessary because those who had conceived the idea of the survey were anxious that particular stress should be laid on the evolution of industrial organization. It was at once obvious that Birmingham, though so many of its industries were peculiar to itself, had the most intimate relations with the Black Country. So the limits of a definite industrial region were carefully drawn. As the work advanced, the preliminary decisions with respect to this area were discovered to be fully justified. The contrast between Birmingham and the Black Country provided a major theme. Many forces which have been at work in effecting the economic adjustments of the last half-century were brought out into sharp relief. Migration of industries within the region has long been a recognized fact. An acute observer some ninety years ago remarked that, " as

[1] In all public references to this piece of research the endowment has always been ascribed to " A Birmingham Firm." Now that the work is complete, the benefactors have agreed that their identity may be revealed. The University would not have been in a position to entrust the Faculty of Commerce with the task of preparing this survey had it not been for the financial assistance of Cadbury Brothers Ltd., Bournville.

the trade in light and fancy articles advanced, machinery and the beneficial division of labour were introduced. Large colonies of ingenious workmen flocked to the town (*i.e.* Birmingham), the simple operations of the hammer and anvil retired. The ' smiths ' and ' lorimers ' retreated to Walsall, Willenhall and Wednesbury—the ' naylors ' were found as constituting the mass of the population in various districts dependent on Dudley and Stourbridge." [1] The present survey illustrates the inter-relations between Birmingham and the Black Country in a more scientific spirit and in much greater detail. Every effort has been made to account for changes and so to exhibit the working of the principles which have wrought far-reaching changes in the industrial structure of the region.

The promoters of the survey, while they wished the method to be historical, made it a definite instruction that it should be brought down to the present day. When we considered what precise interpretation should be placed on the last half-century, which was admittedly only a rough indication, it was decided to make 1860 the point of departure. There were two reasons for this decision. The sixties witnessed the culmination of the industrial development of the first part of the nineteenth century. We also had to hand a valuable account of the position of the chief industries in the early sixties. In *The Industrial History of Birmingham and the Midland Hardware District* Samuel Timmins certainly succeeded in his aim of collecting and preserving " a large and important mass of industrial facts." [2] It is true that the contributions which he included are of unequal merit, but the book as a whole is a mine of information. Without it the present project would have been a much more difficult one. To begin to write industrial history from such a recent date is something of a novelty. Large books which treat the subject as a whole, as well as special studies devoted to particular industries, usually fail to carry the story beyond the middle of the nineteenth century. An attempt is here made to concentrate attention on a restricted area and to present its development in the last sixty or seventy years as a matter of objective history.

Perhaps enough has been said to indicate what our general instructions were and how they were interpreted. A word ought

[1] William Hawkes Smith : *Birmingham and South Staffordshire* (1838).
[2] Samuel Timmins : *The Resources, Products and Industrial History of Birmingham and the Midland Hardware District* (1866).

to be added about the method of procedure. Mr Allen could give all his time to the searching for printed and manuscript material and to arranging interviews with business men who were likely to be able to supply special information. As has been mentioned, he proved himself a most competent investigator. He assumes full responsibility for the survey now presented to the public. But it ought to be added that the endowment of this important piece of research had a stimulating effect on the general research work of the Faculty. Mr Allen has been assisted at certain points by investigations simultaneously undertaken by some of our graduate students. Two holders of the William Morton Scholarship, who were required by the conditions of the award to examine "A Midland Industry," relieved Mr Allen to a considerable extent of the burden of conducting personal inquiries in the subjects they had chosen. Mr J. C. Roche prepared a valuable survey of the history of the Jewellery Trades and Mr D. N. Sandilands of the Glass Industry. These dissertations are frequently referred to in the notes to the present work. We greatly regret that the sudden death of another researcher, Mr Edmund Pritchard, deprived us of the co-operation which he had promised and was so well qualified to give with respect to the history of the South Staffordshire coalfield.[1]

Historical interpretation is simply the presentation of generalizations which are provisionally acceptable. With the advance of knowledge these generalizations nearly always require to be qualified. Possibly economic history has suffered to a peculiar degree from hasty generalization. What was true of one area has been too often assumed to be representative of the country as a whole. When it is discovered that this is not necessarily so, critics are inclined to react too violently against the accepted view. This is what has happened with respect to the " Industrial Revolution." The conceptions which have become current about the economic and social changes of the later eighteenth and early nineteenth century have now been assailed. It is of

[1] Mr Roche's thesis was published in 1927 as a supplement to *The Dial*, by the Dennison Watch Case Company Ltd., in collaboration with the Birmingham Jewellers' and Silversmiths' Association. The typescript of Mr Sandilands' work may be consulted in the Birmingham University Library. Mr Pritchard's papers are in the possession of his friend, Mr James Cossar, of the Oxford School of Geography.

course true that an account of industrial development which is based on selected facts must be inadequate. To get a more just view of the " Industrial Revolution " the regional method should be adopted. Out of a group of such studies the material for new generalizations will emerge. It is a commonplace that the earlier accounts of the " Industrial Revolution " were based too exclusively on the history of the textile industries. The invention of machinery and the application of steam-power to its operation seemed so important that changes were assumed to have taken place more rapidly and more generally than was actually the case. The study of the West Midlands supplies a corrective. Here the textiles played an insignificant part. While it was one of the first areas to be industrialized, it was slow to adopt the " factory system " which is popularly associated with that process. Unlike Lancashire, the West Riding of Yorkshire, the Clyde Valley, or South Wales, it has never had a predominant staple industry. The multiplicity of its activities are at first sight bewildering. It is possible to quote instances of continuity, such as that of the industries of Walsall, of which Plot quaintly remarks in the seventeenth century that they " chiefly relate to somewhat of Horsemanship." [1] There have been migrations into the area, such as the coming of needles to Redditch. Examples of transition from a decaying trade to a new application of the skill of the craftsman are numerous, but perhaps the rise of the jewellery trade on the ruins of the buckle and trinket trades is the best. Some trades have enjoyed considerable reputation and then virtually disappeared. This was the fate of papier mâché, which once commanded a wide market for its products. In the Black Country local mineral resources, particularly of coal and iron, exercised a decisive influence. The consequences of their gradual exhaustion are clearly indicated in its history. But even here industries were established and maintained which, on the face of it, seem surprising developments, such as the making of ships' cables and anchors.

The ingenuity of local historians has been exercised in trying to discover and account for the stages in the industrial growth of the area. As far as Birmingham is concerned, apart from the fact that the small community had the advantage of a market, little is known of its activities in the Middle Ages. We gather

[1] Plot, *History of Staffordshire* (1686), p. 376.

from sixteenth-century references that the raw material of the district was worked up into semi-manufactured or manufactured goods. In the first category falls the preparing of leather by a dozen or more tanneries; and in the second, the output of numerous small forges, where smiths made bits, spurs, nails and other iron articles.[1] It is possible to indicate roughly what additions were made to these occupations of the people in each subsequent half-century.[2] But when it comes to explaining why Birmingham became the centre of so many and such various industries, writers resort either to platitudes or to an enumeration of minor causes, the cumulative effects of which do not strike one as likely to have had any decisive influence. Paradoxes abound. The town, which since it was not incorporated afforded an asylum to Dissenters, who are said to have laid the foundation of its industrial greatness, was also the scene of " Church and King " riots, of which some of the Nonconformists had to bear the brunt. A people whose " virile and enterprising individualism " is alleged to be the key to its prosperity has always been peculiarly susceptible to leadership and mass-suggestion. A place where the skill of the craftsman is given as a reason for its attracting and holding power has made singularly little positive effort to train its workpeople. The question of the localization of industry is much more complicated than it is often supposed to be. Even such an apparently simple case as that of the growth of the cotton industry in Lancashire, particularly the distribution of the different processes within the area, presents considerable difficulties. In the West Midlands one hesitates to be dogmatic. Mr Allen notices some of the explanations commonly put forward; but the general effect of his research is to warn us against generalizations on the subject.

It is obvious that the enterprise of certain individuals made the most of the opportunities which accidentally came in their way. Of this the career of Matthew Boulton is an outstanding example. He inherited a typical eighteenth-century Birmingham business. When he removed from Snow Hill to Handsworth, and occupied his new buildings at Soho, his intention was to

[1] On this question Professor Conrad Gill has kindly allowed me to read his essay on " Birmingham in the Sixteenth Century," which he intends to publish together with other studies of the history of Midland municipal development.

[2] See chapters in R. K. Dent, *The Making of Birmingham* (1894); the rise of the brass and copper trades is dealt with in H. Hamilton, *The English Brass and Copper Industries to 1800* (1926).

develop that business by setting himself to improve the standard of quality of the metal " toys " he was engaged in making. The gradual change-over to engineering and the eventual foundation of Soho Foundry were due to an accidental chain of events. Financial embarrassments led Dr John Roebuck of the Carron Ironworks to transfer his rights in James Watt's engine to Boulton. Otherwise, Watt might never have left Scotland. It may, indeed, be said that the " artificial " nature of this enterprise was demonstrated by the event. That it succeeded at all was due to the genius of Watt, combined with the business acumen of Boulton. Soho was, and continued to be, an exception. The principles which it exhibited had no influence on the general practice of the district. It was a " factory " in an area of small workshops. Problems of lay-out were grappled with, systems of accounting and of the keeping of records of orders were elaborated, methods of wage payment and industrial insurance were adopted; in fact, the organization would do credit to modern business practice.[1] But all this was of no interest to the small masters of Birmingham. Nor had they any use for the products of Soho. When Boulton playfully boasted to James Boswell that he was selling power, which all the world desired, he might have added that there was no particular demand for it in the immediate neighbourhood. Engineering was hardly appropriately placed in Birmingham. There is a curious *lacuna* in its history. Boulton and Watt were pioneers who had no immediate successors in the district.

What may be called the normal process of industrialization in the area followed very different lines, and is marked by some interesting characteristics. Where the " factory system " was adopted outright the employer had to find capital and take upon himself the risks of the enterprise. He usually financed his venture by entering into partnership with a person or persons of means, or by private borrowing. For development he depended on the investment of profits in the business. It has been contended that this fact explains the intense degree of exploitation

---

[1] The records of the Boulton-Watt firm are preserved in the Birmingham City Library. Some indication of the abundance and variety of the material may be gathered from *Capital and Steam-power*, by John Lord (1923), and from *James Watt and the Steam Engine*, by H. W. Dickinson and Rhys Jenkins (1927). It still awaits comprehensive examination. As the means of constructing the history of the pioneer engineering firm in the world its value can hardly be exaggerated.

of labour in the early decades of the nineteenth century. The lower the labour cost the larger the surplus which would be available for capital development. When the mechanism of the joint stock company provided means for mobilizing the savings of the small investor the pressure on the standard of living of the worker was somewhat relaxed.[1] These generalizations hardly apply to this area. The remarkable fact which emerges from a study of organization is the extent to which the entrepreneur evaded the problems which are involved in the direct employment of labour. Proprietors of coal-mines in the Black Country relied on the " butty " system, by which small subcontractors engaged to get coal at an agreed price and employed their own labour for the purpose. They assumed the odium of exploitation and did not shrink from adopting methods in which the proprietors would not have had the opportunity, even if they had had the desire, to indulge. The petty tyrannies of the system, and particularly its intimate connection with the practice of " truck," are amply illustrated in contemporary Parliamentary Reports. Similar arrangements were made in the ironworks, where different classes of " overhands " with their respective gangs undertook the work. It was in effect the application to large unified enterprises of the principles which were appropriate to the domestic system. In the industries where small units survived the factor performed the function of supplying the credit which the outworker required. This was the common organization of the Birmingham trades until the middle of the nineteenth century, and survived to a much later date in some.

Even when workers were collected in factories the practices of the earlier period persisted. One of the most interesting points which Mr Allen makes with respect to the stages in the development of industrial organization is that there was a phase when the factory system was in a state which may be called immature. The employer provided the workplace and its chief equipment, but he did not exercise control through a discipline imposed by foremen appointed by himself. " Overhands " engaged and paid the labour. What wages they received was not the immediate concern of the factory owner. If there was exploitation—and there is every reason to believe that there was

---

[1] There are some suggestive remarks on this subject in G. D. H. Cole's *Short History of the British Working Class Movement*, vol. i., pp. 179-180.

—the responsibility for it rested on the shoulders of the sub-contractors. The defects of this system are fully demonstrated by Mr Allen. No doubt it was to a considerable degree a solution of the problem of regimentation which was a great difficulty in the early stages of the factory system. Outworkers did not take kindly to the discipline of the factory. Complaints of bad time-keeping are constantly made where men who had been brought up in the looser domestic system were introduced into a factory. In the cutlery trades of Sheffield and the felt-hat industry of Stockport and Denton parallels to the Birmingham immature stage of factory development may be found. Employers, since they had not elaborated methods of supervision and costing systems, were attempting to make what they could from the economies of a larger unit of production without embarrassing themselves with the more troublesome questions of wage rates, hours of labour and general factory conditions. Except for a few industries, such as that of pen manufacture in Birmingham, the employers were men of limited resources. When Richard Cobden was commenting on John Bright's election as Member of Parliament for Birmingham in 1857 he drew an interesting contrast between Manchester and Birmingham. " I have always had [the opinion]," he wrote to Bright, " that the social and political state of that town [Birmingham] is far more healthy than that of Manchester; and it arises from the fact that the industry of the hardware district is carried on by small manufacturers . . . whilst the great capitalists in Manchester form an aristocracy, individual members of which wield an influence over sometimes two thousand persons. . . . There is a freer intercourse between all classes than in the Lancashire town, where a great and impassable gulf separates the workman from his employer." [1]

It is impossible to indicate here the significance of the conclusions to which Mr Allen's examination of the later development of the region leads. He reveals the fortunes of the older industries under the strain of the great depression of the late seventies and early eighties of the last century. The rise of new industries and the effects of the Great War and post-war conditions upon them are also carefully studied. In broad terms, adaptation has involved increasing concentration on the production of finished goods of high quality. The West Midlands may be said to

[1] Lord Morley, *Life of Richard Cobden*, vol. ii., chapter viii.

have anticipated the course which British manufactures as a whole seem now to be taking. It has maintained its supremacy in spite of the loss of cruder and heavier types of industry. How this has been done cannot perhaps be fully explained; but the concluding sections of this study offer many suggestions which contribute towards an answer to the question. That is as far as we can go. The present is the outcome of the past and the forerunner of the future. A survey such as the present one brings tendencies to light and enables the student to correct old and enunciate new generalizations. It becomes the basis for a better understanding of industrial evolution. We are also not without hope that this study of the history and structure of industry will appeal to the business man and serve to stimulate his interest in the wider bearings of his everyday activities.

J. F. REES.

BIRMINGHAM,
June 1929.

GEOLOGICAL MAP
OF BIRMINGHAM AND THE BLACK COUNTRY.

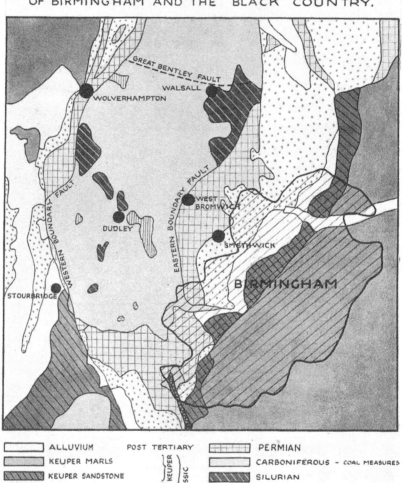

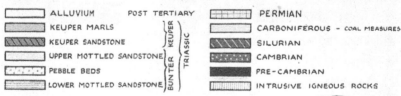

	ALLUVIUM	POST TERTIARY		PERMIAN
	KEUPER MARLS			CARBONIFEROUS - COAL MEASURES
	KEUPER SANDSTONE			SILURIAN
	UPPER MOTTLED SANDSTONE			CAMBRIAN
	PEBBLE BEDS			PRE-CAMBRIAN
	LOWER MOTTLED SANDSTONE			INTRUSIVE IGNEOUS ROCKS

THE AREA OF THE CITY OF BIRMINGHAM IS SHADED THUS

SCALE: 2 MILES TO AN INCH

[To face page 1

PART I
INTRODUCTORY

CHAPTER I

THE AREA DEFINED

THE area with which we are concerned in this survey can be defined with some accuracy and detail, for it has possessed throughout the last sixty years of its history clearly marked characteristics which separate it from the neighbouring districts. This is rather surprising because the area does not form an administrative unit, and its limits are not fixed by physical features of any kind. Neither rivers, hills nor any peculiarities of surface configuration coincide with the line of its boundaries ; and while it is true that the rocks lying beneath its surface have had an important influence on its economic development, its geological structure is not by any means homogeneous. The area is, in fact, to be regarded as a unit solely from an industrial point of view, and the characteristics which enable it to be distinguished are economic rather than physical or administrative. It might be expected that the boundary of a district which is essentially industrial should have changed profoundly between 1860 and 1927. During the course of nearly seven decades, indeed, the larger towns have spread over the surrounding countryside, and the industries of the district have extended to neighbouring centres of population which, at the beginning of this period, were either predominantly agricultural or concerned with manufactures which were in no way connected with those of the area. Yet, although it will be important to notice such modifications as have occurred from time to time with the extension of the industries of the district, or with changes in its economic character, no marked deviations from the boundary line which will now be described have occurred.

Roughly, the area may be said to consist of the City of Birmingham, according to its present limits, and of that part of South Staffordshire and of North Worcestershire which is known as the Black Country. A more accurate conception is arrived at by considering the country enclosed by a line drawn from the north-eastern boundary of Birmingham, near Short Heath, north-west to Walsall and Bloxwich, from there to the north-western outskirts of Wolverhampton, then south through Kingswinford to the western limits of Wordsley and Stourbridge, and from there eastwards through Hales Owen to the western edge of Birmingham. The present boundary of Birmingham forms the south-western and western limits, except where our boundary line takes in Sutton Coldfield, and so parts of the three counties of Stafford, Warwick and Worcester will be dealt with in this survey.

The area thus defined is at the present time concerned almost entirely with industry and commerce, and it is only in the southern section of the City of Birmingham, and on the edges of the district as a whole, that there is a fringe of agriculture. In 1860, the industrialization was not, of course, so complete; but even in parts which were then predominantly agricultural, such as the parishes of Northfield and King's Norton, certain domestic industries typical of the area were extensively carried on, and consequently they and other parishes with similar characteristics may be regarded as forming part of our industrial district then as now. Further, there are certain towns and villages which, though isolated geographically, belong to the area on account of their economic character, and these also fall within the scope of the survey. The most important of these industrial centres at the present time is the City of Coventry; but, for reasons which will be considered later, Coventry is not held to form part of our area in 1860, and it is not until the eighties that it begins to be linked up. On the other hand, the manufactures of Redditch and of the neighbouring villages, such as Alcester and Studley, have borne from early times such a close relationship to those of Birmingham and District that they have been included from the beginning of the survey. These form the most substantial additions to our territory. Several important industries, however, though centred within our boundary line, have been carried on at different periods in outlying agricultural districts, and these will be considered in so far as their manufactures can be regarded as offshoots of those associated with our area. To this limited extent, then, such places as Bromsgrove, Bellbroughton, Brewood and Pelsall will fall within the scope of this history.

When these outlying districts—which may be regarded, from an industrial point of view, as offshoots of the compact area falling within our boundary line—are included, the area coincides so nearly with that defined in the Industry Tables of the Census of 1921 as " Birmingham and District" that this description is worth quoting; for it will afford an indication of the cities, towns and villages to which our attention will be directed throughout the course of this survey. Birmingham and District, according to this authority, consists of the following:—

part of Staffordshire—viz. the county boroughs of Smethwick, Walsall, West Bromwich and Wolverhampton; the municipal borough of Wednesbury; the urban districts of Amblecote, Bilston, Brierley Hill, Brownhills, Coseley, Darlaston, Heath-town or Wednesfield Heath, Perry Barr, Quarry Bank, Rowley Regis, Sedgeley, Short Heath, Tetten-hall, Tipton, Wednesfield and Willenhall; the rural districts of Dudley and Walsall;

part of Warwickshire — viz. the county boroughs of Birmingham and Coventry; the municipal borough of Sutton Coldfield; the rural districts of Coventry, Foleshill, Meriden and Solihull;

part of Worcestershire—viz. the county borough of Dudley; the urban districts of Bromsgrove, Lye, and Wollescote, North Bromsgrove, Oldbury, Redditch and Stourbridge; the rural districts of Bromsgrove and Hales Owen.

Although attention will be concentrated on the area previously described, we shall be concerned incidentally, when not directly, with all these places, with the exception of the rural districts lying to the east of Birmingham.

The district within the boundary line has a total area of about 200 square miles. Its length from north to south ranges from 17 miles between Bloxwich and Rednal to 12 miles between Wolverhampton and Old Swinford; while in width it is about 8 miles in the north between Walsall and Wolverhampton, and 16 miles at its widest point between Kingswinford and the extreme edge of the western boundary of Birmingham. A part of the main watershed of England, which here separates the basins of the Severn and the Trent, runs through this district, and the heights of which it is formed give to the area its main topographical features.[1] In South Staffordshire and North Worcestershire this watershed appears as a series of hills running diagonally to the south-east, and is composed of the heights of Sedgeley, Wren's Nest, Dudley Castle and Rowley. It is continued in the rounded points of Warley and Frankley, and leaves the district in the high and bold ridge of Clent and

[1] For the following account of the topography and geology of the district see C. Lapworth, *The Birmingham Country* in the *Handbook for Birmingham and the Neighbourhood* (British Association Meeting, 1913), p. 549 *et seq.*; C. Lapworth, *The Geology of the Birmingham District* in the *Proceedings of the Geologists' Association*, August 1898; and C. Naden, *The Geology of the Birmingham District* in *Further Reliques*, 1891.

Lickey, which lies just beyond the boundary line. Within our area the watershed nowhere attains a height of more than 900 feet above sea-level; but it suffices to provide the dominant feature of the landscape and to divide the district into two main surface areas. To the north there is a gently undulating plateau of from 400 to 500 feet above sea-level. This rises sharply in the east at Barr Beacon, and it is divided in the extreme west by a secondary watershed which runs by Wednesfield to Bushbury, and separates the basin of the Penk from that of the Tame. The City of Birmingham stands on a transitional belt of country, where the uplands of South Staffordshire break down irregularly into the central Warwickshire lowlands, and its surface consists of an alternation of low, rounded hills and shallow stream valleys. It is drained by the River Rea, which runs through the south-east of the city and, by its affluents, into the Tame. This latter river, which rises in the centre of the Black Country and flows through the Hamstead Gap in the Barr Ridge, just north of Aston, to join the Trent ten miles beyond Tamworth, thus drains the whole of our district (including Birmingham) north of the main watershed. To the south of the divide the country is more varied in its surface configuration, and it contains at Lye and Hales Owen curious hollows which have been washed out of the South Staffordshire plateau. This part of the area is drained by the River Stour into the Severn, while the isolated industrial district of which Redditch is the centre is drained by the Arrow into the Avon.

Physically the streams flowing into the Trent are in marked contrast to those entering the Severn; for while the former have the appearance of maturity, and occupy broad valleys with gentle gradients, the Stour and the Arrow are confined in their upper reaches to ravine-like valleys. This contrast is of importance to the economic historian, for the steeper gradients and the greater and more constant supply of water in the Severn rivers have given them a marked advantage over the others in the provision of water-power.[1]

Over the greater part of Birmingham and the Black Country the original surface features have been so entirely destroyed by industrial activity and urban development that little attention

[1] R. H. Kinvig, *The North-West Midlands* in *Great Britain, Essays in Regional Geography* (1928), p. 212.

need be paid to topography; but the geological structure invites a more detailed consideration because of its influence on the economic development of the area as a whole and on the sites of the chief towns. The rocks which floor that part of South Staffordshire and North Worcestershire which is known as the Black Country have been bent into a long, low, anticlinal arch, from which the originally overlying Permian and Triassic rocks have been denuded, so as to lay bare the coal-measures. These form the " visible " coal-field, and within that part of it which is bounded by Smethwick, Oldbury, Walsall, Dudley and Bilston, thirteen or fourteen seams coalesce to form the " thick," or " ten yard," coal for which the district was long famous. To the south, near Hales Owen, where the measures thin out, the seams become mixed with shale; and they terminate against the red sandstones (or so-called Permian strata) of the Clent Hills. As they pass to the north, the seams become separated by intermediate sandstones and shales; so that at Pelsall and Essington the " thick " coal is represented by fourteen distinct seams resting in a mass of barren rock. Thus there is an important distinction between the southern and the northern sections of the South Staffordshire coal-field. The line of division between the two is determined by the Great Bentley Fault, which runs east and west just north of Walsall. To the south of this is the Black Country coal-field, to which our survey is confined. To the north lies the Cannock district.

The main anticlinal, which is the dominant feature of the Black Country's geological structure, is broken up by three minor anticlinals, and rocks of the underlying Palæozoic systems protrude through the sheet which forms the " visible " coal-field. These outcrops must be briefly referred to, because they have proved of value to the industries of the locality. To the north-east of our district, in the neighbourhood of Walsall and Barr, there is an outcrop of Silurian limestone and shale with a surface area of about two square miles. In the heart of the Black Country the hills of Sedgeley, Wren's Nest and Dudley Castle are similarly formed; and the Netherton anticlinal, in the south-west, exposes Silurian rocks at Lye. In contrast to these are the Rowley Hills, which are composed of basalt. From an economic point of view the anticlinals of South Staffordshire are of great importance. The hills and plains are all related to them—

the former marking the outcrops of the uplifted harder rocks (the limestones), the latter the softer rocks (the shales and clay) ; and the arches have brought within working distance of the surface the coal, ironstone, brick-clay, fire-clay and limestone which have formed the raw materials for most of the local industries.

It has been shown that the boundary of our district coincides with the Great Bentley Fault in the north and with the limits of the " visible " coal-measures in the south-west. Our western boundary, moreover, extends only a short distance beyond the Western Boundary Fault, where the coal-measures are faulted against a narrow band of Permian (so-called) strata. The greater part of Wolverhampton rests on sandstones of that age ; but its suburb, Tettenhall, and Kingswinford and Stourbridge are floored by rocks of the Triassic series. In spite of a few exceptions, then, the limits of the " visible " coal-measures deviate to a surprisingly small extent in the north, south and west from the boundary which has been assigned to the area on economic grounds alone, and this coincidence is an indication of how strongly the geological structure of the district has influenced its industrial development. In the east, however, the matter is more complicated. The Eastern Boundary Fault, against which the coal-measures terminate, runs north from California and Quinton through Oldbury and Swan Village to the north-east of Walsall. East of this fault the coal is overlaid by a broad outcrop of red sandstone of the (so-called) Permian series, on which parts of Oldbury, West Bromwich and Smethwick rest. Beyond this belt of Permian strata there occurs that formation which is " the Birmingham system *par excellence* "—viz. the Triassic formation.[1] Part of Smethwick, Harborne, Handsworth and part of Aston all stand on Bunter Beds of the Triassic series ; but the greater part of Birmingham, including its older and more thickly populated quarters in the east, rests on a wide outcrop of Keuper sandstone, or " waterstone." This " sweeps through the centre of the city, forming all the higher ground supporting the main streets and the chief public buildings, and is continued through Aston and Erdington to Sutton." [2] The significance of this structure deserves emphasis. However great the economic value of the Carboniferous and Silurian rocks of South Stafford-

---

[1] C. Lapworth, *The Birmingham Country* in *Handbook for Birmingham and the Neighbourhood* (British Association Meeting, 1913), p. 590.
[2] *Ibid.*, p. 594.

shire, the influence of the Triassic formations in attracting a dense population can scarcely have been less powerful. The Bunter Beds of the Birmingham neighbourhood, besides being responsible for the excellent casting sand of Hockley and elsewhere, are porous, and, in combination with overlying Keuper sandstone, form a great reservoir of water. Consequently the districts in which these Triassic rocks outcropped could provide a water-supply for a large population, as well as high and healthy sites for residences. " The narrow bands of the Midland country, floored by the outcrop of these ' waterstones,' or Lower Keuper sandstones, rich in springs of good water, relieved by swelling hills . . . and adorned with a luxuriant growth of trees, were . . . naturally selected by the ancient inhabitants . . . as the sites of their earliest permanent settlements." [1] Not only were most of the castles of the nobility, from Tamworth and Warwick in the east to Witley in the west, built on rocks of this kind, but all the older towns of the district—Warwick, Coventry, Nuneaton, Tamworth, Bromsgrove, Birmingham, Sutton, Lichfield and Penkridge—are situated on the " waterstone " formation, and the favourite suburbs of these towns lie along its outcrops.[2] It is important to notice that while many towns in the West Midlands shared the advantages of a situation on Triassic rocks, the outcrop was, in the case of most places near the coal-fields, very small, and that the nearest town to the South Staffordshire coal in which an extensive outcrop of " waterstone " existed was Birmingham. The significance of this fact will be discussed in the next chapter.

It has been shown that a sharp contrast existed between the South Staffordshire and North Worcestershire section of our area, which rested mainly on rocks of the Carboniferous and of the (so-called) Permian series, with here and there exposed beds of limestone, and the district covered by Birmingham and its immediate neighbourhood, which could claim no mineral wealth, but which was floored by a wide bed of water-bearing sandstone. This geological difference between the two subdivisions has been reflected in their divergent economic characteristics, and throughout the survey it will be necessary to emphasize the contrast, produced largely by geological factors, which has existed between

[1] C. Lapworth, *Geology of the Birmingham District* in the *Proceedings of the Geologists' Association*, August 1898, pp. 385-386.
[2] *Ibid.*, p. 386.

the industrial structure of the Black Country on the one hand and that of Birmingham on the other.

Since the survey begins with the year 1860, it is desirable to form some idea of the magnitude of the population which fell within our boundary line at that time, and also to indicate the size of the chief boroughs, townships and sub-districts which made up the various parishes. In Table II. (see Appendix A.) an enumeration of this kind is attempted. It has not been possible to determine precisely the population of the area, for some parishes overlap the boundary line. This is true of the parishes of Walsall, Sutton Coldfield, Hales Owen and Kingswinford. In none of these cases, however, did a large proportion of the inhabitants live beyond the limits of the area, and so this lack of coincidence does not give rise to any serious problem. It will be seen that the total population, thus enumerated, amounted in 1861 to 819,000. In this survey, however, we are concerned solely with the population engaged in, and supported by, industry and commerce, and an attempt to determine the numbers which fall into that category is met with difficulties. Even at the present time the area contains some agricultural workers; and in 1861, when the process of industrialization had not advanced as far as at present, certain districts were still predominantly agricultural. To the east in the parishes of King's Norton, Northfield, Harborne and Sutton Coldfield, and in the west in the Sedgeley and Kingswinford parishes, a considerable number of the inhabitants were working on the land, though it is difficult to form an accurate estimate of the numbers involved. On the other hand, as already mentioned, there was a large body of industrial workers who were engaged in industries typical of the area, but who were living in rural districts beyond its boundaries. This applies not only to the inhabitants of Redditch, who have been included in the total given in Table II., but also to those of the neighbouring villages of Studley and Alcester, which still carried on the manufacture of needles and fishhooks. Further, in the Bromsgrove Poor Law Districts, including such parishes as Stoke Prior, Hagley, Frankley, Bellbroughton, Clent, Romsley, Bentley, Alvechurch and Coston Hackett, there were over 2500 adult men and women returned as nailers ; while there were a few hundred more engaged in other small metal trades.[1] Moreover,

[1] *Census of England and Wales*, 1861, vol. ii., pp. 495, 507.

beyond our boundary, in the neighbourhood of Walsall and Wolverhampton, the inhabitants of several small towns and villages followed callings which were closely allied to those of the Black Countrymen. As far as these people were concerned with mining, they lie outside our scope; for, as already indicated, this part of the survey has been limited to the field to the south of the Great Bentley Fault. But in such places as Rushall, Pelsall and Codsall, branches of the heavy iron trades were carried on; while there was a number of villages, notably Wombourn, Coven and Brewood, in which a large proportion of the population was engaged in nailing and lock-making.[1]

It will be noticed that the population of Coventry has not been included in our Table. At that time its economic life ran in very different channels from those of the trades of Birmingham and District, and in respect of only one industry could the town be held to form part of the area. The watch- and clock-makers, however, should be included in the estimate of population, both because their trade was connected with those of Birmingham, and in view of their influence on later industrial developments. In this Coventry trade there were about 2600 men and boys in 1861.

If one takes into account all the outlying districts which have been mentioned, together with certain small residential suburbs, such as Tettenhall, which lay beyond the boundary, then it would not be an exaggeration to suppose that the whole population supported by industrial employments of the type with which the survey is concerned, but falling outside the parishes and townships enumerated in Table II., amounted to between 25,000 and 30,000. This would go far towards balancing the number of agricultural workers found within the area, and we are thus justified in placing the whole population covered by the survey at not less than 800,000 in 1861. This figure includes the whole population of the area, with the exception of those engaged in agriculture, and also that of the district in the immediate neighbourhood, so far as it was concerned with employments characteristic of the area.

It is interesting to compare the figures shown in Table I. (see Appendix A), as these will illustrate the rapidity of the

---

[1] William White, *History, Gazetteer and Directory of Staffordshire* (1851), pp. 210, 447.

district's development during the first half of the nineteenth century. Its population, which had amounted to only 187,000 at the beginning of the century, was four and a half times as great in 1861; and the percentage increase in each decade had risen from 21·5 per cent. in 1801-1811 to 34·6 per cent. between the years 1831-1841, and in the two succeeding decades it amounted to 28 and 28·7 per cent. respectively. The rate of increase was by no means uniform for all parts of the area. The district comprising the parishes of Birmingham, Aston and Edgbaston, which included in 1861 the Municipal and Parliamentary Borough of Birmingham, had increased from 73,800 in 1801 to 320,000 sixty years later, and was thus more than four and a half times as great. The parish of Harborne, of which the new industrial district of Smethwick formed part, had increased nearly eightfold between 1801 and 1861, and this was true also of Wednesfield and of the parish of West Bromwich. In sixty years the parish of Tipton had multiplied the number of its inhabitants by nearly seven. Willenhall, Wolverhampton and the parishes of Kingswinford, Wednesbury, Handsworth, Dudley and King's Norton had increased between four- and five-fold. These figures alone are sufficient to show the rise of Birmingham and District in industrial importance during the first half of the nineteenth century; and, although we are not specially concerned with the area before 1860, it forms a necessary introduction to our period to consider the reasons for the great increase in population. This will provide an opportunity of forming an idea both of the early history of particular industries and of how they became localized in the places in which we find them in 1860.

CHAPTER II

ECONOMIC DEVELOPMENT BEFORE 1860

WE have no intention of giving detailed attention to the industrial history of the area before 1860. This chapter, therefore, is intended to serve merely as an introduction to a description of the economic structure of Birmingham and District at that date, to explain the increase in population which occurred during the first half of the nineteenth century, and to indicate the main causes which led to the localization of the different industries within the area.

Even before 1800 the district had reached a position of economic significance, and the manufactures of some of its chief towns were renowned throughout Europe. This was the result of the great changes which, about the middle of the eighteenth century, began to transform the metal trades, with which the fortunes of Birmingham and the Black Country have from the first been closely linked. For many years prior to these developments, however, the area had been the home of scattered communities of smiths and miners. As early as the sixteenth century Birmingham itself was manufacturing nails, saddlers' ironmongery, knives and cutting tools [1]; locks were being made in Wolverhampton and Willenhall [2]; coal was mined at Brierley Hill, Dudley, Sedgeley, Wednesbury and Bilston [3]; and the local woods and forests were extensively drawn upon by charcoal iron-smelters. [4] This industrial population had been created chiefly by the presence of the ironstone and wood required in the smelting and " fining " of iron, and of coal which could be employed by the smiths.

During the next century several new industries took root in the locality, [5] attracted there either by the supplies of raw

[1] Leland, *Itinerary, 1538*, ed. T. Hearne, 1711, iv., p. 89.
[2] S. Timmins, *Birmingham and Midland Hardware District* (1866), pp. 85-86; and G. Price, *A Treatise on Fire- and Thief-Proof Depositories* (1856), chap. xx.
[3] *Report of the Committee on South Staffordshire Mines Drainage* (1920), p. 10 et seq.; G. T. Lawley, *History of Bilston* (1868), pp. 78-79; *History of Bilston* (1893), p. 249.
[4] H. Scrivenor, *History of the Iron Trade*, chap. ii.
[5] *Cf.* James Jaffray, *Hints for a History of Birmingham* (1856-1857), chap. v.; S. Timmins, *op. cit.*, pp. 210-211, 526-527; and W. Hawkes Smith, *Birmingham and South Staffordshire* (1838), chap. i.; *Birmingham and its Vicinity* (1838), p. 17 et seq.

materials or by the skill of the ironworkers which could be directed towards the manufacture of new products, expressed both in iron and other metals. By 1700, the glass trade had become established in the neighbourhood of Stourbridge, where both coal and fire-clay for crucibles were available ; the manufacture of leather and of saddlery and harness had grown up in Birmingham, owing to the local supplies of good water and of bark necessary for tanning operations ; and there were many additions to the variety of metal manufactures. In Birmingham itself the production of guns and swords had become an important branch of the town's activities, and the trades which during the eighteenth century were to make it famous had been born. These were the trades producing buckles, buttons and trinkets, which were already being made not only in iron but in steel and brass also. Of these " toys " more will be heard later. Their manufacture had been stimulated towards the end of the seventeenth century by the change of fashion and the growth of luxurious habits after the Restoration, by the prohibition of the importation of French buttons imposed in 1662, and later by the interruption of French trade as a result of war. In the towns of South Staffordshire similar developments had taken place. While many of the older industries had continued to flourish, such as lock-making at Wolverhampton, Willenhall and Wednesfield, new branches of the metal industries had sprung up. Bilston had taken up buckle-making.[1] In 1700, Wolverhampton was manufacturing small brass articles in addition to steel " toys " and iron products ; while Walsall was engaged in making *inter alia* brass and copper wares, including hollow-ware.

It seems likely that the already famous buckle trade of Birmingham owed its origin in some degree to makers who were driven from Walsall, where the trade had once been carried on, by the religious persecutions which followed the Restoration.[2] If this is so, then it is merely an example of the migration of industries from one place to another within the area, to which continual reference will have to be made in the course of this history. Even before 1700, several other instances of this movement had taken place. The most important had occurred in the nailing industry. Originally, as we have seen, the nailers had been

---

[1] S. Timmins, *op. cit.*, p. 214.
[2] H. Hamilton, *The English Brass and Copper Industries to 1800*, p. 130.

found within Birmingham; but by the end of the seventeenth century they had for the most part shifted farther westwards, and were to be found chiefly within the neighbourhood of Dudley and Stourbridge. Most of the "lorimers," or saddlers' ironmongers, too, had departed to Walsall, which was to remain the chief seat of their activity.[1] The causes of these migrations are worth considering, as they throw a light on changes which had occurred in other branches of industry.

Towards the end of the seventeenth century it was stated that "within ten miles of Dudley Castle there be near 20,000 smiths of all sorts, *and many ironworks . . . . decayed for want of wood.*"[2] The decline in the production of iron, which is here indicated, was typical of industrial England at this time; for the industry depended on the supplies of wood for conversion into charcoal, and the destruction of the forests had proceeded so rapidly that by the end of the seventeenth century iron manufacturers were suffering from a fuel famine. This had important effects on the localization of both the iron-producing and the iron-using industries. The smelting of the ore, which had long been carried on in the West Midlands, tended to shift towards Wales, where fuel was still available; while Swedish iron was imported in continually increasing quantities to remedy the shortage in the home supplies, and reached Birmingham and South Staffordshire by way of Bristol and the Severn. It was on the banks of this river and of its tributaries that the manufacturers of finished iron tended to establish their forges, since they were thus able to secure a favourable situation both for obtaining the pig-iron from Wales and abroad, and for dealing with their market in South Staffordshire, whither the iron was conveyed on pack-horses. The sites of the rolling mills and slitting mills for the production of nail rods were affected by similar considerations. Yet, while they had to be within easy reach of the producers of finished iron and of the smiths of South Staffordshire and Birmingham, the mills needed water-power, and they were thus found scattered about the district wherever streams existed. Finally, the smiths who had been originally attracted to our area by the presence of iron and coal, still clung to the locality; for though iron was no longer produced there in sufficient

---

[1] S. Timmins, *op. cit.*, p. 209.
[2] Dud Dudley, *Metallum Martis* (ed. 1854), p. 7.

quantity, the local coal, which could be used in their forges, if not in the production of pig or finished iron, was a sufficient inducement to them to remain. Thus in the early eighteenth century, as a result of the shortage of charcoal and of the dependence of iron producers on rivers for transport and power, the iron industry was scattered in nature. " Mills were rarely found in proximity to forges, and forges were commonly remote from furnaces,"[1] and it was only in the later stages of manufacture, such as engaged the mills and smithies, that the industry could be said to be localized in our area.

Even the smiths, moreover, had not been entirely unaffected by the centrifugal movement which was flinging out the different branches of the iron industry to the west, and their response was indeed reflected in the migration, to which reference has already been made, of certain finished-iron manufactures from Birmingham to South Staffordshire. In the sixteenth century, when the nail industry, to take a typical example, could obtain its iron from producers in the neighbouring woodlands, then Birmingham, although situated at some distance from the coal-fields, was not inconveniently placed for the trade, being somewhat nearer the chief highway from London to Chester than the South Staffordshire towns, besides having other advantages to be presently described. But when the trade came to depend on iron brought up the Severn, the nailers naturally felt themselves impelled to shift westwards, since to the attraction of coal was added the necessity of being as near as possible to Bewdley and the Severn ports. Further, it is probable that as the nail and other iron trades grew, the neighbourhood of Birmingham, though fairly well supplied with streams, had not sufficient to provide power for the increasing number of rolling and slitting mills required, and their proprietors had an inducement to seek elsewhere for suitable sites. These they naturally tried to procure farther to the west, and they found them on the banks of the Stour and its tributaries, in the neighbourhood of Hales Owen and Stourbridge. In these localities the smiths naturally tended to establish themselves. In the meantime, Birmingham was becoming concerned with products of a highly finished kind, such as required a great deal of labour in their manufacture; for while its long industrial tradition had given its artisans

[1] T. S. Ashton, *Iron and Steel in the Industrial Revolution*, p. 22.

superior skill, it was at a disadvantage, compared with other places within our area, with regard to the cost of raw materials. Hence there tended to appear, even at this early date, that distinction between the industries carried on in Birmingham and in South Staffordshire which became much more marked in later years. The former was tending to produce articles which required a great deal of skilled labour, and in which the cost of materials and of transport made up only a small proportion of the total value, while in the district situated over the coal-measures the cruder manufactures were already finding a home.

The eighteenth century, in confirming this tendency, brought about a great development in the economic activities of the area.[1] In Birmingham, the gun trade was stimulated by the wars of the period. The manufacture of sporting guns was taken up after 1714, and by 1800 the production of small arms had become one of the town's staple industries.[2] The " toy " trade, which was concerned with the production of polished iron, steel, brass and plated articles of personal adornment, attained a European reputation ; although one of its most important branches suffered a serious decline just before the end of the century. This was the buckle trade, which, after reaching its zenith in 1770, when 5000 people are said to have been employed in it, was killed by the coming of the shoe-string shortly afterwards. As this industry declined, however, the manufacture of buttons rose to take its place, and many of the 20,000 persons, who in 1791 were said to be in terrible distress owing to the cessation of the demand for buckles, came to depend on this and other metal smallware trades.[3] This was among the first of the many notable industrial transformations which, since then, have affected the Birmingham area.

The brass trade, besides undergoing an expansion, developed several new branches. Before the eighteenth century most of the small brass and copper articles in use had been made by the " battery " process ; but the progress which was made in methods of casting resulted in an improvement in the style of the products, while the application of the stamp and press

[1] *Cf.* James Jaffray, *op. cit.*, chaps. xvii.-xviii. ; R. K. Dent, *The Making of Birmingham*, pp. 93-95, 141-147 ; and *Old and New Birmingham*, p. 111 *et seq.*
[2] *Observations on the Manufacture of Fire-arms for Military Purposes*, 1829 (Birmingham Reference Library), p. 4.
[3] S. Timmins, *op. cit.*, p. 215 ; James Jaffray, *op. cit.*, chaps. xvii.-xviii.

B

to the trade towards the end of the century brought about a great expansion in its scope. This new process, which seems to have been used first about 1769 in the production of coffin furniture, came to be characteristic of Birmingham's productive methods; for stamping and pressing before 1800 had been applied to a wide variety of local trades—from the button and toy industries to the manufacture of picture frames and umbrella-fittings. This development, besides calling into existence a class of die-sinkers and stamp- and press-makers, increased the demand for sheet metal, and so caused the growth in the number of the local rolling mills. In the meantime, Birmingham had also become the seat of another branch of the industry. Up to 1740 the town had depended entirely upon outside sources of supply for its brass, which was then made by the " cementation " process. In that year, however, a firm was founded at Birmingham for making brass, and forty years later the manufacturers of the town, which had now become the chief centre in the country for producing brass and copper wares, combined to erect an establishment for producing the metal they required. It does not appear, however, that they satisfied the whole of the local demand, for the brass users of Birmingham, Wolverhampton and Walsall still continued to purchase part of their materials from Bristol and Cheadle.[1]

In addition to these developments within the older trades of Birmingham the later decades of the eighteenth century witnessed the introduction of several new manufactures. Some of these were offshoots of industries which were already long established; others migrated to the town, either from South Staffordshire or from more distant parts of the country. The jewellery trade, for instance, was beginning to separate itself from the " toy " and buckle trades, which it afterwards entirely superseded, during the last decade of the century.[2] Boulton's coining business was connected with the development of the stamping process in the non-ferrous metal trades; while the smiths were continually driven to produce an increasing variety

---

[1] H. Hamilton, op. cit., p. 224.
[2] J. C. Roche, History, Development and Organization of the Birmingham Jewellery and Allied Trades (1928), chap. i.
The early jewellers of Birmingham did not gain a high reputation for the quality of their work. It was said of them : " Give a Birmingham maker a guinea and a copper kettle, and he'll make you a hundred pounds' worth of jewellery " (J. Jaffray, op. cit., chap. xviii.).

of small iron articles—from screws to wrought-iron hollow-ware. On the other hand, the new glass trade of Birmingham was partly the result of migration and partly due to the increasing variety of materials in which the toy-makers expressed their wares. Glass apparently had been used by the button-makers during the first half of the eighteenth century, and some of them had taken up the production of the material itself; but as far as table-ware is concerned the industry appears to have spread from Stourbridge about 1750.[1] In the eighties a good deal of glass was employed by local spectacle-makers, while a very different branch of the trade, the manufacture of stained glass, was introduced at Soho in 1784. Other trades appear to have been attracted to the town from Sheffield. The most important of these was the silver-plate manufacture, which by 1800 included not only table-ware but buckles and saddlers' metalwork also. As early as 1770 this had become sufficiently extensive to warrant the establishment of an Assay Office in Birmingham.[2] The Britannia-metal and the fender trades appear to have come from the same source. At the same time the pewter trade migrated from Bewdley, and the manufacture of pins[3] and edge tools from Gloucestershire; while the papier-mâché trade, introduced by Henry Clay in 1770, soon reached a position of importance.[4] Thus Birmingham, which at the beginning of the century had been chiefly concerned with iron and steel smallwares, had by 1800 attained a much more diverse industrial life. It had not only developed a wider variety of iron manufactures, but it had come to deal with the non-ferrous and precious metals, with glass and with papier mâché; and at the great factory by the Soho Pool the manufacture of the steam-engine foreshadowed its future greatness as an engineering centre. Meanwhile, on the banks of streams at Northfield, King's Norton and Hockley, the rolling mills had steadily increased in numbers, and wherever water-power was available in the vicinity the hammer and the mill were busy.

[1] D. N. Sandilands, *The History of the Midland Glass Industry* (M. Com. Thesis, 1927, Birmingham University Library), chap. iv.

[2] S. Timmins, *op. cit.*, p. 499.

[3] " The manufacture of pins was started in Gloucestershire by John Tilsby in 1626, and the business soon proved so prosperous that it gave employment to 1500 persons. . . . About the middle of last century wire - drawing and pin - making were commenced in Birmingham by the Rylands family " (*Commissioners of Patents for Inventions' Abridgments of Specifications relating to Needles and Pins*, 1871, p. x).

[4] S. Timmins, *op. cit.*, pp. 617, 656, 207 *et seq.*

In South Staffordshire and North Worcestershire there had occurred even greater developments. The hand-wrought nail industry, which was then centred in South Staffordshire rather than in Worcestershire, and which was extensively carried on in Kingswinford, Sedgeley, Dudley, Tipton, West Bromwich, Oldbury, Darlaston and Rowley, had so increased that 35,000 to 40,000 nailers [1] were said to be working in the district in 1780. The branches of the brass trade which existed at Walsall and Wolverhampton had shared in the growth which had attended that of Birmingham, and the Walsall district had outstripped its greater rival in the production of saddlery and of saddlers' ironmongery. In conformity with the general tendency, already discussed, the manufacture of gun parts, such as barrels and locks, had sprung up in Wednesbury and Darlaston, [2] and these were supplied to the Birmingham gun trade, which was responsible for the assembly and finishing processes. At Bilston, fancy enamel boxes were being made. Both there and at Wolverhampton the manufacture of tinplate wares, introduced about 1720 from Pontypool, [3] was a thriving new industry; and beyond the boundary of our area, on the banks of the Arrow at Alcester, Redditch and Studley, the needle trade was taking root, being in process of migration from Long Crendon in Buckinghamshire. [4]

The most significant changes, however, had occurred in the iron trade, and it is with these that we must now concern ourselves. The decline in the production of iron, which had reduced England to a dependence on imports from Sweden and Spain, was arrested by developments of far-reaching importance. Early in the eighteenth century the Darbys of Coalbrookdale began to use coke for the smelting of iron ore, and achieved the distinction of being the first to employ mineral fuel for this purpose with commercial success. By 1750 charcoal iron production was being sensibly affected by the new blast-furnaces; and then, some thirty years later, Cort invented the puddling process, which enabled mineral fuel to be used in the production of finished iron. Shortly afterwards the steam-engine was applied to the furnace, mill and

[1] F. W. Hackwood, *Oldbury and Round About*, p. 126.

[2] *Cf.* F. W. Hackwood, *Wednesbury Workshops* (1889), pp. 34-40; and *A History of Darlaston* (1887), p. 157.

[3] W. H. Jones, *Story of Japan-Tinplate Working, and Bicycle and Galvanizing Trades in Wolverhampton* (1900), p. 1.

[4] William Shrimpton, *Notes on a Decayed Needle-Land* (reprinted from the *Redditch Indicator*, 1897), pp. 6-7, 17 *et seq.*

forge, and by 1800 these developments had freed Birmingham and District from its dependence on imported iron and had brought into being the Malleable Iron Period, in which South Staffordshire was to hold a position of predominance. In 1750 the various processes of iron manufacture, from the reduction of the ore to the production of finished articles, had seldom been found together in one locality. By 1800 mineral fuel had freed the producer of pig or of finished iron from the necessity of seeking a site for his works near woods and forests, and had drawn him towards the coal-field. The canal and the steam-engine were beginning to destroy the importance of rivers both as sources of power and as means of transport, and the furnace and the forge were shifting from Shropshire and Wales towards the mills and smithies of South Staffordshire. By the end of the century this centripetal movement had created for the district an importance as an iron-producing centre which it was to enjoy for nearly a hundred years. In 1790 there were 21 coke blast-furnaces in operation in South Staffordshire, of which 15 were in the parish of Wolverhampton, 5 were in the neighbourhood of Stourbridge, and 1 was at Tipton. In 1806 in the whole of Staffordshire there was a total of 42 furnaces built, with a production of pig-iron amounting to over 49,000 tons annually out of the total British output of 250,000 tons. Practically all these 42 furnaces were within our area, which was in that year exceeded as a pig-iron producing centre only by South Wales and Shropshire.[1] It was owing to this increased production of iron, as well as because of the local coal supplies, that so many new metal-using trades sprang up in the district during the last two or three decades of the eighteenth century.

The revolution in the iron industry was accompanied by the rise of another class of producer—viz. the ironfounder. Before the great changes which have just been described occurred, the metal most usually supplied to the workers in iron had been malleable sheets, rods or bars; but the fact that coal had been applied to the blast-furnace many years before it was extensively used in the fining process brought about an increased supply of pig-iron which stimulated the production of castings.[2] This stimulus was all the greater because the new iron lent itself readily to use in the foundry. During the era of charcoal-smelting

[1] H. Scrivenor, *op. cit.*, chap. v.   [2] T. S. Ashton, *op. cit.*, p. 38 *et seq.*

it was impossible to make light pots and utensils by the casting process, because charcoal iron ran very thick [1] ; but coke-smelted pig was free from this disadvantage, and its quality made possible the rise of a new industry — viz. the manufacture of cast-iron hollow-ware, which before the end of the century had become established at Wolverhampton and West Bromwich. The general ironfounder, too, increased the range of his products, and Birmingham, Dudley and Wolverhampton became renowned for their fenders, grates and fire-irons.[2] Meanwhile, the rise of the steam-engine had given a stimulus to the production of heavy castings, for which Bilston and Tipton had become the chief centres. It was in this neighbourhood that Wilkinson cast the first cylinders for Watt's engines prior to the construction of the Soho Foundry.

In contrast to the expansion of the iron industry the manufacture of steel in the neighbourhood actually declined during the eighteenth century. Just before 1700 the production of steel had been taken up by several firms in Birmingham with the object of supplying the " toy " makers with a raw material they required ; but the new industry did not have a long life. Soon after Huntsman's invention of the crucible process, steel-making ceased in the town, and Sheffield became the source of supply. There is no evidence to lead one to suppose that the industry existed in South Staffordshire during the eighteenth century.[3]

Just as Sheffield's supremacy in steel manufacture had killed the small local trade, so the rise of Lancashire brought an end to the West Midland cotton industry. It is well known that an early experiment in spinning by rollers was undertaken at Sutton Coldfield, while calico-printing was introduced in 1780. Indeed, in the last decade but one of the eighteenth century a considerable cotton manufacture existed in the locality.[4] Besides this textile, a certain amount of linen manufacture also was carried on. But by 1800 both of these trades had migrated from the district, and for more than a century the Birmingham area was practically devoid of any textile industry.

The increase in iron production and the development of other industries which required fuel were naturally accompanied by a

---

[1] W. Hawkes Smith, *Birmingham and South Staffordshire*, pp. 5-6.
[2] *Ibid.*, p. 12.
[3] S. Timmins, *op. cit.*, p. 212.
[4] James Jaffray, *op. cit.*, chap. viii.

greater exploitation of the coal-field. In the latter half of the seventeenth century there were said to be " within ten miles of Dudley Castle twelve or fourteen coal works, some in Worcestershire and some of them in Staffordshire, now in work ; and twice as many in that circuit not at work ; each of the works mined two thousand tons of coal yearly—some . . . three, four or five thousand." The total annual production, therefore, was presumably in the neighbourhood of 30,000 to 40,000 tons.[1] In 1879, however, " the collieries near the Birmingham Canal and its several branches between Birmingham and Wolverhampton raised at least 15,000 tons of coal a week. Of this quantity about 5000 tons were used in the Walsall, Wednesbury, Bilston, Dudley, Oldbury, Tipton and West Bromwich districts ; 2000 tons were sent to Wolverhampton, Bridgnorth, and other places near the Severn ; and 8000 tons were sent to Birmingham and beyond. . . . The collieries south of Dudley raised 1200 tons of coal a week." [2] Thus the annual output must have been about 840,000 tons. Besides coal, ironstone had been mined from early times in the thick coal-measures of South Staffordshire, and by the end of the eighteenth century 60,000 tons of ore a year were being produced.[3]

It is scarcely necessary to lay further emphasis on the transformation which our area had undergone in the course of a century. In 1700 it was chiefly noted for its smiths and its " toys " —for nails, locks, bolts, saddlers' ironmongery, buckles, guns and swords. By 1800 the production of these commodities had greatly increased and the scope of all the hardware trades had immensely expanded. Brass and brass wares were being produced on a great scale. The pin, jewellery, papier-mâché, tinplate, japanned and enamelled ware trades had been created. The ironfounder had become a figure of importance. The glass trade had spread to Birmingham from Stourbridge, and the needle, silverplate and pewter trades had migrated, or were migrating, into the district from other parts of the country. Birmingham had become a great centre for the production of light finished-metal goods, and was famous the world over for its achievements in engineering. Most significant of all, the last two decades of the

[1] H. Scrivenor, op. cit., pp. 48-49.
[2] T. E. Lones, A History of Mining in the Black Country (1898), p. 30 ; cf. F. W. Hackwood, Oldbury and Round About, p. 132.
[3] T. E. Lones, op. cit., p. 30.

century had seen the little groups of smiths and miners, scattered over a district still largely agricultural,[1] develop into a great industrial community. South Staffordshire, in this short space, had been launched on its career as a leading iron-producing district, had become the scene of extensive mining operations, and had made itself a renowned centre of metal manufactures.

At this point the main forces which had been instrumental in creating this industrial district are worth summarizing, as they are of great interest. As far as the South Staffordshire and North Worcestershire section of the area is concerned, little more need be said, for sufficient indication has already been given of the leading causes which led to the concentration of the iron and other trades within that district. There, indeed, the presence of raw materials was undoubtedly the strongest influence at work. Coal, ironstone and limestone brought the various branches of the iron industry and its associated manufactures; coal and Stourbridge fire-clay were responsible for the glass trade; and the water-power of its streams frequently accounted for the exact site of its factories and workshops. But the problem of Birmingham is more complex. In 1801 the parishes of Birmingham, Aston and Edgbaston alone possessed nearly forty per cent. of the population of the whole area, and if parishes which have since been added to the town are included the proportion is no less than forty-four per cent. Although, as we have seen, the cruder manufactures had gone to South Staffordshire, the town was concerned with a wide variety of finished products of iron and non-ferrous metals. Yet the cause of its economic importance, unlike that of the places situated on or very near to the coal-measures, is far from obvious. It was in a definitely less favourable position for securing supplies of fuel and of raw materials than they, and, although several streams ran through it, the town's supply of water-power was not greater than that of many neighbouring districts. It was situated at some distance from the main road from London to Chester, so it could not claim any important transport advantages; and if a central situation was favourable for dealing with the home market, that privilege was shared by other towns in the immediate vicinity. Thus, although we can easily understand why South Staffordshire became a centre of the iron industry, and how it was that

[1] *Cf.* W. Hawkes Smith, *Birmingham and South Staffordshire*, pp. 12-14.

the heavier manufactures migrated there, it is more difficult to conceive why Birmingham retained such a marked predominance in the lighter metal trades; since even in those the higher cost of fuel and of certain raw materials, as compared with their prices in Dudley, Wolverhampton, Walsall or Stourbridge, must have imposed extra burdens on the Birmingham manufacturers. Except for the foundries of the town, which could draw on the excellent casting sand available at Hockley, we cannot explain the localization of any branch of industry by pointing to the presence of raw materials; and even the foundries had to obtain coal and iron from Staffordshire.

A host of reasons have been suggested by those whose curiosity has been aroused by this problem, but most of them are unconvincing. Some writers have sought an explanation in the fact that, owing to its high altitude as compared with other places in the neighbourhood, Birmingham possessed a bracing climate, which had an invigorating effect on those who were fortunate enough to be born there. Consequently the men of the town became alert and enterprising, while their neighbours were being lulled into degeneracy by softer breezes. Yet there were many places on the West Midland plateau which, though blessed with higher altitudes and still keener winds, remained in comparative obscurity. The climate, in fact, can have had only a very slight effect on the growth of Birmingham, and the fact that it has been offered as a serious explanation affords some indication of how difficult inquirers have found their search for causes.

It is in the human factor that others have discovered a justification of the town's expansion. The original settlement of Birmingham, it is said, had been established on the banks of the Rea at a spot where the river was easily fordable. This advantage, together with the high altitude and rock structure of the neighbourhood, had made the place a desirable site for residence, a market town for agricultural communities in the vicinity, and consequently a point of convergence for local roads and tracks. From this the transition to the manufacture of articles—such as nails, leather goods and saddlers' ironmongery—required by the agriculturists had been a natural one, especially in view of the fact that coal and ironstone were not far distant, and that wood for fuel and bark for tanning were abundant. Thus there had been created at an early period a race of skilled metalworkers, who drew to themselves new industries. This theory is, it is true, adequate as an explanation of the original site of Birmingham, and of its early industrial character; but it gives no indication of the cause of the town's disproportionate growth, as compared with that of other industrial centres in the neighbourhood, during the eighteenth century. How can one explain the failure of the manufacturers to move towards the coal-field when the woods had disappeared and when all their raw materials came from farther west? The cruder manufactures—the trades in which the cost of raw materials formed a high proportion of the cost of production—did migrate in this way; yet others, in which the cost of iron and coal was far from negligible, remained, or were newly established in the town. Sheer conservatism might account for much; but that has not been a quality claimed by any writer for early Birmingham, and it certainly could not explain the introduction of the host of new trades which occurred in the eighteenth century and for its disproportionate increase in size as compared with the South Staffordshire towns.

Other writers have pointed out that Birmingham not only saw the birth of some of the major mechanical inventions of the century, but that it provided an environment peculiarly suitable for their industrial application. In the older corporate towns the regulations which were imposed on industry blunted the keenness of the enterprising, and forced new trades down the old channels of organization. But Birmingham had no corporation and no system of industrial regulation. There was no apprenticeship system to restrict the mobility of labour and to prevent the rapid growth of new trades, or the flow of labour to ancient industries which were being reorganized. The past pressed less heavily on Birmingham than on the older towns of the neighbourhood, such as Coventry and Walsall, and the men of enterprise in the early years of modern industrialism viewed it as a haven of economic freedom. It was, therefore, the resort of the new type of manufacturer who was appearing towards the end of the eighteenth century, and, indeed, of all who were in conflict with the conservative tendencies of the time.

The fact that Birmingham was not a corporate town attracted to it, during the years which followed the persecuting legislation of the Restoration (viz. the Act of Uniformity and the " Five Mile " Act), considerable numbers of Presbyterians and Quakers.

This undoubtedly had a momentous effect on the future character of the town. For the Dissenters were essentially individualists, in spiritual revolt against a State which claimed the right of prescribing the religious doctrines of its members, and it was natural that such of them as were business men should feel that there was much in common between the corporate regulation of industry and official regulation of religion. They had a temperamental and traditional bias towards the individualism which was to be the outstanding characteristic of the new economic régime ; and, since there was this happy coincidence of the needs of industry and their own mental attitude, the Dissenters found the industrial environment of Birmingham particularly congenial.[1] The close connection between Nonconformity and industrialism has received sufficient emphasis from many historians ; so that it is not necessary here to do more than repeat their convincing arguments. Barred by the religious restrictions of the day from the service of the State, the Professions or the Universities, the more intelligent, ambitious and energetic among the Dissenters turned to industry and commerce as affording the only outlet for their abilities. Their religious traditions forbade them to take part in the pleasures of the world, and so induced them to concentrate the whole of their life, outside their chapels, on their business. It was undoubtedly the energy and independence of spirit of these men, confined as it was to one narrow channel and growing in force as a consequence, which contributed largely to the success of many local enterprises during the eighteenth and nineteenth centuries. Their material prosperity, coupled with the thriftiness and plainness of their manner of life, certainly made possible the building up of the great business undertakings which the new era brought with it. The large-scale enterprises of South Staffordshire, such as mining and iron production, had drawn capital from the landlords ; but most of the newer manufacturing industries of the later eighteenth century depended for their capital on the thrift of the Nonconformist middle class. Thus, according to this line of argument, the growth of Birmingham is to be largely attributed to the freedom which it allowed to all comers, and to its success in attracting the enterprising.

[1] *Handbook for Birmingham and the Neighbourhood* (British Association Meeting, 1913), pp. 356-357.

Now, while it is impossible to emphasize too strongly the effects of the incursion of Dissenters on the industrial development of the town, or to deny that the lack of a corporation favoured the introduction of new industries, it would be foolish to assert that these factors are sufficient to provide a satisfactory solution of the problem. If Birmingham alone of the towns in the vicinity of the South Staffordshire coal-field had possessed the advantage of being " within five miles of any city or town corporate or borough that sends burgesses to the Parliament," then the difficulty might be considered solved. But there were many places in the neighbourhood which, in addition to being nearer the source of raw materials, also fulfilled these requirements. Why did not these attract the Dissenters and the new industries to the same extent as Birmingham ? Why did not the Cannock area develop, or, to take the most obvious example, why did not Wolverhampton, which was not a corporate town and which had a long tradition of metalwork, become the "Midland Metropolis "? With all its advantages, though it had grown during the century, its population in 1801 was only about one-sixth that of Birmingham and Aston. It is true that Wolverhampton was less fortunate than Birmingham in the possession of water - power ; but the latter had only a few streams, and its superiority in this respect was not sufficiently marked to provide an explanation for its disproportionate growth.

While, then, the above-mentioned factors must receive their due weight as contributory causes, the determining influences have still to be found. If we look for some factor which exerted itself only in Birmingham we find this in the geological structure of the locality. It has already been shown that while the towns and villages of South Staffordshire and North Worcestershire rest on coal-measures or on Permian sandstones, Birmingham lies on a wide belt of Triassic rock. As indicated in the previous chapter, this ensured for the early inhabitants not only a high and pleasant site, but excellent drinking water. It is probable that in the eighteenth century the presence of a large water-supply, in addition to the other advantages of the town, would be a strong enough influence to counterbalance even the attraction which the raw materials exercised on the site of industry. Parts of Stourbridge and Wolverhampton also rest, it is true, on strata of similar formation; but in both of those places the surface area of the outcrops is very small. Thus it may be argued that multitudes of enterprising manufacturers and craftsmen were attracted to Birmingham in the eighteenth century not only because it was a non-corporate town possessing water-power and an industrial tradition, but owing to the fact that it was the nearest place to the coal-field in which a large supply of good drinking water made possible the settlement of a dense population.

Besides this, it must be remembered that a great part of the increase in the demand for goods during the eighteenth century happened to be directed towards the type of commodity on which Birmingham had previously specialized. This was a powerful contributory cause of its growth, and a glance at the earlier history of the district is necessary in order to view it in proper proportion. It has been shown how, even by 1700, the cruder manufactures were being lost to Birmingham, having been drawn to South Staffordshire by the attraction of coal and iron; while the town was being obliged to devote itself to more highly finished commodities. In consequence, the part of our district now called the Black Country was developing in the early decades of the eighteenth century a labour supply different in kind from that of Birmingham. This divergence was accentuated during the last half of the century, partly by the growth of mining and of the smelting and puddling branches of the iron industry in South Staffordshire, and partly by the continued migration of the mills, foundries and heavier trades which needed water-power; for Birmingham could no longer supply what they required.[1] The increase in the population of South Staffordshire as a result of these causes was naturally not concentrated in one town or confined to a particular district, but it occurred wherever coal, ironstone and water-power were easily available. But while the industries concerned with raw materials or cruder products were developing, there occurred also during the century a vast increase in the demand for highly finished products—for buckles, buttons, " toys " of all kind, brass and copper ware, guns and jewellery. These South Staffordshire, although it continued to produce some of them, could not supply in the quantities

[1] An example of this is to be found in the migration of Messrs Izon & Co., cast-iron hollow-ware manufacturers, to West Bromwich. While this firm had been situated in Birmingham the blast for the cupola had been obtained by a bellows worked by two men and the machinery had been turned by horse-power; but at West Bromwich water-power was available to do the work (S. Timmins, *op. cit.*, p. 104).

required, for its labour supply was being drawn to iron production, mining and cruder manufacture, and so was lacking in the particular kind of skill necessary. So it was left for Birmingham, which had not been directly affected by the revolution in the iron trade, but which was near to the sources of fuel and raw materials, and which had an excellent water-supply, and workers who had a long tradition of skilled craftsmanship behind them, to benefit by this increased demand for their goods. Thus, largely because of the way in which their industrial skill and traditions had diverged, if the South Staffordshire towns each received a share of the new demands for iron and for the cruder iron products, practically the whole of the enormous increase in the demand for highly finished metal articles had to be met by Birmingham.

To summarize, then, the forces which created the town, it may be said that the greatly increased demands for small finished-metal products had to be satisfied by a place which was near supplies of raw materials, and which also had a tradition of skilled metalworking. The South Staffordshire towns which were nearest the coal and iron could not meet these demands, because they were devoting themselves to the earlier processes in iron production and to cruder products ; so that their skilled labour was not of a kind suitable for the purpose. But Birmingham, for reasons which it is not necessary to describe again, had the type of labour required, and at the same time was within easy reach of raw materials. The fact that it was not a corporate town was an added reason for the development of new industries, since it permitted freedom of enterprise and attracted the vigorous Dissenters. And finally, since it lay on Keuper and Bunter sandstone, it had a water-supply which was not only to some extent responsible for the early settlement, but which made possible the existence of a great population on the site. It was this last factor, more than any others, which caused Birmingham to be singled out from all the other places within or near our area as the Midland Metropolis.

The industrial development of the district would have been less rapid if, during the later decades of the century, there had not occurred an improvement in transport which was associated in this area particularly with the construction of canals. Before this, the cost of transporting coal from South Staffordshire was proving a serious hindrance to the growth of Birmingham's industries, and so in 1767 it was decided to construct a canal to link up the town with the colliery district near Wolverhampton, whence the best coal came. When completed, this canal ran from Birmingham *via* Smethwick and Bilston to join the Severn and Trent Canal near Wolverhampton, and the most obvious result was a reduction in the price of coal in Birmingham from 13s. to 8s. 4d. a ton.[1] Before the end of the century the whole district was linked together by canals and was joined to the chief waterways of the country as a whole. Besides confirming the flow of trade into the places which they connected, and so emphasizing the existing localization of industry, the canals also had an effect on the actual sites selected for new factories and on the general direction of industrial growth. Foundries, rolling mills and all concerns which used coal and heavy raw materials tended to become established on the canal banks, and this movement was encouraged by the fact that specially low tolls were granted on coal and cinders going to works adjoining the canals. When more use came to be made of the steam-engine, a site on a canal bank became of even greater advantage, for the owners of factories were given statutory powers to take water free of charge for condensing purposes.[2] Consequently, towards the end of the eighteenth century, works began to extend from Birmingham, and from the South Staffordshire towns through which the canals passed, along the banks, until ultimately there came to be a continuous line of factories along the waterway, running from Birmingham through Smethwick, Oldbury, Tipton Green and Bilston to Wolverhampton.

Although the next sixty years witnessed a great development in industry and an increase in the population of the area from 187,000 in 1801 to 819,000 in 1861, they were not associated with such fundamental economic changes as was the last quarter of the previous century. There was, moreover, in Birmingham and District no rapid transition from small- to large-scale industry, and no general introduction of machinery such as occurred in the textile trades. Some of the producing units in the older industries increased slowly in size; in a few trades complicated machinery began to be used; yet, on the other

[1] James Jaffray, *op. cit.*, chap. xix.
[2] *Handbook for Birmingham and the Neighbourhood* (British Association Meeting, 1913), p. 441.

hand, some of the large factories which existed here and there before 1800 disappeared, and for the most part the industries were carried on without any important changes in methods of production. The period was, indeed, one of development on the lines laid down in the later eighteenth century rather than an era of transformation. There were alterations in the relative importance of the various manufactures and an extension of their variety; the migration of trades from other parts of the country continued, but the area as a whole possessed the same industrial character in 1860 as in 1800, even if its leading qualities had been immensely emphasized. The chief influences on its industrial growth will be considered when the history of the chief trades is dealt with, and they need only be mentioned at this point in the narrative. The first was the increased demand for iron, which was a characteristic feature of this period of the country's development, and which accounted for the growth in number of blast-furnaces, forges and mills in South Staffordshire. The second was the general introduction of steam-power to the heavy trades and the gradual supersession of water-power in the mills and forges, though this was by no means complete in 1860. Next, the construction of railways conferred wider markets on the district and tended to confirm the existing localization of industry; and finally there was the enormous increase in the population and wealth of the country, which necessitated a greater output of metal products for ordinary domestic use. The period during which development was most rapid varied from trade to trade. The industries which were affected by the demands of war, such as the gun trade, showed the most marked increase at the beginning of the century; and the local iron trade seems to have grown most rapidly during the first three decades. But it was the period stretching from about 1830 to the depression of the later fifties which saw the greatest expansion in the output of small finished articles and in the number of distinct industries. It was then that new methods of production in these trades first made themselves felt. This expansion was due largely to the appearance of railways and to the growth in the demand for articles of comfort and luxury which accompanied the rise in the standard of life during the prosperous early Victorian era. The period of greatest industrial development is illustrated by the figures showing the percentage decennial increase of population (see Table I). It will be seen that the maximum percentage increase was between 1831 and 1841, and that a very high rate was maintained till 1861.

An attempt must now be made to consider the particular trades of the district in some detail. In Birmingham itself no change of importance occurred until after the French wars, when the industries which had been stimulated by a temporary demand declined. Of these the most noteworthy was the gun trade. During the war it is supposed to have supplied two-thirds of the arms purchased for the use of the British troops,[1] and its rise to great importance was signalized by the erection of a Proof House in Birmingham in 1813. This, it should be noted, was for private proofs, as the guns ordered by the Government were subject to an official view elsewhere in the town.[2] After 1815, in spite of the extension of the sporting-gun trade and of demands from abroad, the industry was plunged into a prolonged depression.[3] This lasted until the Government saw fit to replace the flint-lock service gun by the type fired by percussion caps—a step which was taken in 1839. Later the adoption of a new type of service rifle capable of firing an expanding bullet, together with the needs of the army during the Crimean War, brought a spell of prosperity to the trade which lasted until the late fifties.[4]

The silver branch of the jewellery trade extended its scope to include the manufacture of silver chains in 1806, and although gold wares were not made in large quantities in the early part of the century, the local production of articles of this material had become sufficiently great by 1824 to warrant the passing of an Act which permitted the local Assay Office to mark gold jewellery as well as silver.[5] The depression of the middle twenties, however, hit the trade hard and it entered upon a period of decline. The turning-point was reached on the accession of Queen Victoria, and from then onwards the trade grew rapidly. The increasing prosperity of the middle classes was largely responsible for this, since they were able to develop habits of

---

[1] *Newspaper Cuttings* on *Birmingham Industries*, 1863-1880 (Birmingham Reference Library), vol. i., p. 9 ; and *Observations on the Manufacture of Fire-arms for Military Purposes*, 1829 (Birmingham Reference Library), p. 18.
[2] R. K. Dent, *The Making of Birmingham*, p. 344.
[3] *Newspaper Cuttings* on *Birmingham Industries*, vol. i., p. 9.
[4] S. Timmins, *op. cit.*, p. 381 *et seq.*
[5] *Ibid.*, pp. 460 and 540.

C

personal decoration to a much greater extent than ever before, and it was for them that Birmingham catered. After 1849, the gold discoveries of California and Australia gave another stimulus to one branch of this rapidly growing industry.[1]

The greatest development of all, however, was associated with the brass trade, which by the end of this period had become the largest of Birmingham's industries. The increased demand for copper and brass articles came from a variety of sources, which were all dependent on the changes which the new industrial era had produced in the mechanical equipment of society and in the standard of life. The steam-engine brought demands for brass cocks and gauges, and the discovery in 1838 of a process for making seamless brass tubes, which were more suitable than the brazed type for boilers, created a new branch. The manufacture of a new alloy, called yellow or Muntz's metal, was begun early in the century to supply the demand for ships' sheathing ; and the production of naval brassfoundry, which had long been carried on to a limited extent by cabinet brassfounders, became a separate and substantial branch of the industry in the middle forties.[2] The introduction of gaslighting in the early part of the century gave rise to another section ; and with the growth in the national wealth and the decline in the national taste there grew up a great trade in elaborate domestic fittings of brass and copper. Finally, the Public Health Acts and the new duties which the municipalities began to assume towards the middle of the century created a large demand for water-cocks. On the production side this expansion of the industry was stimulated by the fall in the price of copper between 1818 and 1851, and by the discovery of a new process for making brass.[3] After 1830, the alloy came to be produced by mixing copper and spelter (zinc) directly in a crucible, instead of by the longer and more complicated " cementation " process previously followed.[4]

Several of the older trades were subject to changes in the relative importance of their different branches. This was particularly true of those which were affected by fashion. The ornamental buckle trade and, indeed, most of the " toy " trades

[1] S. Timmins, *op. cit.*, p. 453.
[2] *Ibid.*, pp. 313, 352-353.
[3] *Ibid.*, p. 259 *et seq.*
[4] W. J. Davis, *A Short History of the Brass Trade* (1892), pp. 5-6.

had gone by 1860[1]; while metal-button manufacture, after a period of rapid growth in the closing years of the eighteenth and the early part of the nineteenth century, began to decline when other kinds of button came into use. It was first affected by the coming of covered buttons during the second decade, and the introduction of the linen button in 1841 and of the vegetable-ivory button in 1850 accelerated its decline. The pearl-button branch of this industry had, however, grown, and, in spite of the above changes, this and the metal-button trades were still the major sections of the industry in 1860.[2]

The old silver-plate trade, together with such small industries as were concerned with the production of pewter and Britannia-metal goods, was also adversely affected, although this was owing to the discovery of a new manufacturing process rather than to a change of fashion. About 1840, the process of the electro-deposition of silver on baser metals was introduced into Birmingham, and from that date the silver-plate trade began to decay. Electro-plating had another effect on local industry, for it resulted in the introduction of a new alloy, nickel silver or German silver, to the town's metalworkers. This was used as a base metal for the new plating industry, in place of copper, from which the old silver-plate articles had been made; and the refining of nickel itself was also added to the list of Birmingham's activities.[3]

During the second quarter of the nineteenth century a variety of new manufactures sprang up in the town. The metal-bedstead trade first achieved importance during the thirties, and the wood-screw trade in the fifties. The manufacture of steel pens became firmly seated in the locality as the result of the introduction of a new process of production in 1829; the percussion-cap industry grew with the decline of the flint-lock guns; and wire ropes began to be produced in the forties.[4] The attraction which Birmingham continued to exercise during this period, and which resulted in the concentration of many trades within the town, is further illustrated by the history of another minor manufacture —viz. rule-making. In the eighteenth century this had been

---

[1] *Labour and the Poor* in *The Morning Chronicle*, January 27 and February 17, 1851.
[2] *Ibid.*, October 21 and November 1, 1850; S. Timmins, *op. cit.*, p. 432 *et seq.*
[3] S. Timmins, *op. cit.*, pp. 477, 617.
[4] James Jaffray, *op. cit.*, chap. l.

extensively carried on at London and Wolverhampton, as well as at Birmingham ; but gradually the trade deserted the other centres and had become almost entirely located in Birmingham by 1860.[1] There was also a development in the range of engineering products. Steam-engines were made during this period by several local firms, and to this trade was added the manufacture of railway rolling-stock in 1838, of sewing-machines in 1850, and of hydraulic machinery in 1857.[2] During the thirties the skilled metalworkers of Birmingham were enlisted in an interesting minor industry, associated with the names of Pugin and Hardman. This was the production of art and " ecclesiastical " metalwork, which was expressed both in wrought-iron and in the non-ferrous metals.[3]

Besides these there were several trades which Birmingham possessed in common with the rest of the district, and which will now be considered in conjunction with the industries that were confined to the Black Country. The leather trades of Birmingham and Walsall, for instance, which were concerned mainly with producing saddlery and harness, were stimulated by the increased colonial and foreign demands following the gold discoveries of California in 1849 and of Australia in 1851 ; while in connection with saddlers' ironmongery an important new process was discovered. Before 1811 bits and stirrups had been forged on the anvil, but in that year a process, which could be applied to the production of many light iron articles of rather complex form, brought into being a new branch of industry, that of malleable-iron castings.[4] In the Birmingham and Stourbridge flint-glass trades an expansion occurred after 1845, when the excise duty on glass was repealed, and several additional branches of the glass industry came into existence. The most important of these was the heavy section of the trade, the history of which may be said to have begun in 1824, when R. L. Chance purchased the works of the British Crown Glass Company of Smethwick. To the original manufacture of crown glass was added that of sheet, plate and optical glass. The pressed-glass trade, producing table-ware of a cheaper kind than the flint-

---

[1] *The Carpenter's Slide Rule* (published by John Rabone & Sons, 1870), p. 14.
[2] S. Timmins, *op. cit.*, pp. 647 and 670.
[3] *Ibid.*, p. 536.
[4] *Ibid.*, p. 125 *et seq.*, and p. 436 *et seq.*

glass makers, appears to have enjoyed only a short life, as it was established at Birmingham in 1832, but most of it had migrated to Newcastle-on-Tyne before 1860.[1]

The iron- and steel-using trades, with a few exceptions, expanded and increased in variety between 1800 and 1861. The edge-tool industry, which was carried on at Birmingham, Oldbury, Wolverhampton and Hales Owen, appears to have benefited at the expense of Sheffield. The same was true also of the manufacture of fenders and fire-irons, which was conducted at Dudley and Wolverhampton.[2] At both Birmingham and Wolverhampton, moreover, the production of tinplate wares was extended ; while after 1850 the discovery of a process for enamelling cast-iron gave rise to a new branch of the West Bromwich hollow-ware industry.[3] At Wednesbury an important new manufacture arose after the decline in the demand for gun-barrels after the French war. This was the welded-tube industry, producing pipes for gas and water. It appears that the gun-barrels on hand after 1815 had been converted into gas-tubes, for which a demand was just springing up, and during the twenties both Wednesbury and Walsall became centres of a substantial tube production.[4] Ten years later the coach-iron makers of the former town turned to railway work, and the neighbourhood began to turn out railway axles and heavy castings. At Darlaston there was a less obvious transition between the old and new industries, for there the manufacture of gun-locks and barrels came to be replaced at the beginning of the railway age by the production of nuts and bolts.[5] In the neighbourhood of Dudley and Tipton, long famous for the manufacture of wrought nails, two new industries took root. The first was the production of chains and cables, introduced about 1824, and this was followed by anchor-making nearly a quarter of a century later.[6] About 1830 the locksmiths of Wolverhampton began to extend their scope of production so as to include wrought-iron safes [7] ; while at West Bromwich a coil-spring and

---

[1] S. Timmins, op. cit., p. 147 et seq., p. 151 et seq., and p. 526 et seq.; also A Hundred Years of British Glass Making (Chance Bros. & Co. Ltd.), pp. 7-9.
[2] S. Timmins, op. cit., pp. 656, 662, 664.
[3] Ibid., p. 193 et seq.
[4] F. W. Hackwood, Wednesbury Workshops, p. 82 et seq.
[5] Ibid., p. 54 ; and A History of Darlaston, p. 157 et seq.
[6] S. Timmins, op. cit., p. 99.
[7] George Price, A Treatise on Fire- and Thief-Proof Depositories (1856), p. 9.

balance trade took its place beside the production of laminated springs for coaches,[1] which had long been carried on there. Several Black Country firms took up the manufacture of agricultural implements and iron fencing after 1840, and heavy forgings and structural ironwork began to be produced at West Bromwich, Tipton and Brierley Hill.[2] About the same time the galvanizing process was introduced into the district and laid the foundation for several new branches of industry.[3]

Another heavy trade in which development was associated both with the growth of population within the area and with local supplies of raw materials was the brick and tile manufacture. This expanded considerably, particularly in the neighbourhood of Birmingham and Stourbridge. In the same period a heavy chemical industry began to develop at Wolverhampton and Oldbury; red-lead production for the flint-glass trade was introduced to Tipton and West Bromwich; Birmingham took up the manufacture of wax matches; and in many towns in the district there arose a considerable production of colours, varnishes and japans to satisfy the needs of the local hardware manufacturers.[4]

The remarkable progress in the majority of the local industries was offset only in a few cases by a decline, and this was generally due to the fact that new manufactures or new processes had displaced those of the early nineteenth century. Several examples have already been given. The most serious decline, as far as Birmingham itself was considered, occurred in the metal-button manufacture, in consequence of the rise of covered and of vegetable-ivory buttons, and in the production of gilt and fancy "toys," which were displaced by jewellery; while electro-plate table-ware had, by 1860, almost superseded silver-plated, pewter and Britannia-metal articles. Several minor trades also decayed. The manufacture of swords was of small importance in the middle of the century.[5] The pottery trade, which had existed in the Wednesbury neighbourhood in the eighteenth century, had left the district for North Staffordshire, and the production of fancy enamel ware had disappeared from Bilston.[6] With the

---

[1] Personal inquiry.　　　　　　　[2] S. Timmins, op. cit., pp. 100-101.
[3] S. Griffiths, Guide to the Iron Trade of Great Britain (1873), p. 93; and W. H. Jones, op. cit., p. 159 et seq.
[4] S. Timmins, op. cit., p. 671 et seq.
[5] Birmingham and her Manufactures in The Leisure Hour, March 24, 1853.
[6] F. W. Hackwood, Wednesbury Workshops, pp. 9-19; and W. H. Jones, op. cit., p. 12.

rise of enamelled hollow-ware, moreover, much of the manufacture of " black " or rough cast-iron hollow-ware was tending
to migrate to Scotland.[1] In the Black Country and its borderland, however, the most serious consequences of industrial
change were felt by the nail trade. During the first quarter of
the century this had been a large and expanding industry, and
employed far more people than any other manufacture in the
locality—it has been stated, indeed, that there were about 50,000
nailers in South Staffordshire and Worcestershire in 1830,
when the trade was at its zenith; but, in view of the size of the
total population of these counties, this is obviously an exaggerated estimate. Yet it was undoubtedly carried on in almost
every quarter of our area and on the fringe of country surrounding it, and nail-making may certainly be considered the staple
trade of the Black Country during the first three decades of the
century. In 1830, however, a new process of manufacture began
to affect the production of hand-wrought nails. Machinery was
introduced for cutting nails from iron strip; factories began to
be established in Birmingham for producing these " cut " nails,
as they were called, and the cost of production was greatly
reduced. For some years, it is true, only a few types of nails
could be made in this way; but the competition of machinery
had become sufficiently serious by 1860 to reduce the number
of nailers in the district and to bring about a condition of chronic
depression in their industry.[2]

We have purposely left until the end of this chapter a description of the development which occurred in iron production and
in coal-mining, for those industries can be conveniently treated
in isolation from the lighter trades. In 1806 our district was
producing about a fifth of the total make of pig-iron in Great
Britain. The next two decades witnessed an enormous expansion; and by 1830 South Staffordshire became relatively more
important as an iron-producing centre than ever before or since,
and rivalled South Wales, then the chief seat of the pig-iron
industry. By that time Shropshire, which at the beginning of
the century had ranked above Staffordshire, was left far behind.[3]
As a centre of finished-iron production the Black Country had
achieved an even higher position, and the application of Joseph

[1] S. Timmins, *op. cit.*, p. 107.   [2] *Ibid.*, p. 111 *et seq.*, p. 613.
[3] H. Scrivenor, *op. cit.*, p. 135.

Hall's method of " wet puddling " or " pig boiling " to this branch of the industry between 1825 and 1832 confirmed the supremacy of the district.[1] After 1830, although the output of pig- and of finished-iron continued to increase, the relative importance of the area declined, as far as the former product was concerned. This was owing, first, to the rise of a Scottish industry, which the introduction of the hot blast by Neilson made possible, and, later, to the growth of iron production in Lancashire, Cumberland and Cleveland, which were more favourably situated than Staffordshire, both for export and for securing supplies of raw materials. Yet, even if the Black Country's share of the total British output of pig-iron fell from 30 per cent. in 1830 to 17 per cent. in 1858, the amount for which it was responsible at the end of this period was nearly three times its production in 1830 and twelve times its production in 1806. As a centre of high-grade wrought-iron manufacture it was still unsurpassed, and it was producing in the fifties from 500,000 to 600,000 tons a year—about one-third of the total British output.[2]

Together with this increase in production there had come about an extension of the area in which the iron was manufactured. At the end of the eighteenth century the blast-furnaces had been found only in the neighbourhood of Dudley, Stourbridge and Wolverhampton. By 1860, however, they were scattered over almost every quarter of the Black Country; and there had been a particularly great development at West Bromwich, which had become an important centre both of pig and of finished iron.[3] The manufacture of blister steel had also been introduced into South Staffordshire during this period, but the amount produced was never considerable.[4] Meanwhile, the mining activities of the area had extended. Although by 1860 the thick coal seams in the older mining districts of Dudley and Wednesbury were approaching exhaustion, the field had been opened up elsewhere, notably at West Bromwich. The annual output of coal rose from some 840,000 tons at the end of the eighteenth century to from 5,000,000 to 5,250,000 tons in the

[1] J. W. Hall, *The Life and Work of Joseph Hall* (reprinted from the *Proceedings of the Staffordshire Iron and Steel Institute for 1916*), p. 12 *et seq.*
[2] R. Hunt, *Mineral Statistics of Great Britain and Ireland*, 1855-1860.
[3] *Ibid.*, 1860, pp. 79-80.
[4] S. Timmins, *op. cit.*, p. 70.

fifties ; while the yield of ironstone, which had been 60,000 tons in 1798, increased to 959,000 tons in 1858.[1]

The growth in the basic industries of the area was due, in the early years of the century, to the demand for munitions in consequence of the French war, but after that time it was associated with the great increase in the mechanical equipment of society which characterized that period. As many writers have indicated, the industrial revolution brought about a great increase in the relative importance of the metal trades, and the Black Country was one of the first districts in the country to benefit by that change. Moreover, just as in an earlier period industrial growth had been made possible by the construction of canals, so during the two decades previous to 1860 the industries of the area received a great stimulus from the development of the railway system. This caused the appearance of new trades and provided the iron industry with an additional customer; so that boiler-plates, though not rails, became one of its staple products. Further, the railway system, by linking up Birmingham and District with other great centres of population, both extended the market for local trades by reducing the cost of transport, and, within the town and the district, confirmed the localization of industries which had been brought there by other causes, even if those causes might have ceased to operate.

In 1860 the new forces, which had begun to affect the industrial structure of the area a century before, had almost worked themselves out. Birmingham had developed from a centre of " toy " and gun production into the chief British centre for hardware of all kinds. The older industries, as demand for certain of their products increased, had split up to form a number of new trades. Manufactures which were merely incipient in 1760 had reached maturity. The brass trade, with its thousand products of the foundry, stamp and draw-bench, had risen to become the town's greatest industry. Almost equally striking developments had occurred in the gun, jewellery, button, edge-tool and glass manufactures, and in a host of small iron trades ; while in the second quarter of the nineteenth century a multitude of new industries, including the manufacture of cut nails, railway rolling-stock, pens, enamelled hollow-ware and electro-plate had been swept within the scope of the town's activities. In the Black

[1] R. Hunt, *op. cit.*, 1858, p. 74.

Country a few of the smaller metal manufactures declined in relative importance with the growth of mining and of iron production. But the district had turned to wrought-iron tubes, nuts and bolts, malleable-iron castings, anchors, chains, chemicals, galvanized ironwork, springs and safes, in addition to its older industries like locks, wrought nails, glass, leather, saddlers' ironmongery and hollow-ware.

In 1760 iron had been the chief raw material with which both Birmingham and the Black Country had been concerned. Such exceptions as existed—for example, the manufacture of glass, leather and brass wares—were found to the same extent in South Staffordshire as in Birmingham. By 1860, however, whereas the former was still almost as exclusively occupied with iron as a century before, two of Birmingham's chief trades—viz. jewellery and brass—were non-ferrous trades, important industries existed in connection with German silver, pearl-shell, glass and leather, and iron was relatively less extensively used as a raw material. This change occurred mainly because the raw materials of South Staffordshire had induced the new branches of the iron-using trades to settle there, while the special skill of the Birmingham manufacturers and artisans could be applied to the production of highly finished goods, no matter what the metal of which they were made. The effect was to confirm the tendency which has already been referred to. In 1860 the Black Country was not only engaged in mining, in pig- and finished-iron production, and in the manufacture of the cruder small iron articles, as it had been at the end of the eighteenth century, but it had added the production of finished or semi-manufactured goods of a heavy type, such as constructional ironwork, tubes and galvanized sheets. Birmingham, however, still remained faithful to the highly manufactured class of commodities, which, when they were not small and light, were composite in character.

It is not without interest to look more closely at the forces which attracted the new industries to the locality, and which led to the increase in the already great variety of its trades. Apart from the influence of raw materials, which of course exercised a determining influence on the establishment of many of the South Staffordshire manufactures, the localization of a new industry in the area frequently depended on the existence of a particular kind of skill and technical knowledge which could be directed towards satisfying the fresh demand. The discovery of a new process of manufacture often immediately preceded the rise of an industry to prominence. And such a discovery would be more likely to be made in a town with a long industrial tradition than elsewhere, because there the analogy between the processes employed in long-established trades and those required for new classes of products would be soon obvious to alert manufacturers, who would be quick to adapt existing productive methods to new industries. Thus in the early years of the century, when several Birmingham men were experimenting in the manufacture of steel pens, it was a toy-maker, Joseph Gillott, who conceived the idea of applying the method of production then followed in the manufacture of buttons to the new article, and so created the steel-pen industry.[1] Similarly it was a retired button-maker from Birmingham who in the first instance suggested the use of the stamp and press to the Redditch needle-makers for piercing the eyes of the needles, and so gave them an advantage over their rival centre of production.[2] Several other trades also grew to importance because of the alertness of local manufacturers in adopting new processes. The introduction of American automatic machinery caused the rise of the wood-screw manufacture. The metal-bedstead trade was created by the discovery of the " dovetail joint and of the method of joining the parts as firmly as if they had grown together by casting in chill moulds "; for this greatly reduced the cost of production.[3] In all these and in many other cases, moreover, the localization was confirmed by the existence within the town of labour, plant and subsidiary industries appropriate to the new trades. For the bedstead manufacturers there were firms to supply them with tubes and stamped brassfoundry. Women and girls accustomed to light press-work could be recruited for the steel-pen manufacture and female machinists for the screw-cutting lathes.

In some cases a depression in one branch of industry induced manufacturers to adapt themselves to satisfy a new demand. An example of this kind was provided by Wednesbury, where, as we have seen, the iron-tube trade grew out of the decaying gun-barrel manufacture. Sometimes there was a natural transition

[1] E. Edwards, *Personal Recollections of Birmingham and Birmingham Men* (1877), p. 92.
[2] S. Timmins, *op. cit.*, p. 199.
[3] W. J. Davis, *A Short History of the Brass Trade* (1892), p. 24.

from the production of goods expressed in one material to the manufacture of articles of a similar nature made of another kind, as from iron and steel " toys " to jewellery, or from metal to other varieties of buttons. The manufacture of highly composite products, made of many different materials, would naturally be drawn to such a town as Birmingham, which had a great variety of industries ; but this factor was to exert a greater influence in later years. Finally, the central situation of the district made it suitable, especially after the construction of the railways, for supplying the small metal wares which found markets in all parts of the country ; while even for the export trade the class of goods produced by the local industries would be less likely than any others to suffer from the added cost of transport to the sea.

At this stage it will be well to utter a word of warning with regard to the generalizations which are made here and elsewhere on the question of the causes of localization. Such statements must be received with caution. It must be remembered that the explanations are given *ex post facto*, and that the economic historian in his search for causes is led inevitably to place his emphasis on the material factors. In the case of industries in which the presence of raw materials, climate or proximity to markets has been obviously the determining cause, this method is likely to lead to truth, because in these instances the individual has his choice of sites severely limited by the existing material conditions. But the entrepreneurs in the lighter industries, such as were characteristic of Birmingham and District, are not so definitely the slaves of geological and geographical conditions. They have a great deal of freedom in the selection of sites. Hence it is often extraordinarily difficult to explain not only why certain industries should have become so highly localized within our area, but also why particular towns or districts within that area, having no obvious advantages over other places in the neighbourhood, should have become the centre of certain trades. When all the material factors have been accounted for, the element of pure chance in many cases remains the determining influence. An energetic or original man happens to be born in one rather than in another congenial environment. An invention leading to the manufacture of a new type of product happens to be made in a certain town, and the trade takes root there, although many other places may be equally suitable for the industry. How else, for instance, can one explain the localization of the new coil-spring trade at West Bromwich, rather than in many other places in the neighbourhood? Again, when a demand for a new class of product arises, a certain centre may happen to be suffering from a depression in a staple industry and to possess an unemployed labour force accustomed to make somewhat similar articles. It may then turn to the new trade. This alone can account for Wednesbury becoming the seat of tube production. Sometimes it may be merely that a manufacturer happens to purchase a particular site for his factory rather than several others which are equally suitable, but which do not chance to be in the market at the time. In all these cases the material environment does not provide the cause, but merely the conditions, of localization. Finally, it must be remembered that in a multitude of instances all record of the factors which originally led to the selection of a particular locality have been entirely lost, and the historian, thrown back on surmise, may arrive at conclusions which would have astounded the pioneer manufacturer. So all generalizations concerning the causes of localization must remain tentative. It can be said, however, that once a town or district has become the site of a particular manufacture, that industry tends to remain there, especially in the case of the lighter trades where the influence of material conditions is at a minimum, because of the growth of a specialized labour force.

PART II
BIRMINGHAM AND DISTRICT IN 1860

CHAPTER I

THE BIRMINGHAM TRADES

SINCE a good deal of attention is to be given to the industrial structure of the area as it appeared in 1860, the reason which led to the selection of that date as a starting-point must be indicated. The preceding chapters will have helped to justify the choice. By 1800, as we have seen, the area had begun to assume a new economic character, and during the first half of the nineteenth century it reached maturity both as a hardware and as an iron-producing centre. The year 1860 thus corresponds roughly to a point of time when the forces which had been set in motion towards the end of the previous century had nearly run their course, and when our district had still to enjoy a further short period of expansion on the old lines before entering upon a second era of transformation.

The previous chapter has served to trace the general growth of the area as a whole up to 1860. In this and the following chapters an attempt will be made to take, as it were, a cross-section of the district's industrial development, to describe the sort of goods with which its different trades were concerned at that date, and by reference to the numbers engaged in the several manufactures to arrive at some notion of their relative importance. It is hoped that, if there is some slight repetition of facts mentioned in the earlier chapters, this will be forgiven, as it is essential that we should have a clear idea of the industries which flourished at the beginning of our period. It will be convenient to deal first with the industries which belonged essentially to the borough of Birmingham, and to leave the few trades which it shared with other parts of our district, together with the staple Black Country manufactures, for later chapters. The mere fact that it is possible to follow this method of classification illustrates the contrast between the two main sections of our area and the divergence of their industrial activities.

In Birmingham itself the four chief manufactures were brass goods, guns, buttons and jewellery. These trades not only afforded a larger amount of employment than any others, but it was in them that the town enjoyed, if not a monopoly, at any rate a marked predominance over the rest of the district. The brass trade was probably the largest of all, though it is impossible to be quite sure on this point in view of the inadequacy of the available statistical data; and it is with this branch of manufacture that we will first concern ourselves. According to the Census of 1861 [1] there were in the borough of Birmingham 8100 males and females of all ages engaged in the brass trade. This figure, however, does not include all who were so employed. Over 400 people were returned as lacquerers, and most of these must have been connected with the industry ; while brass-wire drawers are likely to have been placed in other categories, such as wire manufacture. On the other hand, the Census total probably includes many brassworkers who were connected with specialized trades, such as metal-bedstead making; and so we may estimate the employment in the Birmingham brass industry, as it is defined below, at 8000.

In other parts of the area the trade was comparatively small. It is true that there were some 600 brassworkers in the Wolverhampton Poor Law District, including Willenhall, Bilston and Wednesfield, about 300 at Walsall and 400 at Smethwick, besides smaller numbers at West Bromwich and Dudley ; but Birmingham possessed at least 80 per cent. of the total number employed in the brass trade within our area.[2] Further, while the workers in the Black Country towns were concerned mainly with supplying the staple industries of each locality with brass accessories, as in the case of the lock trade of Willenhall or the harness trade of Walsall, in Birmingham the industry was far from being merely subsidiary, for it produced a wide variety of finished goods.

NUMBERS ENGAGED IN THE BIRMINGHAM BRASS TRADE
ACCORDING TO THE CENSUS RETURNS

1831	.	.	.	.	.	.	.	1800
1841	.	.	.	.	.	.	.	3400
1851	.	.	.	.	.	.	.	6700
1861	.	.	.	.	.	.	.	8100 [3]

The above Table indicates that it had been subject to a remarkable growth since 1831. Practically all its branches had been stimulated by increased demands ; several new types

---

[1] *Census of England and Wales*, 1861, vol. ii., pp. 511, 514.
[2] *Ibid.*, vol. ii., p. 469 *et seq.*
[3] In the three counties of Warwickshire, Staffordshire and Worcestershire the number was 10,400 (*Census of England and Wales*, 1861, vol. ii., pp. 469, 476).

of product had been added, and its expansion had been such that its historian of the early sixties had been led to declare: " What Manchester is in cotton, Bradford in wool, and Sheffield in steel, Birmingham is in brass." [1]

The rise of the brass trade to the position of a staple had, then, been comparatively recent; yet even before the end of the previous century it had been sufficiently important to possess several distinct branches, and the extension of its range of products after 1800 had created a larger number of clearly defined subdivisions. These may with advantage be described in some detail, for the classification has remained with but little alteration down to the present time.

There were two main sections.

The first consisted of the group of trades engaged in producing from the copper and spelter ingots, which formed the raw materials, semi-manufactured commodities, such as brass and copper sheets, strip, tubes and wire. These were supplied both to other branches of the brass trade and to allied industries. Brass wire was the raw material of the pin trade, and was employed in making fireguards, chains for gas-fittings, telegraph cables, and bracelets for the African market. Much of the sheet metal went to the stamped brassfoundry trade, and a special alloy, known as yellow or Muntz's metal, was used for sheathing ships. The tubes varied from the brazed and cased tubes used for curtain rods, balustrades and bedsteads to seamless tubes, which were required for the boilers of locomotives and marine engines. It is difficult to arrive at an accurate estimate of the numbers employed in this section of the trade. There is, however, evidence to show that there were 500 men and boys in the boiler-tube manufacture and 500 in the rolling mills about this time [2]; so that the total number engaged in making non-ferrous sheet, wire and tubes was probably in the neighbourhood of 2500.[3]

The second and larger section of the industry was that engaged in producing finished goods. These varied considerably in character and may be grouped under six heads. The two most

[1] S. Timmins, op. cit., p. 229.

[2] Ibid., p. 316; and Children's Employment Commission (1862), Third Report, p. 151.

[3] The Reports of the Inspectors of Factories (October 1868, p. 116 et seq.) show that 1800 persons were engaged in tube-making in Warwickshire. The greater part of these was in Birmingham, and most of them would be employed in the non-ferrous tube trade.

important were the cabinet brassfoundry and the "lighting" branches. In 1851 these had accounted for nearly half of the total number of people engaged in the whole brass trade, and their relative importance certainly did not diminish during the next nine years.[1] The former included goods used by cabinet-makers, carpenters and builders, and consisted of such articles as hinges, castors, knobs, handles, hooks and window-fastenings, for which the growth of the population and the prosperity of the country during the early Victorian period had created a great demand. The "lighting" branch of the industry was concerned with the manufacture of oil lamps, candlesticks and gas-fittings. In 1851 the brass-candlestick trade had been fairly large, employing between 300 and 500 people; but, although the increased foreign demand had done something towards balancing the great fall in domestic sales, this manufacture was declining steadily.[1] The same must be said of the production of lamps. The railways had brought a demand for lamps for signals and carriage lighting; the shipping industry was a large customer; and a few years later the trade was to receive a stimulus from the introduction of paraffin-lamp manufacture into the town. But in 1860 this branch was failing. The cause was undoubtedly the spread of gaslighting, and the demand for fittings, which accompanied this development, had certainly compensated for the decline in the lamp and candlestick trade.[2]

The improvement in sanitation, which had taken place throughout the country just before 1860, had extended the manufacture of water-taps, plugs, washers and valves; and this had brought into prominence another subdivision of the industry—viz. plumbers' brassfoundry—a branch which produced also small hydraulic machines, pumps and fittings for beer-engines.[3] Closely allied to it was engineers' brassfoundry. At one time the brass steam-cocks, gauges, whistles and lubricating caps required for steam-engines and other types of machinery had been produced in the engineering factories, but as their trade became more firmly established the engineers found it more profitable to purchase these accessories from specialists, and thus the engineers' requirements in this type of

[1] *Labour and the Poor* in *The Morning Chronicle*, January 6, 1851.
[2] *Ibid.*; and S. Timmins, *op. cit.*, p. 331 *et seq.*
[3] S. Timmins, *op. cit.*, pp. 285-291.

product came to be met by Birmingham brassfounders.[1] Another branch of the trade which owed its origin also to this tendency towards specialization by process in the engineering industry was naval brassfoundry. Up to about 1830 brass fittings for ships had been made in the chief shipbuilding centres ; but by the sixties this trade also had migrated to Birmingham.[1] The development is a natural one and may be noticed in progress to-day in the newer industries. In the early years of any industry concerned with a composite product each manufacturer may be obliged to make all the various parts he requires, however small their quantity may be ; while as the trade reaches maturity, specialists appear to supply such parts and accessories as they can produce more economically than the original manufacturer.

In the course of the last chapter the rise of the stamped brass-foundry trade in the latter half of the eighteenth century was described. This became a branch of great importance between 1830 and 1860 because of the application of the stamping process to the manufacture of articles previously cast. It was not only concerned with producing finished goods, such as window-cornices and finger-plates, but it supplied the other branches of the brassfoundry trade with stamped parts.[2] Besides this there only remain to be mentioned the small section of the industry which was engaged in bell-founding and, finally, the general brassfoundry trade, which produced a great variety of articles, from shop-fittings and picture rods to brass furniture-nails and thimbles.

It is evident that the demand for many of the articles produced by the brassfounders was liable to be affected by changes of fashion and of national habits, and that the industry, like many others in the locality, had to be prepared to adapt itself to these conditions. During the decades immediately preceding 1860, however, the trend of fashion and of industrial change was almost entirely favourable, for the development of railways and steamboats, the rise of gaslighting, the prevailing taste in furniture and domestic ornaments, and the new governmental activities and legislative enactments, all contributed to the expansion and the prosperity of the Birmingham brassfounders.

Although of more recent origin than the brass trade, the manufacture of jewellery had in 1860 attained a position of

[1] S. Timmins, *op. cit.*, p. 353. [2] *Ibid.*, p. 292 *et seq.*

almost equal prominence. " Jewellery " is here used in the trade sense and covers more than is commonly understood by the term, for it includes not only workers in the precious metals, but all those who were producing articles of personal adornment or table-ware in silver, electro-plate and other metals. The oldest branch of the industry thus defined was the " toy " trade, from which, indeed, the whole of it had originally sprung. In 1860 the manufacture of iron and steel " toys," once the staple product of Birmingham, had dwindled to insignificance, and this branch was then concerned chiefly with gilt articles.[1] At Wolverhampton and elsewhere in the district the " steel " toy trade had practically disappeared.[2] The old silver-plate trade, too, was dying, and its place had been taken by the flourishing electro-plating industry.[3] Many varieties of table-ware which had been made of pewter or Britannia-metal in the early part of the century had been drawn within the scope of this trade by 1860, and the firms which had previously manufactured those products had changed over to producing such things as wine- and beer-measures.[4] Two other prominent sections were engaged on gold and silver chains, while the largest amount of employment of all was afforded by the jewellery trade proper, which produced gold and silver lockets, links, rings, bracelets, pins and necklaces. These various branches appear to have become clearly differentiated after 1840, when the trade as a whole entered upon a period of great expansion, which was to leave it one of the most important constituents in the town's industrial life. We have already seen that the growing habit of personal decoration was partly responsible for this expansion ; but the growth in the relative importance of the gold sections of the industry as compared with the silver—a growth which was one of the most outstanding features in the years immediately preceding 1860—had been occasioned chiefly by the gold discoveries of California and of Australia between 1849 and 1851.[5] To complete this classification of the different branches certain subsidiary industries should be mentioned, such as metal-refining, stamping, rolling, die-sinking and diamond-mounting, which had developed with the rise of the industry as a whole.

[1] *Labour and the Poor* in *The Morning Chronicle*, January 27 and February 10 and 17, 1851.
[2] G. Price, *op. cit.*, p. 852, n. [3] S. Timmins, *op. cit.*, p. 477 *et seq.*
[4] *Ibid.*, p. 617 *et seq.* [5] *Ibid.*, p. 452 *et seq.*

The Census figures are not of themselves complete enough to enable us to determine the amount of employment in the trade. According to this authority there were, in 1861, 7000 people of all ages returned as goldsmiths, jewellers and platers in the borough of Birmingham[1]; but it is not obvious whether the gilt-toy makers and the members of the subsidiary industries are included or not. An estimate which was made in 1866 is therefore worth quoting.

EMPLOYMENT IN THE JEWELLERY TRADE, 1866[2]

Masters	500 (or 600)
Jewellers proper	3000
Silversmiths	1000
Gold- and Silver-Chain Makers . . .	1500
Gilt-Toy Makers	1000
Box-Makers, Die-Sinkers and Workers in Subsidiary Trades	1000
Total .	8000

Besides these, there were probably more than 1000 electro-platers engaged in making ornaments and table-ware; and so, if the considerable expansion which occurred between 1860 and 1866 is allowed for, the number in the whole industry at the former date can be placed at 7000 to 7500.

At this time most of the country's supply of cheap and middle-class jewellery, and a large proportion of its electro-plate ware, came from Birmingham. In the early nineteenth century the former manufacture had been carried on in Derby and elsewhere, while " toys " had been made at Bilston and Wolverhampton. By 1860 none of these places was of any importance in these branches of industry; and although there appears to have been a fair number of jewellers at Walsall, in no place within our area except Birmingham was the trade of any considerable importance. Further, even within the town it was becoming confined to one small district in the neighbourhood of St Paul's Church, which remains to this day the " jewellers' quarter." [2] The cause of this development is worth attention. In the twenties most of the jewellers appear to have been conducting their business just north of Colmore Row, in Great Charles Street, Church Street and Newhall Street; and with

[1] *Census of England and Wales*, 1861, vol. ii., pp. 511, 514.
[2] S. Timmins, *op. cit.*, p. 457.

small modifications this remained the seat of their activities for the next twenty years. The present jewellers' quarter was then a pleasant lower middle-class residential district, which was largely occupied by the skilled craftsmen employed in the trade, who formed a comparatively well-paid and prosperous class. When the great increase in demand occurred in the later forties, then the artisans began to establish businesses of their own and used part of their dwelling-places as workshops.[1] In this way a large section of the industry was transferred to its present site, and once it was established there, the advantage of a high degree of localization became apparent; for as the trade grew, processes became more highly specialized, and it became necessary for manufacturers who performed complementary operations on some article to be in close proximity to one another. Few makers of finished goods, moreover, were concerned with more than a narrow range of articles, and it was an advantage for them to be grouped together, since the factors through whom the jewellery was sold, and who required to purchase many different types, were then able to get into touch the more easily with their sources of supply. And finally, since the industry was one which attracted thieves, a physical approximation of workplaces made protection comparatively simple. For these reasons, then, much of the jewellery trade was by 1860 already centred round St Paul's Church, although the movement was not yet complete and there were still many manufacturers in other parts of the town. The electro-platers were for the most part to be found, as at present, in Newhall Street and on the fringe of the quarter.

This localization within a particular section of the town was also a characteristic of one of Birmingham's oldest industries, the gun trade. Of the 5800 people [2] engaged in this manufacture within the borough's boundaries in 1861 the majority worked within a small district round St Mary's Church.[3] This was the "gun quarter," which not only had practically a monopoly of the work of assembling or "setting-up" the guns, but which was also the site of the manufacture of much of the "material,"

[1] *Cf.* J. C. Roche, *op. cit.*, pp. 70-71.
[2] The number in Warwickshire, Staffordshire and Worcestershire was 8500 (*Census of England and Wales*, 1861, vol. ii., pp. 467, 471, 474, 478, 509, 513).
[3] S. Timmins, *op. cit.*, p. 393; and *Pictures of the People* in *Birmingham Morning News*, June 20, 1871.

or parts, which were required. The reason for the high degree of localization is not difficult to discover. The manufacture of guns, as of jewellery, was carried on by a large number of makers who specialized on particular processes, and this method of organization involved the frequent transport of parts from one workshop to another. Had the industry been scattered, a great amount of time would have been lost in carrying material to and fro, and the advantages of concentration must have been obvious to all members of the trade. It is curious to find, however, that certain classes of " material-makers," as they were called, were found in greater numbers in the Black Country than in Birmingham. At Darlaston, for instance, there were 300 or 400 lock-makers; at Wednesbury a somewhat smaller number of workers also were engaged in this branch, and at West Bromwich several factories existed for producing bayonets and rammers. In all there were at this time between 1000 and 1500 people employed in making parts for the Birmingham and London gun trade in the various Black Country towns and villages.[1] The course of development which led to this distribution of the trade is interesting. Both Wednesbury and Darlaston were producing barrels and locks in the eighteenth century, and it is possible that the latter may have produced even complete guns then, though this had disappeared by 1800. The manufacture of barrels declined after the Napoleonic Wars, and never recovered, and the barrel-makers turned to new classes of products; but gun-locks continued to be made in those towns in greater numbers than in Birmingham up to the beginning of our period.[2] It should be noticed that this distribution of the different sections of the industry is in conformity with the tendency which has been previously discussed—the tendency for the raw materials of South Staffordshire to attract towards it the cruder manufactures, while the skill of the Birmingham workers brought to the town an increasing share of the finishing processes.

The gun trade was not only subdivided as to its processes, but its products varied considerably in character. In 1860 its two chief branches from this point of view were the military-arms and the sporting-gun trades. The former was subject to great fluctuations of demand, partly because requirements were

[1] *Census of England and Wales*, 1861, vol. ii., p. 486 *et seq.*
[2] F. W. Hackwood, *Wednesbury Workshops*, chap. vii.

liable to be swelled enormously by the outbreak of war, and
partly because governments might suddenly decide to equip
their forces with a new type of arm, and so bring about a large
but temporary expansion. For instance, the adoption of the
percussion cap and the abandonment of the old flint-lock in
1839 brought an increased volume of trade to the lock-makers ;
while the introduction of the expanding bullet and of rifled
barrels into the services after 1851, together with the stimulus
of the Crimean War, kept the gunsmiths very busy throughout
the decade on military work.[1] In spite of the prosperity of the
military section, however, it seems that even in 1860 the sporting-
gun branch was larger. In one respect, indeed, it was also more
advanced ; for at this time the breech-loading principle was
already applied to some types of sporting guns, although military
arms were still muzzle-loaders. Apart from those produced for
the services, the guns were of very varied types, ranging from
the expensive shot-gun down to the cheap flint-lock musket, of
which 100,000 to 150,000 were produced annually for the West
African market.[2] Pistols also were manufactured in Birmingham
and West Bromwich ; and it is worth noting that the former had
four factories making copper percussion caps and employing in
all from 150 to 200 people.[3]

The button trade, though less important than the other three
Birmingham staples, was even more narrowly confined than the
manufacture of jewellery and guns to the town itself. According
to the Census of 1861, of the 5700 button-makers living in the
counties of Warwick, Stafford and Worcester, no less than
5100, or over 90 per cent., were found within the borough of
Birmingham.[4] This is probably an under-statement of the number
employed, for it is likely that a good many workers who were
employed in making buttons of such materials as glass and papier
mâché were enumerated under other headings. However, as it
was estimated in 1851 that between 5000 and 6000 people were
engaged in the industry,[5] and in 1866 that 6000 were so employed,
the Census figure is accurate enough for our purpose.[6]

[1] S. Timmins, op. cit., p. 381 et seq.; and Artifex and Opifex, The Causes
of Decay in a British Industry (1907), chap. i.
[2] S. Timmins, op. cit., p. 381 et seq.
[3] Reports of the Inspectors of Factories, January 1865, pp. 130-131.
[4] Census of England and Wales, 1861, vol. ii., p. 467 et seq., pp. 510, 513.
[5] Labour and the Poor in The Morning Chronicle, October 21, 1850.
[6] S. Timmins, op. cit., p. 443.

The industry, as a whole, had only just maintained itself among the leading trades during the second quarter of the nineteenth century, and it occupied a relatively less important position in the town in 1860 than in 1830, when it is said to have employed 17,000 persons.[1] Several of the older branches had positively declined, partly owing to foreign competition and partly in consequence of a change of fashion. The metal-button section, for instance, which was concerned with a wide variety of products — from elaborate uniform and gilt, plated and enamelled buttons, to cheap articles of japanned iron—was on the down-grade in 1860, and horn and hoof buttons, a Hales Owen speciality, had almost ceased to be produced. The pearl-button trade still remained the largest branch of the industry ; while vegetable-ivory, or corozo-nut, linen and covered buttons had risen to maintain a place for the button manufacture among Birmingham's staples.[2] This account of the rise and decline of the different types of button illustrates how seriously the trade was liable to be affected by changes of fashion. Besides the major sections of the industry, buttons were made from a variety of other materials, such as glass, papier mâché, leather and wood ; but the output of these kinds formed only an insignificant proportion of the total production. The relative importance of the different branches may be judged from the following Table, which has been compiled from the available contemporary evidence.

PROPORTION OF TOTAL EMPLOYMENT IN EACH
SECTION OF THE BUTTON TRADE[3]

	Per cent.
Pearl-Button Trade	35
Metal-Button Trade	20
Covered- and Linen-Button Trade . . .	25
Vegetable-Ivory-Button Trade . . .	10
Glass- and Bone-Button Trade . . .	5
Other branches	5
	100

Two trades which, though employing fewer people than the four great staples, were like them, inasmuch as they were highly concentrated in Birmingham, were the pen and bedstead manu-

---

[1] *Labour and the Poor* in *The Morning Chronicle*, October 21, 1850.
[2] *Ibid.*, October 21 and November 4, 1850.
[3] S. Timmins, *op. cit.*, pp. 462-463.

factures. Both were of recent origin. The steel-pen trade, having overcome the prejudice against the use of its products by 1840, had developed into an important industry during the next two decades, its output increasing from 65,000 gross weekly in 1849 to 98,000 gross weekly some fifteen years later.[1] With the exception of one firm in Walsall, the whole trade of the country was centred in Birmingham, and the amount of employment it afforded appears to have been in the neighbourhood of 2000 [2]; while several hundred others were engaged on the production of holders and boxes.

The bedstead trade had risen to prominence owing to a change of fashion in the later thirties, when the old wooden type began to be superseded for general use by iron and brass bedsteads. Its development had been rapid; for we are told that production increased from 400 to 500 weekly in 1849 to 5000 to 6000 weekly in 1865.[3] This manufacture was almost entirely localized in Birmingham, although it was carried on to a small extent in Wolverhampton, Bilston and Walsall as well. The estimates of employment in the industry are conflicting. According to the Census of 1861, about 530 men and boys were engaged in the manufacture of bedsteads and wire mattresses within Birmingham; while a few years afterwards two authorities [4] estimated the number at 2000-2500. The discrepancy is to be accounted for by the fact that in the Census return many men working in bedstead factories were classed as ironworkers or brassworkers; while there were many women employed in the japanning and lacquering departments who were not included as bedstead-makers. Probably the most correct estimate is that of the Inspectors of Factories, who gave the total employment in 1867 at 1800.[5]

The wire trades also formed a large group. They were concerned with brass and copper as well as with iron and steel wire, and to some extent, therefore, they fall within the brass trade already described. Birmingham was at this time one of the chief

---

[1] S. Timmins, *op. cit.*, p. 633 *et seq.*
[2] The Census report (*England and Wales*, vol. ii., p. 513) gives the employment at only 1224, but all other reliable authorities combine in placing it at a much higher figure (S. Timmins, *op. cit.*, p. 635; *Reports of the Inspectors of Factories*, October 1868, p. 116 *et seq.*).
[3] S. Timmins, *op. cit.*, p. 624.
[4] *Ibid.*, p. 626; *Children's Employment Commission* (*1862*), *Third Report*, p. 151; *Census of England and Wales*, 1861, vol. ii., p. 510.
[5] *Reports of the Inspectors of Factories*, October 1868, p. 116 *et seq.*

manufacturing centres in the country, both for the actual production of these different types of wire, and also for the finished
goods of which wire was the raw material. The iron and brass
sections were ancient industries in the locality, and in 1860 there
were innumerable small trades producing wire articles. Of these
pins, hairpins, fireguards, hooks and eyes, springs for mattresses
and upholstery, and dishcovers, may be cited as composing the
most important. In addition, there had grown up during the
previous decade a large production of steel wire, which was
employed for piano springs, needles, fishhooks, umbrella frames
and ropes. During the forties, moreover, the manufacture of wire
ropes and cables had been taken up by a local firm, and by 1860
a good deal was being produced for hoisting purposes and for
telegraph work. There was a small production within the town
of hempen rope and of twine, and it was from a specialist in those
manufactures that the wire-rope trade had sprung.[1] It is probable
that about 1500 to 2000 people were employed as wire-drawers,
wire-weavers, pin-makers and wire-rope-makers in Birmingham
in 1860, while in the rest of the area the trades were practically
non-existent.[2] Closely associated with this group was the manufacture of umbrella furniture. Birmingham supplied nearly all
the umbrella-fittings used in the country at this time, and about
700 workers were occupied at the trade.[3]

Of about the same magnitude as the above trades were the
rolling-stock, edge-tool, glass, papier-mâché and japanned-ware,
and leather manufactures, each of which employed between
1000 and 2000 workers in Birmingham. These industries, however, were shared to a large extent by the Black Country, and will
be dealt with later; so that there remains to consider the minor
trades which were centred in Birmingham.

The production of wood-screws, though of ancient origin in
the locality, had not formed a considerable feature of the industrial activities until 1854. In that year, however, the introduction
of automatic machinery displaced the older methods of production and resulted in a great extension of the output, without causing a big increase in the number of workers. In 1861
there were about 1000 screw-cutters in Birmingham and a few

---

[1] S. Timmins, *op. cit.*, p. 578 *et seq.*
[2] *Ibid.*, pp. 578-579; *Reports of the Inspectors of Factories*, October 1868,
p. 116 *et seq.* ; *Census of England and Wales*, 1861, vol. ii., p. 511.
[3] S. Timmins, *op. cit.*, p. 616.

hundreds in the Wolverhampton and Walsall districts.[1] A similar development had occurred in the cut-nail industry, which was carried on mainly at Birmingham, although Wolverhampton was a less important seat of manufacture. The output of cut nails was increasing at the expense of the old hand-wrought nail trade of the Black Country, and it seems that this new branch of the industry had been established at Birmingham and Wolverhampton rather than in the nailing centres because it required a fairly costly plant, which the greater towns could supply more easily than other places in the neighbourhood. Over 1000 workers were employed in this trade at the beginning of our period.[2]

Very little can be said of the manufacture of machines within the town. It is impossible to gather any information from the Census reports with regard to its size, for although nearly 2000 people are returned as being engaged as engineers or machine-makers, few of these would be connected with specialist engineering establishments. For the most part the machinery which the Birmingham manufacturer required was made in those days in his own factory, and, with a few exceptions, the local engineering trade had not become differentiated from the industries which it served. Nevertheless there were several firms in the town producing steam-engines, among them the descendant of the Boulton and Watt partnership. Draw-benches, rolling mills, presses, sewing-machines, pumping machinery, coining presses, nailing machinery, weighing machinery and pneumatic hammers also were made, though on a small scale ; and in 1857 there was established the firm which was afterwards to become famous for its hoisting tackle and hydraulic pumps.[3] Both at Birmingham and Wolverhampton, moreover, a certain amount of agricultural machinery was produced. The list of products seems a formidable one, but it must be remembered that the quantity of each type of machine made was very small, and the engineering trade was not considered to be sufficiently important even to be selected as a subject for investigation when Samuel Timmins was gathering material for his survey of West Midland industries in 1866.

The local brush and broom trade was of considerable size at this time, and it supplied not only the West Midland market but

---

[1] *Census of England and Wales*, 1861, vol. ii., p. 514; *Reports of the Inspectors of Factories*, October 1868, p. 121.

[2] S. Timmins, *op. cit.*, p. 616.

[3] *A Brief History of the Cornwall Works* (Messrs Tangyes Ltd.).

users in other parts of the country. There was, moreover, a fair export trade to the Continent, the Colonies and the United States. Birmingham itself had the largest proportion of the industry, and of the 1000 to 1300 persons who found employment in brush-making in the district, nearly 600 lived in that town. Painting, household, and toilet brushes and brooms were all produced there; while in Walsall, the other chief centre, there were about 200 persons, most of whom were concerned with the manufacture of harness brushes—a necessary adjunct of the staple industry of that place.[1]

In concluding this enumeration of Birmingham industries we must not forget the " artistic " trades which had grown with the early Victorian love of spurious mediævalism. Among these was the manufacture of stained glass and of " ecclesiastical " metal-work in brass or wrought-iron. Both were, of course, very small. The manufacture of statuary by electro-deposition was another curious enterprise which had arisen in connection with the electro-plating industry just before 1860. The trade by which Birmingham had once secured notoriety, and which Boulton had practised with such success—the manufacture of coins—was still carried on by two mints. With the exception of the Royal Mint, these were the only establishments of their kind in England.[2] Matches, measuring rules and scientific instruments were also produced in the town. And finally, there were certain small subsidiary trades, such as chemicals, varnish, paint and japan manufacture, and metal-refining. There was die-sinking, which had connection with most of the leading industries, from brass and buttons to jewellery, electro-plate and coining. Of a different nature were the foundries which produced parts for other industries as well as finished articles like hollow-ware, light castings, fenders and hinges.[3] But all these manufactures were carried on in the Black Country to a greater extent than in Birmingham, and they will be considered in the next chapter.

In conclusion, it is worth calling attention to the fact that the staple trades of Birmingham, as well as several of less importance, were not only localized in the town largely to the exclusion of other places in the area, but they were responsible for most of the output of the whole country in certain of their products. It

[1] *Census of England and Wales*, 1861, vol. ii., p. 469 *et seq.*, pp. 511, 514.
[2] S. Timmins, *op. cit.*, p. 555.
[3] *Ibid.*, pp. 610-612, 641-643, 664-666.

is true that the jewellery and gun trades were shared with London, but Birmingham produced practically all the middle-class and cheap jewellery, and its gunsmiths were possessed of a much bigger share of their trade than that enjoyed by the metropolis. They manufactured more finished guns ; they supplied to the London makers many others in a semi-finished state ; and, if the Government factory at Enfield is left out of account, Birmingham had practically a monopoly of the production of barrels for both military and sporting work.[1] In the brass trade, too, particularly in the cabinet and lighting branches, the town was far ahead of any other centre. In the manufacture of buttons, pens, umbrella-fittings, cut nails, pins, screws, bedsteads and electro-plated table-ware, rival industrial districts had an insignificant part to play ; so that the Birmingham of 1860 could boast not only of a diverse industrial life but of many types of product which were peculiar to itself.

[1] S. Timmins, *op. cit.*, p. 381 *et seq.*

CHAPTER II

THE LIGHT MANUFACTURES OF THE BLACK COUNTRY

DURING the last fifty years there has never been a want of writers to lay emphasis on what had become, by the middle of the nineteenth century, the most obvious characteristic of Birmingham's industrial life—viz. the multiplicity of its trades, the variety of raw materials of which it made use, and the widely different types of labour employed. Few, however, ventured to contrast the industrial structure of Birmingham with that of the Black Country, and to show that, if variety characterized the life of the " midland metropolis," uniformity was, in one respect at any rate, the most obvious quality of the rest of our area. In view of the multitude of articles produced by the South Staffordshire towns this might seem a rash generalization. Yet there is a clear antithesis both in the nature of the raw materials employed and in the general classification of the finished products.

In the Black Country iron and coal were practically the only raw materials which counted, and its finished products could be grouped mainly among iron manufactures. Outside this group there were, it is true, such important products as saddlery and harness, glass and chemicals; but the first of these was closely associated with the manufacture of saddlers' ironmongery, while in the production of glass and chemicals coal was easily the most important raw material required, and the localization of the two trades depended almost entirely on the mineral deposits. Such other exceptions as existed consisted of small subsidiary trades, and it can be declared without qualification that all the staple manufactures of the Black Country were directly dependent on the local extractive industries, and that the district was essentially an iron centre. Now Birmingham, though " pre-eminently the town of metal," employed practically every known variety of that material; and, while the town carried on important iron manufactures, these were secondary to the non-ferrous trades. Of the four staple industries, iron was extensively used only by the gunmakers, and several of the industries which were most characteristic of Birmingham, and in which it enjoyed almost a monopoly as compared with the rest of the area, were independent of local supplies of raw materials. It is sufficient to quote the button, jewellery, pen and brass trades as examples. Coal was, of course, required in their manufacture; but its relative importance in the production of the small and highly finished products of Birmingham was much less than in the heavier trades of the Black Country. Thus the distinction which had begun to appear one hundred and fifty years previously between the activities of these two parts of our area had become a definite contrast by 1860. By that date, indeed, the industries of Birmingham and of the Black Country might almost be termed complementary.

Further, while it was to be expected that a town of the size of Birmingham would have a more diverse industrial life than the smaller places in the district (although the multiplicity of its trades was remarkable even for a town of 320,000 inhabitants [1]), most of the Black Country towns specialized not only on iron manufactures but on some specific branch of that group of trades. This point will be illustrated as the chapter proceeds, when it will be seen to what small localities many of the finished manufactures of South Staffordshire were confined. Even Wolverhampton, though possessing several important industries,[2] was much less versatile, relative to its size, than Birmingham; while Smethwick, the other apparent exception, owed its growth and the variety of its manufactures to the extension of its great neighbour's industries to the west.

In a discussion of the industrial structure of the Black Country it is convenient to make a division between the light and the heavy trades; and since it was in the former group that the industries which were common to both Birmingham and the Black Country fell, a further subdivision may be made between the light industries shared between the two sections of our area and those which were peculiar to South Staffordshire and North Worcestershire. The manufactures which, though centred mainly in Birmingham, were carried on to some small extent elsewhere have already been described. It has been pointed out that material-makers for the gun trade were to be found at Wednesbury, Darlaston, West Bromwich and Hales Owen; that sections of the brass trade existed at Wolverhampton and

[1] *I.e.* including the whole of the parishes of Birmingham, Aston and Edgbaston.
[2] *Cf.* L. Faucher, *Études sur l'Angleterre* (1856), tome i., p. 517.

Walsall; that a special kind of button was manufactured at Hales Owen; and that small quantities of iron bedsteads were produced at Wolverhampton, Bilston and Walsall. These and other branches of Birmingham's industries which were carried on in the Black Country did not constitute, however, any substantial part of its economic activities, and it is to the trades that were more equally shared between the two main divisions of our area that attention must now be given.

Among them the edge-tool manufacture ranks high. In 1860, although there was in Birmingham and elsewhere in the locality a small production of such cutting tools as knives, chisels, saws, planes and files, the chief centre of that trade was Sheffield; and the edge tools on which the West Midlands specialized were of a heavier type. They included scythes, axes, hammers, trowels, hoes, shovels, spades, rakes and machetes, and it is said that nearly three thousand varieties were produced. A large proportion of the products were agricultural tools for foreign markets, while bayonets and swords should perhaps be considered to form part of this group of manufactures, since they were produced by the same firms that made machetes for the West Indian plantations.[1] The wide range of patterns was due to the fact that in the days in which no edge-tool industry in the modern sense existed, the village smiths of each agricultural district had been responsible for the evolution of the particular type of implement used there; and so, when agriculturists came to rely on industrial centres, they still demanded the special kind of tool to which traditional use had accustomed them.

Our area had increased its production of this class of commodity at the expense of Sheffield, the other great centre of production, during the years preceding 1860. This was attributed at the time partly to the lower cost of raw materials in Birmingham (though this may be doubted), but mainly to the fact that the " tyranny " of the Sheffield trade unions had raised wages above the local level and had also prevented the application of improved mechanical methods of production.[2] There was certainly a very great development of the industry between 1830 and the early sixties, when it was supposed that over 3000

---

[1] S. Timmins, *op. cit.*, pp. 100 and 656.
[2] *Labour and the Poor* in *The Morning Chronicle*, January 20, 1851.

people were employed. Under half of these were to be found in Birmingham, mainly in Aston, and the remainder were scattered over the Black Country, chiefly at Wolverhampton, Stourbridge, Oldbury and Old Hill.[1] Besides these centres of the trade, Hales Owen specialized on spades, forks and shovels, and Bellbroughton on scythes. It should be remarked, moreover, that one of the most famous firms of edge-tool makers in the country, Messrs Gilpin & Sons, carried on an extensive business to the north of our area, in the neighbourhood of Cannock. This was a very old-established concern, and many of the founders of similar businesses in Birmingham and South Staffordshire had at one time been employed there.[2]

The edge-tool trade is of great interest because of the connection of its manufacturing operations with a process which was of importance to several local industries. Some of the tools — e.g. hammer-heads — were produced by the process of hot stamping, or drop-forging, as it is now called, although for other types the work of the skilled smith at the anvil had not been superseded. This process had begun to be applied also to the manufacture of gun parts, keys, and of other types of article produced in the locality, and there was thus growing up in connection with a variety of industries a class of stamper who was afterwards to play a part of significance in the economic development of the area.

A trade which afforded an even greater volume of employment was the manufacture of glass. According to the estimates of contemporaries there were about 4800 persons in this industry within our area. About half of these were engaged in the production of sheet, crown and plate glass, the heavy branch of the trade.[3] This had been introduced into the district early in the century and had grown up for the most part in the newest industrial centre, Smethwick, although there was in 1860 one factory at Stourbridge. The flint-glass industry, which was concerned with table and decorative ware, was of much greater historical interest. It was one of the oldest manufactures in the West Midlands, and it had long been localized in Birming-

---

[1] S. Timmins, op. cit., pp. 100, 658.
[2] Personal inquiry.
[3] S. Timmins, op. cit., pp. 147, 151, 526. According to the Census of England and Wales, 1861, p. 469 et seq., there were 4500 persons in this trade in the three counties.

ham and in the immediate neighbourhood of Stourbridge, at Wordsley, Amblecote and Brierley Hill. In 1860 it seems that Birmingham had a slightly larger share than the Stourbridge district of the 2000 to 2300 glass-makers, cutters and engravers who made up the labour force.[1] Further, even if much of the pressed-glass trade, which produced cheap table-ware, had passed to Newcastle-on-Tyne, there was one firm near Stourbridge that still carried on the manufacture [2]; while at Wordsley and Dudley bottle glass was produced in small quantities. The great firm of Chance Brothers of Smethwick, though concerned mainly with the heavy branch of the trade, had opened an optical glass department in 1848 [3]; and in Birmingham itself and at Walsall there were a number of small glass-using industries, such as the spectacle trade, in which 200 people were employed, the mirror trade, and the manufacture of microscopes and other scientific instruments.[4]

Just as the flint-glass industry was shared between Birmingham and Stourbridge, so the leather trade was to be found in Birmingham and one Black Country town, Walsall. In the main section of this industry, which manufactured brown and japanned saddlery and harness, over 3000 people were employed, of whom just over half were at Walsall; while the whip trade, employing less than 300 persons, was to be found mainly at Birmingham. In the earlier processes of leather manufacture, such as engaged the tanners and the curriers, Walsall was the chief centre; although neither of these trades was very important in this district, the tanning branch in particular being very small. There was, in addition, a small production of leather shot-belts, powder-flasks, rifle-slings and leggings, by several firms whose main activities were the manufacture of saddlery and harness.[5]

Closely allied to this group of trades was the manufacture of saddlers' ironmongery, which was carried on mainly at Walsall.

---

[1] " In Birmingham there are . . . seventeen furnaces of the larger sort . . . the annual production of which may be taken in round numbers at five million pounds weight of glass. At Stourbridge there are twenty-two furnaces yielding about three and a half million pounds " (S. Timmins, *op. cit.*, p. 532).

[2] D. N. Sandilands, *op. cit.*, p. 84; *Census of England and Wales*, 1861, vol. ii., pp. 511, 514.

[3] *A Hundred Years of British Glass Making* (Chance Bros. & Co. Ltd.), p. 9.

[4] S. Timmins, *op. cit.*, pp. 130, 533-535.

[5] *Ibid.*, p. 125 *et seq.* and p. 463 *et seq.*; also *Census of England and Wales*, 1861, vol. ii., pp. 467, 486, 509, 513.

Wednesbury, Darlaston and Bloxwich, however, had a small share. The last-named town was also a centre of the production of awl-blades, which were employed by the local leather-workers.[1] Saddlers' ironmongery consists of such things as bits, buckles, stirrup-irons, hames, spurs and light chains, which are required by the makers of saddlery and harness; and in 1860 there appear to have been from 1500 to 2000 persons engaged in their production in the Walsall neighbourhood. There, also, a number of small subsidiary industries, such as the brassfoundry, electro-plating and saddle-tree trades,[2] had been called into existence to serve the staple manufactures.

From the point of view of its influence on future developments there was one process in connection with saddlers' ironmongery which deserves close attention. In the manufacture of most of the articles falling within that category the raw material used consisted of pig-iron produced from the hæmatite ores of Cumberland. Bits, stirrup-irons and buckles were first made by casting and then rendered malleable by annealing, and this process, though applied most extensively at Walsall, was also employed in many other trades in the district. The malleable-iron foundries of Willenhall produced keys, and those of Birmingham were responsible for the manufacture of a multitude of articles, which, being complex in form, had given the smith much trouble in fashioning them from wrought-iron, such as gun "furniture," parts for machinery, and fittings for the bedstead trade.[3]

We have already seen that Wolverhampton shared, though in a junior capacity, in the manufacture of many of the staple Birmingham products, such as brassfoundry and bedsteads; but in one industry which was common to both towns, Wolverhampton was at least the equal of its greater neighbour.[4] This was the manufacture of tinplate, japanned-iron and papier-mâché wares, which, since they were usually produced together in the same factories, may be treated together. The tinplate goods consisted of such articles as baths, jugs, kettles and dishcovers. Trays, coal-vases, tea-caddies and cash-boxes were the staple products of the japanned-ware trade, and trays of the

[1] S. Timmins, *op. cit.*, p. 128.
[2] *Ibid.*, p. 125 *et seq.* and p. 463 *et seq.*
[3] *Ibid.*, pp. 645-647.
[4] *Labour and the Poor* in *The Morning Chronicle*, February 3, 1851.

papier-mâché trade. The last two classes of goods varied greatly in value. Some were of a very low quality, but both included expensive articles of an ornamental character. The papier-mâché trade in particular was responsible for elaborate designs in which such unsuitable material as pearl-shell was used for decorative effect on panels and trays; and it appears that the complete lack of artistic merit exhibited by these products had proved too much even for the mid-Victorian taste, for this trade had been on the decline since 1840. The rise of electro-plating was beginning to affect adversely the production of the more expensive types of tinplate and japanned ware, but the development of a demand for coal-vases and baths just before 1860 had had a compensatory effect. The Census figures of 1861 are not sufficiently comprehensive to make possible an accurate estimate of the amount of employment which these trades afforded, but it appears that there were about 3500 persons in the industry within our area. Of these some 1600 were at Wolverhampton, somewhat fewer at Birmingham, about 400 at Bilston and a few at Dudley. The most expensive kinds of tin-plate and japanned wares were produced at Wolverhampton; Bilston and Dudley concentrated on the cheapest types; while Birmingham was the chief centre for the manufacture of papier-mâché and of the medium-priced tinplate and japanned wares.[1]

Many products of the group of industries which has just been described were of a type which could be classified as hollow-ware—a term which covers hollow or concave articles, used for domestic, particularly culinary, purposes. This type of utensil had long been produced in the locality, and in 1860 there were a number of distinct industries engaged in manufacturing the great variety of goods which fell within this category. Some kinds of hollow-ware were made of copper or brass—e.g. coal-scuttles, pans and kettles—other kinds were produced of Britannia-metal, German silver, tinplate, pewter or electro-plate; but these have already been dealt with in connection with other industries. The most important varieties of hollow-ware, however, besides tinplate goods, fell into two main divisions, the wrought- and the cast-iron wares. The industry engaged in producing the latter, as has been described in Part I., first became important during

[1] S. Timmins, op. cit., p. 117 et seq. and p. 638 et seq. W. H. Jones, op. cit., p. 126 et seq.; and G. T. Lawley, History of Bilston (1868), p. 85.

the last quarter of the eighteenth century, and in 1860 there were many foundries in the district making cast cooking utensils, which were either tinned, enamelled or " black." The " black " hollow-ware took the form of native pots and dutch ovens, for the most part, and was produced mainly for distant markets, having been superseded in England by tinned cast wares, which had been made since the end of the previous century. These in turn, however, were at this date being threatened by the appearance of enamelled ware, which, by its resemblance to pottery, was winning the favour of consumers.[1] The wrought-iron goods, besides being produced with a tinned, enamelled or " black " finish, like the cast wares, also took the form of galvanized wares. The wrought goods were all manufactured from sheet-iron, and the first three types consisted of domestic utensils, similar to those produced by the cast-iron and by the tinplate ware trades, although at this time the amount of wrought-enamelled hollow-ware made was very small. The tinned, " black " and enamelled goods were such as were required for the preparation of food; but the galvanized hollow-ware trade, which was in its infancy in 1860, was concerned with articles for outdoor purposes, or for uses unconnected with food preparation, such as cans, buckets, baths and washing bowls. This branch was being favourably affected by the growth of a Colonial demand at this time.[2]

There is nothing but the estimates of contemporaries to serve as a guide in computing the amount of employment in this group of trades. It seems likely, however, that there were about 2500 persons engaged in the wrought and cast sections in 1860. West Bromwich was the chief centre of the latter; but Wolverhampton, Bilston and Tipton also had a number of factories producing not only various kinds of cast wares, but galvanized and tinned wrought hollow-ware as well. Birmingham had only a small share of the industry, and this consisted mainly of the tinned and galvanized branches of the wrought trade.

Closely connected with the hollow-ware group were a multitude of products which, though not falling within that classification, were produced by similar methods of manufacture, or in hollow-ware factories. From 1850, for instance, a small trade

---

[1] S. Timmins, *op. cit.*, p. 103 *et seq.*
[2] *Ibid.*, p. 641; W. H. Jones, *op. cit.*, pp. 163-171.

had grown up in Birmingham and Wolverhampton in the production of enamelled-iron wares, such as street plates, door numbers and notice boards; while the cast hollow-ware factories, which had originally grown out of foundries producing general ironmongery, still carried on that work as a side-line, and large quantities of cast nails, hinges, coffee-mills, latches, handles, scrapers and door-knockers were manufactured in this way at West Bromwich, Wolverhampton and Bilston. Further, there were several foundries engaged in making cast-iron fenders, which had superseded the steel, rolled-brass or sheet-iron fender earlier in the century, and stove-grates. The latter manufacture was one of the group of trades which was growing at the expense of Sheffield just before 1860, owing to the lower labour costs of the Midlands. An older industry, which from the nature of the finished product was associated with the fender trade, was the manufacture of fire-irons. It employed about 500 people, who were fairly evenly distributed between Birmingham on the one hand and Dudley and Wolverhampton on the other, and, like the fender and stove-grate trades, it was making great progress at this time.[1]

With the few exceptions which have been noted, this might, indeed, be said of most of the industries which have been considered in this chapter. Few, however, had reached such substantial proportions in a short time as the rolling-stock industry, which had become one of the great manufactures of the district in just over twenty years. At the beginning of the railway era the trade had been largely in the hands of a few general engineering firms, "which were soon quite unable to procure the large amount of capital required to meet the pressing demands of the railway companies. . . . This led to the establishment of works by the railway companies themselves . . .; but as the mileage increased, and consequently the stock required to work it, they found that the principal part of their business would consist in keeping their existing stock in repair, and that they had little time for building new vehicles. The old system of employing contractors was again resorted to and has been adopted ever since." As a result of this, and also owing to "a new system which sprang up by which rolling-stock was supplied to railway companies," colliery companies and others, either for cash or for deferred

[1] S. Timmins, *op. cit.*, p. 103 *et seq.*, p. 664.

payment, a great increase was occasioned in the number of independent rolling-stock concerns. In Birmingham the industry had been established as early as 1838, and the district, in view of its central position and its proximity to the supplies of raw materials, proved a favourable locality. In 1860 there were four large concerns, situated at Birmingham and Oldbury, for producing railway carriages and wagons, which together employed about 2000 persons. This industry is of interest because it was one of the earliest in the area of the type to be concerned with the larger and more composite products.[1]

Such, then, were the manufactures which were shared in fairly equal proportions between Birmingham and the Black Country. It will be noticed that, with the exception of rolling-stock, these trades produced small finished articles, and rolling-stock was a composite product which drew on the Black Country for wheels, axles and other parts. But, while the manufacture of glass-ware, edge tools, hollow-ware and other foundry products required skilled labour, they needed also greater quantities of raw materials and coal than the typically Birmingham trades. The staple trade of Walsall, which made little demand on local supplies of raw materials, stands as an exception in this respect among the group of industries which have just been examined. Thus the equal division of several of them between Birmingham and the Black Country may be explained by the fact that the nature of the trades was such that neither the superior skill of the former's artisans nor the raw materials of the latter could exercise a determining influence on localization. Each division of our area had in fact sufficient attractions to secure to it a share of these industries.

The above trades, however, though of great importance to particular towns like Walsall, Wolverhampton, Stourbridge and West Bromwich, accounted for only a small proportion of the total employment afforded by the Black Country industries; and we must now consider those which belonged essentially to South Staffordshire and North Worcestershire. Of all the cruder manufactures which had sprung up in the Black Country, or had been driven outside the boundaries of Birmingham by the specializing tendencies to which reference has been repeatedly made, the hand-wrought nail industry was the largest. Although it had been

---

[1] S. Timmins, *op. cit.*, pp. 669-670.

steadily declining in consequence of the competition of cut nails and of machine-wrought nails since 1830, and although it had lost its chief foreign markets, the United States, Canada and Australia, and its profitable contracts with the Admiralty, the Docks, and the East India Company, it still ranked as one of the staple trades of the area at the beginning of our period.[1] In 1861,[2] 19,400 persons were returned as nail-makers in Worcestershire, Staffordshire and Warwickshire, and practically all of these were to be found in the district covered by this survey. The figure included, however, those employed in making cut nails at Birmingham and Wolverhampton, and machine-wrought nails at Hales Owen; so that it is probable that the number of nailers, in the old sense, was not above 18,000.

Earlier in the chapter it was declared that, as far as the manufacture of finished products was concerned, each of the leading Black Country trades was to a large extent confined to a particular town or locality; and it has been shown that even in those industries which the Black Country shared with Birmingham, specialization of this kind was the rule. Thus, outside Birmingham, Walsall was the only important producing centre in the area for saddlery, harness and allied manufactures; Stourbridge for the flint-glass wares; West Bromwich and Wolverhampton for hollow-ware; Wolverhampton for tinplate and japanned articles. The nailing industry appears at first sight an exception to this rule, for it was carried on over a wide area in the Black Country and in its immediate neighbourhood. Yet, even in this scattered trade, specialization was not absent. The hand-made nails produced in the locality were of many different kinds, ranging from tacks to large railway spikes, and by 1860 each nailing district had come to specialize on particular types. Thus Dudley concentrated on horse and mule nails; Sedgeley produced spikes, rose nails and gate nails; while Rowley, Old Hill, Hales Owen and Blackheath made rivets.[3]

A particular interest attaches to this industry because of the change which had occurred in the relative importance of the various producing centres during the first half of the nineteenth

---

[1] S. Timmins, *op. cit.*, p. 110 *et seq.*
[2] *Census of England and Wales*, 1861, vol. ii., pp. 469, 472, 476, 478.
[3] S. Timmins, *op. cit.*, p. 111 ; F. W. Hackwood, *Sedgeley Researches* (1898), p. 104 ; and W. D. Curzon, *The Manufacturing Industries of Worcestershire* (1881), p. 76.

century. In 1800, while Dudley had for long been its chief seat, the trade was carried on in every part of the Black Country, and was in South Staffordshire rather than Worcestershire.[1] The Bromsgrove district had, then, only 400 or 500 nailers.[2] By 1860, however, the manufacture had almost deserted the northern part of our district, and only an insignificant amount of the trade was left to such places as Wednesbury and Darlaston, which once had been important centres. Most of the nailers still remained within our area in the neighbourhood of Dudley and Stourbridge, and the predominance of the former town had not been shaken. But much of the industry had been forced out into the Worcestershire villages beyond our boundary line, and the Bromsgrove district had become a leading centre of production.[3] Further, even within our area the industry had come to be carried on, except in the case of Dudley, not in the larger towns and chief manufacturing centres, but in villages and hamlets which were still largely agricultural. Both the migration of the trade and its localization in 1860 are to be explained by the fact that nail-making since 1830 had been a declining industry, in which wages and prices were continually falling. Consequently it had been driven out of centres in which new or thriving industries existed, and in which the workers could find profitable employment, into the hamlets and agricultural districts where the wage-level was low. Since, however, it depended on supplies of iron and fuel, the industry had to remain within easy reach of the coal-field, and for this reason it could not be driven farther afield. The apparent exception of Dudley, with its 2500 nailers,[4] is to be explained by the fact that the town was occupied mainly with a special type of nail of a high quality, and this branch had not yet been affected by the competition of machinery. The following Table illustrates as accurately as the available statistics permit the distribution of the industry over our area, and confirms the generalizations which have been made:

[1] F. W. Hackwood, *Oldbury and Roundabout*, p. 125 *et seq.*
[2] T. C. Turberville, *Worcestershire in the Nineteenth Century*, p. 14.
[3] *Ibid.*, p. 14; F. W. Hackwood, *Wednesbury Workshops*, pp. 20-24; and *Census of England and Wales*, 1861, vol. ii., pp. 495, 507.
[4] *Census of England and Wales*, 1861, vol. ii., pp. 511, 514.

PROPORTION OF NAILERS IN VARIOUS POOR LAW DISTRICTS[1]

Per cent.

Dudley District (including the parishes of Dudley, Sedgeley, Tipton and Rowley Regis) . . 39

Stourbridge District (including the townships of Hales Owen, Stourbridge, Lye, Wollaston, Upper Swinford, Amblecote, the parish of Kingswinford and most of the parish of Hales Owen) . . 26

Bromsgrove District (including the townships of Stoke Prior, Bromsgrove, Bellbroughton, Clent, Hagley, Frankley, Redditch, Pedmore, Alvechurch, Romsley, Bentley and Coston Hackett) . 20

<u>85</u>

Thus, in three districts — Dudley, Stourbridge and Bromsgrove—the bulk of the industry was to be found. Of the small proportion of the nail-makers found in other parts, about 40 per cent. consisted of those employed in the machine-made nail trade of Birmingham, Wolverhampton and Hales Owen; and the remainder, about 1000 persons, were at Harborne, Northfield, Oldbury and West Bromwich, or scattered in small groups over the northern part of the district. A few still survived at Birmingham. An associated manufacture, that of horse-shoes, was carried on at Dudley and, to a small extent, at Hales Owen.[2]

While the nailers were diminishing in numbers another typical Black Country industry of a somewhat similar kind was expanding rapidly. This was the manufacture of nuts and bolts. From the eighteenth century, Wednesbury had produced coach-iron, which included nuts and bolts; but it was not until the construction of the railways had given a stimulus to their production that the industry began to assume a position of importance in South Staffordshire. In Wednesbury itself, however, where one might have expected the trade to find a home, the population had turned its attention to tubes and axles, and consequently it was in a neighbouring town, Darlaston, that the manufacture of nuts and bolts was centred.[3] Here development had been particularly rapid during the fifties, and by 1860 there

---

[1] *Census of England and Wales*, 1861, vol. ii., p. 494 *et seq.*
[2] S. Timmins, *op. cit.*, p. 116.
[3] F. W. Hackwood, *Wednesbury Workshops*, p. 54; and *A History of Darlaston*, p. 160.

were eight factories employing from 30 to 50 hands each, besides many smaller establishments.[1] New firms for this manufacture had sprung up also at Wolverhampton, West Bromwich and Smethwick,[2] and at the beginning of our period there cannot have been far short of 3000 persons in the area, chiefly in Darlaston, producing nuts and bolts for railway, shipping and general engineering work.[3]

To the north-west of the chief centre of nut and bolt production an industry was being carried on which, though affording a much greater volume of employment, exhibited to the full by its location the geographical specialization so characteristic of South Staffordshire. The lock-and-key trade, not only of the West Midlands but of the country as a whole, was found almost entirely in two neighbouring Black Country towns, and within a very small district adjoining them. This manufacture, as has been already indicated, was an ancient one, having existed since the sixteenth century; and throughout the eighteenth century it had constituted a staple of Wolverhampton and Willenhall, and had been carried on to a smaller extent in Bilston, Wednesbury, Darlaston, West Bromwich and Birmingham. By 1860, although it was still one of the largest industries of the north-west corner of the Black Country, the relative importance of the different centres had changed. The industry had practically died out in Bilston, Wednesbury and Darlaston, and it had come to be located almost entirely at Wolverhampton and Willenhall, although a small quantity of locks was produced at Wednesfield, Walsall and elsewhere. The rise of Willenhall had somewhat reduced the relative importance of Wolverhampton as a lock-making centre, in spite of the fact that it still remained one of the town's leading activities[4]; but in Willenhall and the neighbouring hamlets this manufacture and its subsidiary trades were supreme. Indeed, of all the towns in our area, Willenhall appears at this time to have had the most highly specialized industrial life, and, except for the inevitable coal-mining and iron production, and for the manufacture of curry-combs and such foundry products as gridirons and bolts, lock-and-key making was the sole

[1] Personal inquiry.
[2] *Newspaper Cuttings* on *Birmingham Industries*, vol. ii., p. 190; and S. Timmins, *op. cit.*, p. 609.
[3] *Reports of the Inspectors of Factories,* October 1868, p. 116 *et seq.*
[4] G. L. Strauss, *England's Workshops* (1864), pp. 122-123.

occupation of the inhabitants.[1] The following Table will illustrate the shares of the chief producing centres, besides showing the size of the trade as a whole in 1866. The total employment according to this authority was much higher than that given by the Census, which showed only 3700 locksmiths in Staffordshire.

Place	Masters and Workmen [2]
Willenhall (including Short Heath and New Invention) .	3275
Wolverhampton	1270
Walsall (including Bloxwich)	435
Wednesfield	250
Brewood	180
	5410

It is no part of our purpose to describe in detail the many types of locks which were produced, but it is necessary to pay some attention to them, because each centre specialized in some degree on particular kinds. A classification might be made from several points of view. If the use to which the locks were put is taken as a criterion, then they might be classified as padlocks, till and chest locks, cabinet locks for furniture, and house-door locks, which in turn could be divided into mortice locks, which were let into the woodwork of the door, and rim locks, which were screwed to the face of the door.[3] Besides these, there were fine-plate locks, which were embedded in wooden frames, and which were employed as stable and yard locks. Padlocks appear to have been made in larger quantities than any other variety, though if estimated in value their predominance would have been more doubtful; the till, chest and cabinet locks, and the house-door locks came next, and were of about equal importance as far as output was concerned; and the fine-plate locks ranked last. Each of the producing centres could be associated with certain types. Both Willenhall and Wolverhampton, being the chief seats of the industry, naturally had a fairly wide range of products; but even here a distinction was introduced by the fact

---

[1] L. Faucher, *Études sur l'Angleterre*, tome i. (1856), p. 517; G. Price, *op. cit.*, chap. xx.; and J. Wright, " Directory of Willenhall Trades " in *History of Willenhall*, 1859.

[2] S. Timmins, *op. cit.*, p. 77 *et seq.* There were no less than 400 establishments in the district in the lock, key and subsidiary industries (*Children's Employment Commission (1862)*, *Third Report*, p. 4).

[3] F. J. Butter, *Locks and Lockmaking*, chap. i.

that the fine-plate locks were made only in the latter. Further, while all the locks of Willenhall and elsewhere relied for their security on the older " warded " principle, a large proportion of the Wolverhampton locks were " levered." It would seem, moreover, that on the whole the latter were of a higher quality,[1] and this point is emphasized by the fact that, in a contemporary estimate of the workers' earnings, the average weekly wages of the Wolverhampton artisan in this trade were placed much higher than those of other lock centres.[2] This was doubtless because the larger town naturally possessed a more highly skilled artisan class, and had attracted to it the more enterprising type of manufacturer. On the other hand, it is interesting to see that the lowest and worst-paid class of work had been driven out of the larger places, where there were more opportunities for remunerative employment, to the villages. So Wednesfield concentrated on cheap iron cabinet-locks, and Short Heath and New Invention produced inferior locks of the same type. The parts for the fine-plate locks were made in rural districts to the north of our area, such as Brewood, Pendeford and Coven, and these parts were sent to Wolverhampton to be fitted into their wooden cases.[3] Thus the lock trade presents an analogy in one aspect of its geographical distribution to the nail industry.

The manufacture of keys was carried on in the surrounding district as well as in the two chief centres of the lock trade, although all the products were, of course, sent to the latter for the finishing processes of differing and fitting. Wednesfield was the chief centre of key-making, while Sedgeley also had a fair share of the trade.[4]

In 1860 the lock trade appears to have been in a rather depressed condition, for a writer stated in 1864 [5] that it had been declining fast during the previous twelve years, a fact which he attributed to the decay in the quality of workmanship. This was due in some degree to the way in which the trade was organized, and will be considered in a later chapter.

Unlike this highly localized industry, an allied manufacture, that of safes, was widely scattered, in spite of the fact that it was

---

[1] G. Price, *op. cit.*, p. 858.
[2] S. Timmins, *op. cit.*, p. 89.
[3] *Ibid.*, p. 87.
[4] *Ibid.*, pp. 88-89 ; and A. Hinde, *History of Wolverhampton* (1884), p. 24.
[5] P. Walters, *The Wolverhampton Lock Trade*, p. 1.

comparatively small. Safes were not at this time so complex and forbidding as they have since become, most of them, indeed, being little more than iron chests. Cast-iron safes of this kind had been produced from early times in the foundries of Birmingham and Wolverhampton, but it was not until about 1830 that wrought-iron began to be employed for this purpose in the locality. Several Wolverhampton locksmiths and some mechanics at West Bromwich then took up the manufacture of this new type, which in 1860 was being made at Birmingham, Wolverhampton, West Bromwich, and at a former seat of the lock trade, Bilston.[1]

Before concluding this enumeration of the leading light metal trades we must dwell for a moment on the manufactures which, though falling within the scope of the survey, lay beyond the geographical limits of our area. Of these the needle trade was the chief. This, as we have seen, had originally been centred at Long Crendon in Buckinghamshire; but during the latter half of the eighteenth century many needle-makers had migrated to the towns and villages situated on the banks of the Arrow. Throughout that century, however, Long Crendon retained its position of priority, and it was not until the conclusion of the Napoleonic Wars that its manufactures were seriously affected by the competition of the newer district. From that time onwards its decline was rapid, and by 1850 it had entirely lost the trade in sewing and heavy needles; while the production of needles in the new centre increased six- or eight-fold between 1800-1850.[2] At the beginning of our period, then, the greater part of the industry was being carried on in a number of Worcestershire and Warwickshire villages and small towns, notably Alcester, Studley, Redditch, Astwood Bank, Feckenham, Crab's Cross and Henley-in-Arden.[3] According to the Census of 1861, 1500 persons were returned as needle-makers in Worcestershire and 2000 in Warwickshire [4]; so it appears that at that time less than half of the industry was to be found in its present seat, Redditch, and that the smaller places in the neighbourhood together possessed the greater share of the industry.

The reason for the migration from Buckinghamshire is not

---

[1] G. Price, op. cit., p. 9 ; G. T. Lawley, History of Bilston (1868), p. 82.
[2] W. Shrimpton, Notes on a Decayed Needle Land, pp. 18-25 ; T. C. Turberville, Worcestershire in the Nineteenth Century (1852), p. 13 ; and The Victoria County History of Worcestershire, vol. ii., p. 273 et seq.
[3] T. C. Turberville, op. cit., pp. 13-14.
[4] Census of England and Wales, 1861, vol. ii., pp. 474, 478.

F

difficult to discover, for it seems likely that it was part of that general movement towards the coal-fields from the south of England which brought several industries, such as edge-tool manufacture and certain kinds of buttons, to our area: " The workers of Long Crendon laboured under great difficulties as compared with the workers of Redditch, Alcester and Studley. The cost of freightage for coal, wire, etc., was greater at Long Crendon on account of the great distance it was from Birmingham. Not only so, but the delay in delivery was also a serious item for the manufacturer." [1] The water-power supplied by the Arrow may have been an inducement, but not a determining influence; for that advantage was one shared by Long Crendon, although it was apparently not made use of there.[2] But while the movement towards the coal of the Midlands need occasion no surprise, since it was common to many trades during the later eighteenth and early nineteenth centuries, it is more difficult to discover an adequate explanation of the failure of the industry to attain an even greater proximity to the source of its fuel.[3] All that can be suggested to meet the difficulty is that in the case of a light industry requiring relatively small quantities of coal and raw materials the advantage of a site in the immediate neighbourhood of the mines was overbalanced by the disadvantage of being in a densely populated centre, where land was dearer and where there was keen competition for the water-power needed in this trade. The fact that emery-stone, which was used for grinding needles, was found near Redditch was a contributory cause of the development of the industry in the neighbourhood.[4] Thus, while a reduction in the cost of transporting raw materials may have been sufficient to cause the migration from Long Crendon, it was not a powerful enough factor to counteract the disadvantages of a site within or nearer to the Black Country. And since a highly specialized type of labour was required, the Birmingham District was not likely to have any overwhelming advantages even in this respect. During the two or three decades immediately preceding 1860 the industry was steadily expanding, partly as a result of the growth of the population and partly in consequence of the opening of foreign markets.

[1] W. Shrimpton, *op. cit.*, p. 19.   [2] *Ibid.*, p. 24.
[3] *Commissioners of Patents' Abridgments of Specifications relating to Needles and Pins* (1871), pp. xi.,i xiii.
[4] S. Timmins, *op. cit.*, p. 198.

In the same area the manufacture of fishhooks also was carried on. The origin of this trade is obscure. There is a legend to the effect that it was brought into the neighbourhood from Limerick, but there is no evidence to support this. It is clear, however, that the trade was of more recent introduction than needle-making, and that it had settled in the Redditch district because a supply of labour accustomed to the manipulation of wire already existed there. It was a smaller trade than the needle industry, and employed some 600 persons. Fishhooks were produced both for river and deep-sea fishing, while tackle was also beginning to be manufactured.[1]

The only other industry that we need mention was the Coventry watch-making trade, which had been introduced into the city in the seventeenth century. It was not of much importance till the opening of the nineteenth century, but by 1860 it had become the second largest trade. According to the Census there were then about 2700 watch- and clock-makers in Coventry [2]; while in Birmingham, where the trade had grown up after 1830-1843, some 500 persons were likewise described, although many of these would doubtless be repairers rather than makers.[3] Coventry was also playing a part in the production of artistic or ornamental metalwork.[4]

[1] S. Timmins, *op. cit.*, pp. 203-204.
[2] *Census of England and Wales*, 1861, vol. ii., pp. 509, 513.
[3] C. J. Woodward, *Manufacturing Industries* in the *British Association Handbook* (Birmingham Meeting, 1886), p. 211.
[4] S. Timmins, *op. cit.*, p. 550.

CHAPTER III

THE HEAVY INDUSTRIES

WHILE the manufacture of each type of light metal article and, as will be seen later, that of certain of the heavy finished products also were usually confined to a small area within the Black Country, the industries which were concerned with the production of raw and semi-manufactured materials were widely scattered. This was especially true of the extractive industries; and since these still formed the basis of the economic activities of the West Midlands, they deserve detailed attention. The most important minerals produced in the area consisted of coal, ironstone, limestone and fire-clay, and each of these may be considered in turn.

In 1860 coal was being obtained from almost every part of South Staffordshire and of North Worcestershire which lay on the exposed coal-measures, while a successful attempt had been made to find coal under the red rocks in the neighbourhood of West Bromwich.[1] The coal-field could be divided into three main sections, the first lying south of a line drawn from West Bromwich through Tipton to the Boundary Fault near Sedgeley. North of this lay the middle part of the field, with a northern boundary running through West Bromwich, Wednesbury, Darlaston, and just south of Wolverhampton. Beyond this, again, was the third division, which was bounded on the north by a line joining Rushall, Bloxwich and the Western Boundary Fault at Wednesfield Heath. The chief types of coal to be found within these districts consisted of brooch coal, thick or ten-yard coal, heathen coal, new-mine coal, fire-clay coal and bottom coal. The brooch coal was mined only in the southern division and, being a quick-burning variety, was employed exclusively for domestic purposes. It was of a high grade, but was at this time approaching exhaustion. The heathen coal was found in all sections of the field, although in the two southern districts it was of a higher quality and easier to work than in the north. It was the best coking coal in South Staffordshire, and it was employed extensively in gasworks, besides being used raw for smelting. The new-mine coal was of a poor quality in the southern division,

---

[1] T. E. Lones, *op. cit.*, pp. 47-48.

and it was there employed only in the mills and forges; but it was considered a valuable seam in the middle section, where it was found in connection with the fire-clay coal, and also in the north, where it was termed the " yard " coal. There it was placed just above the four-feet coal, corresponding to the fire-clay coal of the second section. The coal from all these seams was burnt raw for smelting, manufacturing and domestic purposes, except the four-feet coal, which was used only in mills and forges. The bottom coal, which was inferior in quality to the seams just described, was confined to the middle and northern sections, being mined chiefly in the latter. It was the cheapest coal in South Staffordshire, and was in demand for the mills and forges and for the brick-kilns. Up to the present only the thin seams have been described; and the coal for which the district had long been famous has still to be mentioned. This was the thick or ten-yard coal, which, lying near the surface and outcropping in many places, had been worked for centuries, particularly near Wednesbury, Dudley and Sedgeley. It was found only in the two southern sections, where it had been formed by the coalescence of 13 or 14 seams, and its thickness ranged from 24 feet at Hamstead to 42 feet at Claycroft.[1] Although the coal mined from this great seam varied in quality, much of it was of a very high grade, and it was extensively employed uncoked in the blast-furnaces and for " the most delicate manufactures of the Midland counties, from the annealing of a needle to the welding of a gun-barrel." [2] The fortunes of the Black Country had been closely linked with the ten-yard coal, to the valuable properties of which the high quality of the local iron was in no small measure due. At this time, moreover, the Birmingham manufacturers relied for their supplies of fuel on this coal, which they purchased from the mine owners of Tipton, Bilston, Oldbury, West Bromwich, Wednesbury and Dudley—places which were all situated on canals communicating with Birmingham. The largest quantity came from West Bromwich; but the highest grade coal was still brought from Wednesbury, one of the oldest sources of supply.

By the middle of the century, owing largely to the wasteful and inefficient methods by which the thick coal had been worked,

[1] S. Timmins, *op. cit.*, p. 27 *et seq.*; and *Report of the Committee on the Staffordshire Mines Drainage*, 1920, p. 7.
[2] S. Timmins, *op. cit.*, p. 29.

it was in many places showing signs of exhaustion[1]; and in the fifties the South Staffordshire production of all kinds of coal appeared to be on the decline. In 1855 the output was estimated to be 7,323,000 tons, and from then onwards there was a steady fall, until in 1859 only 4,450,000 tons were produced. There was a recovery during the next year, when the output was 5,272,000 tons—about 7 per cent. of the total British production.[2] While this decline was due in a great measure to the approaching exhaustion of many seams and to the increased cost of production, the depression in the iron trade, which began towards the end of 1857, was a powerful contributory cause. The prosperity of the South Staffordshire coal trade was closely associated at this time with the fortunes of the iron industry, which was its most important customer, and any decline in the demand for iron was soon reflected in a diminished coal output.[3] Another factor which was just beginning to exert an influence was the competition of certain South Staffordshire mining areas which lay beyond the Black Country's borders. Among these was the Aldridge and Wyrley districts, lying just outside our boundary line; while a new mining area had begun to be opened up in the neighbourhood of Cannock.[4] Unfortunately the available statistics do not separate the produce of the Black Country mines from that of South Staffordshire as a whole, and therefore it is not possible to indicate the proportion of the total output, quoted above, which could be assigned to the South Staffordshire field north of the Bentley Fault. It was certainly not large at this time, but the fact that the Black Country was already feeling the competition of these other districts was an indication of the change to come.[5] The distribution of mining activities in 1860 is illustrated by the Table on the opposite page.

The close association of ironstone and coal had contributed largely to the rise of South Staffordshire as a great iron-producing centre, and in 1860, while a great deal of ore was brought from other districts, the local production was still important. Iron-

---

[1] G. T. Lawley, *History of Bilston* (1868), pp. 79-80.
[2] These figures must be regarded as estimates. It was impossible at this time to arrive at an exact figure, owing to the fact that no regular statutory weight was in use in South Staffordshire. It is probable that the production was underestimated. (R. Hunt, *op. cit.*, 1855, p. 79 ; 1859, p. 116 ; 1860, p. 112).
[3] T. E. Lones, *op. cit.*, p. 78 *et seq.*
[4] *Ibid.*, p. 78 ; S. Timmins, *op. cit.*, p. 25.
[5] T. E. Lones, *op. cit.*, p. 68.

stone was mined along with coal in almost every part of the field, and, though varying in quality, yielded from 30 to 50 per cent. of metal.[1] The annual output had been declining for nearly a decade; but in 1860 it still amounted to 786,000 tons—nearly 10 per cent. of the total British production.[2]

District	No. of Collieries [3]
Bilston	64
West Bromwich	52
Dudley	46
Walsall	39
Corngreaves	30
Willenhall	30
Oldbury	27
Wolverhampton	26
Tipton	24
Wednesbury	21
Brierley Hill	21
Rowley Regis	19
Sedgeley	13
Darlaston	11
*Wyrley	15
*Rugeley	3
	441

* Districts lying beyond the Great Bentley Fault.

Besides the coal and ironstone a number of other minerals were obtained from the district which were of no small importance in the local manufactures. Limestone, for instance, which was required in the blast-furnaces, was found in close connection with the coal-measures. In 1860 it was mined mainly from the hills between Dudley and Sedgeley by shafts which penetrated the coal-measures, and also from the Wenlock district. Two measures of this mineral were worked, the thin or top limestone, which was employed as a flux in the blast-furnaces, and the thick or lower limestone, which was converted into lime for building and agricultural purposes. Further, the deposits of fire-clay, which were found in a small area in the neighbourhood of Stourbridge, were of great importance to the glass trade, and had been a primary cause of its localization in that district. The best clay was used for making glasshouse pots, in which the ingredients were melted, and other qualities were employed for gas-retorts, firebricks and crucibles of various

[1] S. Timmins, op. cit., p. 33. [2] R. Hunt, op. cit., 1860, p. 57.
[3] Ibid., p. 112.

kinds, the manufacture of which was conducted chiefly at Lye and Cradley. Besides these special manufactures, bricks, pipes and tiles were made from local clay quarried in many parts of the district, particularly at Stourbridge and Walsall. Furthermore, basalt was obtained from the Rowley Hills, where it was known as Rowley Rag, and was melted and cast for use as paving-stones and tiles. Sand for casting purposes was found in many localities, notably at Hockley, near Birmingham, and a mineral suitable for grindstones was found at Bilston.[1] Thus in 1860 the district was rich, not only in the major raw materials like coal and ironstone, but also in minerals which, though of less importance, were extensively used in the neighbourhood.

It is not possible to arrive at an accurate estimate of the number of persons to whom mining and quarrying afforded employment, but such evidence as can be obtained from the Census of 1861, and from the *Reports of the Inspector of Mines* for 1865, seems to warrant the conclusion that the number of coal-miners was about 24,000, and of iron-miners about 2500.[2] It was estimated a year later that the clay quarries employed 1500 or 1600 persons.[3]

Since the raw materials for iron-making were so widely scattered over our area, it was to be expected that the actual production of that metal should be carried on in practically all parts of the coal-field. As far as pig-iron was concerned the manufacture had penetrated into many districts lying beyond our boundary line, particularly to the north; but although the statistics on page 89 cover a somewhat larger area than that with which we are specially concerned, the proportion of pig produced in these outlying parts was very small. The two chief centres of this manufacture were Bilston, with 42 blast-furnaces built, and Dudley, with 40; but Tipton, Wolverhampton and Walsall also were of great importance, having respectively 21, 17 and 13. Besides these, practically every town in the Black Country, whatever its staple trade might be, had a share of this industry. From Stourbridge in the south-west to Walsall and Bloxwich in the north, from Kingswinford in the west to West Bromwich, Smethwick and Oldbury on the

[1] S. Timmins, *op. cit.*, pp. 33-34, 41 *et seq.*; T. C. Turberville, *op. cit.*, pp. 9-12; and R. G. Hobbs, *A Midland Tour* in *The Leisure Hour* (1872), pp. 172, 429.
[2] *Census of England and Wales*, 1861, vol. ii., p. 469.
[3] S. Timmins, *op. cit.*, p. 136.

eastern border, the skies were lit up at night by the flames of multitudinous furnaces.[1]

As indicated in an earlier chapter, the production of pig-iron had increased rapidly throughout the first half of the nineteenth century, until in 1856 South Staffordshire and North Worcestershire possessed 147 furnaces in blast, and was responsible for an output of 777,000 tons—nearly 22 per cent. of the total British production. Up to September 1857 the trade continued to expand; but in the later months of that year a depression set in, and the iron production of this area, which was more seriously affected than any other, began to decline. This tendency continued, in spite of the expansion of the British iron trade as a whole during the later years of the decade; and in 1860 the Black Country produced only 470,000 tons of pig, its proportion of the whole country's output having sunk to just over 12 per cent. This misfortune was caused partly by the increased cost of production—a consequence of the failing supplies of raw materials in the locality—and partly by the rapid development of newer producing centres, such as Lancashire, Cumberland and Cleveland, which had an advantage in possessing cheaper supplies of raw materials, more up-to-date plant and proximity to the sea. The following Table [2] shows the position of the local industry relative to that of the country as a whole in 1860.

	Tons of Pig-Iron produced	No. of Works	Furnaces built	Furnaces in blast
South Staffordshire and Worcestershire . .	469,000	72	181	109
Great Britain . . .	3,827,000	268	872	583

In the manufacture of finished iron the district still maintained its lead. Although the trade had been depressed since 1857, and although the number of puddling furnaces had fallen, in 1860 the Black Country probably produced more than a third of the total British output, and it possessed 1588 puddling furnaces in operation out of the total for the whole country of 4147, or 38 per cent.[3] These figures do not, however, sufficiently

[1] R. Hunt, op. cit., 1860, pp. 89–90. [2] Ibid., p. 70 et seq.
[3] Ibid., pp. 88–90.

emphasize the relative importance of our area in this branch of the industry; for since much of the finished iron was of a higher grade than that produced elsewhere, the proportion of South Staffordshire's output to the total, if expressed in value, would have been much higher. The iron consisted for the most part of sheets and plates for engineering and shipbuilding purposes; bars for chains, cables and for general use; nail rods, tinplates, sheets and hoops. Rails were not produced in any considerable quantity, for a high-grade iron was not needed for that purpose, and so the manufacture had become centred in districts where lower-quality metal was manufactured.[1]

Like the blast-furnaces, the mills and forges of the Black Country were widely scattered, though in an even greater degree. They were found in much the same places as the blast-furnaces; but the relative importance of the various producing centres for pig- and finished-iron respectively was not always the same. For instance, while both Bilston and Tipton were leading centres for both classes of iron, and while Wolverhampton also ranked high, West Bromwich and Smethwick, which had comparatively few blast-furnaces, were among the most important seats of finished-iron manufacture. Stourbridge also was a finished-iron rather than a pig-iron centre.[2] The reason for this grouping is not difficult to discover. The blast-furnaces naturally tended to cluster in close proximity to the supplies of raw materials, and the finished-iron producers were thus forced towards the edges of the coal-field. The rise of Smethwick and West Bromwich as centres of puddling furnaces may be attributed also to the fact that producers in those towns were not only conveniently placed for receiving supplies of pig-iron, brought by canal from the heart of the Black Country, but they were also near to the large market for finished-iron lying to the east of the coal-field.

The amount of employment afforded by the blast-furnaces, forges and mills is difficult to judge, because the Census definition of " iron manufacture " is too vague to afford any help. From the information given by a contemporary authority, however, it appears that the average number of persons employed in connection with each furnace was about 40.[3] The annual average of furnaces in blast between 1856 and 1860 was 136,

[1] S. Timmins, op. cit., p. 70.
[2] R. Hunt, op. cit., 1860, pp. 79-80, 89-90.
[3] Children's Employment Commission (1862), Third Report, pp. 1-2.

and one would not be far wrong, therefore, in assuming that there were between 5000 and 5500 persons engaged in the production of pig-iron in our district. In the finished-iron trade the labour force was much larger, being estimated at 21,000 in 1862 and at 17,000 in 1866.[1] The actual production was said to be between 800,000 and 900,000 tons a year.[2]

We have already seen that, in spite of South Staffordshire's prominence as a seat of the iron industry, it had never been important as a steel-producing centre. In 1860 Bessemer steel had been as yet scarcely heard of, and blister or crucible steel was the only kind made. Up to 1850 a firm at Oldbury had supplied the Birmingham penmakers with steel strip; but that market had been lost to Sheffield, and at the beginning of our period the small quantity of steel manufactured in the locality went to supply the edge-tool makers and the umbrella-frame industry.[3]

The South Staffordshire manufactures which fell within the category of finished products were tending, during the first half of the nineteenth century, to become distinctly heavier in type. The development was particularly marked after 1840; and in 1860, besides the lighter trades already described, there were several industries producing finished articles which fell definitely within the heavy group. In Wednesbury, for instance, two manufactures of this kind rose to importance between 1840 and 1860. The larger of these was the trade which was responsible for making gas-, water-, bedstead- and steam-tubes, of which the first-named were produced in greatest quantity. As already explained, the gun-barrel makers of Wednesbury, after the Napoleonic Wars, found themselves with a stock of old barrels for which there was no demand. These were converted into gas-tubes, and from that time onwards the gun-barrel welders turned to tube manufacture whenever the demand for their original products slackened. The coach-iron people of the neighbourhood also found a new market in satisfying the call for tube-fittings. A new process of tube manufacture, invented in 1825, lowered the cost of production and improved the quality; so that gradually many makers came to concentrate on what previously had been a side-line and to give up barrel manufacture.

---

[1] *Children's Employment Commission (1862), Third Report*, p. 2; and S. Timmins, *op. cit.*, p. 70.

[2] S. Timmins, *op. cit.*, p. 70.

[3] *Ibid.*, p. 212; and E. Burritt, *Walks in the Black Country* (1868), p. 164.

The demand grew very rapidly during the decades preceding 1860, as may be illustrated by the fact that between 1838 and 1858 the output of Wednesbury's largest firm increased from 793,000 to 4,228,000 feet of tube.[1] The railways bringing a demand for boiler-tubes, the spread of gaslighting, the rise of the iron-bedstead trade, and the beginning of town water supplies all gave a stimulus to the industry, to such local trades as made forgings and fittings for tubes,[2] and to the firms conducting subsidiary processes like galvanizing and enamelling. Although Wednesbury continued to remain the chief seat of the trade, factories had sprung up at Walsall and Wolverhampton[3]; while in 1860 a firm, which was afterwards to obtain a predominant share of the market, was established at Hales Owen. The employment afforded by the industry was in the neighbourhood of 2000.[4]

In connection with the manufacture of coach-iron work the production of springs for carriages had long existed in West Bromwich, Wednesbury and Birmingham; and the coming of railways had induced the smiths who made them to turn to the production of heavy springs for rolling-stock. By 1860 the trade had become centred at West Bromwich and Wednesbury.[5] Besides these heavy springs light coil-springs also were being made in the neighbourhood, though only to a small extent. This industry appears to have arisen in the early twenties, when John Salter, of West Bromwich, invented a spring-balance which made it necessary for him to secure light steel springs of high quality. At the beginning of our period the production of these springs and of spring-balances was carried on at West Bromwich in association with bayonet manufacture; for since at that time the quantity of coil-springs required did not warrant steel-makers producing a special metal for the new trade, bayonet steel was used, having proved most suitable for the purpose.[6]

Another industry which had been created by the presence of the old coach-iron workers on the one hand and the growth of a new demand on the other was that concerned with the manu-

---

[1] F. W. Hackwood, *Wednesbury Workshops*, p. 94.

[2] *Midland Captains of Industry* in *Birmingham Gazette and Express*, December 16, 1908.

[3] *Children's Employment Commission (1862), Third Report*, p. 5.

[4] *Reports of the Inspectors of Factories*, October 1868, p. 118.

[5] F. W. Hackwood, *Wednesbury Workshops*, pp. 55-57.

[6] Personal inquiry.

facture of axles, wheels and iron tyres for railway rolling-stock. The axle trade began in the thirties, when a new type of " faggoted " axle was invented in the locality. This was suitable for both coach and railway use, and as time went on, and the demand for these products expanded, Wednesbury gathered to it more and more of the trade.[1] It was conducted also at West Bromwich and elsewhere.

Here, moreover, and at many other places in the Black Country — at Tipton, Wolverhampton and Smethwick — a beginning had been made before 1860 of structural ironwork, and bridges, turn-tables and girders were becoming important products; while at Spon Lane the manufacture of lighthouses involved the use of heavy iron materials. Heavy forgings, produced under the steam-hammer and including armour plates for warships, were among the products of Brierley Hill, Tipton and Bilston. Steam-boilers, tanks, cisterns, salt and sugar pans, galvanizing baths, plating vats, canal barges and gas-holders were made in the Wednesbury and Tipton neighbourhoods, as well as by a large concern at Birmingham; anvils and vices were among the staple products of Dudley and Lye; and Wolverhampton, Bilston and Brierley Hill manufactured iron hurdles and fences.[2]

Among the newest of the heavy industries in 1860 was the production of galvanized and corrugated sheets. The galvanizing process had been introduced into England in 1837 and had been applied six years later to the production of sheets for roofing by a Birmingham firm. The corrugated process, which was adopted shortly afterwards, had the effect of making galvanized sheets more suitable for this purpose, and during the fifties several firms were established at Wolverhampton and Bilston to take advantage of the Colonial demand which was just growing up. By 1860 it had become one of the leading trades of the district. While the galvanized process had been taken up by manufacturers of many different classes of commodity in all parts of our area, those who made roofing sheets had become centred at Wolverhampton.[3]

No statistical evidence exists to enable any estimate to be made of the employment which the foundries, forges, rolling

[1] F. W. Hackwood, *Wednesbury Workshops*, p. 54 *et seq.*
[2] S. Timmins, *op. cit.*, p. 93 *et seq.*
[3] W. H. Jones, *op. cit.*, chap. xii.

mills and engineering shops engaged in producing the above articles afforded; for although figures showing the numbers employed by the leading firms have been secured, in most cases these include men who were concerned with manufacturing pig- and finished-iron, with which the above trades generally are combined.

Evidence exists, however, for a more satisfactory treatment of the chain and cable industries. Both trades were of comparatively recent origin. It is true that light chains for agricultural purposes had been made in the district from early times,[1] but the manufacture of heavy chains and cables for the shipyards was not introduced until about 1825. During the next thirty-five years there was a great development, due not only to increased demands from agriculture and shipping, but also to the greater use of chains in mines. So, in 1860, besides the trace and curb chains which were turned out at Walsall in association with saddlers' ironmongery, common chain was made for mines and agricultural purposes, and cables were produced in quantity for ships.[2] While the lighter section of the industry strongly resembled the nail trade in the type of labour employed and in the methods of production, it came into contrast with the older trade in one respect. The nailers were found, it has been shown, in many parts of the Black Country and its borderland; but the forges of the chain-makers were for the most part concentrated within an area of two or three square miles. The chief centres of their activities were Cradley and Netherton, and more than half of the total number of chain-makers in Worcestershire, Warwickshire and Staffordshire were to be found in the adjoining parishes of Dudley, Sedgeley, Tipton and Rowley Regis, most of the remainder being to the south-west of Dudley in the neighbourhood of Lye and at West Bromwich.[3] The two most highly localized branches of the trade appear to have been the manufacture of ships' cables and heavy chains, which was confined to the immediate neighbourhood of Dudley, and the production of harness chain, which was among the Walsall trades.

Associated with this industry, both in organization and local-

[1] *Midland Captains of Industry* in *Birmingham Gazette and Express,* January 15, 1908.
[2] S. Timmins, *op. cit.,* pp. 99-100.
[3] *Ibid.,* p. 99; and *Census of England and Wales,* 1861, vol. ii., p. 469 *et seq.,* p. 494 *et seq.,* p. 511 *et seq.*

ization, was the production of anchors. Brought to South Staffordshire by a ships' cable-maker, Noah Hingley, in 1838, by the late forties the manufacture had taken a firm root and was beginning to migrate from the coast. Like the chain trade, this had been drawn to the Black Country through the presence of the local brands of wrought-iron; and it had become localized at Netherton, near Dudley.[1] In 1861 there were, according to the Census, about 2900 persons engaged in the cabin and anchor industry of Staffordshire and Worcestershire, and practically all of these must have lived within our area. The anchor section alone accounted for about 200.[2]

The multifarious manufactures of the district had created a large local demand for various kinds of chemicals. Acids were required, for instance, in the galvanizing baths and the plating vats, and for " pickling " or cleansing the products of the brass-foundry trade; potassium cyanide was needed for the plating industry; red lead was an important constituent of flint-glass; and phosphorus was used in the production of matches. These demands led naturally to the establishment of chemical manufactures in the neighbourhood, especially as the raw materials required to produce many of the chemicals were found locally. Besides the essential commodity, coal, a supply of pyrites could be obtained from the South Staffordshire mines for the production of sulphur; while salt was close at hand at Droitwich and Stoke for the manufacture of alkalis. Consequently, having both a local market and a supply of raw products, the chemical industry had attained a position of some importance by 1860. Heavy chemicals were then produced at Oldbury, which had become the chief local centre for the manufacture of acids and alkalis for industrial purposes,[3] and which had almost a national monopoly of the production of phosphorus.[4] Nickel and cobalt, both raw materials for the German silver trade, were refined at Birmingham. Artificial manures were made at Wolverhampton and King's Norton, red lead at Tipton and Smethwick, and medical and photographic chemicals were made at several centres,

---

[1] S. Timmins, op. cit., p. 100.
[2] Ibid., p. 100. This authority places the employment in the chain and anchor industries at 4200 in 1866.
[3] R. G. Hobbs, op. cit., p. 142 ; and G. L. Strauss, England's Workshops (1864), pp. 133-141.
[4] Midland Captains of Industry in Birmingham Gazette and Express, December 9, 1908.

notably Wolverhampton and Birmingham.[1] At the last-named town and at Smethwick a small quantity of soap also was produced.[2] No contemporary estimates of the employment afforded by this group of trades are available, but the number of workers can have been scarcely less than 2000, for we are informed that one Oldbury factory alone employed 600 persons in 1864.[3]

Outside this group, but closely allied to it, was the manufacture of paint and varnish. The raw materials for this trade were not, of course, found in the locality; but the requirements of the metal manufacturers had created a number of concerns in Wolverhampton and in other parts of the Black Country, as well as in Birmingham, for the production of these commodities. The japanned- and the hollow-ware makers, and the manufacturers of umbrella-fittings, buttons and hairpins, all employed " black tar varnish," or japan. The stove-, range-, bedstead- and fender-makers needed other kinds of black varnish. The lockmakers used a special kind, called " Willenhall lock varnish," and the brassfounders required great quantities of lacquer. In the manufacture of these commodities the district's production exceeded that of any other centre, with the exception of London. Its output of paints and colours, on the other hand, was still very small. The paints made in Birmingham and the Black Country were used mainly for industrial purposes, the chief consumers being the rolling-stock, boiler, gasometer and bedstead trades.[4]

The relative importance of the various industries of Birmingham and the Black Country may be illustrated by the Table on the opposite page, which shows them grouped according to the employment which they afforded in 1860. For a definition of the scope of the various trades reference should be made to the preceding chapters.

[1] S. Timmins, *op. cit.*, p. 671 *et seq.*
[2] *Ibid.*, p. 168.
[3] G. L. Strauss, *op. cit.*, p. 141.
[4] S. Timmins, *op. cit.*, p. 680.

[TABLE

EMPLOYMENT IN BIRMINGHAM AND DISTRICT INDUSTRIES

20,000 to 30,000 Persons	*15,000 to 20,000 Persons*	*7000 to 10,000 Persons*	*3500 to 7000 Persons*
Mines and Quarries	Wrought-Nail	Brass	Button
Pig- and Finished-Iron		Gun	Saddlery,Harness, Whips, and their Components
		Jewellery (including " Toy " and Plate)	Needle and Fishhook
			Lock and Key
			Bolt, Nut, Screw and Rivet

1500 to 3500 Persons	*Minor Trades (under 1500 Persons)*
Chain and Anchor	Chemical
Tinplate, Japanned and Papier-Mâché Ware	Brush
Rolling-Stock	Cut-Nail
Pen	Paint and Varnish
Watch and Clock	Paper and Paper Box
Wire (Drawing, Weaving and Rope-Making)	Weighing and Testing Apparatus
Edge-Tool	Umbrella and Stick
Hollow-Ware (Cast and Wrought)	Ornamental Metalwork
Bedstead	Measuring-Rule
Bricks, Tile, Clay Retort, etc.	Spectacle
Iron-Tube	Pin
	Curry-Comb
	Hempen Rope and Twine
	Optical and Mathematical Instrument
	Coinage
	Safe
	Fender and Fire-Iron
	Tin Toy
	Awl-Blade
	Saw, File and Plane
	Machete
	Spring
	Axle and Wheel

In addition, there was an indeterminate number of persons engaged in the constructional and general engineering trades, in general ironfoundries and smithies, and as die-sinkers and tool-makers.

G

The following Table provides some idea of the localization of the leading industries within the area:

SITUATION OF THE LOCAL TRADES

Town or Village	Industries
Birmingham, Aston and the Immediate Neighbourhood	Brass and other non-ferrous, Gun, Jewellery, Button, Pen, Edge-Tool, Flint-Glass, Tinplate, Japanned and Papier-Mâché Ware, Rolling-Stock, Wire, Pin, Cut-Nail, Saddlery and Harness and Whip, Bedstead
Wolverhampton	Tinplate, Japanned and Papier-Mâché Ware, Lock, Edge-Tool, Hollow-Ware (cast and wrought), Galvanizing, Cut-Nail, Iron-Tube, Iron-Fencing, Brass
Dudley and Immediate Neighbourhood	Wrought - Nail, Chain and Anchor, Fender and Fire-Iron, Constructional Engineering
West Bromwich	Hollow-Ware, Safe, Constructional Engineering, Spring
Walsall	Leather, Saddlery and Harness, Saddlers' Ironmongery, Lock, Brush, Iron-Tube
Tipton	Chain, Wrought-Nail, Heavy Engineering
Bilston	Tinplate and Japanned Ware, Hollow-Ware (cast and wrought), Galvanizing
Wednesbury	Iron-Tube, Gun-Lock
Willenhall	Lock and Key, Curry-Comb
Oldbury	Chemical, Rolling-Stock
Smethwick	Screw, Sheet - Glass, Constructional Engineering
Darlaston	Nut-and-Bolt, Gun-Lock
Stourbridge and Immediate Neighbourhood	Flint-Glass, Crown-Glass, Firebrick and Retort, Edge-Tool
Wednesfield	Lock and Key
Bloxwich	Awl-Blade and Saddlers' Ironmongery
Redditch	Needle and Fishhook
Lye	Firebrick and Retort, Chain, Anvil and Vice
Cradley	Chain
Hales Owen	Wrought-Nail, Edge-Tool, Button

Besides the above distribution of trades there were the wrought-nail, heavy engineering and edge-tool trades, and the iron and coal industries, which were carried on in most parts of the Black Country.

CHAPTER IV

RAW MATERIALS AND MECHANICAL EQUIPMENT

NOTHING illustrates more clearly the decline in the strength of the forces which had originally created South Staffordshire as a great iron centre than the facts which indicate the extent of its reliance on outside sources of supply for the raw and semi-manufactured materials required by the iron producers. It was the coal, ironstone and limestone which had drawn iron manufacture in all its stages to the Black Country; but the drive of these influences was weakening by 1860, and the importance of the industry was being maintained largely by other factors—the presence of skilled labour and organizing ability and by its natural inertia. As far as coal was concerned, however, this change had not yet gone very far. Many of the mines, it is true, were becoming waterlogged: in the former thick coal-mines only the pillars and remnants of the seams remained; and in the older districts, like Dudley and Wednesbury, exhaustion was in sight.[1] But the development of the West Bromwich mines and the working of the new seams in other districts were sufficient to maintain the production at a high level. Nor was competition from neighbouring mining areas yet proving dangerous, and the output of the new districts, such as Cannock, was still very small when compared with that of the Black Country.

The construction of canals had enabled South Staffordshire to sell its coal in other parts of the country, even before 1800, and the coming of the railways opened new markets during the two decades preceding 1860; but in spite of these facilities, and of the fact that the district was conveniently situated for supplying the south of England, only a small proportion of its coal was sent beyond the boundaries of Birmingham and District. In the early sixties, indeed, more than half the coal mined in South Staffordshire was used in the local blast-furnaces, forges and mills—a fact which emphasizes how intimately the fortunes of the coal and iron trades were linked at this time.[2] This does not mean, however, that the district was self-sufficing, as far as the coal for local manufacturing purposes was concerned.

---

[1] S. Timmins, *op. cit.*, pp. 25-26 ; T. E. Lones, *op. cit.*, p. 81.
[2] R. Hunt, *op. cit.*, 1860, p. 112.

While the heathen and the thick coal could be burned in a raw state in the blast-furnaces, there was little good coking coal or gas coal in the neighbourhood. Consequently the gasworks had to find sources of supply elsewhere; and, since the majority of the pig-iron producers used coke rather than raw coal in their furnaces, Welsh coal and tar had to be brought to South Stafford-shire and mixed with local coal in the coke-ovens in order to provide a suitable fuel. In addition, coke itself came in large quantities from Wales and the North of England.[1] Thus, owing to the nature of the South Staffordshire coal, although the district had a surplus to send to Birmingham and elsewhere, the iron industry had to obtain part of its fuel from distant sources of supply.

For their ore the ironmasters were still more dependent on other mining centres. It was estimated in 1866 that the Black Country's output of ironstone amounted at that time to only about half of the total consumption in the locality [2]; and although in 1860, which was a depressed year, the local mines satisfied a larger share of the demand, even then, while 785,000 tons were produced in South Staffordshire, no less than 500,000 tons were imported. The main external source of the supply was North Staffordshire, which accounted for about four-fifths of the total. Small quantities came also from Cumberland, Northampton-shire, the Forest of Dean and Cleveland.[3] Of these, Cumberland deserves particular notice because it was the sole source of supply of red hæmatite, which was employed in making pig for the malleable-iron foundries, where saddlers' ironmongery and many gun parts were manufactured. In addition, about 150,000 tons of " cinder pig " were used annually in the production of a cheap grade of foundry iron.[4] This " cinder pig " or " puddlers' tap " consisted of waste iron produced in the course of the puddling process, and as this had not been employed in the blast-furnaces till the forties, great quantities had accumulated in South Stafford-shire. For the other mineral required in pig-iron production—viz. limestone—the local supplies had become inadequate by 1860, and by far the larger part of the 250,000 tons used annually in the district was brought from North Staffordshire and North Wales.[5]

Since the proportion of locally produced raw materials was

[1] S. Timmins, op. cit., pp. 40 and 65.   [2] Ibid., p. 60.
[3] R. Hunt, op. cit., 1860, p. 60 et seq.
[4] S. Timmins, op. cit., p. 64.   [5] Ibid., p. 66.

declining as compared with that brought from elsewhere, the transport question was becoming more and more intimately connected with the maintenance of the district's importance as an iron centre. A midland situation had from the first demanded good transport facilities and the canals had done much to open distant markets to the heavier products. But now that a large part of the essential raw materials had to be acquired from external sources, the necessity of widespread channels of communication was emphasized, and it seemed scarcely too much to say that had it not been for the development of railways, which were used in 1860 to a much greater extent than canals for the transport even of the heavier products, except where the haul was short, South Staffordshire would have been rapidly sinking to a position of obscurity as a seat of pig-iron production. The same would probably have been true of that branch of the trade in which the district still maintained a priority—viz. malleable-iron production; for in the early sixties about 300,000 tons of pig had to be carried into the area annually for use in the foundries and forges, for the needs of which the output of the South Staffordshire blast-furnaces, ranging at this time from 400,000 to 700,000 tons a year, was insufficient. The imported pig came mainly from Wales, Derbyshire and the Forest of Dean.[1] Another product which several of the local metal trades required, but of which only insignificant quantities were produced within the district, was crucible steel. Consequently the pen, needle, edge-tool, awl-blade, bayonet, coil-spring and steel-wire trades had to purchase the larger proportion of their raw material from Sheffield.

Now, in spite of the reliance of its industries on other districts for certain raw materials and semi-products, the Black Country could still provide the larger share of its requirements. But the leading trades of Birmingham, on the contrary, besides some of those which it shared with the rest of our area, depended almost entirely on distant sources of supply. The brass-using trades purchased their copper and spelter, mainly in the form of ingots, from London merchants. Of the copper, some still came from Devon and Cornwall; but Chile and North America, particularly the former, constituted the chief countries of origin. The greater part of spelter was obtained from Silesia. Tin, employed in the

[1] S. Timmins, *op. cit.*, p. 68.

manufacture of bronze, gun-metal and Britannia-metal, came from Cornwall and Germany. The electro-plate industry relied on the ores of Scandinavia and Switzerland; while the jewellery trade proper, of course, drew most of its raw materials—gold, silver, pearls and precious stones—through London from distant sources. Even the gun trade could not be supplied wholly from the neighbourhood, for the beech stocks, used in the cheaper products, were brought, cut roughly in the form required, from Herefordshire and Gloucestershire; and walnut stocks, for the better class of gun, were imported from Italy and Germany. The button industry made use of a. wide variety of materials, and practically all of these were of external origin. The covered- and linen-button manufacturers went to the textile districts for supplies. The makers of vegetable-ivory buttons obtained their material—corozo-nuts—from Central America. Pearl-shell, both for buttons and papier mâché, came from the East Indies and from many parts of the Pacific. Fontainebleau supplied the sand for the flint-glass manufacturers; China, Russia, South America and Africa the bristles and fibres for the brush trade; while the tropics furnished the gums and Scandinavia the turpentine for the varnish and paint industry. A certain amount of tinplate was manufactured in the neighbourhood of Wolverhampton, but the tinplate- and japanned-ware industry had to buy most of its materials from Stourport and South Wales. As for the saddlery and harness trades, pigskins for the saddles were obtained from Scotland, as pigs were not flayed there as they were in England. The cowhides, on the other hand, were mainly of English origin, and in this respect the industry came into contrast with the boot and shoe manufacture, in which American hides were most commonly used. This was because the saddlers and harness-makers needed soft hides, which were to be obtained from English rather than American beasts, since the former were usually killed at an earlier age.[1]

In view of the fact that the district relied on foreign countries or on distant parts of Great Britain for many of its raw materials, its central situation might have been expected to prove a great disadvantage. Yet in the majority of the Birmingham trades, in which the chief materials came almost wholly from abroad, the expense of transporting them from the coast added only an

---

[1] S. Timmins, *op. cit.*, for source of raw materials.

insignificant amount to the total cost of production, which was influenced mainly by labour charges. Even in the case of the glass trade the initial expense of the raw material was small compared with the price of the finished article, which was determined mainly by the cost of fuel and labour. In the case of subsidiary industries, like paint and varnish, the convenience of being near to a large group of customers more than balanced the transport charges on raw materials; while all the trades which catered chiefly for the home market benefited by a midland situation in the distribution of their finished products. It was, curiously enough, only in the iron trades, to which alone the area furnished any considerable proportion of the raw materials required, that the cost of transport was proving a serious burden in 1860. The expense of bringing large quantities of heavy materials from a distance was by that time becoming a menace to the Black Country's prosperity, and the difficulties of the local iron manufacturers in securing any share in the great increase in the British export trade, which occurred after the middle of the century, was bringing home to them the handicap imposed by the long haul to the coast. So, by 1860, South Staffordshire was taking alarm because of the competitive advantages possessed by the newer centres on the seaboard, and agitations were already in being for the reduction in railway rates and for the development of canal communication to the sea.[1]

In one respect, however, the central position was an advantage, even from the point of view of raw-material supplies. A great deal of the metal used by the local industries consisted not of new metal but of worn-out products or of scrap. The brushmakers, for instance, made use of waste wood, which they purchased from the railway-carriage works.[2] The gun-barrel welders often employed metal which they had not purchased direct from the forges and steelworks, but which consisted of old horseshoe nails and waste iron from the nailing shops, and of scrap steel from the spring and bayonet factories. There were, of course, vast supplies of scrap metal of this kind in the locality.

[1] Cf. *ibid.*, p. 72 *et seq.*; and S. Hill, *Present Rates of Freight to London and Liverpool from Staffordshire Iron District* (Simpson & Steen, Wolverhampton, 1865).
[2] *Report of the Chief Inspector of Factories and Workshops*, October 1879, p. 116.

Similarly, the smaller firms in the brass trade commonly manufactured their brass by melting down old sheathing, boiler-tubes, filings and scrap from the mills and press shops, and by "revivifying" the metal so produced with an admixture of copper. The fact that brass does not disappear in use, but is available ultimately as scrap, has had throughout the history of the industry an important influence on the cost of the raw material. For whenever the price of copper has tended to rise to high levels, then worn-out brass and copper products have flowed into the foundries from all parts of the country[1]; and Birmingham and District, both because it has been itself a great consumer of brass articles and therefore an enormous reservoir of the material, and also because of its geographic relation to other metal centres, has been in a favourable position for securing the scrap. Even the jewellery trade was affected in much the same way; for many of the manufacturers, besides using new gold and silver and sovereigns, were accustomed to melt down obsolete ornaments and jewellery, which were obtained from all parts of the country.[2]

A description of the economic structure of the area would be incomplete if no account were taken of the type of machinery and of power which were employed there; and so an attempt will now be made to deal in a general way with the mechanical equipment of the local industries. This will serve as an introduction to a treatment of the actual organization of production, which is the subject of the following chapters. Compared with the textile centres of the north, Birmingham and District could scarcely claim in 1860 to have reached a high degree of mechanical development; and although the area had been a pioneer in the manufacture of the steam-engine, power was by no means generally applied to the local trades. Except in one important group, indeed, it was as true in 1860 as in earlier times that such machinery as had been introduced was to replace strength rather than skill,[3] and it was consequently confined in the metal trades to the earlier sections of the productive process. An examination of the chief methods of manufacture will provide

---

[1] G. W. Mullins, *The Economics of the Copper, Brass and Nickel-Silver Industries* in the *Proceedings of the Empire Mining and Metallurgical Congress*, 1924, pp. 34-35.
[2] S. Timmins, *op. cit.*, p. 458.
[3] *Cf.* H. Hamilton, *op. cit.*, p. 129.

an opportunity both of illustrating this generalization and of indicating the type of tool or machine of which the leading industries made use.

The basic process in many trades took place in the foundry, where a wide variety of ferrous and non-ferrous metal articles were cast in moulds of sand. This method of manufacture had been pursued for centuries, and it was from its nature not susceptible to great mechanical changes. A multitude of brass products, lock cases, light castings and general ironmongery, cast-iron hollow-ware, metal parts for the saddlery, engineering and gun trade, and certain classes of nails were all produced in this way. The non-ferrous rolling mills possessed foundries in which the brass formed by the mixture of copper and spelter was poured from the crucibles, in which they had been melted together, into iron moulds; while in the bedstead trade a variation of the normal process had been introduced in 1835, when iron, or chill, moulds came to be used instead of sand.[1] This method reduced the cost of production by rendering it unnecessary for moulds to be remade after each operation, and by producing more finely finished articles it minimized the use of the file. Chill-casting, however, could be applied profitably only when large quantities of standardized products were required, and only in this one trade had it been generally adopted by this time. Relatively, the casting process was much more important in the finished-metal trades than it afterwards became; for many articles which in later years could be made more cheaply from sheet metal, owing to the improvement of the press and stamp and to the introduction of metals which could be easily manipulated, were in 1860 produced in the foundry.

Thus one of the most important of the earlier manufacturing processes in the local trades was from its nature independent of power-machinery. In the production of sheet metal, on the other hand, a fairly large plant was necessary; and during the previous half-century steam-power had been generally applied to the rolling mills, and had in most places superseded water-power. In the wire and weldless-tube mills, also, steam-engines provided the motive force; while in the heavier trades engaged in manipulating sheet metal, power-driven machinery was common. Mechanically operated guillotine shears were usual

[1] S. Timmins, *op. cit.*, p. 625.

in all the larger factories, and punching and shearing presses, raised by steam- or by hydraulic-power, had been introduced after 1840.[1] During the fifties, moreover, machinery had been invented to perform the corrugating process in the galvanized-sheet industry [2]; while the manufacture of rolled gun-barrels and welded tubes took place in steam-driven mills.[3] While steam had in many of these industries entirely displaced water-power, the latter was still made use of by the needle, spade, scythe, wire and gun-components manufacturers, particularly in the district lying south of the main watershed; for here, in the valleys of the Stour and the Arrow, the streams were fairly swift.[4]

In the production of finished-metal goods the two machines common to most of the local industries were the press and the stamp, and in the lighter trades these were nearly always operated by manual power. In the pen trade, for instance, the actual manufacture of nibs from steel strip was undertaken mainly on the hand-press.[5] The most typical of the tools employed in Birmingham itself, this was found not only in pen manufacture, but in the production of gilt jewellery, certain kinds of buttons, needles, small chains and countless other metal smallwares.[6] The power-press, on the other hand, had a much less extensive application in the lighter trades, though it was used in the manufacture of coins, brass chain links and door knobs.[7]

Like the hand-press, the stamp had a great part to play, and its use was increasing; for some articles which in the early years of the century had been forged on the anvil were in 1860 produced in part, if not entirely, by hot stamping. This applies to certain edge tools, parts for guns and swords, and keys.[8] Before 1840, moreover, all tinplate articles had been made by hand and soldered together; but during the next twenty years many of the chief products of the industry, such as tea-trays and dish-covers, were stamped out of sheet metal. The larger articles produced by the electro-plate trade, spoons and a multitude of

---

[1] S. Timmins, op. cit., pp. 96 and 657.
[2] W. H. Jones, op. cit., chap. xii.
[3] S. Timmins, op. cit., p. 389.
[4] Reports of the Inspectors of Factories, October 1868, p. 116 et seq.
[5] G. L. Strauss, op. cit., pp. 6-8.
[6] Birmingham and her Manufactures in The Leisure Hour, February 3, 1853.
[7] S. Timmins, op. cit., pp. 303, 552, 640.
[8] W. C. Aitken, British Manufacturing Industries, vol. iii., pp. 19-21, 54 et seq.

brass products also were dependent on this process.[1] But it was not possible at the time to produce deep stampings, and so most of the wrought hollow-ware was still made by hand. And even where the stamp was used it could not, in any case, supersede the skilled handicraft required in the finishing processes.

In the small metal trades, in which a heavy stamp was unnecessary, the type commonly employed was the " dead-weight kick-stamp," with a hammer weighing up to 20 lb. This was raised solely by man-power; but in the industries in which large masses of metal had to be manipulated the " kick-stamp " had, between 1840 and 1860, come to be aided by a power-driven shaft, which enabled the weight to be increased to 10 cwt. Steam-hammers,[2] also of a very heavy type, were used to forge boiler plates, anchors and other massive products of the Black Country, as well as in the production of tinplate wares and edge tools.[3] The only other machine which was common to a wide variety of local industries was the lathe. This was still simple in design, and even in the larger factories the substitution of the power- for the treadle-lathe was by no means complete.[4]

Thus, even the machines which were widely used in the locality were still crude, and were driven by steam-power only in the heavier trades. A glance at the leading light finished-metal trades will show what a large part the skilled craftsman had still to perform. In the gun trade the bayonets, it is true, after being forged under steam-hammers, were drilled and planed mechanically. But the production of guns themselves owed practically

[1] W. C. Aitken, *British Manufacturing Industries*, vol. iii., pp. 123, 292, 640 ; and G. L. Strauss, *op. cit.*, pp. 51 *et seq*, 80.

[2] The distinction between the steam-hammer and the drop-hammer or stamp should be noted. When the former is used, the anvil block is placed on timber and the blow is cushioned. Where dies are used, a certain amount of initial forming is necessary, and the article is thus merely finished in the die. With the drop-hammer, on the other hand, the anvil is much more massive than when the steam-hammer is used, and it is placed directly upon an unyielding foundation. The blow given is thus sharp and keen, the metal " flows " on the impact of the die, and little initial forming is required. The latter process is very economical, because it enables an accurate finish to be obtained and eliminates machining to a large extent. For the production of forged goods, however, the steam-hammer was much more commonly used than the drop-stamp until the beginning of the present century ; and the slow progress of hot-stamping, or drop-forging as it is now called, is generally attributed to the fact that engineers were prejudiced against the process, which, they thought, adversely affected the quality of the metal.

[3] S. Timmins, *op. cit.*, p. 93 *et seq.*, pp. 656-657; and W. H. Jones, *op. cit.*, chap. iv.

[4] *Newspaper Cuttings* on *Birmingham Industries*, vol. i., p. 22.

nothing to machinery. Certain parts were made under the " kick-stamp," the military barrels were rolled and ground by steam-driven plant, but the rest of the process was performed entirely by hand. In the jewellery trade the best articles were made throughout by skilled craftsmen, and even the cheap stamped and pressed wares had to be assembled and finished by skilled manual workers. The brassfounders, too, might employ stamps, and power-driven lathes for polishing and burnishing; but other-wise their trade was mainly one of hand-processes. The leading Black Country industries were of the same nature. The nailers, for instance, received their rods, which had been cut at the mills from plate-iron by rolling shears, or rolled from malleable bars, and worked without any subsequent aid from machines. The chains of Cradley, the bolts and nuts of Darlaston, the springs of West Bromwich, were all forged on the anvil.[1] At Willenhall and Wolverhampton lock-making was a manual process; and although sewing-machines were used to a small extent in the manufacture of harness, the local leather trades in all their branches were essentially handicrafts.[2] The flint-glass makers followed methods handed down from ancient times, and only in the cutting shops, where power-driven cutters were used, was there anything in the nature of machinery.

Thus, over this wide field of industry, the mechanical equip-ment was extremely small. In the early or cruder processes of manufacture, in the rolling, tube and wire mills, and for certain subsidiary operations, like grinding and polishing, steam-power was extensively employed. But in the later processes of manu-facture the only machines in general use were the press, the stamp, the hammer and the lathe, and these, in most instances, were not steam-driven. The power-press was in its infancy; the lathe was still simple in construction and was worked often by a treadle; and the " dead-weight kick-stamp " was the common type used.[3] Many of the leading industries were carried on entirely by hand. The remainder, while relying on power-machinery for a few processes, still required skilled manual labour to perform the greater part of the work.

The insignificant part which machinery played in the manu-facture of the staple finished products of Birmingham and

[1] *Children's Employment Commission (1862)*, Third Report, pp. 8-9.
[2] *Ibid.*, p. 7.   [3] *Ibid.*, p. 55.

District—in jewellery, guns, buttons, brassfoundry, locks, nails, wrought chains, saddlery and harness, hollow-ware and flint glass—brings the single group of trades of which this was not true into great prominence. The group in question consisted of the wire-using industries, which were all, though in varying degrees, highly mechanized. The pin trade affords the best example. During the first quarter of the nineteenth century pins had been made by a series of hand-processes; but in 1824 a patent was taken out by an American, named Wright, for a machine which enabled a complete pin to be produced in one operation. This machine was first employed in factories at London and Stroud, though without great success. During the next two decades, however, it was perfected, and by 1860 it had been generally adopted by Birmingham manufacturers.[1] Only special types of pin, of which large quantities were not required, were still made by hand.[2] In the production of hooks and eyes, moreover, automatic machinery had been in use since 1846; hairpins and wire gauze also were produced mechanically; and for the heavier types of woven-wire work, such as was used for fireguards and wire-netting, complicated machinery had just made its appearance.[3] Wire ropes, too, were being woven by machinery similar to that employed in twine-making; and, most important of all, a process had been introduced into Birmingham from the United States in 1854 which enabled wood-screws to be produced from iron wire by automatic machines.[4] The needle trade of Redditch, though a member of the wire-using group, had not reached the same degree of mechanical development as the above industries, for needles were more complicated articles to produce than the other wire products. Nevertheless the process of their manufacture was no longer a handicraft. At the end of the previous century the stamp and press had been adopted for piercing the eye, on the suggestion of a Birmingham

---

[1] Of all the Birmingham manufactures the pin trade was declared in the early sixties to be best equipped with steam-driven machinery. Other industries which were said to make use of mechanical power on a considerable scale were the hook-and-eye, eyelet, cut and patent nail, screw, rivet, light-chain, coin, wood-, bone- and ivory-button manufactures (*Children's Employment Commission (1862), Third Report*, p. 55).

[2] S. Timmins, *op. cit.*, p. 591 *et seq.*; and *Commissioners of Patents' Abridgment of Specifications relating to Needles and Pins* (1871), p. x.

[3] S. Timmins, *op. cit.*, p. 596 *et seq.*; *Birmingham and her Manufactures* in *The Leisure Hour*, February 10, 1853.

[4] S. Timmins, *op. cit.*, p. 604.

button-maker and a visiting factor—an illustration of how new processes might pass from one trade to another in a district of diverse industrial activities; and in 1860 mechanical power was used for burnishing the eye, and a beginning had been made of pointing needles by machinery.[1] The needle district was still one in which water-power had continued to survive, and it was reported in 1854 that the "good-sized and useful stream," the Arrow, was turning a number of old mills, used in grinding and scouring needles.[2]

The high degree of mechanical development in the wire trades may be attributed to the fact that they were producing large quantities of small standardized products of simple design, and that wire was a material which lent itself readily to manipulation by machinery. In certain branches, however, like wire-weaving and wire-rope making, it is possible to account for the development by pointing to the similarity which existed between their productive process and that of the textile industries; for that would naturally suggest to manufacturers the adoption of mechanical processes which had long been followed by cotton weavers and hemp-rope makers.

Outside the wire group the only trade which could be considered highly mechanized was the manufacture of cut nails. These were produced on automatic machines, which cut the nails from cold iron strip. Here again the stimulus to invention had been provided by the existence of a very large demand for an article of simple and standardized design.[3] With the exception of these few trades, however, machinery in the industries of Birmingham and District was a mere accessory to manual skill, and, as a French observer said: "A Birmingham . . . le travail est purement manuel. On emploie les machines comme un accessoire de la fabrication; mais tout dépend de l'adresse et de l'intelligence de l'ouvrier."[4]

The horse-power (steam and water) used per head of workers employed was as follows for factories under the Factory Acts Extension Act of 1867. Workshops—i.e. places in which less than 50 persons were employed—were not included, and as these used less power per head than the factories, the Table exaggerates

[1] S. Timmins, op. cit., p. 197 et seq.
[2] Victoria County History of Warwickshire, vol. ii., p. 234.
[3] S. Timmins, op. cit., p. 613.
[4] L. Faucher, op. cit., p. 503.

the amount of power employed in industries in which the small
workplace was common.[1]

Industry	District covered by Table	H.P. used per Head of Workers
Smelting	Staffordshire	1·14
Other branches of Iron Trade .	Staffordshire	0·59
Wire	Warwickshire	0·81
Boiler, Axle and Anchor . .	Staffordshire	0·43
Tube	Staffordshire and Warwickshire	0·35
Chain	Staffordshire	0·29
Bolt, Nut, Screw, Rivet . .	Staffordshire and Warwickshire	0·25
Gun and Pistol . . .	Warwickshire	0·20
Bedstead	Warwickshire	0·12
Pen	Warwickshire	0·12
Glass	Warwickshire	0·11
Chandelier	Warwickshire	0·05
Button	Warwickshire	0·04
Lock	Staffordshire	0·04
Jewellery	Warwickshire	0·03

[1] *Reports of the Inspectors of Factories*, October 1868, pp. 116-125.

CHAPTER V

THE SCALE OF INDUSTRY

CONFINED as our attention has been to the general growth of industry, we have not as yet attempted to examine the individual business units of which each trade was formed. But we must now try to distinguish the representative firm within such leading industry, so that we may gain some idea of the scale of manufacture, of the range of products with which the typical unit was concerned, and of the degree to which it was self-contained. Complex as these problems are, the data available are sufficient to permit fairly accurate generalization. In this chapter only the industries producing finished products will be our concern, the iron and coal trades being considered separately at a later stage.

From the last quarter of the eighteenth century the manufactures of the area had been of peculiar interest because of the marked contrasts which existed between them in the scale and method of production. From the time of the application of coke to the smelting and " fining " processes the producing units in the iron industry had been large, and it was not uncommon to find a manufacturer controlling blast-furnaces, forges and mills, as well as coal- and iron-mines. Great integrated concerns, indeed, had existed from the beginning of the malleable-iron age in the Black Country, and it was estimated in 1812 that there were no less than ten ironworks, each of which had been established with a capital of over £50,000; while in several of them as many as 300 to 500 men, besides colliers, were employed. Thus, from the outset, the primary processes in the iron trade were organized according to modern capitalist methods.[1] This was true also of several of the newer industries of the later eighteenth century. The brass-houses, where the crude metal was produced, were comparatively large; and many products, the manufacture of which was protected by patent rights or special knowledge, were necessarily monopolized by a few factory owners. Clay, for instance, is supposed to have employed 300 men in his papier-mâché manufacture [2]; while the great Soho establishments of Boulton and Watt were typical of the modern factory era.

[1] T. S. Ashton, *op. cit.*, pp. 100, 163.
[2] E. Burritt, *op. cit.*, p. 101.

It was stated in 1799, however, that, comparing Birmingham manufacturers with those of Leeds and Manchester, "there are very few that may be called large capitals. There are many manufactories in Birmingham which do not employ £100; some about £1000, and, speaking in general of the higher descriptions of manufactures, about £6000 or £7000."[1] Indeed the vast majority of the finished-metal products, from buttons and jewellery to guns and ironmongery, were made by small producers in workshops adjoining their homes, or in part of the dwelling-houses themselves. The "garret-master," not the factory owner, was in 1800 the typical figure in the finished-metal trades; while the great businesses which drew the attention of the world were in the nature of magnificent exceptions rather than samples of the prevailing industrial pattern. And the great factory by the Soho Pool, even if it had endured for half-a-century, would still have been prophetic rather than typical.

The changes of the next sixty years did little to modify the contrast between the scale of production of the iron industry on the one hand and that of the trades producing finished goods on the other. Certain of the new heavy trades were necessarily conducted in factories; a few industries had been transformed by the introduction of machinery, or of new processes; some old-established firms had grown gradually in size; but there had been no "industrial revolution" in Birmingham and District. Its great economic development was marked by a vast increase in the number of producing units rather than by a growth in the size of the existing few, and the factory still remained unrepresentative of the majority of the concerns producing finished goods. Of Birmingham itself it was said in 1856 that nothing was on a large scale, and that the manufacturing class had not raised itself in any large degree. The concentration of capital and the development of large-scale enterprises had not taken place there as in the northern centres of industry, and most master manufacturers, it was declared, employed only five or six workers.[2] And this was equally true of the Black Country's small metal industries.

Thus, at a time when the cotton- and wool-using trades had

[1] *House of Commons Committee Reports*, x., p. 663.
[2] L. Faucher, *op. cit.*, p. 502 *et seq.*

H

passed under the sway of the machines, the industries of Birmingham and District, except in the case of the heavy manufactures, were for the most part unchanged in their productive
methods. In 1860 there were, it is true, some great concerns in
almost every local industry; for at that time, as in the eighteenth
century, the organizing genius could operate on a large scale
successfully, even in trades where the factory owner had no
obvious advantage over the small master.[1] But in the industries
producing finished goods the former was not typical, and the
expansion of industry during the first sixty years of the nineteenth
century had meant for our area an increase in the number of
small manufacturers rather than the concentration of its activities
within great factories. To find a reason for this is not difficult.
The economics of large-scale production are much less substantial in the small metal trades than in the textile group, or
in industries where bulky raw materials are used. The variety in
the design of the metal articles is so great, the opportunities for
standardized production are so few, and the importance of skill
so evident, that the small unit is naturally to be preferred. Up
to the present time, indeed, the transition to the factory in those
trades has been very slow and is still far from complete. Nor
must technical factors be ignored. Even the metal industries in
which large-scale production is now practised require much
more complicated machinery than do the textile trades, and
their reorganization on modern lines has had to await the more
recent developments of engineering and metallurgy.

Before examining in detail the productive methods of the
leading trades we may with advantage attempt to distinguish
between the different types of workplace existing in the district.
This classification can be only a rough one, but it is based on
fundamental differences. In the first place there was the large
factory, employing upwards of 150 persons and making an extensive use of power-machinery. Usually this type of workplace

---

[1] An example of how dependent on the genius of an individual is the existence of a large unit in any industry in which conditions were not specially
favourable for it is provided by the history of the great brass firm which had
been built up by Robert Winfield. " Old men remember the little stucco
building . . . where that eminent manufacturer commenced business in a very
small way ; saw it gradually overtopped by huge piles, which time after time
were added, till the place became, as it is said, ' a little town ' ; watched the
growth of the concern as one new thing after another was originated or taken
up . . . and looked sadly on at the decline and decay which seemed to set in
when . . . the master spirit was removed from it " (W. J. Davis, *op. cit.*, p. 35).

had been specially erected for the purpose it served, but it was not a common form at the time. Then came the small factory, with numbers ranging from 30 or 40 to 150. In some instances these factories may have been built as such, but many of them had been extended slowly with the growth of the business, and often they consisted of a chain of converted dwelling-houses. They, too, had in most cases a power-driven plant. After the factory was the workshop, which employed up to 30 or 40 persons. This usually consisted of a dwelling-house or outhouse, where no power was used. Finally, there was the outworker, " garret-master," or domestic worker proper, who used part of his own home, or a shed or brewhouse adjacent to it. He was assisted only by members of his family and by an occasional apprentice or journeyman.

This classification may be discussed in greater detail. The broad division between the factory owner on the one hand and the shop owner and domestic worker on the other is based to some extent on the greater size of the former's establishment and on his use of power-machinery. But a more fundamental distinction lies in the methods of industrial organization. Both the shop owner and the domestic worker were dependent on a factor or merchant, not only for the distribution of the products, and often for the raw materials, but also for financial assistance during the process of production. The factory owner could provide his own working capital and treat directly with the banks when he needed credit; but the various types of small manufacturers relied on the weekly advances of money which were obtained when the goods were taken to the factor's warehouse each week-end. The main distinction, then, is found in the degree of financial dependence on a merchant intermediary. The division between the shop owner and the domestic worker proper is determined by the fact that whereas the former is concerned mainly with administration, the latter is both the organizer and the leading craftsman. The shop owner, in fact, exercises some of the functions which belong to the factor in the domestic system. He is still financially dependent on the factor to a large extent, but he has assumed the task of co-ordinating the labour of the journeymen, whether they are engaged in his own establishment or as outworkers.[1]

[1] Examples of a form of industrial organization which falls logically between the domestic system and the shop-owner system are to be found in the hook-

Bearing these distinctions in mind, let us first turn to a detailed examination of each of the leading small-scale industries. The four Birmingham staples were all of this type, although there were exceptions to be found in each of them. In the gun trade the small unit was almost universal—a surprising fact, because there the principle of the division of labour had been applied to an extreme degree in the manufacture of a complicated product. The master gun-maker—the entrepreneur—seldom possessed a factory or workshop. In the few instances in which he did so the establishment was small and the operations were performed by skilled craftsmen without mechanical aids. But it was only in the production of very high-grade guns that the employer had taken this step. Usually he owned merely a warehouse in the gun quarter, and his function was to acquire semi-finished parts and to give these out to specialized craftsmen, who undertook the assembly and finishing of the gun. He purchased materials from the barrel-makers, lock-makers, sight-stampers, trigger-makers, ramrod-forgers, gun-furniture makers, and, if he were engaged in the military branch, from bayonet-forgers. All these were independent manufacturers executing the orders of several master gun-makers.[1] Some of the parts were produced by little masters who employed only one or two assistants; others were made by workshop proprietors, who might perform some of the task in their own establishments and give the rest to outworkers; while certain accessories were produced in small factories. Thus, at Darlaston, the centre of the gun-lock trade, there were five or six workshops employing about 20 journeymen each, and 20 or

and-eye, button and pen trades. In these it was common for a "fogger" to take out the finished goods from the factories, to undertake to card them for a certain price, and to employ a number of outworkers for the purpose. Again, in the Coventry silk trade of the early nineteenth century the factor commonly contracted with an "undertaker," who did part of the work himself, and who had other processes performed by outworking journeymen. Occasionally, however, this "undertaker" employed the craftsmen in his own workshop; and here we have an illustration of how a shop owner might arise from an intermediary of this type to whom the factor had delegated his task of co-ordination. The following quotation concerns the Coventry silk trade : "The master gave out the whole silk in the hank to an 'undertaker,' who undertook the responsibility of winding, warping and weaving, and to return the silk to the warehouse in the shape of ribbons. . . . The 'undertaker' provided winding and warping, and employed a journeyman to do the weaving. Of the sum paid the 'undertaker' took one-third, the weaver received two-thirds, providing his own shute-filler. . . . The 'undertaker' frequently had a shop of looms in his own dwelling, where he employed the journey-hands" (B. Poole, *History of Coventry* (1870), p. 359 *et seq.*).

[1] S. Timmins, *op. cit.*, pp. 387-393.

30 little masters.[1] The barrel-welders, who produced the barrels for the better class of sporting gun, were commonly craftsmen working at domestic forges. Theirs was a very highly skilled and laborious task, for their work consisted in welding together strips of metal varying greatly in carbon content and made from scrap iron and steel, and then in winding and welding the bars, so formed, spirally so as to produce " damascened " barrels.[2] The barrels for the military and the African markets, on the other hand, were rolled from iron strip, and finally drawn to the required length.[3] This process required a fairly large power-driven plant for rolling, boring and grinding, and had, in consequence, become a small factory trade. Similarly, bayonet- and rammer-makers needed machinery for rolling, stamping, grinding and polishing; and one firm in the trade, which was concerned also with sword and edge-tool production, employed some 400 persons.[4] Once the parts had been purchased from the " material-makers," as they were called, the next task was to hand them out to a long succession of " setters-up," each of whom performed a specific operation in connection with the assembly and finishing of the gun. To name only a few, there were those who prepared the front sight and lump end of the barrels; the jiggers, who attended to the breech end; the stockers, who let in the barrel and lock and shaped the stock; the barrel-strippers, who prepared the gun for rifling and proof; the hardeners, polishers, borers and riflers, engravers, browners, and finally the lock-freers, who adjusted the working parts.[5] Some of these were individual outworkers, employed by a particular master; others were shop owners working for several employers. It was not uncommon, moreover, for a craftsman who had no workplace of his own to hire shop-room, a bench, a vice, and a gas-jet from one of these workshop proprietors, and to work quite independently for some gun-maker.[6] Nor did the craftsmen rely only on the Birmingham masters. In the more highly skilled branches of the trade, such as barrel-straightening and setting,

---

[1] *Children's Employment Commission (1862), Third Report*, p. 7.
[2] J. W. Hall, *Presidential Address to Junior Institution of Engineers* (Midland Section), February 1917 (reprinted), p. 6.
[3] S. Timmins, *op. cit.*, p. 389.
[4] G. L. Strauss, *op. cit.*, p. 26.
[5] S. Timmins, *op. cit.*, p. 393 ; W. C. Aitken, *British Manufacturing Industries* (1878), vol. iii., pp. 15-21.
[6] *Reports of the Inspectors of Factories*, October 1868, pp. 265, 269.

certain men had, and still have, an international reputation, and were employed by gun-makers in London and abroad; while many classes of " material - makers " produced parts for the London trade.[1]

The system of organization involved the constant transport of materials to and from the master's warehouse and the craftsmen. Besides this, the barrels had to be taken to the Proof House in Banbury Street for a provisional proof before they were set up, and for a definitive test when the guns were completed; and an army of boys was to be seen hurrying to and fro about the gun quarter, performing the functions of porters.[2]

As the system of manufacture has survived with but small modification down to the present time, it has been possible to check the evidence of authorities by conversation with contemporary workers in the industry; and a description of a typical corner of the gun quarter will illustrate how this once great trade was carried on sixty years ago. A passage from a main street communicates with a courtyard, from which two blocks of three-storied buildings rise facing one another, and at intervals staircases lead up from the courtyard to the workshops, of which the buildings are entirely composed. Each shop consists of one or two small rooms, in which the various operations in connection with the " setting-up " of the guns are performed. In one shop two women will be found engaged in barrel-browning; in another a single workman is shaping the gun stocks from a pile of roughly cut wooden blocks delivered to him by the master gun-maker. Elsewhere a lock-filer is working with one assistant, and in another shop leading from the same staircase an engraver and his sons carry on their trade. Farther down the street a narrow alley communicates with an ill-lighted room, where two barrel-filers, whose work is known throughout Europe, are engaged; and near by is a tiny workshop, with the name of the proprietor roughly chalked on the door, which forms the establishment of one of the most famous hardeners in the trade. Each craftsman works for one or several gun-makers, and receives the material and parts from them; but he hires his own workshop and pays his own assistants. In 1860, not only the " setting-up " but much of the " material-making,"

---

[1] *Observations on the Manufacture of Fire-arms for Military Purposes*, p. 5.
[2] *Pictures of the People* in *Birmingham Morning News*, June 20, 1871.

which has since passed into the factories, was carried on in this way. Then only in the manufacture of a few parts, like rolled barrels or bayonets, was production on anything like a large scale. Otherwise trade was essentially a skilled handicraft, and over the greater part of the industry the stamp and the foot-lathe were the only machines employed.

In an earlier chapter it was shown that the output fell into two main groups—sporting guns and military arms. In 1860, although there were certain processes which were peculiar to one or the other, there was no fundamental difference in methods of production, and, while some gun-makers might specialize on a particular branch, most of them were concerned with both classes of product. But, in view of later developments, it is important to notice that those sections of the industry which were carried on in factories, in marked contrast to the prevailing methods of production — e.g. rolled barrel and bayonet manufacture—were connected with the military arms trade.

At first sight it seems surprising that, in view of the specialized nature of the processes and the high degree of the division of labour, attempts had not been made to group workers in factories; for it was acknowledged that the frequent transport of materials to and from the warehouses added to the cost of production, and the co-ordination of the activities of a multitude of outworkers must have been a difficult task.[1] The fact that the trade made little use of machinery and that the craftsmen objected to factory routine is of itself insufficient to account for the prevalence of the small unit. As far as the high-class sporting guns were concerned, the real reason seems to be that each product was individual, in the sense that it was made to suit the special requirements of the purchaser. But in the military arms trade the cause lay in its liability to extreme fluctuations in demand.[2] Consequently, until the introduction of machinery compelled the gun-maker to establish a factory, he would have no inducement to take that step; for in times of depression he would then have been obliged to bear the cost of keeping his plant idle. Under the existing system he could throw the burden

---

[1] " The workman who brings up the gun to his own particular stage of completion is required to put a certain finish and smoothness on his work, which the workman who follows him proceeds immediately to destroy " (*Pictures of the People* in *Birmingham Morning News*, June 20, 1871).

[2] *Pictures of the People* in *Birmingham Morning News*, June 20, 1871.

on the workers themselves. The trade showed at this time a remarkable power of expansion and contraction. Certain branches, such as barrel-welding and straightening, it is true, required specialized training and experience rather than general skill, and it was difficult for labour to be found for these operations in times of increasing demand. But many Birmingham artisans, accustomed to work in hard wood, could turn to stockmaking; while hundreds of metalworkers, skilled in the use of the file and lathe, could, when occasion arose, hire shop-room, and engage in one of the multifarious sections of the industry.[1]

The jewellery trade was similar in character—*i.e.* a small-scale industry for the most part, with factories operating in a few branches. The workshops were, it was said, among the closest and worst arranged in Birmingham,[2] for they had all developed from dwelling - houses situated in what had once been a lower middle-class residential quarter. In the manufacture of high- and medium-class jewellery the operations were commonly performed throughout by skilled craftsmen, working either as independent outworkers or more frequently in workshops containing from ten to twenty employees. Most of the masters originally had been workmen themselves, and in nearly all branches of the trade conditions were unfavourable for the growth of factories. The work was performed largely by hand: a bench, a leather apron, a few tools, a blow-pipe and a gas-jet, supplied on credit by the Gas Company, comprised all the plant necessary; and the artisan who wished to set up on his own had only to rent a room in the quarter; while for the manufacturing of gold or gilt articles a convenient supply of raw material of reliable quality was available in the shape of sovereigns.[3]

Since the production of many of the gold and silver ornaments was a manual process which could be undertaken by a single craftsman, there was less subdivision of labour than in the gun trade. Yet even here the rolling of gold leaf for gilding, jewel-setting, die-sinking, engraving, case-making and many other processes were distinct trades carried on in separate establishments.[4] Many parts for the gilt jewellery, moreover, were

[1] *Newspaper Cuttings* on *Birmingham Industries,* vol. i., p. 9.
[2] *Children's Employment Commission* (*1862*), *Third Report,* p. 54.
[3] S. Timmins, *op. cit.,* p. 454; *Children's Employment Commission* (*1862*), *Third Report,* p. 151; and *Pictures of the People* in *Birmingham Morning News,* July 3, 1871.
[4] J. C. Roche, *op. cit.,* p. 74.

produced by the stamp or hand-press, and this operation was commonly conducted by specialists before being completed by the maker. So in this trade also a considerable subdivision of labour was not inconsistent with the survival of the small unit.

There were one or two branches of the industry, however, which had attained the small-factory stage. Among these was the manufacture of gold, silver or gilt chains. Although automatic machinery had not yet been introduced into this branch, semi-skilled labour could be employed in cutting out the links from the strip on presses and in joining them together. Concerned with a standardized commodity, and providing an opportunity for the employment of power-machinery, the trade was one in which the productive process could be divided among a number of unskilled workers. Consequently, although much of the chain manufacture was still conducted in workshops, some masters had factories of a considerable size.[1] In one, no less than 400 persons were employed.[2]

The manufacture of electro-plate and German-silver wares was carried on in establishments varying greatly from one another. Spoons and forks were made in little workshops from blanks supplied by the rolling mills, and ornamental wares of German silver were produced by garret-masters, who had their stamping and plating done out by specialists. But there was at least one instance of production on a very large scale. This was at Messrs Elkington's, where the electro-deposit process had first been applied commercially; and, partly because of their position as pioneers in the new industry, they operated a factory in which no less than 1000 persons were employed.[3] Here all the processes of manufacture were combined, and power-machinery was used for stamping out articles from German-silver sheets and for spinning and polishing them on the lathe. Providing a marked contrast to the prevailing scale of industrial organization, this firm included within its scope of production not only table and ornamental plated ware, but electro-deposit statuary as well. An opportunity for the large unit had been given both by the expensiveness of the plant needed for plating

[1] S. Timmins, *op. cit.*, p. 460.
[2] *Children's Employment Commission* (*1862*), *Third Report*, p. 118; and *Birmingham and her Manufactures* in *The Leisure Hour*, March 3, 1853.
[3] E. Burritt, *op. cit.*, p. 114.

and for fashioning certain classes of article, and because a large firm could cover a wide field and employ skilled modellers, designers and die-sinkers. But the small man could still survive in the trade, not so much because he could concentrate on a particular type of article, but through the possibility of splitting up the productive process among specialists.

With no important contrasts to the manufactures already described, the button trade need not receive detailed attention; for it merely provided another example of the small-scale industry characteristic of the town. In the metal - button section the stamp was used, and machine-production was the rule in the three factories in which linen buttons were made; but the manufacture of the other chief types—viz. pearl and vegetable-ivory — was conducted almost entirely by manual labour or on hand-presses, owing to the delicate nature of the raw material. In these branches, in particular, the garret-master flourished.[1] In the pearl-button trade the employer seldom had a factory of his own, but he gave out pearl-shell to the domestic workers. Even the firms which maintained manufacturing establishments commonly obtained the larger share of their requirements from outside. It was said that anyone could set up as a pearl-button maker for a few shillings. He could hire tools for four shillings a week, and after obtaining shell on credit could sell his products weekly to the factors.[2] In contrast to the methods of production pursued over the greater part of the trade a few large factories had sprung up. In the linen-button manufacture there was a concern with no less than 250 employees [3]; but this, it should be remembered, was a trade which was a recent introduction into Birmingham, and which made use of machinery. A firm which was engaged in several branches of the industry is said to have employed 470 factory operatives and 100 outworkers; another had as many as 800 employees, though probably some of these were outworkers; and there were four or five more with 100 to 150 employees.[4]

---

[1] S. Timmins, *op. cit.*, p. 441; *Newspaper Cuttings* on *Birmingham Industries*, vol. i., p. 22 ; and *Children's Employment Commission (1862), Third Report*, pp. 55, 91.
[2] *Labour and the Poor* in *The Morning Chronicle*, November 4, 1850 ; and *Reports of the Inspectors of Factories*, October 1868, p. 269.
[3] S. Timmins, *op. cit.*, p. 436.
[4] *Children's Employment Commission (1862), Third Report*, p. 91 *et seq.*; and *Newspaper Cuttings* on *Birmingham Industries*, vol. i., p. 22.

The organization of the brass trade is a more complicated matter, owing to the great variety of manufactures which fell under that head. It was said that in 1800, with two or three exceptions, the workplaces had consisted of dwelling-houses, in which the manufacturers continued to live [1]; but by 1860 the size of the representative establishment had grown and had become in most branches the workshop employing 20 or 30 hands, or the small factory. In 1866, 17 brass-houses provided information concerning the number of their employees, which was an average of 115 per establishment. Another firm employed 700 to 800; and so, even if these were the only large units, it is evident that a considerable section of the industry was conducted in factories.[2] The scale of production naturally varied according to the branch of the industry. The firms engaged in the earlier process—viz. the wire, tube and rolling mills—needed a foundry, annealing ovens and a steam-driven rolling or drawing plant, and consequently there was no opportunity here for the little master. In the manufacture of yellow-metal sheathing one very large concern existed.[3] The production of gaseliers, moreover, was a comparatively complex process, and in this branch the small factory was common. But in the cabinet and cockfounding trades a lathe, a vice and a few tools provided the manufacturer with an adequate plant, and so the workshop proprietor and the garret-master flourished.[4]

The existence of the small unit in these and other sections of the brassfoundry was encouraged by the fact that the processes of production could be split up and carried on in separate establishments. This feature was common to many of the Birmingham trades in which small and large units existed side by side, and it was reported of the area in 1862 that few processes were carried on in the factories which were not also conducted in small workshops.[5] For instance, there was a class of brass-casting manufacturers who produced castings for makers of finished brassfoundry according to patterns supplied by them. Sometimes these " casters for hire," as they were called, were provided with the metal by their customers; but generally they

[1] S. Timmins, op. cit., p. 359.
[2] Ibid., p. 356.
[3] Ibid., p. 313.
[4] Labour and the Poor in The Morning Chronicle, January 6, 1851.
[5] Children's Employment Commission (1862), Third Report, p. xix.

purchased what they required to carry out their orders, and they commonly worked for the small manufacturers who had no foundries of their own and who confined themselves to assembling and finishing operations. Similarly, in the stamped branch of the trade, there was a division of process among a variety of specialist concerns. Besides producing finished articles certain manufacturers, called " stampers in the rough," supplied stampings to the smaller makers of cabinet brassfoundry, gas-fittings or bedsteads, who did not possess dies or stamps of their own. Another class, the " stampers for hire," merely owned stamping appliances, and were furnished with the dies and the metal by their customers, to whom they returned the finished product.[1] Furthermore, brassfounders who required to polish articles, but had no power-machinery, could send them out to firms of polishers, who undertook the task. Thus it was not only usual for the brassfounder to obtain his sheet metal, tubes and wire from specialists, but the small man found the industry organized in such a way that he could buy out both castings and stampings, rely on other firms for polishing, and devote himself merely to assembling and finishing.

Concerns such as these naturally confined themselves to a very narrow range of products, and even the small factory owner usually specialized on some specific branch of the trade, such as lighting or cabinet brassfoundry. But one firm followed a very different policy, and since it employed about ten per cent. of those engaged in the industry it deserves special attention. This was Messrs Winfield, the number of whose employees had grown from just over 100 in 1835 to 700 or 800 in 1860.[2] Particular interest attaches to the firm not only because it was concerned with a wide variety of articles, which were normally manufactured by distinct sections of the trade, but because it was integrated in structure as well. It produced sheet metal, wire and tubes in its own mills and castings in its own foundry, and it then went on to manufacture gas-fittings, bedsteads and general brassfoundry. But this concern was as exceptional in the Birmingham brass trade of 1860 as the Soho factory had

[1] S. Timmins, *op. cit.*, pp. 271 and 303.
[2] *Ibid.*, p. 361 ; and *Children's Employment Commission (1862), Third Report,* p. 69 *et seq.*

been three-quarters of a century before.[1] A man of great organizing ability, if he possessed the necessary capital, could at both periods carry on with success a wide variety of operations within his factory, especially if his wares had earned a high reputation for quality; but for the general run of manufacturer there was little advantage in the large unit.

If the small concern was widely prevalent in the Birmingham staples, it was even more characteristic of the chief finished manufactures of the Black Country. While the domestic worker proper was still common in Birmingham, his place in most industries was being taken by the shop owner. There the majority of the establishments consisted of " separate and detached buildings occupied solely as places of work," and " real housework " was reported to be growing less. But in the Black Country the domestic system proper was typical of several of the leading industries.[2] Wrought-nail making, for example, was carried on almost entirely in forges within or adjacent to the worker's house. " The nail-shop," said a writer, " is generally a small and dirty shanty, about ten feet by twelve feet, ventilated only through the doorway, and lighted by one or two unglazed apertures." [3] Assisted only by his wife and children, the nailer provided his own fuel and the simple tools he required, such as the hammer, the heading tool, the bellows and the anvil, and in some cases he purchased the nail rods from the local factors. More usually, however, the iron was given to him weekly by the nail-master, who possessed warehouses in various parts of the district, and its cost was deducted from the price paid for the nails when they were " weighed in." [4] The iron rods were provided usually

[1] This firm had been started " in a comparatively small way " by Robert Winfield about 1820. " In addition to his brassfoundry trade he gradually added the manufacture of brass, copper and tin tubing, gas-fittings and chandeliers, iron and brass bedsteads, ship's fittings, brass fittings for shopfronts and general architectural ornamental metalwork of all kinds. He afterwards purchased the large establishment near his own works, called the Union Rolling Mill, where he carried on a very extensive trade in rolled metals of every kind, and brass and copper wire of all descriptions ; and he was for forty years largely engaged in the coal business. For a long period Mr Winfield was the sole proprietor of the business he had created " (E. Edwards, *Personal Recollections of Birmingham and Birmingham Men*, 1877, pp. 118-120). *Cf.* p. 114, n.

[2] *Children's Employment Commission (1862), Third Report*, p. xix.

[3] F. W. Hackwood, *Wednesbury Workshops*, p. 20 ; *cf.* also *Reports of the Inspectors of Factories*, October 1868, pp. 298-301.

[4] *Birmingham and her Manufactures* in *The Leisure Hour*, January 6, 1853 ; *Children's Employment Commission (1862), Third Report*, p. 53 ; and E. Burritt, *op. cit.*, pp. 210-217.

in bundles weighing 60 lb., and an allowance varying from 6 to 28 lb., according to the size of the nails, was made to the worker for waste.[1] The larger nail-masters, who owned many warehouses scattered over the Black Country, often had several hundreds of outworkers dependent on them. One is reported to have had as many as 450[2]; while another had 1800 to 2000, whom he served from eight warehouses.[3] This system had existed for centuries in the trade, and a Parliamentary Commission reported that the lapse of one hundred and fifty years had not improved the dwellings, working conditions or habits of the nailers.[4]

Although the nailer and his family usually owned their own forge, sometimes the masters provided shops, which were rented to their workers. At Dudley, for instance, a firm had erected a block of nail-shops behind their warehouse, each of which was let to one of their outworkers. Frequently, moreover, the nailer who had no shop of his own would rent a "standing" from a fellow-worker and carry on his trade quite independent of the occupier—a practice common to many of the local trades. At Lye, for instance, hearths could be rented for fourpence per week, the landlord finding the bellows and fireplace, while the tenant provided his own tools.[5] As there was a tendency for labour in the rural districts to fluctuate between agriculture and nail-making—a great efflux of nailers to the hopfields of Hereford occurring each year at harvest-time—it is probable that many of those who rented "standings" were workers of this type.[6]

The conditions which prevailed in this large and ubiquitous manufacture—employing in 1860 some 18,000 persons—were paralleled by those of the smaller and more highly localized chain trade. But there were certain important differences. The chain-maker always had a hearth to himself, whereas the nailers worked sometimes four or five at a fire.[7] Further, in the chain trade there were a few factories in which large chains and ships' cables were produced. Several of these establishments manufactured anchors, besides in some instances producing the

---

[1] E. Burritt, *op. cit.*, pp. 213-214.
[2] *Reports of the Inspectors of Factories*, October 1872, p. 114.
[3] *Newspaper Cuttings* on *Birmingham Industries*, vol. ii., p. 38.
[4] F. W. Hackwood, *Wednesbury Workshops*, p. 21.
[5] *Children's Employment Commission (1862), Third Report*, p. 143 ; *Daily Telegraph*, March 10, 1872 ; and *Reports of the Inspectors of Factories*, October 1872, p. 113.
[6] *Reports of the Inspectors of Factories*, April 1874, p. 55.
[7] *Ibid.*, October 1868, p. 300.

wrought-iron they required, and so were of considerable magnitude. But all the smaller types of chain, which did not require the blast-engine, were made either by workshop proprietors employing up to 25 persons, or by single-handed workers in the forges adjacent to their homes. The factory owner usually acted as a factor or intermediary between the merchants and the different classes of chain-makers. Having received an order for a variety of chain, he proceeded to manufacture the heavy types in his factory and to give out orders for the rest, together with the iron required, to shop owners and to single-handed workers. Often the shop owners, in turn, would distribute part of their work among domestic makers.[1] As an illustration of the type of factory owner existing in the trade, we are informed that at Tipton a large manufacturer employed 50 men in his own establishment and 80 outworkers.[2] The methods of production did not vary greatly whether the chain was made in the factory, the workshop, or at the domestic forge. In every case most of the work was performed by hand, and it was merely the necessity of having power to drive the blast that had drawn the workers into the factories.

Neither the nail nor the chain trade was well organized. The fact that a large proportion of the Black Country population had learnt one or the other in their youth meant that in time of general depression, ironworkers, colliers and their wives used to rent hearths and eke out a livelihood by producing chains or nails, to the detriment of the regular members of these industries.[3] Working as many of them did, moreover, in country districts, the nailers found it difficult to improve their position by combining together, while the fact that many branches of their trade were in competition with the Birmingham and Wolverhampton cut-nail factories intensified the chronic depression of their wages. The similarity between the conditions of the workers in the highly localized and expanding chain trade on the one hand, and those in the scattered and decaying nail trade on the other, seems to indicate that what was chiefly responsible for the low wage-level was the weakness of the workers' bargaining position as compared with that of the employers. The absence

[1] R. H. Tawney, *Minimum Rates in the Chainmaking Industry*, chaps. i. and ii.
[2] *Children's Employment Commission (1862), Third Report*, p. 8.
[3] *Reports of the Inspectors of Factories*, October 1868, p. 295 ; October 1872, p. 114 ; and October 1888, pp. 108-109.

of effective unions meant that masters could set the nailers or chain-makers in competition with one another with regard to the price at which the work was taken out. In the nail trade the average earnings of a family, consisting of a man and his wife, a son or daughter, was as low as twenty shillings weekly,[1] from which they had to provide their own fuel, rent and tools. At Hales Owen it was declared that a nailer, his wife and four children could not earn more than twenty-two shillings a week, even if they worked 14 to 18 hours a day.[2]

The weak bargaining position of the workers had called a figure into existence who was common to most of the ill-organized domestic industries of the Black Country—viz. the " fogger." The proprietor of a public-house or a " tommy-shop," the " fogger " supplied the workers with iron on credit and bought back the nails from them, paying largely in kind, or insisting that part of the wages should be spent in his shop adjoining the warehouse.[3] The poverty of the nailers and the fact that they often had difficulty in getting the nail-master to buy their products forced them to go to the " foggers," who would take small quantities of nails from such necessitous people as could not afford to wait the pleasure of the masters. " If the nailer worked for a head warehouse—i.e. a respectable firm or merchant of position—then he was paid according to the current list of prices at each week-end, when his work was counted in. But the improvidence of the nail-makers called into existence a class of factor or nail-fogger who preyed on the necessities of these poorly paid workers."[4] As they could make an additional profit out of their " tommy-shops," the truck-masters were in a position to undersell the respectable employers,[5] and their practices nullified any attempt to raise wages, or to secure general agreement to a list of prices.

The staple trade of Willenhall and Wolverhampton was conducted in much the same way as Disraeli had described it twenty years before.[6] Locks and keys were made almost entirely in domestic workshops by craftsmen who seldom had more than

---

[1] E. Burritt, op. cit., p. 214.
[2] R. G. Hobbs, op. cit., p. 638.
[3] Ibid., p. 638 ; Reports of the Inspectors of Factories, April 1875, pp. 82-84.
[4] F. W. Hackwood, Sedgeley Researches, p. 104.
[5] Report of the Chief Inspector of Factories, October 1879, p. 75.
[6] Disraeli, Sybil, Book III., chap. iv.

half-a-dozen journeymen and apprentices.[1] The lock cases in those days were of cast- or wrought-iron, and if of the former type were purchased out from the foundries. Key-stamping, performed by the " dead-weight kick-stamp," also was a specialized trade.[2] Yet, although the locksmith might buy castings and keys from small masters who produced under conditions similar to his own, most of the lock parts were forged on the anvil, and the finished articles were put together by the craftsman himself. Even in the few larger establishments which existed, the division of labour had not gone very far, and it was still usual for them to be staffed by skilled craftsmen who made the lock throughout by hand. There were six or seven factories or large workshops in the trade at Willenhall; but the leading firm did not employ more than fifty men, and in such establishments the manufacture of door furniture, curry-combs and general hardware was combined with lock-making.[3] For the production of high-grade locks a much larger factory, employing some 200 workers, existed at Wolverhampton. This, however, was exceptional, and had been created, not by the application of machinery or by the division of processes, but solely because of the necessity of securing control over the materials and workmanship by a firm of high repute. It was said that, even at this factory, not a single machine was employed—a fact which was generally true of the trade, except for the few cases in which the steam-hammer was used for forging.[4] Of this industry it was, indeed, true to say that " no extensive branch of local industry has taken less advantage of the recent progress of mechanical science than the lock trade "[5]; and the conditions of work in this, as in many of the other domestic industries of the district, were such as to justify the criticism of a contemporary observer: " C'est le travail en famille, moins la sainteté de mœurs domestiques; c'est l'atelier moins les vertus sociales qu'il engendre."[6]

From the standpoint of industrial organization, the leather and allied trades of Walsall and Birmingham were of even greater interest. Although the saddlery and harness were composite products, the manufacturing process was split up among a

[1] G. L. Strauss, *op. cit.*, pp. 122-123 ; and S. Timmins, *op. cit.*, p. 88.
[2] G. Price, *op. cit.*, pp. 862, 865 *et seq.*
[3] *Children's Employment Commission* (*1862*), *Third Report*, p. 4 *et seq.*
[4] G. L. Price, *op. cit.*, pp. 871-872.
[5] S. Timmins, *op. cit.*, p. 90.
[6] L. Faucher, *op. cit.*, p. 536.

I

number of domestic craftsmen, each of whom specialized on a
narrow range of articles. Thus the making of bits, curbs, the
various types of buckle, hames, rosettes, crests, saddle nails,
harness furniture, stirrups and spurs all formed distinct trades,
and were for the most part carried on by specialists in small
workshops employing less than six persons. Occasionally several
branches might be combined, as when, for instance, the bit-
maker also produced stirrups; but it was unusual for many lines
to be associated. The leather- and wood-work, too, were similarly
subdivided. Collar-making, tree-making and bridle-cutting were
distinct trades, and there was a division between the " black
saddlers," who made saddles for harness, and the " brown
saddlers," who produced riding saddles. The cart-gear trade
comprised several distinct occupations carried on in separate
workshops; there was a group of small concerns engaged in
tanning and currying the leather for local use; and finally there
were firms which performed the close or electro-plating for the
industry.

Thus, as in the gun and jewellery trades, division of labour
carried to an extreme limit had failed to modify, over a large
section of the industry, its domestic character. This was partly
because skilled hand-labour had not been superseded by
machinery to any considerable extent and partly because little
power was needed. It is true that the sewing-machine had been
introduced; but it was not suitable for all classes of work and
was not extensively used. The metalwork was produced either in
the foundry or on the anvil, the best bits, hooks, rings, swivels,
chains and hames being forged; while the cheaper stirrups, bits,
hames and buckles consisted of malleable-iron castings.[1] Though
the stamp was used in producing harness ornaments, it did not
play a large part in the industry as a whole. These trades were,
then, handicrafts in which the manufacturer required very
little capital for the purchase either of raw materials or of his
plant. Further, most of the home demand was not for finished
saddles or sets of harness, but for parts, which the local saddler
in every part of the country used to make up to suit the needs
of individual customers.[2] To bridge the gap between him and
the producer in Walsall or Birmingham there existed an im-

---

[1] S. Timmins, op. cit., pp. 131 and 478, n.
[2] Ibid., p. 471.

portant class of factor, termed the " saddlers' and coachbuilders' ironmonger," who bought the saddlery and harness, either in a finished form or in parts, from the multitude of little masters, and supplied the local saddlers in various parts of the country. Sometimes these factors themselves took up the manufacture of certain classes of goods while still continuing to factor the lines which they did not themselves produce. Besides these functions they had another of equal importance. A maker who specialized, as was usual, on particular leather articles did not require the whole hide of a beast, for he could use only part of it in his work. For instance, a man who produced reins would require only " backs," where the leather was strongest, and he would generally get these, not direct from the currier but from the factor, who had purchased the whole hide, and who supplied his dependent craftsmen with the particular parts of it which they needed. Thus, as in the gun trade, the factor's task was to co-ordinate the activities of a multitude of small producers of parts and of finished articles, and his functions were of great importance because of the composite nature of the product.

It has been said that the home market required parts rather than finished saddles and harness; but, in addition, there were two sources of demand of which this was not true—viz. first, the foreign and colonial markets, and secondly, Government requirements. These deserve attention; for the export trade had become large by 1860, while the War Office demand, which was liable to be swelled suddenly on the outbreak of war, introduced an element of instability into the saddlery and harness, as into the gun trade. From the point of view of organization, however, the importance of these two markets lies in the fact that the demand was in each case for finished standardized commodities. An opportunity for large-scale production was thus provided, especially in view of the fact that the merchant, in placing a large order for finished saddles and harness, would prefer to give it to a manufacturer capable of dealing with quantities rather than go to the trouble of distributing it among a multitude of little masters. So, much of the trade in finished goods was in the hands of makers who usually bought out their curried leather and ironmongery, and who conducted the rest of the manufacturing process in a factory. Even in this section of the trade, however, it was common for much of the leather, which was cut out by men, to be stitched by female outworkers, although the increasing use of sewing-machines was tending to draw more of them into the factories at this time.[1] In Walsall there were fifteen small factories, which are said to have employed from 50 to 100 persons each,[2] though probably some of these were outworkers; while there were a few large establishments at Birmingham also.

In all these trades engaged in producing the staple finished products of the locality—in the manufacture of guns, jewellery, brassfoundry, buttons, nails, chains, locks, and saddlery and harness—the small unit was the typical form; and in many of the minor trades also this was equally true. In the production of awl-blades, nuts and bolts, springs, fenders and hearth furniture, watches, dies, brushes,[3] needles and fishhooks, either the domestic craftsman or the small workshop proprietor employing less than 40 persons was the representative figure; and since these trades together provided the bulk of employment in the finished manufacture, it was they who stamped the character of the area as a whole.

Against the prevailing industrial pattern the manufactures in which large-scale production was normal stood out in sharp relief; but, if only because of the contrast they provided, they occupied a far from insignificant position. Most of them owed the exceptional character of their organization to the fact that they were concerned with massive or complicated products, which from their nature had always involved the close association of large bodies of men. Only in a few instances had the manufacture of small and simple articles been drawn within the factory as a result of mechanical changes.

The heavy branch of the glass industry, which involved the manipulation of great masses of material, was typical of the large-scale manufactures of the area. We have already seen that the industry took root in the district when R. L. Chance purchased a crown-glass factory in 1824. In 1832 he took up the manufacture of sheet glass for window-glazing, and, as this had not been previously carried on in England, he secured the

---

[1] S. Timmins, *op. cit.*, pp. 132 and 471.
[2] *Children's Employment Commission (1862), Third Report*, p. 7.
[3] In the Birmingham and Walsall brush trade the range of employment per firm was from 1 to 38 persons, the average being 8. These figures apply to both journeymen and apprentices (*A List of Legal Journeymen Brush-Makers and Apprentices for the Year 1874*, Wertheimer, Lee & Co.).

assistance of a French manufacturer, Georges Bontemps, and of a number of Continental workmen. Such a step was obviously only in the power of a large capitalist, and from the beginning, therefore, the trade was confined to a few hands. Before 1860 the same firm had taken up the production of rolled plate and optical glass and lighthouse equipment in addition to the other manufactures; and this association of products, any one of which required a great capital outlay for plant, resulted in the growth of one of the largest concerns in the Midlands.[1] In 1852 Messrs Chance Bros. employed 1200 persons in their factory, and the number had risen to 1700 in 1868. There were only two other firms in the heavy-glass trade in the neighbourhood, one of which employed about 170 and the other some 600 hands.[2]

This, then, was a trade reserved exclusively for great factories. In the manufacture of flint-glass, moreover, if the large unit was far from universal, even here the capitalist employer was the typical figure; for the productive process was of a complicated nature, and a considerable plant was required for the manufacture of most kinds of ware. Usually the establishment consisted of a foundry, in which the ingredients for the glass were melted and the products shaped, and of a grinding and cutting shop, in which the articles were embellished with designs and finished. Occasionally, it is true, the second group of processes was carried on in separate works; but these could not operate successfully unless they possessed a steam-engine, and so garret-masters were necessarily excluded. A sketch of the productive methods of the foundry will throw into relief the peculiarities of the trade. The materials, consisting of white sand, red lead, potash, saltpetre, cullet (*i.e.* broken glass), and certain bleaching agents, were mixed together in troughs, then placed in pots of Stourbridge clay, purchased out from specialists, and finally melted in the foundry. The last process usually began on Friday or Saturday, and took from 36 to 40 hours, after which 8 or 10 hours were allowed for the metal to cool down to working heat. The hours common to most industries could not be followed in this trade; for when the metal in the pots was ready, then it had to be used continuously until the supply was

---

[1] *A Hundred Years of British Glass-making* (Messrs Chance Bros. & Co. Ltd.), pp. 7–20.

[2] *Birmingham Glass Works* in *Household Words*, March 1852; and S. Timmins, *op. cit.*, p. 147 *et seq.*

exhausted. Consequently the workers in the foundry were divided into two shifts, which worked in " turns " of 6 hours each. The first shift usually began at 6 A.M. on Monday and worked till noon, when it was relieved by the second shift, which continued until 6 P.M. At this hour the first shift came on again until midnight, and this alternation was pursued till the metal was used up. Each shift commonly worked eight " turns " a week, and as, in practice, the nominal 6-hour period was reduced often to 5, the normal working week consisted of about 40 hours, and the glass-makers would usually finish their week's labours on Thursday night. The men worked in groups, or " chairs," of four, consisting of the " workman " (or maker), the " servitor," the "footmaker" (or "blower"), and the "taker-in." Each had a definite function to perform in the manufacture of the ware, rising from the " taker-in," who was a boy in the first stage of his career, to the " workman," who sat on a wooden trestle and completed the article, on which each of his assistants had performed some operation according to his place in the hierarchy of glass-makers. It was usual for every " chair " to specialize on some particular class of goods.[1]

In 1849 it appears that in a Birmingham glass-house, one of the largest which ever existed in the trade before or since, some 400 hands were employed; but this was exceptional in size.[2] In the neighbourhood of Stourbridge there were in 1852 twelve flint-glass works, employing on an average 90 persons each,[3] and their size probably increased in the next eight years. Two of the most important glass-houses in Birmingham in 1862 had 11 and 12 " chairs " respectively.[4] This would mean that there were 88 and 96, counting both shifts, actually engaged as makers; while many more must have been employed in preparing the ingredients, in attending to the firing in the foundry, and in cutting and engraving. The substantial flint-glass firm of the time, then, employed probably between 100 and 200 persons. Besides a number of smaller factories there were also a few little masters in the industry, who were assisted by less than six persons, and who produced the smaller and commoner types of

---

[1] *Children's Employment Commission, (1862), Fourth Report*, p. 188 et seq.
[2] D. N. Sandilands, *op. cit.*, p. 67; *Pictures of the People* in *Birmingham Morning News*, July 24, 1871.
[3] T. C. Turberville, *Worcestershire in the Nineteenth Century* (1852), p. 9.
[4] *Children's Employment Commission (1862), Fourth Report*, pp. 220, 226.

glass-ware. In these "cribs," as the small glass-houses were called, a different method of production from that of the factories was followed, for the materials were melted usually at night and the pots worked out the following day.[1] The "cribs" had increased in numbers during the period of sudden expansion in demand which followed the repeal of the glass duties; but by 1860 their numbers were declining, both at Birmingham and Stourbridge, and by far the larger part of the trade was being carried on in factories.[2]

The Black Country trades producing heavy finished products were naturally unsuited to any save the large producing unit. In the welded-tube manufacture a great firm at Wednesbury appears to have employed nearly 1000 persons [3]; and although the other concerns in the trade were not comparable in size, they were all of the factory grade, for the productive process necessitated a steam-driven rolling plant and a large staff of workers. The forging of tube-fittings, however, was a separate branch of the industry, and was organized in a different way, being carried on mainly by outworkers at domestic forges.[4] The manufacture of galvanized and corrugated sheets was another heavy trade which needed, even when makers did not roll their own iron, a plant for galvanizing and a considerable number of workers for handling the material. The production of railway wheels and axles, boilers, heavy forgings and constructional ironwork were also factory industries; but as many of these articles were manufactured by integrated firms it is impossible to estimate the employment provided by a representative unit. It is sufficient, indeed, to point to the contrast which existed between the scale of production of the small finished-iron goods, like locks and nails, and the necessarily large plant required for the above manufactures. Statistical data are, however, available to enable us to gain an idea of the size of the unit in the rolling-stock industry. The four firms existing in 1860 used "the most expensive and costly plants of machinery," and one employed no less than 1200 to 1300 persons.[5]

In the edge-tool trade the forces at work were very different

---

[1] *Children's Employment Commission (1862), Fourth Report*, p. 229.
[2] S. Timmins, *op. cit.*, p. 542.
[3] F. W. Hackwood, *Wednesbury Workshops*, p. 85.
[4] *Ibid.*, p. 109.
[5] S. Timmins, *op. cit.*, p. 670; and *Children's Employment Commission (1862), Third Report*, p. 132.

from those in the heavy industries. Here factories had sprung up for reasons which had little to do with the cost of the plant or the complicated nature of the productive process; while alongside the large establishment the small unit continued to flourish. The explanation of the phenomenon is to be found in the existence of two distinct markets for edge tools, one consisting of the home trade and also of the foreign demand for cheap goods, and the other the " branded " trade. Certain old-established firms had built up a reputation for reliability, and their products, distinguished by a trade-mark such as a crocodile or a bull, were easily recognizable, even by the illiterate natives of South America and India, which were large markets for tools. Intensely conservative in their demands, these customers, having once become used to a particular " brand," would continue to purchase it, even if cheaper but unfamiliar makes were available. So, as the foreign markets for " branded " goods expanded, the result was not to call into existence a greater number of producers, but to bring about a growth in the size and output of concerns with an established reputation and a well-known trade-mark. These firms, moreover, tended to confine themselves to the production of high-grade articles for foreign markets; for they found that the skill of their operatives deteriorated if they were set to produce cheap qualities as well. Consequently there had arisen by 1860 two types of maker—the manufacturer with a large factory, producing high-grade " branded " goods in quantity for the conservative native buyer, and the small producer of cheap tools. These two types tended, indeed, to form non-competitive groups, and the power of the larger manufacturer to exclude the small man from distant markets was increased by the fact that the former could more easily adapt his plant to the production of the special and individual designs required by each locality. Thus, although the division between the " branded " and " non-branded " trade was not then as clear as it has since become, it was sufficiently marked to account for the co-existence of factory and small workshop production. The large firms usually made a wide variety of articles, such as machetes, spades, hoes, picks and trowels; while in some cases edge-tool manufacture was combined with the production of the raw materials required. One or two factories employed as many as 400 hands, although it is probable that some of these would be outworkers.[1] Even as carried on by the larger firms, the trade was not highly mechanized. Steam-power might be employed for working the tilt hammer, the stamp, the shears and the grindstone; but a great part of the work was still a hand-process.[2]

In the hollow-ware industry somewhat similar conditions existed. Small foundries could still operate successfully in the " black " cast-iron-ware trade, and many little masters were occupied in making up wrought sheets into buckets and other articles, which afterwards could be either galvanized on the premises or sent out for the purpose. But the manufacture of tinned and, above all, of enamelled hollow-ware was reserved largely for the factories. The enamelling of iron was a comparatively new process, and could be undertaken only by men with considerable capital and a high degree of technical knowledge. So the trade was in the hands of two firms in the neighbourhood, one of which employed over 400 persons.[3] Both of these, as well as several smaller factories, combined the production of various kinds of cast hollow-ware with " odd-work "— i.e. general ironmongery, such as hinges, latches and coffee-mills.

The tinplate- and japanned-ware trade also was conducted for the most part on a large scale. At Wolverhampton there were several firms employing over 250 persons [4]; and both there and at Bilston and Birmingham a number of smaller factories flourished. The large size of the producing units in this trade was no recent development, for the Old Hall factory, originally a residence of the Leveson-Gower family, had been operating on a considerable scale from the early part of the century, and many of the businesses in existence in 1860 had been founded by enterprising workmen, who had been trained at the Old Hall, and who followed its methods of production.[5] Doubtless one reason for the existence of factories was the necessity for the special knowledge of decorative principles and methods in the manufacture of the japanned wares; while, since similar processes of ornamentation could be applied both to iron and papier mâché, the production of both classes of goods were commonly

---

[1] G. L. Strauss, *op. cit.*, p. 90.
[2] S. Timmins, *op. cit.*, p. 656.
[3] *Ibid.*, p. 103 *et seq.*; and *Birmingham Official Industrial and Commercial Handbook* (1919), p. 88.
[4] *Children's Employment Commission (1862), Third Report*, p. 6.
[5] *Ibid.*, pp. 6, 22 *et seq.*, and p. 133 ; and W. H. Jones, *op. cit.*, chaps. i. and vi.

carried on in the same establishments. Further, although power-machinery was not extensively employed, certain classes of article, such as trays, could be produced under power-stamp,[1] because of their standardized shape; and here the large manufacturer had an advantage over the small man. But there were, nevertheless, a good many garret-masters who specialized on a few classes of tinplate wares, in the production of which machinery and a high degree of technical knowledge were unnecessary.[2]

The few industries which had been recently revolutionized by the introduction of new mechanical processes were confined almost entirely to Birmingham and its immediate neighbourhood. Among these the pen manufacture was perhaps the best example of a large-scale industry, for in it the small unit was non-existent. The number of producers was small, and the average number of persons employed in each factory attained the remarkably high figure of 200,[3] while the two leading firms had about 500 workers each.[4] One factory was described by a contemporary as " an immense brick building which looks something like a large asylum." [5] Strangely enough, the reason for the large size of the typical concern was not to be found in the extensive use of power-machinery; for although some of the manufacturers employed power for rolling down the steel strip to the gauge required, this was not the practice of the majority, and no other operation needed the aid of the steam-engine. The explanation lies in the fact that the manufacturing process consisted of a large number of separate operations which had to be carefully co-ordinated. To cut out the blanks from the steel strip, to pierce the hole and slit the pen, to form the nib and to emboss the pattern, each involved an operation on a hand-press or light stamp. Like Adam Smith's pin, the Birmingham pen manufacture, once conducted by craftsmen in the domestic workshop, might have been given as an example of the economies of the division of labour; for that principle certainly had been as extensively applied to it as to any trade in the locality. This might seem an insufficient reason for the existence of factories; for, as we have already

[1] W. H. Jones, *op. cit.*, chaps. i. and iv.
[2] *Labour and the Poor* in *The Morning Chronicle*, February 3, 1851.
[3] S. Timmins, *op. cit.*, p. 635.
[4] *Labour and the Poor* in *The Morning Chronicle*, December 16, 1850 ; and *Newspaper Cuttings* on *Birmingham Industries*, vol. i., p. 163.
[5] G. L. Strauss, *op. cit.*, p. 5.

seen, in certain other local trades a high degree of division of labour was not inconsistent with the survival of the domestic system. But between these and the pen trade there was an important distinction. Gun and saddlery parts were complicated articles in themselves and were produced by skilled craftsmen, each of whom was concerned with making a complete part for a composite whole. But pen manufacture made use of semi-skilled workers, most of whom performed merely a single press operation. Further, in the pen trade there was a very important and specialized class of tool-maker, who could not be drawn from the general die-sinkers of Birmingham, but who had to be accustomed to the work from boyhood. Only a large manufacturer could train these men and co-ordinate their activities with those of a mass of semi-skilled operatives. Pen-holders and paper boxes were sometimes produced in a department of the pen factory; but this was not usual, and more frequently they were manufactured by specialist concerns.

Another trade, typical of the factory era, was the manufacture of machine-made nails, which naturally had been drawn into large establishments because of the expensive plant required. In the case of machine-wrought nails the shank was cut and the heading and pointing were performed by a die and a roller while the iron was hot; whereas the cut nails were made from cold iron strip and afterwards annealed. The latter were produced in larger quantities, since the process was much cheaper, and the typical Birmingham or Wolverhampton factory employed from 150 to 200 workers.[1]

We have seen that the wire trades provided the most important exception to the generalization that power-machinery was employed in Birmingham as a substitute for strength rather than skill. Making use of the most complex machines found within the district, this group of industries provided small scope for the skilled domestic craftsman, and the units of production within it were necessarily large. In the manufacture of steel wire one maker employed 250 workers, and another, who made hempen rope and twine as well as wire ropes and cables, was operating on an even larger scale.[2] Several great factories also existed for the production of iron and brass wire articles. One

[1] *Children's Employment Commission (1862), Third Report*, p. 6.
[2] S. Timmins, *op. cit.*, p. 591 *et seq.*

firm which manufactured pins, hairpins, bottling wire, and hooks and eyes had 300 employees [1]; and as in these sections of the industry, particularly in the pin trade, expensive power-driven machinery was essential, there were very few exceptions to the prevailing large scale of the business unit. Yet even in these highly mechanized industries the outworker had a function to perform, if only in the subsidiary processes; for many women and children were employed to sew buttons, hooks and eyes and similar articles on to cards, and this work was carried on at home. [2]

The most recent instance of a change from small-scale to factory production was, however, to be found in the wood-screw trade. Before 1854 screws, though they had long ceased to be made solely by hand-processes, were turned out by a series of operations on different machines which could be set up in workshops or in small factories; but the new machinery, which was automatic in character, was too expensive for any save the great capitalist. Consequently, after its introduction the tendency was for more and more of the trade to be concentrated in a very few factories employing several hundreds of workers. [3] The advent of machinery had a similar effect on another minor trade. Up to about 1840 rule-making had been carried on by many little masters who worked by hand; but the introduction of mechanical methods swept them away and threw the trade into the hands of a few large manufacturers. [4]

Thus in the early sixties the greater part of the local industries were conducted on a small scale. Some trades, like nailing, were conducted almost exclusively by domestic workers proper; but the majority were in the hands partly of domestic workers and partly of shop owners. And even in trades of which the factory was typical, the little masters had still an important place. Just as the rise of the iron industry, itself conducted on a large scale, had enabled a great increase to take place in the number of small makers who used the iron, so in 1860 the growth of certain factory trades provided openings for garretmen, who performed subsidiary operations. Thus, while pens,

[1] S. Timmins, *op. cit.*, p. 600.
[2] *Children's Employment Commission* (*1862*), *Third Report*, p. 103.
[3] S. Timmins, *op. cit.*, p. 604 *et seq.*
[4] *The Carpenter's Slide Rule* (published by Messrs John Rabone & Sons, Birmingham, 1870), p. 14.

hooks and eyes, and certain kinds of buttons were produced in factories, the carding of those articles was performed by out-workers.[1] Large units were common only in the heavy industries, in the few highly mechanized trades, and in those which required the co-operation of a series of semi-skilled workers. Occasionally large concerns were to be found in industries which were given over mainly to little masters. Such firms, however, were usually associated either with an employer of exceptional ability or with the existence of a special demand for goods of high quality or of standardized character. This last point may be illustrated by reference to the military demand for saddlery and harness and to the " branded " edge-tool trade, both of which fell within the scope of factories, although a great part of those industries were in the hands of small men. It is seldom that we find the large and small units producing precisely the same class of goods and serving identical markets.

[1] *Children's Employment Commission (1862), Third Report*, pp. 128, 152.

CHAPTER VI

PRODUCTIVE METHODS IN THE COAL AND IRON TRADES

LYING at the foundation of all the economic activities of the area, and affording a greater volume of employment than any other, the coal and iron industries necessarily claim special and detailed attention. It had been coal and ironstone which originally had created the great industrial community of the West Midlands, and the mines of the district still formed in 1860 the main source of fuel supply for the multitudinous local trades. In view of its importance it is remarkable that the organization of mining was in such a primitive state. The 5,250,000 tons of coal and the 800,000 tons of ironstone produced annually were mined together in small, shallow and ill-equipped collieries which numbered about 440.[1] Over a large part of the field the thick coal, owing to its existence just below the surface, was worked either along the outcrops or in shallow shafts; and " extensive mining of the most elementary character, vigorously prosecuted for centuries, with no regard to the damage done to the surface or contiguous seams," had caused much of the area to resemble a " water-logged rabbit warren." [2] South Staffordshire was dotted with innumerable shafts, which usually were sunk two together at 6 or 8 yards apart, and which commonly had a diameter of only 6 or 8 feet.[3] Few mines were more than 200 yards deep [4]; while the majority were very much less. Even the larger type of thick coal-pit raised only 800 tons a week and employed as few as 60 hands in the pit and on the bank.[5] Where outcrops were worked, the operations were, of course, on a much smaller scale.[6]

Over the greater part of the field the mechanical equipment was in a very backward state. In some collieries atmospheric

---

[1] R. Hunt, *op. cit.*, 1860, p. 112.
[2] *Report of the Committee on South Staffordshire Mines Drainage* (1920), p. 10.
[3] *Records of the School of Mines* (1853), vol. i., part ii., pp. 339-340.
[4] T. E. Lones, *op. cit.*, p. 37.
[5] R. Kettle, *The Ten-Yard Coal* (1864), p. 9.
[6] " Ten acres is considered about an average quantity to raise at one pair of pits . . . and 20 acres would be a medium-sized colliery, while 50 or 60 acres is set down as a large colliery " (S. Timmins, *op. cit.*, p. 22).
Cf. also *The Black Country* in *The Edinburgh Review*, April 1863, p. 412 *et seq.*

engines were still used for driving the winding-gear; others worked with inefficient beam-engines; and in the small units a horse supplied the power. Skips, drawing only from half-a-ton to two tons, were commonly used for raising and lowering men and materials, owing to the narrowness of the shafts and the weakness of the engines; and in 1860 the total number of guides and of cages employed numbered only 20. Many of the shafts had defective linings and only in a few instances had covers been fitted to protect the men in descending. For winding purposes, in the deeper pits, the heavy " wood " chain, which had three flat links joined by wooden stays, was the usual type; and in some places the dangerous single-link riveted chain was used. Natural ventilation, moreover, was the rule.[1]

The backward state of the mining equipment was to be attributed to the ease with which men of small capital could engage in the industry. Mines could be operated temporarily without an expensive plant or a heavy capital outlay, which would have required owners with a permanent interest in their success. So in periods of excited trade a small man would sink a shaft and work a mine, which he could abandon without much capital loss when the depression came. Thus the self-interest of the typical mine owner coincided with a most inefficient and wasteful method of operation; for the system resulted in large quantities of coal being crushed or flooded in abandoned workings.[2] Even in the mines which were controlled by ironmasters the equipment and methods of production were little better; for many of those firms worked with small capital, and even the greatest ironmasters had little inducement to improve the organization of an industry which was not their main concern. Nevertheless, the collieries owned by the large integrated firms appear to have been better equipped than the others.

The existence of the thick coal had introduced special problems into mining operations and necessitated a peculiar system of working. In contrast to the " long wall " method, applied in this district and elsewhere to the thin seams, the thick coal was mined mainly by what was known as the " square work " system—that is to say, the mineral was worked

[1] *Records of the School of Mines*, vol. i., part ii., pp. 340-341. T. E. Lones, *op. cit.*, p. 55 *et seq.*
[2] *Report of the Committee on the South Staffordshire Mines Drainage*, 1920, p. 11 ; *Records of the School of Mines*, vol. i., part ii., p. 341.

out in a series of rectangular chambers, separated by ribs of coal, the internal support for the roof being afforded by square pillars. Under this system the mineral could not be removed in one operation, two or more being required, and a long period might elapse between the working of the " whole " (as the first operation was termed) and the final extraction of the ribs and pillars.[1] Owing to careless mining often the roof collapsed after the first working, and vast quantities of coal were lost by crushing. In the older parts of the field, collieries were occupied in 1860 with working the remnants of thick coal-measures, as few virgin seams remained at shallow depths.[2] Moreover, the trouble which was afterwards to overwhelm a large section of the Black Country had in the fifties already begun, and the mines of the Tipton neighbourhood were already threatened with inundation.[3]

In the larger pits the organization of the workers resembled the system practised in the mining industry generally and in many other local trades. Only in a very few collieries did the owners undertake the entire control and supervision of the operations. Usually they contracted with " butties," who engaged, managed and paid the workers required for getting the coal from a section or from the whole of a mine, and for carrying it to the shaft. In return, the " butties " received a price per ton of mineral raised. The owners' function was to maintain the winding machinery, to bear the expense of raising coal to the pithead, and to pay the engine-drivers and banksmen. But the workers underground were entirely under the control of the " butty," being responsible to him and not to the owner.[4] Not infrequently serious abuses arose in connection with this system. Subcontractors or their relatives often kept public-houses or " tommy-shops," and forced their employees to spend part of their wages in them. Though some colliery owners refused to contract with this type of " butty," all were not so conscientious, for he could naturally offer them advantageous terms.[5]

In the iron trade about fifty-five firms were engaged in operating the furnaces which produced forge or foundry pig.[6] Here also

---

[1] *Report of the Committee on the South Staffordshire Mines Drainage*, 1920, p. 12.
[2] T. E. Lones, *op. cit.*, p. 55.   [3] *Ibid.*, pp. 77, 80, 89, 103.
[4] *Ibid.*, pp. 36-37; and *The Black Country* from *The Edinburgh Review*, April 1863, pp. 425-426.
[5] T. E. Lones, *op. cit.*, pp. 60-61.
[6] *Children's Employment Commission (1862), Third Report*, p. 1.

much of the plant was old-fashioned, and this did not help the district in its competition against the northern centres with their more modern equipment. Many of the Staffordshire blast-furnaces were small and isolated, with an output of only 100 tons per week; but the typical firm worked furnaces with a capacity of 130 to 150 tons each in groups of three. There were some which could produce as much as 180 to 250 tons; but these were very few.[1]

The materials commonly were raised to feed the furnaces by the agency of small stationary engines, and only in a few instances were hydraulic or pneumatic lifts employed. Usually of the " open-top " variety, only here and there could furnaces of the new type be found, in which the top was closed, and the waste gases were used for heating the blast and for raising steam in the blowing engines.[2] For many years to come, indeed, nearly every blast-furnace in South Staffordshire " was a huge torch flaring to the heavens, making the Black Country almost as light by night as it was by day."[3] Since 1835 the hot blast had been superseding the cold blast in Staffordshire, and it had enabled " cinder pig " to be made from the slags tapped off from the puddling and reheating furnaces. First produced by Gibbons of Corbyns Hall, near Dudley, in the thirties, this " cinder pig " had been so extensively manufactured that by 1860 enormous heaps of slag had been worked up into iron.[4] Although by this time the hot blast was in general use, there were still in the Black Country a number of cold-blast furnaces, the make of which was very small.[5]

It has been shown in an earlier chapter that the South Staffordshire coal was of a non-coking variety, and that consequently much of it was burnt in the furnaces in a raw state. The most common practice, however, was for it to be converted into coke by admixture with tar and with Welsh coking coal[6]—an expensive process, especially as the methods employed were primitive and wasteful, and as no attempts were made to utilize the by-products. Thus, in pig-iron production the Black Country was paying dearly for its position as a pioneer. Much of its plant was antiquated, and the prospects of the district, which were not brightened by the depression of the later fifties, were not such as to induce

[1] S. Timmins, op. cit., pp. 66-67.   [2] Ibid., p. 67.
[3] J. W. Hall, op. cit., p. 12.   [4] Ibid., p. 10.
[5] S. Timmins, op. cit., pp. 67-68.   [6] Ibid., p. 65.

K

manufacturers to renew their plants, even when they could afford to do so.

The administration of the ironworks was typical of the methods generally followed in the local industries. The ironmaster commonly contracted with a " forehand," or " overhand," to supply labour to perform the various operations. The upper part of the blast-furnace was in charge of a subcontractor, called a " bridge-stocker," who kept horses, employed a gang of men, women and boys (termed " fillers "), and whose duty it was to supply the furnaces with the necessary materials. He was paid so much a ton on the produce of the furnace, and he made his own arrangements with his underhands. The " stock-taker " was the subcontractor in charge of the lower part of the furnace, and his men prepared the sand and looked after the casting and the weighing of the pigs.[1] The number employed at each furnace naturally varied according to its size and mechanical equipment; but usually there were about 12 men on each shift at the furnace, and from 10 to 20 more who were engaged in carrying materials. The typical ironworks, with three blast-furnaces, thus employed 100 to 130 persons.[2] The units, consisting of single cold-blast furnaces, were much smaller; while the large ironmasters, with several groups of furnaces, must have had 300 to 400 men. Among these were the Chillington Iron Company, with 9 furnaces; B. Gibbons, with 7; and N. Hingley & Sons, the Earl of Dudley, the New British Iron Company, Philip Williams & Sons and John Bagnall, with 6 each.[3]

It was, however, on its high-grade finished iron that South Staffordshire based its claim to be numbered among the leading metallurgical centres of the country. The key-process in this industry was performed by the puddler, who was required to bring to his task a high degree of strength, skill and experience; and a description of the development of the puddling furnace is necessary for an understanding of the organization of a finished ironworks. In 1784 Cort had invented " dry puddling," and so laid the foundations of the malleable-iron period. Six years later Homfray, of Tredegar, devised the " refinery," or " running-outfire," to get rid of the surplus silicon, and carried the process of finished-iron manufacture a stage nearer perfection. On the

---

[1] *The Black Country* from *The Edinburgh Review*, April 1863, pp. 409-411.
[2] *Children's Employment Commission (1862)*, *Third Report*, pp. iv., 2-3.
[3] S. Griffiths, *Iron Trade Circular*, 1862.

combination of the " refinery " and the " dry-puddling furnace " the bar-iron trade of South Wales was built up, and in the early part of the nineteenth century this method of production was employed also in South Staffordshire. It is still used for treating the cold-blast pig, from which high-grade Yorkshire iron is made. But progress did not rest here. Between 1825 and 1832 Joseph Hall, of the Bloomfield Ironworks, brought to perfection another method of puddling, which by 1860 had been generally adopted by all the Staffordshire houses engaged in producing high-grade bar-iron. This was the system of " wet puddling," or " pig boiling," according to which the furnace was lined with slag rich in oxide, together with the scale which fell from the iron while it was being hammered and rolled. Hall's process dispensed with the " refinery," and yet produced a purer and more uniform metal from practically any normal pig; although the best results were obtained from forge pig, prepared specially for the purpose. From 5 to 7 heats, each of 25 cwt., could be worked in a 10-hour shift at this type of furnace. After the puddling operation the iron left the furnace in the form of a ball. It was then reheated and hammered, or " shingled," as it was called, under a steam-hammer in order to remove the slag. From the " shingler " the iron passed to the " forge train," where it was rolled out into " puddled bars." These were then cut up in the mill department and piled together in " boxes," each of which consisted of four pieces of " puddled bar " and some scrap-iron. The piles were brought to welding heat, and finally were rolled down into finished bars.[1]

In 1861-1862 nearly 100 ironworks, controlled by about seventy-five firms, were in operation in the Black Country; while 12 or 15 more were " standing." The size of these firms may be indicated as follows [2]:

Number of Puddling Furnaces per Firm	Number of Firms
Over 50	10
21 − 50	19
10 − 20	29
Under 10	16

The plant of a typical unit consisted of between 10 and 20 puddling furnaces, a " balling-up " furnace, a steam-hammer,

[1] J. W. Hall, op. cit., pp. 13-15.
[2] S. Griffiths, Iron Trade Circular, 1862; also Children's Employment Commission (1862), Third Report, p. 1.

a " forge train," 2 or 3 reheating furnaces and 2 sets of rolling
mills, and it gave employment to about 250 men.[1] The largest
firms were John Bradley & Co., with 95 puddling furnaces;
Barrows & Hall, with 89; John Bagnall & Sons, with 85; and the
British Iron Company, G. B. Thorneycroft & Co., and the
Chillington Iron Company, with over 70 each.[2] The larger firms
specialized in the higher grades of iron, and the bars which
they produced were stamped with their registered marks. The
imprint of these " marked bar " houses, among which the
Bloomfield Ironworks, with its famous B.B.H. brand, held the lead
for quality, had an international reputation.[3] The existence of a
number of very large concerns in this industry, in which it was
possible for the comparatively small maker to survive, is not to
be attributed to any economies of production which the large
unit could secure; for inasmuch as puddling was a manual
operation, the growth in the output of a firm was to be achieved
merely by a duplication of its existing processes. It was because
wrought-iron varied greatly in quality, and because certain firms
had achieved a high reputation, that some of them were able to
extend the scale of their operations beyond that of the majority.
While most of the larger makers manufactured iron in many
forms, and for various uses, the majority had some special line.
Some were concerned chiefly with nail rods, some with boiler
and ship plates, others with gun-barrel iron; and several, as
we shall see later, produced metal mainly for use in their own
tube mills, edge-tool works or engineering shops. As in the
blast-furnaces, the subcontracting system was common in the
finished-iron works. The puddler usually employed one or
two men and boys as assistants at the furnace; the " shingler "
had an underhand to help him move the iron; and in the rolling
mills the work was done on contract between the employers and
the master-rollers, who themselves hired and paid the hands they
required.[4]

It is obvious that the representative works engaged on the
production of pig or finished iron was in 1860 conducted on a
much larger scale than the typical producing unit in most of the

---

[1] Cf. J. W. Hall, op. cit., p. 15.
[2] S. Griffiths, Iron Trade Circular, 1862.
[3] J. W. Hall, op. cit., p. 15.
[4] Children's Employment Commission (1862), Third Report, pp. 2-4; and
Reports of the Inspectors of Factories, April 1876, p. 74.

other local trades. Compared with the modern steel plant the normal finished-iron works of the sixties might seem insignificant and its output small. But it turned out 200 to 250 tons a week of finished iron, which had passed through a long and complicated process, and its initial cost was in the neighbourhood of £15,000 or £20,000.[1] Even the small works with less than 10 puddling furnaces had to be equipped with power for its " shingling " hammer and its mills, and to employ a variety of skilled labour. As we have already seen, from the early days of South Staffordshire's iron trade, firms had existed which, in addition to blast-furnaces and puddling furnaces, owned extensive mining properties. This type of concern had become more common during the first half of the nineteenth century, and in 1860 about twenty of the leading businesses in the industry were integrated in structure.[2] This end had been achieved by different paths. Sometimes a firm, having begun as a manufacturer of some special metal commodity, such as edge tools, later took up the production of the materials it required in order to ensure the quality of its goods. This was an obvious policy for a manufacturer who was situated in the heart of a coal and iron district, and it was particularly easy to carry out in the Black Country, because mining operations did not require heavy capital expenditure and were not, therefore, necessarily confined to specialists. In other instances, men who began business as colliery owners extended their activities to include blast-furnaces, or, more usually, the proprietors of blast-furnaces attempted to secure a market for their pig-iron by setting up forges and mills. Thus the Brades Iron & Steel Co. at Oldbury was primarily engaged in the production of edge tools; but its plant included also blast-furnaces and a finished-iron works, with 8 puddling furnaces. It manufactured the sheer and cast steel which it needed in its edge-tool factory, and it had sunk " seven pairs of coal-mines round the works." [3] John and Edward Bagnall, to give another example, had begun business as mine owners in the eighteenth century, and just before 1800 had acquired iron-works. In 1860 the firm possessed numerous mines in several parts of the Black Country, besides six blast-furnaces and three

[1] J. W. Hall, *op. cit.*, pp. 15, 24.
[2] *Children's Employment Commission (1862)*, *Third Report*, p. 1.
[3] E. Burritt, *op. cit.*, p. 162 *et seq.*

finished-iron works at Wednesbury and West Bromwich.[1] The most recent example of a movement towards integration was provided by the great concern controlled by the Earl of Dudley. Engaged until 1855 solely in mining, quarrying and pig-iron production, the Earl in that year constructed the Round Oak Works, which consisted of 28 puddling furnaces, 2 hammers, 2 forge-trains and 5 mills, for the manufacture of high-grade finished iron. The specified reason for taking this step was to provide an additional customer for the thick coal which was being raised in increasing quantities on the Himley Estate, and also to find a market for Lord Dudley's All-Mine pig-iron made at the Level Furnaces.[2] Integrated firms of this character must have been responsible for a large proportion of the total iron output; for of the leading producers of finished iron, Messrs Barrows & Hall, of Tipton, was the only concern which did not control blast-furnaces and mines.

Thus in 1860, even more than in earlier times, there was an immense difference between the scale of production of the small metal trades and that of the iron industry. In the former not only was the small unit ubiquitous, but the productive process often was divided among a multitude of firms. To the iron trade, on the other hand, men with large capital had been attracted; and highly integrated concerns with coal and ironstone mines, with limestone quarries, and with large plants for pig- and finished-iron manufacture—concerns employing not only hundreds but, in some instances, thousands of men—had leading parts to play in the industry.

[1] S. Griffiths, *Guide to the Iron Trade of Great Britain* (1873), chap. v.; and *Newspaper Cuttings* on *Birmingham Industries*, vol. ii., p. 200.
[2] Personal inquiry.

CHAPTER VII

GENERAL FEATURES OF INDUSTRIAL AND COMMERCIAL ORGANIZATION

PERHAPS the most remarkable feature of the industrial structure of the district in 1860 was the co-existence in many trades of highly subdivided processes of production and the small unit. The gun, jewellery, brassfoundry, and saddlery and harness trades exhibited this characteristic in a marked degree; and although in some of them the individual nature of the product, the absence of any need for machinery and the fluctuations to which the demand was subject may help to explain the survival of the shop owner or the domestic craftsman, it is surprising that the employer or factor was able to co-ordinate efficiently the operations of great bodies of outworkers. The same problem existed in the early textile industries; but in those the number of processes was much fewer and the task of co-ordination was therefore less difficult than in several Birmingham trades. In the manufacture of guns, for instance, there were nearly fifty distinct processes, each of which might be performed by special groups of outworking craftsmen.[1]

The survival of the small unit was aided in trades producing finished goods of a complex character by the extent to which the manufacturer could rely on specialists for the performance of subsidiary processes. As we have seen, the garret-master in the cabinet brassfoundry trade, to quote only one instance, could buy out his stampings and castings from men who were working on the same scale as himself, and, having made up the article, could have the polishing and other processes done out by specialists. Even the application of power-machinery to certain operations had not revolutionized the local industries, except in a few instances; for the industrial organism reacted to this new element by creating opportunities for its employment without necessitating any fundamental change in the scale of manufacture. Buildings were erected which were divided into a number of separate workshops, through each of which shafting, driven by a steam-engine, projected. Here garret-masters and others who required power for certain of their operations

---

[1] S. Timmins, *op. cit.*, pp. 392-393.

could hire the facilities they needed, and it was common at this time to see the notice, " Power to Let," affixed to mills in the neighbourhood. In the Coventry silk trade another method was followed, and there steam-power was made available to the domestic weavers by means of shafting which was carried through the ranges of workshops that formed the upper stories of their houses. The extension of this practice of hiring power was said to have been responsible for an increase in the number of garret-masters during the first half of the nineteenth century, and so to have brought about an enormous fall in the price of commodities.[1] Frequently, moreover, the small manufacturers used to hire room and power from a large factory owner, and in this way several of the leading businesses in the district were begun.[2]

It is, however, in another direction that we must look for a complete explanation of the universality of the small unit and of its survival even in the highly subdivided trades. Only by an understanding of the " factor system " can we discover how production was initiated and controlled within each industry, and how the output of the little masters found its way to the market. In Birmingham and District the term " factor " applied to middlemen who catered for the home market, or who acted as intermediaries between the manufacturers and the export houses; and only those who were concerned with foreign trade were called " merchants."[3] Both classes had functions of the utmost importance in 1860 and during the next few decades. They occupied, indeed, a key-position in the economic life of the time, and they were far from being mere wholesale dealers in the modern sense. Upon them the workshop proprietor or the garret-master depended, not only for the marketing of his

[1] L. Faucher, *op. cit.*, pp. 505-507 ; *Children's Employment Commission* (*1862*), *Third Report*, pp. 54-55.

[2] *Reports of the Inspectors of Factories*, October 1872, p. 121.

Coventry provides another example of how steam-power might be made available to the comparatively small manufacturers. In 1835 a number of masters in the silk trade combined to erect a factory and a steam-driven plant with the object of sharing both the expense and the unpopularity of this method of production. It was proposed to allot each story in the factory to a different manufacturer, as in the company mills of Yorkshire ; but this aim was never realized, and the establishment was ultimately taken on by one firm (B. Poole, *op. cit.*, p. 360). In this connection it is worth remarking that when motor-car manufacture was first introduced into Coventry, it was conducted in an old textile mill, each story of which was for a time occupied by a different firm.

[3] *Cf.* S. Timmins, *op. cit.*, p. 454, n., and L. Faucher, *op. cit.*, pp. 504-505.

goods and for financial help during the period of manufacture, but for the actual organization of production. Even in the sphere of marketing the merchant and factor were then more important than they have since become; for whereas the large manufacturer of to-day can study market requirements himself, can impress his name on the public, and can treat the merchant and factor as mere intermediaries, the little master must rely on them for information as to the type of commodity required. In 1860, besides the general factors who dealt in a wide variety of small-wares there were several specialized classes, which have already been mentioned—viz. the saddlers' and coachbuilders' iron-monger, the nail-master, the gun-maker.

The functions of the factors naturally varied according to the industries with which they were concerned. In the nail trade we have an example of the domestic system in its simplest form. The nail-master usually possessed warehouses in each centre which specialized on a particular class of product. Through these he distributed the rods and orders to the domestic nailers, and received back the nails at each week-end. Here and there the factors had erected in the vicinity of their warehouses nail shops, which they rented to nailers who had no forges of their own; but this was the extreme limit to which the capitalist had gone in this industry. The lock-makers of the Willenhall neigh-bourhood disposed of their output to factors at Wolverhampton and Birmingham, to whom they took their products each Saturday, and from whom they returned with orders for the following week.[1] And, with some modifications, these practices were followed in the majority of the hardware trades.

In the more complex industries, however, the factor had other duties to perform. Thus the master gun-maker was required to have an intimate technical knowledge of his trade, and also, since he had to co-ordinate the activities of a multitude of " material-makers " and " setters-up," he had to come into close contact with the manufacturing operations. Similarly the " saddlers' and coachbuilders' ironmonger " was responsible for bringing together in his warehouse the various components which were produced by the little masters, and also for pur-chasing hides and for supplying such of his craftsmen as were leatherworkers with the particular section of the hide which

---

[1] G. Price, op. cit., p. 877 et seq.; L. Faucher, op. cit., p. 531.

they needed. In the jewellery trade, on the other hand, the co-ordination of the work of specialists was done in most branches by the shop owner and not by the factor. Even in divisions of the trade in which the garret-master or single-handed craftsman flourished, such as wedding-ring manufacture, the maker was independent of the factor for his supply of raw materials, because a readily available supply was present in the shape of the sovereign. In the jewellery trade, indeed, the factor's part was confined largely to the distribution of the products and to providing the masters with credit.

There was, then, a gradation from the factor who was concerned only with the distribution of the products and with the financing of the little masters to the type who exercised an intimate control over the materials supplied to the workers, and who had to co-ordinate the labour of many dependent craftsmen. The distinction which has been sometimes drawn between the system of industry in which the factor supplied the materials and that in which the worker found his own can be perceived in the structure of Birmingham industry; but it is not here that we must look in any attempt to classify the various types of industrial organization. This distinction did not correspond to any fundamental contrast in forms of industrial organization, or in the relations of factor and craftsman; for it depended mainly on the kind of raw material with which the latter was working. The most important difference lies in the factor's position in the trades dominated by the shop owner and those in which the factor himself co-ordinated the various processes. In the first group of industries the factor tended to devote himself to merchanting, allowing the task of co-ordination to be assumed by others. In the latter group he came into close touch with the manufacturing operations. Nor must it be assumed that there was a necessary chronological progression from one stage to the other; for the nature of the finished products was often responsible for the distinction. In the industries producing simple types of article there was no need for a shop owner. It was in trades such as brassfoundry and jewellery, where production was of necessity split up among a number of specialists, that the shop owner was required, although he might appear in any trade in which the plant was comparatively expensive. In certain trades, notably the gun and saddlery and harness manufactures, the existence of the shop owner was not inconsistent with the need for the factor's co-ordinating functions; for those trades required both the co-ordinating of processes in the production of each component and the assembly of those components which were turned out by a variety of distinct trades. In gun-making, for example, while shop owners might be concerned with the manufacture of certain finished parts, the master gun-maker still had much to do in the co-ordination and direction both of their work and that of single-handed outworkers.

As was shown in the previous chapter, the chief link between the divers forms of organization which were comprehended in the factor system is to be found in the financial dependence of the manufacturer and the factor. Indeed an understanding of industrial finance during the nineteenth century is impossible unless this is taken into account. The factor acted as a link between the banks and the small makers who could not then resort to them for credit. Through the factor, industry was supplied with its working capital; for though the domestic workers and shop owners might not all receive their materials from the factor, they all depended on him for weekly advances, from which they might meet their expenses of production.[1] Further, the able workman who was anxious to set up on his own often would receive financial assistance from the factor, who would sometimes furnish him with a loan for the purchase of the required tools. Many flourishing establishments still in existence were started in this humble way in the middle of the nineteenth century.

In many industries, moreover, the small producers did not invariably deal through a man who was exclusively a factor or merchant. Frequently they took orders from, and sold their output to, a manufacturer himself, who, in addition to producing goods in his own establishment, had also taken up the factoring of goods. This combination of functions might arise in several ways. In some cases women, when leaving the factory of their employer on marriage, might continue to work for him at home. Sometimes lack of capital or the inconvenience of site might prevent a manufacturer from extending his factory, and

---

[1] " One great advantage possessed by the manufacturers of Birmingham having but small capital is the practice which has long existed among factors and merchants of paying cash every Saturday for supplies of the whole week " (R. Tangye, *The Rise of a Great Industry*, p. 91).

so he might continue to deal with increased orders by the employment of outworkers. In certain trades, such as linen-button or hook-and-eye manufacture, some operations might be economically performed within a factory; while others, like the carding process, might provide an opportunity for home work. Again, in fluctuating industries the manufacturer might try to keep his overhead charges low by having an establishment large enough to deal with a normal demand, and he might extend his output by employing garret-masters. Finally, an employer who had created a valuable connection with customers for the particular class of goods he made might try to take advantage of his position by factoring other lines which he purchased from outside. In all these instances it is assumed that the factory owner who also dealt in goods produced by others was primarily a manufacturer, and doubtless this was often the case. But sometimes the conjunction of interests would be achieved in a different way. A factor who was concerned, say, with a wide variety of metal smallwares, might find that he could with advantage take up the production of one particular line himself. He might be induced to do this because he found it difficult to obtain the quantity of goods he required from domestic producers,[1] or because the extension of the demand for that commodity had made large-scale methods of production economical. And so from manufacturing one line himself he might slowly assume the production of more and more articles, while he continued to factor those which he still purchased from outworkers. This combination of functions was to be observed in a multitude of local industries, from the chain trade of Cradley to the jewellery and pearl-button trades of Birmingham[2]; and it should be observed that the movement from selling to manufacturing was one of the chief sources of new producing units at this period.

[1] An example of this is provided by the needle trade. " For some time previous to 1850 Messrs Kirby, Beard & Co., of London and Birmingham, were buyers of Crendon needles. They bought from Emmanuel Shrimpton two-thirds of the output of this firm. Their needle business was now rapidly increasing—so much so that Emmanuel & Sons could not produce sufficient to meet the demands of Kirby, Beard & Co. In consequence of the delays in the execution of their orders this firm decided to commence making needles themselves. . . . This new firm . . . built a mill, erected a steam-engine of eight horse-power, with scouring apparatus and all appliances necessary for needle-making . . . and appointed one of the Shrimptons manager" (W. Shrimpton, *op. cit.*, p. 22).
[2] Cf. *Pictures of the People* in *Birmingham Morning News*, July 3, 1871; and W. J. Woodward, *op. cit.*, p. 190.

Finally, there were many little masters who never came into contact with the factor because they were concerned with performing special operations for other manufacturers.

Monopolizing, as he did in many trades, the functions of initiating enterprise and the marketing of the products, the factor occupied a strong position in bargaining with the small manufacturer. In times of excited trade it might be possible for the latter to extract high prices from the factor for whom he was accustomed to work by threatening to take his goods elsewhere. But the factor had no great overhead charges to burden him if his men struck; and in trades which suffered from a permanent oversupply of producing units, like nailing, and generally in times of depression, the workers could be pitted against one another by their employers.[1] Certain factors were known as " slaughtermen," from their practice of forcing down the workers' prices in this way.

It was repeatedly asserted, both by factory owners and by their employees who were engaged in trades in which large and small units flourished side by side, that the greatest evil from which they suffered was the competition of the garret-masters, whose necessities were taken advantage of by " slaughtermen," and who were compelled to produce goods at prices with which the large manufacturer could not compete.[2] The situation was at its worst in the Black Country, where the truck system was prevalent. Even some of the largest firms kept " tommy-shops " in connection with their factories and induced their men to deal there [3]; but the evils of the system were most evident in the domestic industries, where the " foggers," standing as an intermediate class between the factor and the outworker, insisted that the wages should be spent in their public-houses or at their shops, in which the provisions sold were generally of a very bad quality.[4]

The fact that the craftsman in certain trades worked mainly for one master must not be taken to imply that his position was more subservient than that of the worker who was less permanently attached to a particular factor. The degree of the

[1] R. H. Tawney, *op. cit.*, p. 16.
[2] *Labour and the Poor* in *The Morning Chronicle*, November 4, 1850; *Birmingham and her Manufactures* in *The Leisure Hour*, February 3, 1853.
[3] F. W. Hackwood, *Wednesbury Workshops*, pp. 75-80.
[4] R. G. Hobbs, *op. cit.*, p. 638; *Report of the Chief Inspector of Factories and Workshops*, October 1879, p. 75.

employer's control over the industry, moreover, had little bearing on the economic strength and well-being of the small manufacturer. The latter's position was determined mainly by the amount of skill required by his trade and by the ease with which outsiders could enter it. In the highly skilled industries the craftsman was in a position to make a good bargain with a factor, who would be loath to lose a valuable workman to a competitor. It was in the less skilled trades, which were liable to suffer from an oversupply of labour, that the worker's position was weak, and that the evils described above usually made their appearance.

It may sound paradoxical to state that the industrial organization of the area was nowhere more clearly illustrated than in those large units which, though they had long existed in the heavy trades, were exceptional among the lighter finished manufactures. This was because even in trades in which large-scale production was common the habits connected with the older types of workplace survived. Even where it existed the factory was regarded as something exceptional, and this attitude of mind influenced the methods of organization which were followed there.

Before considering what these methods were we may pause for a moment to consider the origins of the factory and its evolution from other forms of organization. It is true that the history of some industries shows no progression from one stage to another, for these, from their inception, had been conducted on a comparatively large scale. But in many of the lighter trades we may trace the rise of the factory from two sources. From below we may watch the outworker, who depends upon the factor for his materials and for the co-ordination of his work with that of others, develop into a shop owner who employs several workmen and who has assumed the task of co-ordinating the labours of independent specialists, and then into a factory employer, who can contract with the factor as between equals, and who depends upon the latter merely to distribute his goods. Or, from above, we can see the factor advance towards the position of a manufacturer when he builds workshops and rents these, together with the tools required, to his outworkers. He goes a stage farther when, finding the demand for a certain class of goods outstripping the capacity of his men, or seeing that a particular line may be produced more profitably by machinery, he erects a factory for manufacturing that line while still continuing to factor other classes of goods. Finally, as he takes up the production of other lines his functions as a factor become subordinate.

Yet, having arrived at the factory, we have not arrived by any means at the modern type of factory. We have arrived at a stage in its organization which may be called the "subcontracting system." The significance of this method of organization which once prevailed throughout the majority of industries and which still survives in many, in some form or other, has received less recognition than might have been expected. But it must be considered in any study of industrial evolution, because it represents a definite stage in the growth of the modern factory. The idea that the employer should find, as a matter of course, the workplace, plant and materials, and should exercise supervision over the details of the manufacturing processes, did not spring into existence as soon as the men had been drawn within the factory; and in the larger establishments of the period, arrangements came into being which were obvious survivals of the earlier forms of organization and which represented a transitional stage of development. Just as the manufacturer who had grown out of the factor remained at heart in his earlier capacity, and tried to hold himself aloof from the details of the productive process, so the employees brought into the factory the traditions of the domestic workshop.

The various compromises which reflected the struggle of the employer and worker to maintain their ancient relationship in a period of change are worth examination. The idea that the former's function was to supply materials and to pay for and market the completed articles, whereas the worker's was to provide workshop and tools, survived in the factories in the custom of charging deductions. Even in large factories it was common for sums to be subtracted from the employee's wages for shop room, gas and power, just as if these were nominally provided by the worker and not by the capitalist. In the nail trade, as we have seen, the master sometimes constructed nail shops and let them to his workers for a weekly rent, chargeable against the price they received for their products. This, however, represented an earlier transitional stage towards the factory, and a better illustration is provided by the fact that, in the few large establishments in the lock trade, deductions were made for " standings and light "—*i.e.* shop room and gas. In the brass-foundry trade charges were made against wages to cover the cost of power and light—1s. to 3s. 6d. for the former and 4d. to 6d. a week for the latter.[1] In the foundries the head casters had to pay for use of the sandmill, which had superseded the pestle and mortar; while a rent for shop room often was required from the head of a gang.[2] Finally, in the glass-cutting shops a deduction of 12s. or 12s. 9d. was made from the workers' weekly wage to pay for the power which had been introduced to replace the old method, according to which the machinery was set in motion by a boy who turned a handle.[3]

Of greater interest and of more vital significance to the system of industrial organization, however, was the method of engaging the workers and of supervising them. Common not only to the trades of Birmingham and District, but to those of many other industrial areas, this has received but little attention from econ-omic historians. Yet it occupies a definite stage in the transition from domestic to modern large-scale production, and in 1860 it had long existed in all industries in which the large unit flourished, from the coal and iron trades to the manufacture of brass goods and buttons.

The chief feature of this system of organization was the exist-ence of an intermediate class of men who acted as a buffer be-tween the employer and the workers. Termed " subcontractors," " overhands," " fitters," " charter-masters," " butties," or " piece-masters," according to the industry in which they worked, they all had much the same general function to perform. This was to contract with the factory owner to produce a certain quantity of output for a fixed sum, and then to engage, pay and supervise workers for the task. The details of their duty varied according to the nature of their trade. Sometimes they had large numbers of men under them; in other cases they had only three or four underhands. Occasionally they provided their men not only with tools and equipment but also with certain raw materials. Thus subcontractors in some industries possessed a good deal of capital and relieved the employer of much responsi-bility; elsewhere they were little more than skilled men who,

[1] *Brass Trades Arbitration Report*, 1900, First Day's Proceedings, p. 6.
[2] *Ibid.*, Fifth Day's Proceedings, pp. 33, 47, 60-61.
[3] *Labour and the Poor* in *The Morning Chronicle*, December 23, 1850.

though having a few assistants, relied on the factory owner for all the tools and materials required.[1]

The practice of subcontracting involved the wage-system in all kinds of complications. After the overhand had made his bargain with the factory owner the former alone was concerned with fixing the wages of his subordinates. But he could not claim payment from the employer until the quantity of work contracted for was completed, yet neither he nor his men could afford to wait for several weeks without money in cases in which the work was spread over a long period. Consequently, to meet such difficulties, it became customary for the subcontractor to draw on the employer at each week-end for a sufficient sum to provide a reasonable wage for himself and his underhands. When the work was completed, then the price contracted for was balanced against the weekly drawings and the remainder paid over to the subcontractor, who, if he had obtained his labour cheaply, or if he were a good organizer, might make large profits for himself. But sometimes, in order to secure the work in competition with others, the subcontractor might have agreed to perform it at such a low price that the balance was against him when settling-day came round. He might, in fact, be in debt to his employers at the end of the job. When this occurred, the overhand might get into the employer's power and become " tied " to him. In any case, however, subcontracting involved a double wage-contract—that between the employer and the overhand, which was a piece-wage, and that between the overhand and his subordinates, who usually were paid day-rates.

The origin of this system is not difficult to surmise. When the employer first decided to establish a factory, he would naturally engage subcontractors, since he would thus avoid the trouble of supervising the process of production; and his position would still approximate to that of the factor. The subcontractor, indeed, was a logical development from the shop owner. Their relation to the employer was identical, except that, whereas the shop owner had his own workplace, the subcontractor worked in the employer's establishment. In those days, moreover, the employing class had as yet worked out no managerial system by which control could be centralized. If wide

[1] *Labour and the Poor* in *The Morning Chronicle*, October 7, 1850, and articles in subsequent issues.

L

functions devolved on the overhands, then the manufacturer had no need to concern himself about the supervision of his labour and about wages. He required no large office staff and no costing system, and he could keep his overhead charges at a minimum. The method of organization might not be applicable to industries in which the productive process required the co-ordinated activities of large numbers of semi-skilled workers, but few of the local trades in 1860 were of that type. In such as did exist—e.g. the pen trade—the subcontracting system was non-existent.[1] The existence of large gangs in certain trades, such as brass-foundry, does not need an elaborate explanation. There the overhand, who began with only two or three assistants, might find the demand increasing for the products on which he was specializing, and he would, therefore, gather round him a large staff of men to deal with the additional output.

That there were serious disadvantages attending the system cannot be denied. It was frequently declared that the overhand sweated his men and often made disproportionately high gains himself. The first complaint was probably true enough; but the employer in some industries was partly responsible, for he had every inducement to drive a hard bargain with the subcontractor, since the odium of the low wages which necessarily resulted could be directed against the subcontractor rather than against the employer. The fact that the employer was a more remote figure in the wage-contract, as compared with the position to-day, is of great significance; for in the comparatively small factory the public opinion of the workers has a more powerful influence on business policy than is generally realized. As to the overhand's high earnings, which frequently were in sharp contrast to the wages of his subordinates, it must be remembered that the former possessed wider functions and suffered greater risks than the modern foreman.

From the standpoint of business efficiency the system had many faults. Since the whole process of producing a finished article had to be performed by the subcontractor and his gang, it was impossible to set up separate departments within the factory for performing each operation, or to take advantage of the economies of the division of process among specialist workers. Each subcontractor might have certain machines solely allotted

[1] *Labour and the Poor* in *The Morning Chronicle*, December 16, 1850.

to his use, and while he and his underhands were performing other operations these would be idle. Much time was lost, moreover, when the subcontractor was making his bargain with the employer and in obtaining materials for his work; and finally, since the overhands worked according to traditional methods, the enlightened employer found it almost impossible to make improvements in the manufacturing process. The overhand, like the modern foreman, would almost invariably be sceptical of the success of new methods; and the employer, fearing to arouse the hostility of his key-men, could exercise little control over them. Thus the system was disadvantageous inasmuch as the principle of the division of labour was not followed out, an uneconomical use was made of the plant, and reforms in productive methods were difficult to effect. As was pointed out by a trade union secretary in an industry in which subcontracting was universal, " if a workman has to superintend a large shop, he is supposed to look out his work, look up patterns, and do a great deal which could be done for him by a general man " in a modern type of establishment.[1] Yet in the early days of the factory, when no costing system, no trained office and works staff, and no experience of centralized management existed, it is hard to see how the subcontractor could have been dispensed with. Once established, the system was difficult to change; and any attempt on the part of the employer to relegate his overhands to the position of a modern foreman would arouse their bitter opposition.

This generalized account can be illustrated with advantage by a description of conditions in the leading trades. We have already seen that there was a gradation from the subcontractor, who employed 20 or 30 men and provided materials and tools, to the type who was merely a skilled worker, employing a few assistants for the rougher parts of his task. An example of the latter kind was the smith, who commonly employed a boy to work his bellows and an adult striker. In the chain factories the overhand usually had two or three strikers.[2] In the edge-tool works and stamping shops the stamper was assisted by two boys, one to look after the fire and the other to hold the iron.[3] As already explained, the puddlers and shinglers engaged one or

[1] *Brass Trades Arbitration Report*, 1900, Third Day's Proceedings, p. 57.
[2] *Children's Employment Commission (1862)*, *Third Report*, pp. 6-8.
[3] *Souvenir of Thos. Smith & Sons* (Works Publication).

two assistants, and the relationship between them is illustrated by a clause in the rules of the Tipton puddlers, stating that no underhand should receive any benefit if he should strike against his overhand. In the gun-lock factories each skilled man had his boys or youths to help him. The moulders in the brickyards employed two or three children, called " pages," to fetch the clay from the pit and to carry off the bricks.[1] The women in the button factories each had a few girl assistants, and it was said of that trade that " the manufacturer . . . has merely a nominal control over the large proportion of his workpeople. He neither engages them, pays them nor dismisses them. They are the servants of his servants." [2] A variation of the system was when women carders took out buttons, hooks and eyes, and pens from the factories, and sewed them on cards at home, with the assistance of a number of girls. One of these " foggers," as they were sometimes called, had eleven girls to help her.[3]

The " bridge-stockers " and the " stock-takers " at the blast-furnaces, whose functions have already been described, were much more substantial types of subcontractor. And the same was true of the " butty " in the coal-mines, who sometimes had as many as 150 men under him, and who himself would employ a " doggie " to help in the work of superintendence.[4] In the rolling mills, in both the ferrous and non-ferrous trades, the master-roller undertook to turn out a quantity of metal at a fixed price, and engaged his own labour for the task; and a similar practice was followed in the tube mills.[5] In the establishments where machine-made nails and washers were produced, the masters contracted with a few " fitters," who hired the labour and superintended the machinery and the work [6]; and variations of the same system existed in the bedstead, saddlery and harness, hollow-ware and tinplate-ware factories, and in the iron foundries.[7]

Perhaps the best illustration of subcontracting was afforded by the practice in the brassfoundry trade, to which the system was well adapted. An overhand in this industry commonly

---

[1] E. Burritt, *op. cit.*, p. 207.
[2] *Labour and the Poor* in *The Morning Chronicle*, October 21, 1850.
[3] *Children's Employment Commission (1862), Third Report*, p. 128.
[4] R. G. Hobbs, *op. cit.*, p. 266.
[5] *Children's Employment Commission (1862), Third Report*, pp. 3, 11.
[6] *Ibid.*, p. 11.
[7] *Ibid.*, pp. 52-53.

specialized in some particular class of article and employed about 7 underhands, although 20 or 30 was not an uncommon number.[1] Usually he would contract with the master to turn out articles at a fixed price, which, in the case of those of traditional pattern, would be determined by custom. When the price had been fixed in the days of candles and treadle-lathes, then, in factories where gaslight and power had been introduced, it would be subject to deductions to pay for these innovations. Occasionally a charge was made against the subcontractor's price for shop room. Often the overhand undertook to supply the tools, aqua fortis and other " loose " materials; while the firm provided space, power, machinery and metal. When the job was a long and complicated one, requiring a variety of skilled labour, then two or more overhands would sometimes go into partnership with each other, and would pool their resources for the duration of the particular contract. In the foundries the head caster usually had four " tubs," and 8 to 10 persons under him, and he produced castings at so much a hundredweight, with deductions for the use of the sandmill. As already indicated, the subcontractor, both in the foundries and in the other shops, generally paid his subordinates day-wages; but in exceptional cases might put his men on piecework. In connection with the system of " drawing " on the employer for weekly sums during the course of a contract which happened to extend over a long period, a practice had arisen which was bitterly resented by the overhands. Sometimes, it appears, the masters fixed the total price for the work and the weekly " drawings " without consulting the overhands, and the latter alleged that this " blind piecework," as it was called, often resulted in their being in debt to their employers at the end of their jobs. Probably the practice was most common in highly competitive lines, where the bargaining position of the subcontractor would necessarily be weak.[2]

An equally significant illustration of the character of the factory system then in existence was to be found in the refusal of the men to accept the employer's discipline, and in their restiveness under the yoke of factory routine. In this respect

---

[1] In a few instances the subcontractor employed as many as 70 underhands.
[2] *Brass Trades Arbitration Report*, 1900, First and Second Days' Proceedings, pp. 75-86.

also they carried the habits of work which they had acquired in their domestic workshops into the larger establishments, or perhaps it would be truer to say that the methods of labour existing in the multitude of small workshops set the standard to which the factory hands tended to conform. In the majority of the small-scale industries it was customary for the men to " play away " on Monday, and often on Tuesday as well, and to concentrate the whole of the week's labour into the next three days and nights, so as to be ready to hand over their products to the factor on Saturday.[1] A factory inspector once declared: " The tendency to make six days' labour into three days is most prevalent among the chain-makers "[2]; but similar habits were to be found among the workers in most industries.

Observers of industrial conditions who came from the " respectable " classes in mid-Victorian England invariably expressed their abhorrence at this alternation of idle merry-making and prolonged and concentrated labour. But it is difficult to find a priori grounds for regarding a whole week of monotonously regulated toil more socially desirable than a few days of careless idleness, followed by bouts of unremitting work; and Mr G. K. Chesterton might even draw a moral from the fact that the workers referred to their days of leisure as " Saint Monday " or " Saint Tuesday." In the domestic workshop it is doubtful whether even efficiency suffered from such a division of the week's labour. But in the factories it was different. There the temporary absence of certain men who occupied a key-position in the productive progress might hold up output; and where large plants were employed, a few days' idleness, which could not be easily balanced by overtime, might increase the burden of overhead charges. Yet few of the factory owners could induce their men to forgo on occasions the observance of Saint Monday and Saint Tuesday; and this ingrained habit was largely responsible for the slow development of large-scale productions in trades to which it was applicable, and also of modern methods of organization within such factories as were set up. Here and there employers made determined attempts to lay the ghost of the domestic system. At Messrs Gillotts' pen factory subemploying and the observance of Saint Monday

---

[1] *Children's Employment Commission (1862)*, *Third Report*, p. 57 ; and L. Faucher, *op. cit.*, p. 501.

[2] *Reports of the Inspectors of Factories*, April 1874, p. 56.

were forbidden.[1] Of a large Wednesbury works it was stated that all the boys, even though they were engaged as assistants to adults, were employed direct by the owner; but the report went on to say that this was exceptional.[2] It was, indeed, only in the trades where a large proportion of unskilled or female workers were engaged that the employer had managed to put down this voluntary absenteeism and had introduced modern methods of management. The skilled craftsmen were not amenable at this time, nor indeed for many years afterwards, to the strict discipline of the present type of factory.[3]

In conclusion, something must be said about the composition of the labour force and of its organization. In Birmingham the brass, gun, engineering, edge-tool, rolling-stock and tinplate trades, the foundries and the mills, employed male labour almost exclusively, although there were a few processes, such as lacquering in the brass shops, japanning in the tinplate-ware factories, and barrel-browning in the gun trade, which were conducted by women. On the other hand, in the manufacture of pens, and in many other trades which made use of the hand-press, while the skilled tool-makers and " setters-up " were men, the greater proportion of the labour force consisted of females. In the button trade the cleavage was mainly between the older and more skilled branches on the one hand as such, the metal- and pearl-button sections, and the newer covered- and linen-button manufacture on the other. The former relied largely on men, the latter on women. In the production of jewellery the same principle of division could be observed; for the men made the high-class jewellery, while women and girls worked on the hand-presses in the manufacture of cheap gilt articles and of chains. Thus in Birmingham, which afforded such an immense variety of occupations, there was a fairly clear distinction between the operations conducted by each of the sexes.[4] The men worked in the heavier and more highly skilled industries ; the women were found in lighter and semi-skilled occupations. But in the Black Country the distinction was by no means so clear.

[1] *Labour and the Poor* in *The Morning Chronicle*, December 16, 1850.
[2] *Report of the Chief Inspector of Factories and Workshops*, October 1888, p. 311.
[3] *Children's Employment Commission (1862), Third Report*, p. 21.
[4] *Labour and the Poor* in *The Morning Chronicle*, October 7, 1850 ; and February 10, 1851 ; *Children's Employment Commission (1862), Third Report*, p. 51 *et seq.*

It is true that the miners, the workers in the pig- and finished-iron works, the locksmiths, the tinplate-ware and edge-tool makers were almost exclusively males; but women worked beside men on the pit-banks, and in the manufacture of nails, chains, saddlery and harness, and hollow-ware. Sometimes a distinction existed, based on a difference of process or on the class of work, as when the men cut out the saddlery and harness and the women did the light stitching.[1] But this was not always the case. It was a source of conflict in the nail trade that women should be set to make the same class of nail as the men at cheaper rates [2]; and the former were found in many occupations, such as the wrought-chain manufacture, which required great strength and endurance.[3] The contrast to the conditions in Birmingham was brought out most clearly by the practice in the brickyards. Whereas in Birmingham women seldom were found employed in them, in the Black Country 75 per cent. of the employees were females.[4] In the former centre the light trades afforded ample employment of a kind peculiarly suitable for women; but in the Black Country, for lack of fitting occupations, they were driven into the heavy industries.

In 1856 it was said that Birmingham had as high a proportion of juvenile labour as any in the country; and this was borne out six years later, when it was stated that work became general in the district at the age of nine or ten, and that about 2000 children under ten years of age were employed in Birmingham alone.[5] Like the adults, whose labours they assisted, they commonly worked twelve hours a day, and even longer in the domestic trades. Boys were employed to assist the casters in the foundries, where they prepared the sand, helped in the filling of the moulds, dusted and cleaned the castings, and carried them to the warehouse. In the forges both boys and girls were set to working the bellows, and in the pig- and finished-iron works there were said to be 1200 boys under the age of thirteen

---

[1] *Children's Employment Commission (1862), Third Report*, p. 7.
[2] *Report of the Chief Inspector of Factories and Workshops*, October 1892, p. 105.
[3] *Work and Wages in East Worcestershire* in *The Globe*, August 12, 1880.
[4] *Newspaper Cuttings* on *Birmingham Industries*, vol. ii., pp. 134-135; E. Burritt, *op. cit.*, p. 205 ; and *Reports of the Inspectors of Factories*, October 1868, p. 123 *et seq.*
[5] *Letter* from Rev. G. M. Yorke to J. Chance (Birmingham Reference Library); *Children's Employment Commission (1862), Third Report*, p. 52; and R. G. Hobbs, *op. cit.*, p. 142.

who worked on the night- as well as the day-shift.[1] Two-thirds of the female employees in the Black Country brickyards were girls between the ages of nine and twelve, who worked twelve hours a day during the week, and often on Sundays as well.[2] In the match and percussion-cap factories the larger part of the labour force consisted of children.[3] Just as in the men's trades boys were employed as assistants by the operatives themselves, so in the light industries—in the manufacture of buttons, jewellery, boxes, toys, umbrella-fittings, and saddlery and harness—girls were engaged by the adult female workers.[4]

The extensive employment of children was not only the consequence of the fact that in most trades which employed skilled workers there were certain processes which could be satisfactorily performed by child assistants; for the actual system of organization was partly responsible. In the domestic trades the children, naturally, would assist their parents; while in the factories the subcontractors had every inducement to obtain the cheapest labour possible. An employer who attempted to subject a whole factory to centralized control might have difficulty in superintending the labour of child employees; but the overhand could exercise a minute supervision over the details of their work. It is no part of our purpose to discuss the obvious social evils connected with child employment; but one point may perhaps be emphasized. Under the conditions of work which prevailed at the time the position of children was much worse than it would be in a modern factory. It has been shown that, both in the domestic workshops and in the majority of the factories, the men and women worked irregular hours, and often tried to concentrate the whole week's labour into three days. Whatever may be said of these habits from the adults' point of view, the effect on the children was most injurious. For, since their hours of work necessarily coincided with those of the adults whom they assisted, they were obliged to work night and day during the latter half of the week. This evil was particularly common in the nail and chain industries.[5] Conditions generally were better in the larger factories, particularly in those where

[1] *Children's Employment Commission (1862), Third Report*, p. 2.
[2] E. Burritt, *op. cit.*, p. 205 *et seq.*
[3] *Children's Employment Commission (1862), First Report*, p. 105 *et seq.*
[4] *Labour and the Poor* in *The Morning Chronicle*, October 7, 1851, and in subsequent issues.
[5] *Reports of the Inspectors of Factories*, April 1874, p. 56.

the subcontracting system did not prevail. Some of the leading factory owners would not permit the employment of children under the age of twelve, and, although the Factory Acts did not apply to this district, several of the larger concerns had established factory schools for their young workers.[1]

In 1860 Birmingham and District was essentially a free labour centre, and was as typically individualist in this respect as in the highly competitive character of its business life. Not only were the industries free from legislative interference, but only in one or two trades did powerful unions exist. The absence of strong labour organizations is to be accounted for by the small scale of the typical enterprise. There was no inevitable conflict of interest between the workshop or small factory proprietor and his employees, and a dissatisfied workman could, in many trades, set up as a garret-master without any considerable capital outlay. In those domestic industries in which the relation of the worker and the factor was practically one of master and servant, the isolation of the men from one another, and the ease with which newcomers could enter the trades, prevented such unions as existed from becoming powerful.[2] On the other hand, many of the larger factories were controlled by benevolent employers, who provided schools for their child workers and gave financial assistance to the sick, superannuation, burial, dress, boot and " gypsy " (*i.e.* picnic) clubs, which commonly were formed among their employees. This paternalism militated against the growth of unions among workers who would otherwise have been drawn into them.

Most of the owners of the workshop or the small factory, moreover, originally had been workmen themselves, and this was a powerful factor operating against labour unrest. It is commonly assumed that the employer who has risen from the ranks is a harder master than one who is drawn from the middle class; but the truth of this assumption is to be doubted. The

---

[1] *Labour and the Poor* in *The Morning Chronicle*, December 2, 1850.

[2] It was said in 1866 of strikes in local industry : " These in the Birmingham trades proper . . . are neither frequent nor disastrous. The gun-makers occasionally suffer, so do the flint-glass makers, and sometimes there are strikes in one or other department of the brass trades. . . . None of these partial strikes, however, are of much practical importance." The non-existence of co-operative manufacture was explained in much the same way as the absence of serious industrial disputes. " Co-operation in manufactures has not been attempted probably because in most trades it is easy for the workman to start on his own account as a ' little master '" (S. Timmins, *op. cit.*, pp. 687-688). There were, however, a few instances of co-operative enterprise in the Black Country manufactures.

former has inevitably a more intimate knowledge of his men's psychology and is thus more capable of dealing with them and of understanding their attitude to himself; while, since he comes from the same social grade and has the same education, the men have no sense of class distinction, which destroys frankness and engenders suspicion. Further, the existence of a buffer between employer and workman in the shape of the overhand tended to make the former a more distant figure in the wage-contract. Indeed, just as the clash of interest between employer and workman was modified in certain types of small-scale industry by the existence of the shop owner, so in the factories this antithesis was obscured by the presence of the subcontractor. Besides this, the subcontracting system provided a stepping-stone by which many men could rise to establish businesses of their own.[1] Naturally all these factors had an adverse influence on trade-union development.

Yet some organizations had been formed. In the nail trade, for instance, in which repeated strikes had occurred between 1830 and 1860, a union of horsenail-makers had been formed in 1850, and had succeeded in raising wages; but it succumbed to a determined attack on the part of the Dudley Nailmasters' Association ten years later.[2] In the chain trade a union, known as the Chain and Trace Makers Anti-Truck and Price Protection Society, had been formed in 1844 to abolish truck, to restrict the number of assistants employed by journeymen and to establish standard rates of pay.[3] But it was found almost impossible to secure permanent agreements in this as in other domestic trades. A list of prices would be followed for a time, and then certain masters would bring pressure on their outworkers to take work at lower prices. This tendency would slowly communicate itself to the whole industry, and wages would fall, until a strike resulted in the re-establishment of the list price.[4]

The lack of powerful labour organizations over the greater part of the local industries was sharply contrasted with their great power in a few isolated skilled trades. Of these the flint-glass industry provides the best example. Here there were two

---

[1] *The Black Country* in *The Edinburgh Review*, April 1863, p. 426.
[2] K. Henn, *History of the Wrought-Nail Trade* (M. Com. Thesis, Birmingham University Library).
[3] G. I. F. Lloyd, *The Cutlery Trades* (1913), p. 405.
[4] *Report of the Chief Inspector of Factories and Workshops*, October 1894, p. 208.

unions, the Flint Glass Makers' Union and the Glass Cutters' Union. Both were powerful associations of highly skilled men. They were strong enough at this time to secure the limitation of the number of apprentices which a master might employ, the ratio being fixed at one apprentice to five workmen. They maintained their unemployed by levies during periods of depression, and they established Tramp Societies to encourage the mobility of labour. These were interesting organizations. The glass-cutters, for instance, paid a penny a mile to unemployed members who left their homes in search of work, and when a member " on tramp " reached a town where glass-cutters lived he received board and lodging free from one of them. Nor was this encouragement to the movement of surplus labour restricted to English glass-making districts. In 1850 the glass-makers had set up an Emigration Committee, whose object was to send six men a year to the United States, and the cutters also used to pay the passage of members to foreign countries. It was said that some Midland workers had been employed in many parts of England, France and the United States. Besides their emigration and unemployment funds, these unions had funds for superannuation, which were raised mainly from the profits of dances, tea-parties and " gypsy " parties.[1]

In the edge-tool trade also a strong union existed, and had secured from the employers a general acceptance of a uniform list of prices.[2] The tinplate-workers were powerfully organized, and all the men in the Britannia-metal shops belonged to a branch of a Sheffield union.[3] In the brass trade the only union which existed was the cockfounding branch, and even this was very small.[4] At Walsall the saddlers who worked in factories were strongly enough organized to enforce a limitation on the number of apprentices; while in the finished-iron works of the Black Country the skilled men, like the shinglers and puddlers, together with their underhands, belonged to local branches of the National Association of Puddlers, Shinglers, Rollers and Millmen.[5] But, except in these and a few other industries, trade unionism had no part of importance to play in the life of the district.

---

[1] *Labour and the Poor* in *The Morning Chronicle*, December 23, 1850.
[2] *Ibid.*, January 20, 1851.
[3] *Ibid.*, February 3, 1851.   [4] *Ibid.*, January 6, 1851.
[5] *General Laws of National Association of Puddlers, Shinglers, etc.* (Wolverhampton Public Library).

PART III

PROSPERITY AND DECLINE
1860-1886

CHAPTER I

THE SEEDS OF CHANGE, 1860-1870

THE seventh decade of the nineteenth century was one of security and of tranquil growth for Birmingham and District. No striking or dramatic series of events disturbed the course of its history. There was no rapid progress in any trade. There was no sudden decline. The tendencies which were active during the years preceding 1860 were still at work; and although there was some change in the relative importance of the various industries during these ten years, the transitions were gradual. Yet, even if the contemporary observer could scarcely have detected them, events did occur which foreshadowed the future transformation, and certain new tendencies appeared which, while of small account at the time, were later to refashion the character of the area.

Before dwelling in detail on the progress of the different trades we must try to view the locality in its general economic setting, and to regard briefly the broad stream of national development which bore along the industries of the area. In the first place, the course of the trade cycle demands attention. In 1860 the country was recovering from the depression into which its industries had been plunged since 1857; but the normal period of active trade was disturbed between 1861 and 1864 by the American Civil War. The indirect economic results of this struggle on local industries will be referred to later; but here certain obvious and immediate influences may be indicated. While some trades, notably the manufacture of needles and buttons, found their American market closed for the duration of the war,[1] others expanded in a marked degree as a direct consequence. The gun trade, for instance, was subject to an enormous increase, while the edge-tool industry received a stimulus from the greater demand for plantation hoes from Egypt and India, where larger quantities of cotton were being grown to remedy the shortage in the American supplies.[2] A boom which was common to most industries in 1864 and 1865 came to an abrupt end in the financial crisis of 1866, which

---

[1] S. Timmins, *op. cit.*, pp. 201, 441; E. Burritt, *op. cit.*, p. 316.
[2] S. Timmins, *op. cit.*, p. 658.

175

was followed by a depression. Not till 1869 was a slight recovery noticeable; but by the next year it was evident that a period of great activity was at hand.

Such, then, was the course of the cyclical movement, with which the local trades were associated in a greater or less degree; and from this we may turn to consider certain legislative enactments which, though applicable to the county as a whole, were of special importance to our area. In 1862 the Companies Act was passed, which consolidated and amended earlier legislation and made incorporation by registration possible. Little advantage was taken of the Act during this period, partly because of the small scale of the majority of local enterprises and partly because of the tradition which favoured private individual enterprise. But a few companies were formed, and among them were some which were of supreme importance to future development. Of more immediate significance, however, was the application during this decade of the principle of the Factory Acts, until then restricted to textile establishments, to the whole field of industry. The first extension beyond the textile and allied trades took place in 1864, when certain dangerous and unhealthy trades were brought within the scope of the regulations. Two small Birmingham industries were affected—viz. the manufacture of wax matches and of percussion caps—both of which employed a large proportion of female and of non-adult labour. As far as the latter trade was concerned, the restriction which the Act imposed on the employment of children had an almost immediate influence on industrial organization; for we learn that mechanical methods of production were adopted by one manufacturer at least almost as soon as the measure had become law.[1] Three years later, when the Factory Acts Extension Act and the Workshops Act were passed, the whole of the area's industry, until then practically free of any form of legislative control, passed under the regulations. The first-named Act, which covered all places where 50 or more persons were employed, and also certain enumerated places, such as glassworks, provided that children between the ages of eight and thirteen should be given 15 hours of schooling a week, and should have their weekly hours of labour limited to 30. The working period of women and young persons between the ages of thirteen and

---

[1] *Reports of the Inspectors of Factories*, October 1865, p. 91.

eighteen was limited to a maximum of 10 hours a day and 58 a week. In the case of workshops—*i.e.* places where less than 50 persons were engaged—young persons and women were permitted to work 10½ hours daily, and the schooling of children need not exceed 10 hours a week. These provisions have been quoted because they were of exceptional importance for our area. It has been shown that, in most of the industries, boys and girls were extensively employed as assistants to adults; and the Acts, though they might not at first be strictly observed, created a shortage of child labour, for the half-time system meant that in some trades twice as many boys and girls would be required as previously. Besides this the Act, in addition, fixed the hours of young persons in factories at 10 hours daily, and although this may not have been less than the normal working day in the larger establishments, the provision meant that adult employees could no longer rely on the assistance of youths after the specified hours. This, in itself, was a strong inducement to the men to modify their habits of irregular work, described in the previous chapter; while the employer for his part received an incentive to take a greater interest in the discipline of his factory.[1] Thus a change in industrial organization was foreshadowed. In the particular case of the mining industry a legal decision, given in the case of Regina *v.* Cope in 1866, tended towards a like result. Up to this time the " butties " had been held responsible for mining accidents; but it was decided that henceforth the onus should be on the consulting engineer, who was, of course, the owner's agent.[2] Thus the proprietors were compelled to concern themselves more intimately with the actual mining operations and to assume some of the functions previously entrusted to the " butties." This legislation tended to have a further effect on factory organization. Many children and youths had up to this time been employed to provide motive-power for the simple machines at which the adult worked, whilst others had performed operations for which mechanical methods could be substituted. The appearance of a shortage of child labour naturally gave a great stimulus to the introduction both of steam-power and of machine tools.

[1] *Reports of the Inspectors of Factories,* October 1865, p. 91 ; *ibid.,* October 1868, p. 239.
[2] T. E. Lones, *op. cit.,* pp. 88-89.

M

During the seventh decade, however, the tendencies which have been indicated were not very obvious; for the adjustment of industry to these new conditions was hindered both by the conservatism of the employers and workers, and by the difficulty of enforcing the Acts, particularly in the workshops.[1] Since the employer did not in most instances engage the non-adult labour in his factory, the overhand often could evade the provisions of the Act by sending a boy over thirteen for the required examination as to age. Having obtained the medical certificate in this way he would then substitute a younger child.[2] Nevertheless the pressure of these enactments was gradually giving rise to new tendencies in industrial organization.

The two developments which knowledge of later events show to have been of most consequence occurred in the gun and iron trades. The history of these industries between 1860 and 1870 stands out in contrast to the gradual changes and uneventful progress which characterized the economic life of the area as a whole; and that contrast can be best emphasized if the other manufactures are first considered, for their history will form a tranquil background, against which the events in the two exceptional industries are outlined. Unfortunately the Census reports do not afford much help in effecting a comparison between the numbers employed in the various industries in 1861 and 1871 respectively, for in some instances the figures are not comparable through differences in compilation; and in certain trades the employment in 1871 was swollen temporarily by the war boom. However, ignoring for a moment the gun trade, we find that during this decade the staples of Birmingham—jewellery, brassfoundry and buttons—still retained their predominant positions; but, relative to each other, their importance changed. Even before 1860 the button trade had been decaying, in spite of the appearance of new varieties of that article, and this tendency continued throughout the decade; so that there were two or three hundred button-makers less in Birmingham in 1871 than there had been ten years before.[3] The decline was not due,

---

[1] *Reports of the Inspectors of Factories*, October 1868, pp. 198, 265, 268, 270.

[2] *Newspaper Cuttings* on *Birmingham Industries*, vol. i., p. 55.

[3] *Census of England and Wales*, 1861, vol. ii., pp. 510, 513 ; 1871, vol. ii., pp. 321, 324.

Comparisons based on the Census returns between the amount of employment afforded by the various local industries at different periods should be considered in connection with the note to Table V. in the Appendix.

as in the middle of the century, to any change of fashion, but rather to the growth of industry in foreign countries. During the period of the Civil War the American market was lost, the gilt and the vegetable-ivory button trade was seriously affected by German competition after 1863,[1] and in 1867 it was reported, with particular reference to the French industry, that the Continental button had advanced, while that of Birmingham was stationary.[2] But this was not all. Towards the end of the decade the shortage of pearl-shell, due to the failure of the South American supplies, brought depression to one of the chief sections of the trade.[3]

In the brass industry, however, progress was maintained. A large number of new firms were established in the heavy branch of the trade. The demand for wire increased during the sixties, when the cables manufactured in Birmingham were successfully laid across the Atlantic.[4] The growing popularity of metal bedsteads meant a larger output of brass-cased tubes, and the rolling mills benefited by the continued extension of stamped brassfoundry. Nor were the branches which were concerned with finished products stationary. Stimulated not only by the increased use of gas-fittings, but also by the introduction into Birmingham in 1861 of paraffin-lamp manufacture,[5] the " lighting " section made particularly great progress. In consequence the numbers in the industry, which were estimated to have increased from 8000 in 1861 to 9500 in 1866, probably were not less than 10,000 in 1870.[6]

The jewellery trade was subject to a much greater expansion. In 1860, as we have seen, there were within the borough of Birmingham some 7000 to 7500 persons, including electro-platers and those engaged in subsidiary processes, in the industry; by 1866 the number had increased to 9000; and by 1870-1871, although exactly comparable figures are not available, employment had

[1] S. Timmins, op. cit., p. 432 et seq.; Newspaper Cuttings on Birmingham Industries, vol. ii., pp. 212-213.
[2] W. C. Aitken, Report to the Birmingham Chamber of Commerce on the International Exhibition at Paris, 1867, p. 43.
[3] Newspaper Cuttings on Birmingham Industries, vol. i., pp. 87-88.
[4] W. E. Hipkins, The Wire Rope and its Applications (1896), p. 10.
[5] S. Timmins, op. cit., pp. 336-337.
[6] Ibid., p. 362. The figures cover employment in Birmingham and Aston only. In Staffordshire, Warwickshire and Worcestershire the total number in the brass and allied trades increased from 10,700 in 1861 to 11,400 in 1871 (Census of England and Wales, 1861, vol. ii., p. 469 et seq.; 1871, vol. ii., p. 315 et seq.).

reached probably 9500 to 10,000.[1] Thus, in consequence of favourable fashions and of the national prosperity, the jewellery trade had now equalled, or even surpassed, brassfoundry, and both of these ranked far above the declining button manufacture. A significant change, however, occurred in the relative importance of the different branches. In the early sixties the production of gold jewellery and of electro-plate had increased at the expense of silver-ware, which had risen in price since the gold discoveries of 1849 and 1851. In the middle of the decade, however, this tendency began to be modified by the silver discoveries in Nevada, in consequence of which the world's average annual output of that metal rose from nearly 29,000,000 ounces between 1851-1860 to 35,000,000 ounces between 1861-1865, and to 43,000,000 ounces between 1866-1870.[2] After 1866, therefore, the silver branch of the trade expanded to a much greater extent than the gold section, though the advance of the latter was far from negligible, and the last few years of the decade saw the beginning of the silver jewellery period. Those who were adversely affected by this development were the manufacturers of gilt and imitation jewellery, together with producers of low-standard (12 and 9 carat) gold wares.[3] Meanwhile the increasing use of precious stones brought about a growth in the stone-setting section; and just before 1870 a new manufacture, that of mayoral chains and civic insignia, became a prominent branch of the jewellery trade—a development which was associated with the rise of the municipalities.[4] Thus, if the industry as a whole made a marked advance during the decade, that progress was not shared in an equal degree by all its branches.

The allied trade of coin manufacture also increased. Carried on intermittently by only one concern before 1860, the industry was joined by another producer, and was busily engaged throughout the seventh decade on minting work for the British, Colonial and Continental Governments.[5] By 1870, however, prosperity

---

[1] S. Timmins, *op. cit.*, pp. 457, 495 ; *Census of England and Wales*, 1871, vol. ii., pp. 322, 325.

[2] J. C. Roche, *op. cit.*, p. 26 *et seq.*

[3] *Ibid.*, p. 28 ; C. J. Woodward, *Manufacturing Industries* in *British Association Handbook* (Birmingham Meeting, 1886), pp. 188-190.

[4] *Newspaper Cuttings* on *Birmingham Industries*, vol. i., p. 118 ; C. J. Woodward, *op. cit.*, p. 188.

[5] " Changes of dynasties abroad rendered new coinage necessary ; while established Governments were recoining the old money in circulation " (S. Timmins, *op. cit.*, p. 555 *et seq.*).

was being threatened by the competition of the Government Mint, which had begun to produce coins not only for domestic but for foreign requirements; and the "itch for Government manufacturing" in this and in another industry was arousing the opposition of Birmingham's industrialists.

At the same time the minor industries of Birmingham showed for the most part a steady growth, while the manufacture of pens, screws, bedsteads and wire products flourished exceedingly. To these trades new markets were thrown open by the development of the Colonies and by the liberal tariff policies of the Continental Governments, particularly the French. The growth of telegraphy and the increased use of wire ropes in collieries gave a stimulus to the local wire-drawing and wire-rope industries, and there was an advance in engineering. The more extensive employment of steam-power in the factories was partly responsible for this expansion; but it was due also to the growth of trades which required machinery, like those producing wire, tubes, stamped and pressed goods, and, most important of all, guns. During the sixties one engineering firm alone, Messrs Tangyes, developed from a small concern with 28 employees to one of the largest in the town, and found employment in 1870 for nearly 1000 persons.[1] Like the other engineering establishments of the period, the scope of its manufacture was wide, and it produced steam-pumps, pulley blocks and hydraulic presses. Another product which had been taken up by the Birmingham engineering trade was the manufacture of marine engines.[2]

While these trades were growing in size, and were steadily adding new branches, a group of manufactures of a very different type was slowly emerging from obscurity—viz. the food and drink trades. A vinegar company had been established in 1860, and during the next ten years one or two others grew up; while towards the end of the decade the brewing industry showed signs of change. Before this time such brewing as took place in Birmingham was conducted in the household, or in a few concerns which employed only 20 persons; but by 1870 projects for establishing great breweries were in the air and a

---

[1] *Newspaper Cuttings* on *Birmingham Industries*, vol. ii., p. 130 ; and Sir R. Tangye, *The Rise of a Great Industry*, 1903, pp. 80-117.
[2] *A Factory of Quick Revolution Engines* (Belliss & Morcom Ltd.), 1908.

transformation of the trade was imminent.[1] The cocoa and chocolate manufacture had been carried on since 1835, but it was still of small importance.

With the exception of button manufacture, then, the trades which were specially associated with Birmingham expanded during the decade, although no sudden or dramatic developments occurred in any of those which have been mentioned. About the Black Country industries and about those which were shared between that district and Birmingham itself it is less possible to generalize. Some of them went ahead more rapidly than any of Birmingham's typical trades, with the possible exception of jewellery; but several seemed stationary or on the decline. The lock industry, which had been in a far from satisfactory condition in 1860, was counted among the most prosperous before the end of the decade. In spite of its loss, in certain classes of locks, of its once important American market,[2] the home and Colonial trade had grown so that the numbers engaged in the manufacture in 1870 were well ahead of those of a decade previously.[3] The allied branch of safe manufacture was subject to an equally great advance.[4] The increase in exports to the Colonies also was responsible for a great development in the saddlery and harness trade [5]; but the Census figures, which show an increase in employment of over 2000 between 1861-1871, exaggerate the growth which occurred up to 1870, because numbers [6] were temporarily swelled in the Censal year in consequence of the Franco-German War. The flint-glass trade was equally progressive. Exports expanded suddenly during the early sixties, and although the high level of 1864-1865 was not maintained during the rest of the decade, in 1869-1870 they were in value 50 per cent. above those of 1859-1860. The heavy branch of the industry also grew, and consequently the number

---

[1] *Newspaper Cuttings* on *Birmingham Industries*, vol. ii., p. 141; *The Pictorial World*, March 31, 1887; and *Midland Captains of Industry* in *Birmingham Gazette and Express*, March 19, 1907.

[2] E. Burritt, *op. cit.*, p. 197.

[3] The Census reports show an increase from 3700 to 5200 between 1861-1871; but other authorities place employment during the sixties at a considerably higher figure (*Census of England and Wales*, 1861, vol. ii., p. 468 *et seq.*, and 1871, vol. ii., p. 315).

[4] R. G. Hobbs, *op. cit.*, p. 463.

[5] *Midland Captains of Industry* in *Birmingham Gazette and Express*, September 17, 1907, and September 23 and October 14, 1908.

[6] *Census of England and Wales*, 1861, vol. ii., p. 467 *et seq.*; 1871, vol. ii., p. 313 *et seq.*

of glassworkers in the district rose from about 4500 to 5400 during the inter-Censal period.[1]

Thus the period brought added prosperity to the staples of Stourbridge, Walsall and Willenhall; but for a leading industry of Wolverhampton and Bilston it was less favourable. This was the tinplate- japanned- and papier-mâché-ware trade. The papier-mâché section had long been failing, and so its continued decline was not surprising; but depression in the other manufactures requires an explanation. Producing a great variety of elaborate and expensive articles for domestic use, this branch had been very prosperous up to the middle of the century. By the sixties, however, its products, particularly the japanned ware, began to be displaced by electro-plate, and although manufacturers turned to the cheaper types of article, and occupied themselves with new products, such as japanned coal vases, the industry was suffering in 1870 from this change of fashion.[2]

The hand-wrought nail and chain industries, which bore such a close resemblance to one another in the physical conditions of production, pursued opposite courses. The tendency of the former to give way to the machine-made-nail trade was accelerated, and branches which previously had been unaffected began to suffer. During the fifties and early sixties the horse nail-makers, who, being uninjured by the competition of machines, seemed in a secure position, succeeded, by determined efforts on the part of their union, in forcing a large increase in wages from their masters. But their success was short-lived; for the incentive which was thus given to the introduction of machinery resulted in the successful production of certain types of horse-nails in factories, and after 1864 there was a slump in wages. About the same time the machinery for producing the ordinary type of cut nail was improved, and it now became possible to cut four nails from the iron strip at each operation, whereas previously only one had been produced.[3] With their competitive power thus strengthened the factory owners of Wolverhampton and Birmingham entered upon a period of greater prosperity; while henceforth practically every branch of the

[1] *Census of England and Wales*, 1861, vol. ii., p. 469 *et seq.*; 1871, vol. ii., p. 315 *et seq.*

[2] G. Lindsey, *British Manufacturing Industries* (1878), vol. iii., p. 175 *et seq.*; W. H. Jones, *op. cit.*, chaps. vii.-viii.

[3] S. Timmins, *op. cit.*, pp. 115-116 and 613 *et seq.*

unfortunate hand-wrought trade had to face the menace of machine production. In 1871 the nail-makers in Warwickshire, Worcestershire and Staffordshire numbered 17,700, as compared with 19,400 at the previous Census.[1] As these figures include the factory workers (*i.e.* those employed in making cut and machine-wrought nails), who had increased in numbers during the decade, the decline in the older section of the industry was greater than the Census returns indicate. The chain and anchor trade, on the other hand, was subject to a great expansion in consequence of the development of shipping and of agriculture, which were its two chief customers, and the employment in the industry rose by 25 per cent. between 1861-1871.[2] Apart from the stimulus which was given by the Civil War, the increase of the export trade, together with agricultural prosperity at home, was responsible for a steady advance of the edge-tool manufacture [3]; while the hollow-ware trades expanded,[4] and the nut-and-bolt manufacture was stimulated by the development of engineering and of constructional ironwork.

Nor did the outlying districts escape from the current of change. By 1870 needle-making had completed its long period of migration and was firmly established in the Redditch neighbourhood.[5] But difficulties were beginning to appear. Swelled to large proportions just after the Civil War, the American sales had dwindled by the end of the decade; while the manufacturers of Aix began to compete with local firms, particularly in the lower grades of product.[6] In spite of these adverse factors, however, and although the rise of sewing-machines was affecting the demand for hand-sewing needles, the trade had nevertheless increased in size during the inter-Censal period, the numbers having risen from 3600 to 4300.[7] At Coventry the watch trade showed a much smaller expansion.

[1] *Census of England and Wales*, 1861, vol. ii., p. 469 *et seq.* ; 1871, vol. ii., pp. 315 *et seq.*

[2] *Ibid.* ; and 1871, vol. ii., pp. 315, 318.

[3] S. Timmins, *op. cit.*, p. 658 ; and *Newspaper Cuttings* on *Birmingham Industries*, vol. i., p. 114.

[4] W. H. Jones, *op. cit.*, chaps. viii.-xii.

[5] When Messrs Kirby, Beard & Co. transferred their business from Long Crendon to Redditch, four-fifths of the Buckinghamshire needle-makers migrated with them (W. Shrimpton, *op. cit.*, p. 25).

[6] E. Burritt, *op. cit.*, p. 316 ; *Midland Captains of Industry* in *Birmingham Gazette and Express*, December 23, 1908 ; and W. C. Aitken, *op. cit.*, p. 45 *et seq.*

[7] *Census of England and Wales*, 1861, vol. ii., p. 474 *et seq.* ; 1871, vol. ii., pp. 320, 324, and *Newspaper Cuttings* on *Birmingham Industries*, vol. ii., p. 9.

Thus, over a wide range of local industries no important new tendencies were introduced during the sixties. In the expanding trades, even where the growth was large, the forces at work were similar to those which had existed before 1860. The industries which were on the decline in the earlier period, such as the hand-wrought-nail, button, silver-plate and papier-mâché trades, continued to pursue their downward course. Further, in the manufactures which have been discussed no substantial development occurred in mechanical equipment and the scale of production. Nor in the foreign markets which the district served were any great changes evident. It is true that certain ominous signs had appeared. The American Civil War represented for several industries the end of their export trade to the United States, for after the struggle the Government began to impose heavier tariffs on imported manufactures. Continental competition, moreover, which had affected the button industry first about 1850, had become increasingly keen during the next twenty years; while in the sixties gilt jewellery began to be imported into England, and European producers began to compete in foreign markets in such widely different manufactures as needles and rolling-stock.[1] But this rivalry was merely incipient and was serious in only one or two trades. In 1867, indeed, it was reported that Birmingham manufacturers had little to fear from foreigners, as far as the majority of their products was concerned[2]; and even in the few cases in which Continental rivalry had caused a loss of trade, compensation had been found in the rapidly increasing demand from the Colonies. There was, in fact, no hint of danger from abroad in most of the contemporary accounts of industrial development.

In two industries, however, events of moment occurred which did much to modify the general impression of easy prosperity and tranquil growth. The gun trade, to take the first instance, was subject to great changes, which were not only to have far-reaching effects on its future, but which were to exercise a powerful influence on the industrial structure of the area as a whole. In the early years of the decade the most obvious feature

[1] S. Timmins, op. cit., p. 437 et seq., pp. 201, 455 ; Midland Captains of Industry in Birmingham Gazette and Express, December 23, 1908 ; Newspaper Cuttings on Birmingham Industries, vol. i., p. 123.
[2] W. C. Aitken, Report to the Birmingham Chamber of Commerce on the International Exhibition at Paris, 1867, p. 21 et seq.

of the industry was its exceptional prosperity, occasioned by
the call for arms from America. Hindered at first by the embargo
on shipments during 1861, the expansion of the trade in 1862,
when the prohibition was removed, brought a period of un-
exampled progress to the gun-makers. In that year alone at least
380,000 guns were sent to America from Birmingham, which,
before the end of the war, had exported about 730,000 to that
market.[1] Even before peace had been declared, however, the
demand had slackened, as the American factories had become
capable of dealing with the output required; and in 1864 depression seized upon the swollen industry. The stimulus which
it received from the Prussian-Danish War in 1865-1866, and
from the Austro-Prussian War in 1868, was slight and short-
lived; and in the meantime changes had occurred in foreign
producing centres. In 1860 a French report had declared that
Saint-Étienne could not compete with Birmingham because
the English had the advantage of manufacturing more cheaply.
Indeed their methods were so economical that even Liège, the
chief centre of the trade in Europe, imported a great number of
component parts.[2] But the rise in prices and the interruption in
the supply of arms to the Continent during the term of the
Civil War had been a boon to the Belgian competitors, and had
induced other countries to take up the production of the arms
they required.[3] Besides this, the Americans, after 1864, began
to supply arms, which were produced by mechanical methods
in large factories, not only to their home market, but to countries
which previously had been served by Birmingham. Even the
British market was invaded by foreign makers. Large quantities
of unfinished parts of rifles were imported into the country;
while the bayonet and sword trades were lost almost entirely to
Germany.[4] Nor was the military trade the only one to suffer.
During the period of active demand for service arms the gun-
makers had neglected the sporting-gun section; and when the
demand for the former fell off and the makers reverted to the
" birding trade " they found it difficult to win back their
customers, many of whom were now served by the Belgians.[5]

[1] S. Timmins, op. cit., p. 418.
[2] Artifex and Opifex, The Causes of Decay in a British Industry (1907),
pp. 5-6, 37.
[3] E. Lander, The Birmingham Gun Trade, 1869, pp. 4-8.
[4] Ibid., pp. 4, 8, 20.
[5] F. W. Hackwood, Wednesbury Workshops, chap. vii.

So, after a great expansion between 1861 and 1864, employment steadily decreased throughout the decade.

Yet however serious the growth of foreign competition may have been, a fact of far greater significance was the appearance during the sixties of a definite cleavage between the military- and the sporting-gun sections of the industry. In 1860 there was no sharp contrast between the methods of production pursued in those two branches; but by the end of the decade, while sporting guns continued to be made by traditional methods in little workshops, a great part of the military trade was being conducted in large factories equipped with plants of complex machinery. The manufacture of military rifles, in fact, was ceasing to be the concern of the craftsman and was becoming a task for the engineer. By 1870 the change was not complete, for the factories were not yet capable of satisfying the entire demand. But the old Birmingham gun trade had lost what only a short time previously had been its chief source of profit.

In order to obtain a clear idea of the cause of this transformation we must look back to the early fifties.[1] Before the outbreak of the Crimean War the attention of the Government had been called to the American method of producing guns by machinery on what was called " the interchangeable principle "; for it appeared that guns manufactured in this way and assembled from standardized parts were suitable for military purposes. Moreover, if machine-production were resorted to, output could then be increased more rapidly in time of war than by the Birmingham methods of manufacture. Under the influence of a report drawn up by a Commission which visited the Government factory at Springfield in 1853 the British War Office decided to erect an establishment at Enfield where guns might be made on the interchangeable principle. The opposition not only of the members of the gun trade but of all the active exponents of *laissez-faire* was aroused by this proposal; but the outbreak of the Crimean War led to the erection of a factory at Enfield on a much larger scale than had been originally intended. Machinery was brought from America and the first guns were turned out in 1858. The parts of which these arms were made

---

[1] For the following account of the gun trade the author is chiefly indebted to the *Private History of the Birmingham Small Arms Company, Limited*; also S. Timmins, *op. cit.*, p. 381 *et seq.*

were produced in a series of operations on special machines, and although a certain amount of hand-labour was needed for finishing off, and for assembling, the work of the skilled craftsman was largely dispensed with.

The Birmingham gun - makers naturally viewed this new factory with alarm, and a group of them soon took steps to meet the danger to their prosperity. In 1854 an association, known as the Birmingham Small Arms Trade, had been formed. It consisted originally of sixteen firms, which had been selected by the Government to supply arms on the outbreak of the Crimean War, and which had come to a mutual agreement to fix the wages of their workers and to determine selling prices. This step had been necessary, because in times of excited trade a master, having contracted to deliver arms at a certain price, often found himself deserted by his workers, who had been drawn away from his service by offers of higher wages. But soon the association had begun to act for other purposes. It was through its efforts that the Proof Act of 1855 received its form, and, most important of all, it was the members of this association who organized a company in 1861 to erect a factory at Small Heath, and to equip it with machinery capable of producing interchangeable arms comparable to those manufactured at Enfield. " Stocking " machinery was purchased from Massachusetts and rifling and boring machinery from Leeds, and thus the famous Birmingham Small Arms Company, Limited, was set upon its long career. The critical nature of this enterprise was fully realized by those who had undertaken it, and in 1864, before the new company had completed a contract, it was declared in a letter from the Chairman to Lord Palmerston: " If failure attends the present effort, the trade will be taken from them [*i.e.* from the Birmingham gun-makers], either by the cheap hand-labour of Belgium, or by the vast mechanical resources of the American gun manufacturers." [1]

The fact that it was in the manufacture of rifles that large-scale production first made its appearance in the local engineering industry is in conformity with what we should expect. The conditions which are necessary for such forms of enterprise were all present, inasmuch as very large quantities of standardized commodities were to be produced. But the division between the

[1] July 30, 1864.

two sections of the trade, which was an inevitable result, was not without grave disadvantages. Under the old system the gun-makers could devote themselves to the sporting demand in times of slack military trade, and although fluctuations could not be wholly obviated within the industry, their effects could be modified. But the new cleavage meant not only that the old gun trade was robbed of a large group of customers, but that factories were erected which, after being swelled to a great size during periods of active trade, were left without any means of employing their plants when military demands fell off. The difficulty of adapting the specialized tools and machinery to the production of other commodities, indeed, left the military-gun manufacturers during slack periods with a heavy burden of over-head charges. Further, the recruitment of suitable labour for their new factories was no easy task, and one instance of this may be quoted, as it illustrates the difficulties which attended the introduction of mechanical methods into old-established trades. A number of Darlaston lock and spring filers were engaged by the Birmingham Small Arms Company, and a struggle immediately took place between them and their foreman, who tried, with little success, to induce them to give up old-time methods and prejudices. " These men still followed the practice of a hundred years previously . . . they still resorted to ' fiddle-drilling ' (i.e. bow and breast drilling), when, by going a few yards, they could use power-machinery. They still used tallow-dip candles (purchased by themselves) when tempering springs, though the Company had offered to supply them with best Russian tallow free. They would not do tempering after ten o'clock in the morning, owing to their superstitious belief . . . that springs tempered after that hour would break." Under such circumstances it can well be understood why masters in other skilled trades, where the advantages of mechanical production were somewhat less obvious, should refrain from introducing machinery.

In spite of these difficulties the prospects of the Company at the time of its formation seemed favourable; for fundamental changes in the type of arm used by the military forces of Europe were imminent. This point must receive a word of notice. In 1855 the Enfield rifle had superseded the Minie rifle and the old percussion musket in the British services. These three types were all large-bore muzzle-loaders, fired by percussion caps. By the end of that decade, however, experiments were being made with breech-loading rifles, firing cartridges which carried their own ignition. Various types of breech-loading carbines were issued experimentally to the cavalry between 1859 and 1861; but the British Government was anxious to find a means of converting its Enfield muzzle-loaders into breech-loaders. In 1866 it was finally decided to adopt the Snider breech action and to convert the whole supply of Enfields. This proved a turning-point in industrial history. Although the old gun trade had suffered before this from the competition of the Government factory at Enfield, the cleavage between the military and the " birding " work till then had only been incipient. As the new Company had not been ready to begin work the workshops had received the full benefit of the American War, and had dealt with three-fifths of the order for 50,000 Enfields which had been placed by the Turkish Government in 1862, while early in 1866, on the other hand, the Company had considered taking up the manufacture of double-barrelled sporting guns. This latter project was, however, abandoned when the Government in the same year ordered the Company to convert 100,000 Enfields into Snider breech-loaders, and the matter was not seriously considered again for half-a-century. The old gun trade received no benefit from the great orders which the Government placed in 1866—a new phenomenon in its history. As was declared at the time, there was a boom in Government work, but the old gun trade remained plunged in depression. A new stage in the history of a Birmingham staple had begun; but there was still to be one final period of coalescence before the two branches of the industry were irrevocably sundered.

In spite of its encouraging start the military-arms factory failed to maintain its prosperity during the rest of the decade. Having completed its first Government contract in 1868 the Company found that it was impossible to keep its plant occupied on the small orders which were then received from the British, Turkish and Colonial Governments. A large order which was obtained from Russia could not be entirely carried out owing to disputes between the parties to the contract; while other European Powers, which had adopted the breech-loader, placed their orders on the Continent. The absence of British Government orders after 1868 was to be accounted for partly by the fact that the War Office was considering the adoption into the services of the small-bore breech-loader; but it had become evident that the existence of the Government factory meant that the normal demand for the services could be dealt with at Enfield, and that the trade would be called on only in times of exceptionally great demands. Even at this early stage the burden of fluctuations was being thrown on to the shoulders of the private manufacturers.

The repercussions of the developments which have been described were far-reaching. The introduction of the breech-loader, for instance, gave a stimulus to the ammunition trade, and by 1870 there were several firms in Birmingham engaged in manufacturing cartridge cases, which provided a new market for the brass-rolling mills. But the effects were wider than this. It cannot be too strongly emphasized that the Birmingham Small Arms Company was the first of the local factories to turn out highly finished complicated metal articles by mass-production methods. This meant that certain kinds of complex machinery began to appear for the first time in large quantities in a Birmingham factory, while new methods came into existence for the production of standardized parts. For instance, it now paid to sink dies and to stamp out rifle parts which previously had been forged by the smith on the anvil. Thus the coming of the interchangeable rifle brought not only the machine-shop and the tool-room in their modern forms, but also a development of hot stamping. This process, previously confined to such products as keys and edge tools, now began to play a much more important part in Birmingham's manufacturing operations.

If the significance of the changes which occurred in gun manufacture was recognized by contemporaries, the forces which were working to transform the basic trades of the area—the iron and coal trades—were less obvious. To the casual observer, indeed, they appeared to be continuing their course of steady expansion, and the available statistics seem at first sight to bear out that conclusion. The output of pig-iron, which amounted to 470,000 tons in 1860, after falling during the next year, rose to reach a maximum of 693,000 tons in 1865; and, though it declined during the depression of 1867-1868, it stood at 570,000 tons in 1869.[1] This branch of industry, in fact, made a

---

[1] R. Hunt, *op. cit.*, 1865, p. 69; 1869, p. 76.

substantial advance. The finished-iron industry was similarly affected, as may be judged from the increase in the number of puddling furnaces in operation. There was a rise from 1588 in 1860 to 2116 in 1865 [1]; and though a decline occurred during the depressed years, the number at work during the latter half of the decade was well above that of 1860 to 1863. But the expansion was greater in the coal industry, which appears to have pursued a steady course of development without being adversely affected during the years of depression, and the output rose from about 5,250,000 tons in 1860 to nearly 9,000,000 tons in 1869.[2] The apparent independence of the local coal trade from the fluctuations experienced by the iron industry during this period is remarkable, for in earlier times their fortunes had been intimately connected. The explanation is doubtless to be found in the fact that, owing to the development of other manufactures and to the growth of the population of the area, the relative importance of the demands of the iron trade had declined, and that when it was depressed, there was less difficulty in finding alternative markets, especially in view of the improved transport facilities.[3]

Besides an expansion of output the decade witnessed important technical improvements, which seemed to confirm an estimate of the progressive character of the basic industries. There was a great advance in mining equipment. In the early sixties shafts began to be fitted with cages and guides; covers were provided for the cages; the use of safety-chains increased; single-link chains were superseded; wire ropes took the place of hempen ropes; the winding-gear was greatly improved and steam-brakes came to be more generally employed; while the construction of inclined planes, which permitted the use of trams and tubs, was pressed forward. Owing to these improvements, and to a greater use of timber, the loss of life in mining accidents was considerably reduced during the decade.[4] In the pig-iron industry the hot blast came into more general use, while the practice of closing the furnace top and of using waste gases

[1] R. Hunt, op. cit., 1865, p. 80.
[2] The production in 1860 was probably underestimated. Many of the smaller mines evidently had ceased to produce during the decade; for there was a decline from 422 in 1859 to 326 in 1869 in the number of South Staffordshire mines (R. Hunt, op. cit., 1869, pp. 96, 111).
[3] T. E. Lones, op. cit., p. 105.
[4] Ibid., p. 69 et seq. and p. 82 et seq.

to heat the blast, which had been first tried in the district at Darlaston, spread to all parts of the Black Country.[1] About the same time an improved type of coke-oven came to be employed; and these developments resulted in a greater economy in the use of fuel. In consequence, the cost of producing a ton of South Staffordshire pig declined from £3, 11s. 11d. in 1857 to £2, 12s. 10d. in 1869.[2]

Moreover, the future prosperity of the iron-producers seemed more assured because of the expansion between 1860 and 1870 of the heavy iron-using trades. It was particularly rapid during the years of depressed prices which followed the crisis of 1866, for the low cost of iron encouraged its use for constructional purposes.[3] New plants for dealing with heavy forgings were laid down at Hales Owen and elsewhere, and there was a great advance in the manufacture of iron bridges, gas-holders, boilers, and of all kinds of constructional work; while the amalgamation in 1867 of the two great Wednesbury firms—the Patent Shaft and Axletree Company and Lloyd Fosters, which produced not only their own raw and semi-products but also railway wheels, bridges, girders and tyres—marked an important stage in the progress of the manufacture of railway material in the district.[4] In the galvanized-sheet industry, too, there was a marked expansion. Demand had been stimulated at one time by the sale of galvanized sheets by auction in the Colonies; and, by the sixties, this method of attracting customers had had its desired effect.[5] Meanwhile the tube trade had been favourably influenced by the spread of gaslighting, and the largest firm, which had produced 4,200,000 feet of tube in 1858, increased its output to 5,300,000 in 1865 and to 6,700,000 in 1871.[6]

Yet if, on the surface, the fortunes of the heavy trade seemed secure enough, actually there was cause for alarm. The great increase in the coal output would seem to rule out one industry at any rate from the list of those threatened, but that was not the case. The figures quoted cover the whole of South Staffordshire and Worcestershire, and most of the increased output was due, not to a great expansion in the yield of the older coal

---

[1] T. E. Lones, *op. cit.*, p. 84.
[2] *Ibid.*, p. 85 ; and F. W. Hackwood, *Wednesbury Workshops*, pp. 117-119.
[3] S. Griffiths, *Guide to the Iron Trade of Great Britain*, pp. 12-13.
[4] F. W. Hackwood, *Wednesbury Workshops*, chaps. xi. and xii.
[5] W. H. Jones, *op. cit.*, p. 164 *et seq.*
[6] F. W. Hackwood, *Wednesbury Workshops*, chap. xiii.

N

centres, but to the development of the Cannock mines and to the opening of new pits in the Rowley neighbourhood.[1] As an illustration we may quote the statement, made in 1872, that the population of Chase Town had increased from 200 to 2000 during the previous ten years, owing to the rapid increase in the number of collieries. It is interesting to remark, in passing, that the mining population of Cannock was still migratory. Men flocked into the mines during busy periods, and returned to other occupations in the neighbourhood when a depression came.[2] While these new districts were growing, many of the older mining centres were on the decline as a result of the exhaustion of the thick coal and of the flooding of the mines. The trouble from water will be dealt with at length in the next chapter. Here it is sufficient to state that since the fifties the Dudley and Tipton districts had been water-logged, and efforts to clear the mines by co-operative pumping had not met with complete success. At Oldbury it was said that the pits were rapidly approaching exhaustion; while, most significant of all, the population of Bilston actually declined between 1861-1871 in consequence of the closing down of the local mines and of ironworks which depended on them.[3]

Since it is not possible to separate the output of the Black Country from that of South Staffordshire as a whole, other forms of evidence cannot be reinforced by statistical data in the case of the coal industry; but the exhaustion of the local supplies of raw materials can be illustrated by the figures for the production of ironstone, which was not mined in any considerable quantity in the Cannock region. In 1860 the ore obtained from our area amounted to 786,000 tons, and during the boom in the middle of the decade the output rose to 949,000 tons [4]—nearly 9 per cent. of the total British production. This was the largest annual output of ore which had ever been obtained in South Staffordshire, and the figure was never again reached. After 1865 there was a sudden decline, and the output was only 341,000 tons in 1868 and 350,000 tons in 1869.[5] An increasing quantity of ore had, in consequence, to be brought from Northampton-

[1] T. E. Lones, *op. cit.*, pp. 90, 99-100.
[2] R. G. Hobbs, *op. cit.*, p. 319.
[3] *Ibid.*, p. 142 ; *Census of England and Wales*, 1861, vol. i., p. 119 ; 1871, vol. i., p. 352 ; T. E. Lones, *op. cit.*, p. 103 *et seq.*
[4] Output for 1864.
[5] R. Hunt, *op. cit.*, 1864, p. 52 ; 1868, p. 63 ; 1869, p. 62.

shire, North Staffordshire and the West Coast,[1] and the local iron trade was thus forced to bear the additional burden of transport charges on one of its chief raw materials.

It could ill afford to do so. The production of pig-iron had increased, but not nearly so rapidly as in the newer centres. In the depressed period, 1860-1862, South Staffordshire produced 11·1 per cent. of the total British output; in the active years, 1863-1865, 14·3 per cent.; and in the second depression, 1866-1869, 10·9 per cent. These figures are of interest, because the fluctuations which they indicate are what we should expect from an old centre which was struggling to maintain itself against better-equipped rivals. During periods of active trade the output of South Staffordshire rose more rapidly than that of other districts, because it possessed a greater surplus capacity than they ; a surplus capacity which was the legacy of its earlier prosperity, but which could not be worked profitably during the lean years. In other words, the Black Country had more blast-furnaces than other centres which were on the margin, and a movement in the price of iron had consequently an exceptionally great effect on the number of plants in operation.[2]

The reputation and quality of the South Staffordshire finished iron were maintaining that section of the industry; but complaints of the disadvantage at which the long haul to the coast placed the local ironmasters became louder as the decade progressed. " A few years ago," it was said in 1866, " South Staffordshire had the entire north European trade; but it cannot now compete with Middlesbrough." [3] The London market, moreover, was being severely contested by the northern manufacturers, and even France and Belgium are reported to have supplied it with iron in the depressed years.[4]

But the most significant development of all, though it had little effect on output during the sixties, was the coming of the new steel. Bessemer converters had been operated since the late fifties, and between 1863 and 1867 Dr Siemens carried on an experimental works in Great Hampton Street, Birmingham. His success resulted in the establishment of the first open-hearth plant at Landore, South Wales, in 1868; while in the Black

---

[1] T. E. Lones, *op. cit.*, p. 90.
[2] *Reports of the Inspectors of Factories*, October 1868, p. 181.
[3] S. Timmins, *op. cit.*, pp. 73-74.
[4] *Ibid.*, p. 74 ; G. T. Lawley, *History of Bilston* (1868), p. 83.

Country an early attempt to manufacture Bessemer steel was made by the Patent Shaft and Axletree Company, which constructed a works for producing steel tyres and axles.[1] But, largely through the prejudice against its use, steel was made only in small quantities during the latter part of the decade.

The threat (and it was no more at this time) which the introduction of steel held out to the Midland iron trade was based on the fact that only non-phosphoric ores could be used in the converter or in the open-hearth furnace, and these were only found, as far as Great Britain was concerned, in Cumberland. Consequently steel-makers were compelled to set up their works either in the neighbourhood of the scanty British supplies or near the coast, where they would be conveniently situated for obtaining the imports of Spanish hæmatite. Thus, inevitably, Cumberland, South Wales and the North-East Coast tended to become the new steel centres. But this new factor did not exercise much influence on the metal trades during the sixties, and the only use in which steel had supplanted wrought-iron to any large extent was in the manufacture of rails. Iron rails were not produced in quantity in South Staffordshire, which was, therefore, not affected by the change; and although steel plates had been rolled and a steel ship built as early as 1859, it was long before iron plates, which were among the chief products of the Black Country, were superseded.[2] The same was true of most of the other types of iron which were produced there. Nevertheless it was evident that steel would prove a more formidable rival to wrought-iron in the near future, and that Staffordshire had not the advantages which would attract the new plants.

Thus the approaching exhaustion of the local supplies of ore, the flooding of many of the most valuable thick coal-measures, the rise of an iron industry in districts more suitable for dealing with the foreign trade, and the dawn of the steel age—all these pointed to the ultimate decline of the South Staffordshire iron manufacture. But in 1870 the industry was still advancing, and it was to enjoy one further short burst of prosperity before it was finally overwhelmed.

[1] S. Timmins, *op. cit.*, p. 70; and F. W. Harbord and E. F. Law, *The British Iron and Steel Industry* in the *Proceedings of the Empire Mining and Metallurgical Congress*, 1924, part iv., pp. 181, 185.
[2] F. W. Harbord and E. F. Law, *op. cit.*, p. 183.

CHAPTER II

THE CULMINATION OF THE OLD INDUSTRIALISM, 1870-1875

IN 1870 Birmingham and District held a pre-eminent position in the hardware and small metal manufactures, and was one of the chief iron-producing centres in the country. For a hundred years or more it had been steadily advancing towards that goal, and the forces which had created it were gathering themselves for a final effort before they slackened and failed. We have seen that at the beginning of 1870 the cyclical movement of trade was on the up-grade, and it was expected that during the course of the year the county would enter upon the early stages of a boom. But the outbreak of the Franco-German War, after steadying for a moment the upward movement, sent both output and prices soaring far above the level which would otherwise have been attained. Birmingham and District received the full force of this great impetus. Increased demands for its goods came not only from the belligerents but from the Colonies and distant markets, and in many industries exports exceeded all previous records. So the older trades reached a level of importance which they were never afterwards to attain, and in the early seventies the area achieved its zenith both as a hardware and as an iron-producing centre.

It would be tedious to recount the progress of each trade in turn, as development was for the most part on the lines described in earlier chapters. The hollow-ware, bedstead, pen, wire, brass, screw and chain trades all expanded. The number of factories in the tube trade doubled between 1868 and 1873. The flint-glass firms were responsible for a larger export trade than was ever reached before or since. The edge-tool makers were exceptionally busy with orders for distant markets, particularly for India,[1] and the nickel- and cobalt-using industries, such as minting and electro-plate manufacture, received an added stimulus from the discovery of ores in New Caledonia in 1870. Previously these metals had been obtained from the arsenical ores of Hungary, South America and Russia; but by

---

[1] *Newspaper Cuttings* on *Birmingham Industries*, vol. i., p. 72 ; *Reports of the Inspectors of Factories*, April 1871, p. 63 *et seq.*, and October 1873, p. 86.

1872 the new supplies were beginning to affect the industry, which received further benefits from the exceptionally large demand for nickel coins at the time.[1] The engineering trade also grew steadily with the gradual introduction of power-machinery into the factories; while the food and drink industries, though still small, were swelled by the establishment of several large breweries.[2] As was to be expected, the jewellery trade was peculiarly sensitive to the general prosperity. It had been among the most progressive trades during the sixties, but during the boom even that rate of advance was exceeded. This applies particularly to the silver jewellery, although expansion was not confined to that section. There was a growth in the output of high-quality gold jewellery and a great increase in the use of precious stones. Even the decline in imitation- and gilt-jewellery production seemed to be checked.[3] Several new branches, moreover, were added to the trade. In 1872 a factory was established for producing watch-cases by machinery,[4] and during the same year diamond-cutting was introduced. Previously the practice had been either for stones to be purchased from Amsterdam or for jewellers to send their rough diamonds to be cut and polished in London; but now it was hoped that a part of this trade would be retained by Birmingham.[5]

Even stationary or declining industries were revived. The tinplate- and japanned-ware manufacture recovered its former prosperity, both because of the opening of foreign markets and owing to the rise of a demand for a new type of product. This was the japanned travelling trunk, the output of which responded rapidly to the development of the seaside-holiday habit and of the demand from abroad.[6] Consequently there was an expansion in the size of the Wolverhampton and Birmingham factories, where, moreover, methods of production were affected by the introduction of the power-press after 1870.[7] Even the hand-wrought nail industry felt the effects of the boom, and in 1875 it was reported to be flourishing — probably the only occasion

[1] *Handbook for Birmingham and the Neighbourhood* (British Association Meeting, 1913), pp. 413-416.
[2] *Newspaper Cuttings* on *Birmingham Industries*, vol. i., pp. 73, 121; vol. ii., p. 11.
[3] J. C. Roche, *op. cit.*, chap. iv.
[4] *Newspaper Cuttings* on *Birmingham Industries*, vol. ii., pp. 131-138.
[5] *Our Industries* in *Hardware, Metals and Machinery*, January 25, 1876.
[6] W. H. Jones, *op. cit.*, chap. viii.
[7] *Ibid.*, chap. ix.

after 1830 on which this could have been said of this unfortunate manufacture.[1] Only one trade failed to respond—viz. the pearl-button industry, which was grievously affected by the shortage of pearl-shell, and appeared to be rapidly declining in consequence.[2]

Throughout 1871 and 1872 the rise in prices continued; and between September 1871 and midsummer of the next year the following increases were reported to have taken place:

Commodity	Percentage Increase in Price,[3] Midsummer 1872 over September 1871
Iron Tubes	117
Tinned Hollow-Ware	33
Iron Wood-Screws	50
Galvanized Buckets	42
Chains	55
Wrought Nails	50
Cut Nails	95
Brassfoundry	30
Frying Pans	67
Locks	25
Wrought Hinges	33
Curry-Combs	40
Washers	100
Brass Tubes	33
Brass Wire	44
Copper Wire	43
Fenders and Fire-Irons	25
Paraffin Lamps	10
Gas-Fittings	20
Coffin Furniture	17
Light Edge Tools	14
Spades and Shovels	30
Anvils	25
Japanned Ware	30

The upward movement lasted until the autumn, when there was a slight set-back; but in the early part of 1873 prices were again rising, and they remained high throughout this and the next year.[4] One authority spoke of 1872 as being " rarely equalled and never surpassed for its great and general prosperity." [5]

If these were the conditions in industries which were not directly influenced by the demands of the war, it can be under-

---

[1] *Reports of the Inspectors of Factories*, April 1875, p. 76.
[2] *Newspaper Cuttings* on *Birmingham Industries*, vol. i., pp. 87-88.
[3] *Ibid.*, vol. i., p. 72.
[4] *Ibid.*, vol. i., p. 72 ; G. H. Wright, *Chronicles of the Birmingham Chamber of Commerce* (1913), pp. 250-251, 255 ; *Reports of the Council of the Birmingham Chamber of Commerce*, January 1872, p. 6 ; August 1872, p. 6 ; January 1873, p. 6.
[5] *Newspaper Cuttings* on *Birmingham Industries*, vol. i., pp. 71-72.

stood that the activity of those which manufactured munitions was unprecedented. At Walsall and Birmingham the saddlers and harness-makers were flooded with orders from the Continent, and there was a great increase in their numbers [1]; while the small-arms trade rose from its depression during the later sixties and entered upon one of the most prosperous periods in its history. On the outbreak of the war the only Birmingham factory manufacturing interchangeable rifles was engaged on a Russian contract; and, as it received large orders also from the British Government, it could not meet the demands of either belligerent, except from stock. Consequently the whole of the gun trade was swept for breech-loaders, and some 20,000 were immediately shipped abroad, mainly to France. When the supplies of this type of arm were exhausted every muzzle-loading Enfield which could be found, and all parts which could be hurriedly assembled, were also exported. After this, since the Birmingham Small Arms Company and the only other private rifle factory in the country, the London Small Arms Company, were not in a position to accept orders from the Continent, the old gun trade was overwhelmed with demands, and a great shortage of skilled workmen was experienced. The next year brought no relief; for in the spring of 1871 the British War Office decided to adopt the Martini-Henry rifle for the services. This type, however, was not manufactured in quantity before 1874, and until then the Government orders, which continued to pour in, were for Sniders. But the decision of the War Office, and of several Continental Governments also, in favour of the small-bore breech-loader, together with the active character of the small-arms trade during the war, resulted in the formation of a second great firm, the National Arms and Ammunition Company, which in 1872 proceeded to establish four factories in Birmingham for the production of Martini-Henry rifles and for the manufacture of the brass, ammunition and machinery required. At the same time the older concern was reconstructed, and became the Birmingham Small Arms and Metal Company, having acquired a factory where brass could be rolled and the new type of cartridge manufactured. Several other ammunition firms grew to importance during this period, and although the

---

[1] *Midland Captains of Industry* in *Birmingham Gazette and Express*, September 23 and October 14, 1908; and *Census of England and Wales*, 1861, vol. ii., p. 467 *et seq.*; 1871, vol. ii., p. 313 *et seq.*

old gun trade had become slack again before 1875, the rifle and munition factories remained busy on orders from the British and Prussian Governments. Thus the boom years, 1870-1875, had been of great consequence to the whole industry. The Birmingham Small Arms Company had extended its plant; a second great rifle and ammunition concern had been established in the town; and the manufacture of cartridges had become an important local trade. Although the old gun trade, as carried on in workshops, did not attain the output of 1862-1864 when it had reached its zenith, the period of the Franco-German War had proved one of the most prosperous in its history.

Meanwhile, in the Black Country, the iron trade had been swept by the war into a culminating period of triumph. In 1870 the industry, which was just emerging from " as flat a period . . . as can well be remembered,"[1] was caught by the boom, and entered upon three years of remarkable activity. The official price per ton of " marked bars " was £8 in 1870. By December 1871 this had advanced to £11, and from then it rose by leaps and bounds till, in July 1872, the price stood at £16.[2] The advance in sheets was even greater; and the *pro rata* scale, which for more than half-a-century had regulated the relative prices of bar- and sheet-iron, was abandoned, because the demand for the latter had risen far beyond the capacity of the South Staffordshire mills to roll.[3] For this the great expansion of the galvanized-sheet trade was largely responsible.[4] Thus the phenomenon was no mere price boom. The number of puddling furnaces in South Staffordshire rose from about 1700 in 1869 to 2155 in 1872—the highest total achieved during the century—and the mills from 282 to 329. Nor was the finished-iron branch alone affected. The output of pig soared from 570,000 tons in 1869 to 726,000 tons in 1871, and for the next two years remained as high as 673,000 tons. The figure for 1871 represents the maximum production of the district throughout its history and amounted to nearly 11 per cent. of the total British output. During the same period (1869-1871) the furnaces in blast increased from 95 to 114.[5]

[1] S. Griffiths, *Guide to the Iron Trade of Great Britain*, pp. 12-13.
[2] *Ibid.*, p. 18 ; and *Newspaper Cuttings* on *Birmingham Industries*, vol. i., p. 71.
[3] S. Griffiths, *Guide to the Iron Trade of Great Britain*, pp. 9, 18 *et seq.*
[4] W. H. Jones, *op. cit.*, chap. xii.
[5] R. Hunt, *op. cit.*, 1869, pp. 76, 90 ; 1871, pp. 90-91 ; 1872, pp. 121, 167 ; 1873, p. 95.

Under these circumstances the whole resources of the extractive industries were called upon, and the response in the case of ironstone mining was shown in the rise of the output from 350,000 in 1869 to 706,000 in 1871.[1] Yet this effort, great as it was, yielded 250,000 tons less than during the previous boom year—1864—and enormous quantities of ore had to be brought from North Staffordshire, Northamptonshire and Cleveland to satisfy the needs of the blast-furnaces.[2] The failure to attain the previous peak of production was an obvious indication of falling resources. The coal output increased by nearly 1,250,000 tons, and stood at 10,550,000 tons in 1872, after which there was a fall.[3] The rise in the price of this mineral was of equal magnitude to that of iron, for it was said in 1872 that during the previous twelve months the advance had amounted to 80 per cent.[4] New mines were sunk in the Rowley district, and the increased demand led to attempts to obtain coal from beneath the red rocks beyond the Eastern Boundary Fault. In 1870 the most important of these efforts, the Sandwell Park sinking, was begun, the thick coal-measures being reached in 1874.[5] At the same time there was an extension of mining activities in the Cannock district, where, during this period, about 1,300,000 tons were produced annually.[6] In part, the extension of operations over the field was the result of the increasing exhaustion of the older centres, which was illustrated by the fact that, in spite of the greater output of Cannock, the production of South Staffordshire as a whole rose by only 10 per cent. during the boom. As far as the Black Country itself was concerned the output, for all the increased demand and high prices of the years 1870-1873, must have been practically stationary. The inundation of an increasing number of mines, moreover, brought the question of providing adequate pumps to a head. From 1854 arrangements had existed among the Tipton owners, each of whom had agreed to bear a proportion of the expense of clearing the mines in their district from water; and in 1870 the Old Hill Mines Drainage Company Limited was formed to pump dry the collieries in the Old Hill area. But these attempts had not proved satisfactory, and by

[1] R. Hunt, *op. cit.*, 1869, p. 62; 1871, p. 69.
[2] *Ibid.*, 1871, p. 69 *et seq.*; and T. E. Lones, *op. cit.*, p. 90.
[3] R. Hunt, *op. cit.*, 1872, p. 145.
[4] R. G. Hobbs, *op. cit.*, p. 351.
[5] T. E. Lones, *op. cit.*, pp. 95-99, 100.
[6] *Ibid.*, p. 99.

1873 the danger of flooding had become so great that the South Staffordshire Mines Drainage Act was passed to deal with the matter. With the object of freeing the threatened mines of water the Act set up a body of Mines Drainage Commissioners, who included among their numbers coal owners, ironmasters and representatives of public bodies and canal companies, and were given powers to introduce a system of drainage at the expense of the mining industry.[1]

The situation with which the Commissioners had to deal deserves a detailed examination. As the coal-field was of a higher altitude than that of the surrounding country, the main part of the surface waters were the result of the rainfall on the field itself; while, since the visible measures were bounded by faults and the dip of the beds was away from the field, the underground waters to be dealt with were due almost entirely to percolation from the surface. South Staffordshire was, in fact, self-contained as regards its drainage; but owing to the subsidence of the ground, for which centuries of mining operations and the damage done to the surface by industrial activities were responsible, a great part of the rainfall, instead of being carried away by streams, flowed into the mines. The trouble was particularly acute to the north of the watershed, as there the streams were sluggish, and many of them had become choked up by road silt and by sewage deposition. In the Tipton area, which was the centre of the trouble, most of the mines were shallow, and the removal of 20 to 30 feet of solid coal had resulted in 7000 acres of the area sinking to such a level as to prevent the natural outlet of the water. It was discovered, moreover, that there existed a number of isolated " pounds," or subterranean basins, which, being separated by faults, had to be drained independently. The problem which was presented to the Commissioners was, therefore, twofold. The first part of their task was to improve the surface drainage so as to limit the amount of water flowing into the mines—a task which took the form of straightening, embanking and making water-tight the main streams and of clearing away the silt and debris. To cover the expenses of this work the Commissioners were empowered to charge a penny per ton on all coal, ironstone and fire-clay brought to the surface. Besides

[1] A. Underhill, *A Popular Survey of the South Staffordshire Mines Drainage Act, 1873*, p. 2 *et seq.* and p. 10 *et seq.* ; *Report of the Committee on the South Staffordshire Mines Drainage* (1920), p. 13 *et seq.*

this, they had to set up pumps to clear the water which had accumulated in the " pounds." It was decided to acquire the pumps of the Tipton Drainage Company and to set others to work; and it was hoped that these official efforts, in addition to the private pumping operations which were already carried on, would keep the mines free of water. For this part of their task the Commissioners were permitted to levy a drainage rate of 3d. a ton on fire-clay and limestone, 9d. a ton on ironstone, and 6d. a ton on coal and other minerals. The field was divided for administrative purposes into five districts—Bilston, Tipton, Oldbury, Old Hill and Kingswinford.[1] This attempt to deal in a corporate fashion with the common problems of the mining industry was not greeted with unanimous enthusiasm by the coal owners of the neighbourhood, and the attitude of many of them is an illustration of how often the self-interest of the industrialist is directly opposed to what may ultimately benefit industry as a whole. As already indicated, most of the pits were in the hands of small owners or contractors, who were concerned only with getting what tonnage they could at a minimum cost, and not with developing the mining resources of the Black Country; while many other mines were controlled by ironmasters, who were interested in the coal trade as consumers rather than as producers. Both these classes objected to the drainage rates, which were imposed in the common interest.[2] The history of these new drainage operations, however, must be left to a subsequent chapter, as by 1875 little of importance had been done.

Since the boom may be said to have coincided with the last years of the Malleable Iron Period, during which South Staffordshire had been the most famous producing centre, it is of interest to glance at the structure of the typical firm in the industry. This has been dealt with to some extent in an earlier chapter; but since the features of the industrial organization, which were there emphasized, had become more pronounced between 1860 and 1873, the subject may with advantage be referred to again. The integrated concern was still characteristic of the trade. At Wolverhampton Messrs Thorneycroft & Co. were the principal producers, and turned out about 700 tons of finished iron a week in the form of plates, angle-iron, T-iron, girders, sheets,

[1] *Report of the Committee on the South Staffordshire Mines Drainage* (1920), pp. 14-15.
[2] *Ibid.*, p. 21.

hoops and bars from their 74 puddling furnaces and 12 rolling mills. In addition, they owned mines and blast-furnaces; they made most of the machinery which they required in their own works; and they even constructed their own canal boats. Some 2000 persons found employment in the various branches of their business.[1] The Earl of Dudley was an even greater magnate and operated the " model works of the Black Country." He possessed limestone quarries and iron- and coal-mines, blast-furnaces, forges and mills, and a factory in which he produced machinery and locomotives; while he employed no less than 5000 persons. The Patent Shaft and Axletree Company of Wednesbury mined coal and ironstone, manufactured pig-iron in its blast-furnaces and finished-iron in its 86 puddling furnaces, and operated a steel plant, foundries and engineering shops, where railway wheels, axles, turn-tables and structural work were produced. This company employed about 4000 persons.[2] The Darlaston Iron and Steel Company owned 850 acres of mines and a plant consisting of 3 blast-furnaces, 43 puddling furnaces, 17 reheating furnaces and 8 rolling mills; and in addition it produced Bessemer steel on a considerable scale. The New British Iron Company, which carried on business at Brierley Hill and Corngreaves, worked 6 blast-furnaces and 64 puddling furnaces, besides mines. William Hunt & Sons, of the Brades Works, had blast-furnaces, mines, 7 puddling furnaces and 3 mills, and they produced also cast-, shear- and blister-steel for use in their large edge-tool factory. Another great ironmaster, Mr David Rose, of the Moxley and Albert Iron Works, mined his own coal, ironstone, sand and fire-clay, manufactured fire-bricks and pig-iron, produced finished iron on a large scale and operated a works for turning out galvanized sheets. A Wolverhampton firm, the Chillington Iron Company, which also had interests in the Walsall neighbourhood, owned 7 blast-furnaces, besides several finished-iron works and extensive mining properties.[3] Finally, there was the famous concern of William Barrows & Sons (formerly Barrows & Hall). Unlike the other great iron firms of the Black Country, this was not integrated in structure, for it had no blast-furnaces and it purchased its pig from the Earl of Dudley and from the Lilleshall Works,

---

[1] R. G. Hobbs, *op. cit.*, p. 463. [2] *Ibid.*, p. 282.
[3] S. Griffiths, *Guide to the Iron Trade of Great Britain*, pp. 50-79.

Shropshire. But it was the largest finished-iron producer in the district. It operated no less than 100 puddling furnaces in its three works; it employed over 1000 persons, and it turned out more than 1000 tons of finished iron a week.[1] Such, then, was the type of firm which was responsible for the prosperity of the area's greatest industry.

Let us now turn to another aspect of industrial development. The effect of the Factory and Workshops Acts on the local industries has been discussed in the last chapter, and the new tendencies which they introduced were reinforced after 1870, not only by new factory legislation but by the Education Act. This, by rendering factory schools obsolete, dealt a blow at paternalism, and by depriving workmen of cheap assistants tended to undermine the subcontracting system. The Act so accentuated the shortage of young labour that workmen were forced to employ older boys, who required higher wages. Indeed, owing to these legislative measures, the price of boy-assistants' labour was said to have risen from 4s. or 5s. a week in 1860 to 10s. a week in 1875.[2] In the trades in which production took the form of a long, continuous process, as in the blast-furnaces and the flint-glass works, serious difficulties were encountered. Boy assistants, instead of working according to the men's hours, now had to be engaged in relays, and there were insufficient boys to cover the needs. In consequence, their earnings were more than doubled.[3] The men naturally attempted to recoup themselves by asking for higher wages, and the prosperity of the boom years made them a favourable period for bringing forward these proposals. So, in a wide variety of local trades, organized labour grew in strength, and there was a general demand for higher wages, which were in most cases conceded, though not without serious disputes. For instance, 10,000 nailers struck in 1872 for a 20 per cent. addition to the list price.[4] The edge-tool workers formed themselves into a union (The Heavy Steel Toy, Gimblet and Brass Bit Makers Association) to press for a 15 per cent. advance in wages.[5] In the iron and coal trades, so it was declared in 1873, apprehension had been

---

[1] J. W. Hall, *The Life and Work of Joseph Hall*, p. 25.
[2] *Newspaper Cuttings* on *Birmingham Industries*, vol. ii., p. 37 ; *Reports of the Inspectors of Factories*, April 1876, p. 79.
[3] *Newspaper Cuttings* on *Birmingham Industries*, vol. ii., p. 42.
[4] R. G. Hobbs, *op. cit.*, p. 639.
[5] *Newspaper Cuttings* on *Birmingham Industries*, vol. i., p. 74.

caused by the frequent and exorbitant demands of the workers for higher wages, demands which had been stimulated by the employers' inordinate greed for profits.[1] There was a long colliers' strike in 1874; but serious disputes were avoided in the iron industry by the adoption of a sliding-scale, according to which wages varied with the selling-price of bars and by the establishment of a Conciliation Board.[2] The most interesting example of labour activities during the period, however, was the formation of a union in an industry hitherto unorganized—viz. the brassfoundry trade. The existence of a multitude of garret-men and small employers, and the difficulty of drawing up a list of piece-prices in a trade in which products had an indi-vidual character and could not be graded, had prevented the growth of labour organizations, and were for long to place the employees in a weak bargaining position. Nevertheless in 1872 the National Society of Amalgamated Brassfounders was formed, on the initiative of W. J. Davis, to press for an increase in wages to compensate for the rise in the cost of living and the dearness of underhand labour.[3] An advance of 15 per cent. was conceded in most branches of the industry, although the tube- and bedstead-workers, who failed to obtain the increase, soon left the union.[4]

Associated with the successful attempts to secure higher wages was the demand for a shorter working day; and the "nine-hour movement," which was taken up by the A.S.E. in 1870, was widely represented in the Midlands.[5] There was con-siderable resistance offered to the movement by some employers, but several of the larger firms in the neighbourhood welcomed it, and in a number of trades the result was the reduction of the normal working week from $67\frac{1}{2}$ to 54 hours. This change did not have much effect on the small-scale industries, where the practice of crowding most of the week's work into three days was still followed, and the factory inspector still had to keep a look-out to see that children were not worked towards the end of the

---

[1] G. H. Wright, op. cit., p. 244.

[2] R. G. Hobbs, op. cit., p. 352; and Newspaper Cuttings on Birmingham Industries, vol. i., p. 71.

[3] Annual Report of National Society of Amalgamated Brassworkers, 1872-1873, pp. 5-8.

[4] Ibid., 1873-1874, p. 5.

[5] Reports of the Inspectors of Factories, October 1872, pp. 113-117; R. Tangye, op. cit., pp. 110-113; R. G. Hobbs, op. cit., p. 382.

week longer hours than were permitted by law.[1] In the factories, however, the reduction of hours strengthened the new tendencies which had begun to appear in some industries; for, with a shorter working day at their disposal, the employers were necessarily bound to concern themselves with improving their methods of organization, to subject their men to stricter discipline, and to insist on the observance of more regular hours. In a sense, it might be said with justice that better discipline and an improvement in factory organization were the necessary conditions of a reduction in the length of the working day.

In 1872, when the boom was at its height, it was obvious to many observers that the great rise in prices before long might prove dangerous to the local trades. By the next year the upward movement was checked, and although most of the local industries remained busy, there were already signs of a reaction in certain of them.[2] The foreign markets were the first to be affected. During the early years of the boom, exports of produce had greatly increased, especially to Australia, France, Brazil and the United States.[3] But the continued advance in prices up to the beginning of 1873 resulted in the American hardware-makers and the Belgian iron-producers capturing a share of the district's foreign markets during that and the following years. It was said, indeed, that the Belgians even had succeeded in selling iron to Birmingham manufacturers in competition with South Staffordshire [4]; while the Chamber of Commerce reported in July 1873 that, though trade was active, the enhanced price of labour and fuel was causing loss of business to foreign countries, and that the United States was becoming independent of Great Britain for its iron and was even supplying the Colonies.[5] This development was associated with the increase in costs which inevitably accompanied the boom. A considerable reduction had been effected in the length of the normal working week; money wages had risen enormously; and, as a result of the Factory and Education Acts, a supply of cheap labour, within a comparatively short time, had been removed. However socially necessary they might be, these changes, although they might

---

[1] *Reports of the Inspectors of Factories*, October 1872, pp. 114-117.
[2] G. H. Wright, *op. cit.*, p. 251 ; *Reports of the Inspectors of Factories*, October 1873, p. 86 *et seq.*
[3] *Newspaper Cuttings* on *Birmingham Industries*, vol. i., pp. 60, 72.
[4] *Ibid.*, pp. 100, 115, 143.
[5] G. H. Wright, *op. cit.*, p. 251.

benefit industry in the long run, were likely to be disadvantageous until the necessary adjustments had been effected. Further, the years of excited trade had seen a wave of company-promoting, and many private concerns, particularly in the iron industry, had been converted into limited companies. Since these conversions had occurred during a period of high prices, and of excessive optimism, many of the firms were over-capitalized, and were led to follow a mistaken price-policy during subsequent years.[1]

It was natural that the basic industries, which had received the greatest stimulus from the boom, should suffer sooner than most of the others from the inevitable reaction. In July 1873 iron bars were selling at £2 a ton less than during the spring, and though even then their price was far above that of 1870, this was the first hint that a depression was about to overtake the trade.[2] By 1874 a rapid decline in the volume of output had set in, as may be judged from the fact that South Staffordshire's production of pig-iron fell from 670,000 tons during 1872 and 1873 to 450,000 tons in the next year.[3] Although there was a slight rise to 470,000 tons in 1875, by that time the industry was sunk in depression and only 76 furnaces were in blast as compared with 114 five years before.[4] The decline in coal prices, which accompanied the blowing out of the furnaces, resulted in a reduction of miners' wages, which the men resisted in a four-months' strike in the early part of 1874. The coal output fell from 10,550,000 tons in 1872 to 9,460,000 in 1873, and was down to 8,390,000 tons in the year of the strike.[5] The production of ironstone was similarly affected.[6]

Yet, while as early as 1873 there had been signs of incipient depression in the heavy Black Country industries, the lighter trades of the area remained prosperous for several years. The brass trade was not seriously affected, and as late as 1875 one section of it, the hinge-dressing branch, managed to secure a rise in wages.[7] Great vitality was reported in the hardware, tube

---

[1] *Newspaper Cuttings* on *Birmingham Industries*, vol. ii., p. 200.
[2] *Ibid.*, vol. i., pp. 96-97.
[3] R. Hunt, *op. cit.*, 1872, p. 107 ; 1873, p. 95 ; 1874, p. 94.
[4] *Ibid.*, 1875, pp. 93, 100.
[5] *Ibid.*, 1872, p. 145 ; 1873, p. 140 ; 1874, p. 142.
[6] *Ibid.*, 1872, p. 85 ; 1874, p. 74.
[7] *Annual Report of the National Society of Amalgamated Brassworkers*, 1875-1876, pp. 6-7.

and edge-tool trades of Wolverhampton at the beginning of the same year,[1] and as late as September 1875 edge-tool makers were reported to be well employed.[2] The screw and the nut-and-bolt manufacturers also remained busy up to that time[3]; and, while the old gun trade had been slack since the end of the Franco-Prussian War, the military arms and ammunition factories were actively engaged on Government orders.[4] The nail trade was remarkably prosperous, and a writer stated that it had never been better than during the half-year ending April 1875.[5] The masters were quite unable to satisfy the demand, and were obliged to increase the number of their warehouses so as to get into touch with larger bodies of workers. Further, since the trade had been relieved of its oversupply of labour, partly by the activity in the other industries and partly because legislation had done something to limit the competition of non-adult workers, the nailers themselves were able to obtain several advances in wages, and from 1870 to 1875 they enjoyed greater prosperity than they had done for many years, or were ever to do again.[6] Gradually, however, more and more trades passed under the cloud. Early in 1875 the chain-makers were without sufficient orders, and most of the hardware trades began to suffer after the crisis of June of that year.[7] Towards the end of the year the small-arms factories also were slack, and then the brass trade began to fail. By 1876 the depression had spread to the greater part of local industry, prices had fallen, unemployment was rife and the export trade had greatly diminished.[8]

[1] *Newspaper Cuttings* on *Birmingham Industries*, vol. i., pp. 113-114.
[2] *Ibid.*, p. 161.
[3] *Our Industries* in *Hardware, Metals and Machinery* (1874), Nos. 3 and 4.
[4] *Private History of the Birmingham Small Arms Company.*
[5] *Reports of the Inspectors of Factories*, April 1875, p. 76.
[6] *Our Industries* in *Hardware, Metals and Machinery*, October 25, 1875.
[7] G. H. Wright, *op. cit.*, pp. 260-262.
[8] *Ibid.*, p. 268 ; *Reports of the Inspectors of Factories*, April 1876, p. 71.

CHAPTER III

THE GREAT DEPRESSION AND THE HARDWARE TRADES, 1876-1886

IN 1876 the country as a whole passed under the cloud of depression which persisted, with a short period of activity in 1880-1882, until 1886. The significance of the slump has received little attention from historians, in spite of the data provided by the Royal Commission which investigated it in 1885; but probably it will be regarded by future generations as marking a turning-point in the industrial history of Great Britain. For the great depression divides the period of the country's unchallenged predominance—when its metallurgical trades supplied the world with their products, when new markets continually were being opened to British goods, and when serious rivalry from Continental and American manufacturers was unknown—from the age in which Great Britain lost her lead in the metal industries, and in which her producers had to struggle, not only in the foreign but in the home market, with the well-equipped industries of other lands. The depression is, indeed, the watershed between the era of British industrial supremacy and the era of international competition.

No detailed examination of the underlying causes of the long slump can be undertaken here. Powerful contributory causes were doubtless to be found in the rise in the value of gold, in the depreciation of silver, and in the decline in agriculture. In some degree the prolonged nature of the depression may be attributed to the fact that the period was one of transition, in which the necessity for a redistribution of productive resources in consequence of the rise of foreign competition, and for the introduction of new plants as a result of technical changes, raised costs over a wide field. But, whatever the causes to which we assign priority, the effect was certainly to seek out the weak places in the armour of British economic life and to overwhelm trades which were on the margin of efficiency. Since, moreover, the depression was exceptionally severe in the manufactures which were most characteristic of nineteenth-century industrialism —viz. the metal trades—it was the older iron centres which suffered most seriously, and where the pains of transition and of adjustment to a new economic equilibrium, were greatest and most prolonged. And Birmingham and District was, in consequence, an area in which the changes associated with the slump were most obvious, and where its effects on the industrial structure could be most clearly observed.

If scarcely any local trade escaped from the effects of the depression, all were not influenced in the same degree. While the iron and coal industries shrank in size to an abnormal extent even for such highly fluctuating trades, and while the output of some of the finished manufactures was subject to a great and, as it afterwards proved, to a permanent decline, certain trades hardly faltered in their progress. On the whole, moreover, the Black Country was much harder hit than Birmingham.[1] This was not only because the heavy trades were centred in the former district, but because even its light finished manufactures were, generally speaking, among those which suffered most severely. Further, it has already been pointed out that whereas Birmingham was distinguished by the multiplicity of its trades, there was in the finished manufactures of South Staffordshire a high degree of specialization according to locality. So it was difficult for workers in any Black Country town where the staple trade was depressed to pass to other employments; and since in many industries men and women were employed on the same processes, the low earnings of the head of a family during the depression would be shared by all its members. In Birmingham, on the other hand, the existence of a multitude of trades meant that, even if several were affected, there was a chance of employment in others; and as there was a greater differentiation between men's and women's labour than in South Staffordshire, the various members of a family usually would be engaged in distinct manufactures. Thus family earnings might remain comparatively high. The contrast between the position of the worker in Birmingham and in the Black Country needs to be emphasized; but the advantages which lay in the possession of a diverse industrial life have been so laboured by writers that they have tended to be exaggerated. It has been suggested, for instance, that as the use of the hammer, file and lathe was common to many trades, then it was an easy

[1] *Report of the Chief Inspector of Factories and Workshops*, October 1879, p. 17.

matter for men to pass from one to another, according to their relative prosperity. It is true that a certain amount of shifting of this kind took place; but to imagine that it occurred rapidly and on a large scale during depressions is to show ignorance of methods of industrial organization. As we have already seen, men accustomed to working in hard wood might be drafted into the gun trade during its periods of activity and flow back to vehicle-building when the demand for arms ceased. Stampers and die-sinkers could change over to new classes of work without much difficulty. Polishers and burnishers might leave the brassfoundry for other metal trades, and girls who operated presses might change from one industry to another. But most manufactures required specialized workers, and in the brass, jewellery, pen, glass and saddlery trades, to mention notable examples, the labour force, at any rate in the skilled grades, had little mobility. A button-stamper was always a button-stamper, and his like could not easily be recruited from men who had been used to other classes of work. The tool-makers in the pen trade had to be trained from their youth, and other types of skilled die-sinkers could not be substituted for them.

Thus, while there might be some movement of semi-skilled and of a few classes of skilled workers, it is an exaggeration to affirm that any general flow of labour from one trade to another took place during such periods as we are now discussing. The only opportunity which most types of specialized craftsmen had of changing over to another trade was when a new industry, which had not yet acquired a distinct labour force, was introduced. Except when this happened the movement of adult labour would be small. But where Birmingham had an advantage over other towns in the district was in the fact that its boys and girls when entering industrial life had a greater choice of occupation. In many localities in the Black Country, on the other hand, non-adult labour was forced into certain trades, however depressed they might be, merely because of the lack of other openings. This not only accentuated the decline in earnings during slack periods, but, by enabling wages to be forced lower and lower, it kept alive dying industries much longer than was possible in Birmingham, where the recruitment of chronically depressed trades soon ceased. Thus industrial transitions were likely to be more rapidly accomplished in Birmingham than in the Black Country, solely because of the former's greater variety of manufactures.

As we have already observed, the depression struck at the weakest parts of the industrial structure; and so, while the trades which had developed rapidly between 1860 and 1875 continued to progress, or at any rate maintained themselves, those which had been stationary during that period received a blow from which many of them never recovered. The history of the four Birmingham staples alone affords an illustration of the truth of this generalization. Of these, two—viz. the jewellery and brass trades—had grown during the fifteen years of prosperity that followed 1860; the small-arms trade, though subject to great fluctuations, had just about maintained itself, while the button manufacture had been slowly declining. The effects of the great slump on the jewellery trade were complicated, because the manufacture was one which was very sensitive not only to the movements of trade but also to changes of fashion, and it is therefore difficult to disentangle one set of causes from the other. Naturally, being engaged in a luxury trade, the jewellers suffered from the decline in national prosperity; but all of them were not affected in the same degree. During the first part of the depression—1876-1880—the branch of the trade which was most seriously injured was that which produced expensive gold wares.[1] It was declared in 1877 that even the best type of jewellery was simpler in design and had fewer jewels than a few years previously, and the dealers and workers in precious stones were very hard hit.[1] Since, moreover, in this, as in many other trades, changes of fashion were more rapid in bad times than in good, owing to the fact that manufacturers made repeated efforts to stimulate their failing markets, costs must have risen considerably in those branches.[1] But the demand for silver jewellery and for cheaper goods remained large, and for a time the trade continued to benefit by the fall in the price of silver.[2] Thus, to some extent, the loss of the high-class trade was compensated for by the demands for cheaper qualities. " More brooches, lockets, chains and necklaces were sold . . . than previously, but the quality was different " (*i.e.* lower than it had been).[1] This

---

[1] *Newspaper Cuttings* on *Birmingham Industries*, vol. ii., p. 169.
[2] C. J. Woodward, *Manufacturing Industries* in *British Association Handbook* (Birmingham Meeting, 1886), p. 188 ; *Report of the Chief Inspector of Factories and Workshops*, October 1880, p. 9.

development, however, contained within it the seeds of disaster. As makers tried to cut their costs by adopting mechanical methods of production and by employing cheap female labour to produce on presses articles similar to those which the skilled craftsman previously had made by hand,[1] so qualities deteriorated; and this, together with the decrease in the national income, occasioned by the prolonged slump in the staple trades, brought about a change of fashion. Towards the end of this period, in fact, the habit of wearing jewellery, which had been growing since the accession of the Queen, began to decline. This tendency was strengthened by the fact that the continued fall of silver rendered jewellery of that metal so cheap that it lost popularity; while the gilt-ware trade, which had been injured by the competition of silver in the later sixties, received a further blow as a result of American rivalry.[2] Consequently, in the second period of the great slump—in 1885-1886—jewellery was declared to be the most depressed of all the local industries.[3] But some branches escaped. The new manufactures, such as the production of official insignia, presentation caskets and watch-cases, flourished; while the electro-plate and nickel-silver trade continued to expand in consequence of the development of hotel life and of the more luxurious equipment of railways and steamships.[4] The increased supply of raw materials which the New Caledonia ores afforded was also a factor in maintaining the prosperity of this section of industry. Thus, although the manufacture of gold and silver jewellery was plunged in deep depression at the end of the period, during the greater part of the slump all the branches of the trade, with the exception of expensive gold jewellery and gilt-ware production, were active.[5] Even the condition of affairs in 1885-1886 was due to a temporary change of fashion rather than to any enduring cause, and, except in the gilt-jewellery branch, there was no hint that foreign competition was proving a menace during these years. The amount of employment afforded actually increased from nearly 10,000 in 1871 to over 14,000 at the next Census, and it was estimated

[1] C. J. Woodward, *op. cit.*, pp. 188-190.
[2] J. C. Roche, *op. cit.*, chap. iv.
[3] *Report of the Chief Inspector of Factories and Workshops*, October 1887, p. 48.
[4] C. J. Woodward, *op. cit.*, pp. 188, 203, 211.
[5] *Ibid.*, p. 188 ; *Report of the Chief Inspector of Factories and Workshops*, October 1887, p. 48.

that there were probably from 14,000 to 16,000 persons in the trade in 1886.[1] It is doubtful, however, whether the value of the output showed a corresponding expansion; for during the depression the relative importance of the high-class jewellery section declined, and there was an influx of female and of semi-skilled workers into the trade at the expense of the skilled craftsman.[2] Nevertheless, up to 1885 fortune had been kind to this industry as compared with many others in the locality.

The brass trade, including the manufacture of other non-ferrous products, also showed an independence of the normal cyclical movement of trade which has ever since distinguished it. This is not to say that the manufacture was not subject in any degree to the fall in prices between 1875 and 1886; but the depression did little to impede its expansion. In the first place, brassfoundry was not affected as early as the other industries. In 1878 the Council of the Birmingham Chamber of Commerce reported that it was one of the few trades in which slackness did not prevail,[3] and early in August 1879 unemployment among Birmingham brassworkers was said to have fallen to 200.[4] The reports showing the amount of unemployment benefit paid by the trade union bear out this statement; for not till 1878-1879 did it reach a high figure, which was maintained for only two years.[5] Further, it will be remembered that the brassworkers had secured a wage advance of 15 per cent. during the boom. This remained in force up to 1879, and even then the reduction which occurred consisted of only one-third of the previous increase.[6] During the short general revival in trade after 1880 advances ranging from 10 to 50 per cent. were obtained; and although the industry was depressed again in 1885-1886, it is evident that the slump was of shorter duration than in most other trades.[7] Moreover, the reports of the men's union, which have been quoted, tend to exaggerate the severity of the depression

---

[1] C. J. Woodward, op. cit., p. 187 ; Census of England and Wales, 1881, vol. iii., pp. 250, 254.

[2] C. J. Woodward, op. cit., p. 188.

[3] Report of the Council of the Birmingham Chamber of Commerce, February 1878, p. 9.

[4] Newspaper Cuttings on Birmingham Industries, vol. ii., p. 234.

[5] Annual Report of the National Society of Amalgamated Brassworkers, 1875-1887.

[6] Ibid., 1878-1879, p. 5.

[7] Ibid., 1879-1880, pp. 8-9 ; 1880-1881, pp. 12-13 ; 1881-1882, p. 5 ; 1884-1885, p. 5 ; 1885-1886, p. 5.

as judged by the volume of output, for during this period changes in organization and productive methods displaced certain classes of workers. Between 1876-1886 the stamp and the press came to be applied on a great scale to the production of articles which previously had been cast, and this change threw out of employment many casters and other skilled workers.[1] So the trade continued its progress, and, as far as can be judged, numbers increased from about 11,000 in 1871 to nearly 19,000 in 1881, and probably were well over 20,000 in 1886.[2]

The cause of this buoyancy, despite the general slump, lay largely in the fact that many of the chief branches of the trade were essentially " sheltered " industries; for foreign competition was practically non-existent in the home market, because other countries did not produce goods which accorded with English taste.[3] So, although their export trade might decline,[4] brassfounders had little to fear from America or Germany. A great stimulus was given to all branches of this industry, moreover, by the marked decline in the price of the chief raw material which it employed — viz. copper. The movement was to be attributed mainly to the development of the Lake Superior ores, and the extent of the reduction may be judged from the fact that whereas the price of copper was £88 a ton in 1875, it was only £48 a ton ten years later.[5] Further, the growth of population and of housing, the spread of sanitation and of gaslighting automatically provided the brass houses with a steadily increasing demand; while the more general adoption of power-machinery during this period provided the weldless-tube makers with a larger market for boiler tubes, and the engineers' brassfounders with an increased demand for steamcocks and gauges. Again, the development in bedstead manufacture, which was illustrated by the fact that the local output rose from 5000 a week in 1865 to 20,000 a week in 1886, brought greater calls for cased tubes and brass mounts.[6] The bedstead trade, indeed, seems to have been

---

[1] *Annual Report of the National Society of Amalgamated Brassworkers*, 1887-1888, p. 8.
[2] *Census of England and Wales*, 1881, vol. iii., pp. 246, 254; 1891, vol. iii., p. 255.
[3] *Newspaper Cuttings* on *Birmingham Industries*, vol. ii., p. 234; and E. A. Pratt, *Trade Unionism and British Industry* (1904), pp. 108-109.
[4] *Report of the Chief Inspector of Factories and Workshops*, October 1880, p. 10; *Annual Report of the National Society of Amalgamated Brassworkers*, 1886-1887, p. 7.
[5] C. J. Woodward, *op. cit.*, pp. 180-181.
[6] *Ibid.*, pp. 178-179.

quite unaffected by the depression; for during its course not only did the production of wire mattresses become an important subsidiary industry, but there was a big increase in exports to North America, the Colonies, the East and West Indies, China and Egypt.[1]

But if the jewellery and brass trades had suffered no serious check to their progress, the gun-makers were less fortunate. The inherent instability of their industry had, as we have seen, been masked by a series of fortuitous events. The Crimean War in the fifties, the Civil War, the various Continental struggles and the adoption of the breech-loader in the sixties, the Franco-German War and the change from the large- to the small-bore rifle in the early seventies had all resulted in an expansion of productive capacity, which could not be employed when a long period of peace arrived, or when stability in design was attained. On the conclusion of the Franco-German War, moreover, the old gun trade had to face fierce competition from two quarters. It could no longer hope to receive any share of the orders for military arms, for they could now be produced in the factories; while the gunsmiths of Belgium were in a position to turn out the cheaper type of sporting gun and the African musket more economically than the Birmingham craftsmen. So the old workshop trade had to adjust itself after the Franco-German War (the last conflict from which it benefited) to a permanent shrinkage of demand. The factories absorbed the whole of the military trade, and Belgium captured the foreign markets for cheap sporting guns and muskets. In the high-class gun trade Birmingham still retained the greater share, and sales to the United States continued to be substantial throughout the seventies; but even that market declined after 1880, when the tariff on imported arms was raised from 30 to 35 per cent. *ad valorem.*[2]

As for the military section of the trade, for some years after the Franco-German War the two Birmingham firms were busy supplying British and foreign Governments with the new types of breech-loader; but after 1876 the cloud descended on them also. The leading Continental Powers had by that time equipped factories of their own for meeting their needs, and Enfield proved capable of satisfying the peace-time demands of the British

[1] C. J. Woodward, *op. cit.*, p. 179.
[2] Artifex and Opifex, *op. cit.*, pp. 16-18, 28, 37-39, 228-230.

services. Consequently the orders received by the trade were insufficient to occupy more than a small part of their plant. To strengthen their position the three chief firms in the county formed an agreement for dealing jointly with the Government and for allotting to each a fixed proportion of the output required. An arrangement of this kind had existed between the Birmingham Small Arms Company and the London Small Arms Company since the formation of the latter in 1867; but it was not till 1878 that the National Arms and Ammunition Company joined in. According to the agreement the Birmingham Small Arms Company was to make 40 per cent., the National Arms and Ammunition Company 33 per cent., and the London Small Arms Company 27 per cent. of the total number of arms ordered by the Government from the trade in each year. But, far from helping the small-arms factories, the agreement aroused the hostility of the War Office, which was moved to protest against the combine, as it had done against the association of Birmingham gun-makers at the time of the Crimean War. The shortage of orders continued. The Birmingham Small Arms Company was unable to declare any dividend for several years, and on one or two occasions the whole of its plant was shut down. In despair it turned to the manufacture of bicycles in 1880; but the financial results of this experiment were unsatisfactory. The other Birmingham company was even less successful, for it had to be wound up in 1882, and its four factories were sold. The military section of the industry was, indeed, sunk in depression from 1876 to 1883. During the next year, however, just when the area as a whole was sinking into the deepest trough of the slump, prospects began to improve owing to the proposed adoption by the War Office of the magazine rifle; and then, in 1885, both the Enfield and the private factories were roused to a sudden activity by the danger of a rupture between Russia and England. The Birmingham Small Arms Company gave up its production of bicycles and concentrated its energies on the manufacture of arms for the Indian Army and for the Afghans. So great were the demands that a shortage of labour was experienced in Birmingham, and gunsmiths were brought over from Belgium.[1] Yet, although the period ended in a burst of prosperity for the rifle factories, the depression had brought great loss to

[1] *Private History of the Birmingham Small Arms Company, Limited.*

the military arms trade. One great concern had collapsed; the other had for years failed to make profits. The manufacture of bayonets had disappeared and only one sword-maker remained.[1] The continued depression in all branches of industry had a serious effect on the Darlaston and Wednesbury lock-makers, most of whom had to abandon their trade and to drift into the nut-and-bolt or railway-material factories.[2] Except, indeed, for the introduction of revolver manufacture and for the extension of the ammunition-making plants, the period was disastrous for this industry.[3] The Census returns alone are sufficient to indicate the decline. In 1871 the trade had employed in Staffordshire and Warwickshire 8200 persons; by 1881 the number had fallen by over 3000.[4] And it is probable that during the next five years an even lower level of employment was reached; for, in spite of the revival in the military section, there was a progressive decline in the output of sporting guns.[5]

In the button manufacture the fall in employment was smaller. Between 1871 and 1881, indeed, the numbers rose slightly—from 5300 to 5500—although after that they fell, and we hear of a steady decrease between 1883 and 1886 in several branches of the trade.[6] This may be attributed chiefly to competition from abroad, both in the foreign and home markets. Whereas in earlier years, however, France had been the chief rival, after 1876 Germany stepped into that position, and her competition, besides resulting in an almost complete cessation of gilt-button production in Birmingham, dealt a severe blow at the makers of vegetable-ivory and covered buttons.[7] By 1883, moreover, it was reported that the glass-button section practically had disappeared, and that pearl-button manufacture was steadily declining. The misfortunes of this latter branch were due partly to American

---

[1] J. D. Goodman, *The Military Arms Trade* in *British Association Handbook,* 1886.
[2] *Report of the Chief Inspector of Factories and Workshops,* October 1887, pp. 44-45 ; and F. W. Hackwood, *Wednesbury Workshops,* pp. 48-49.
[3] C. J. Woodward, *op. cit.,* p. 199.
[4] *Census of England and Wales,* 1871, vol. ii., pp. 315 *et seq.* ; 1881, vol. iii., pp. 242, 250.
[5] *Report of the Chief Inspector of Factories and Workshops,* October 1887, p. 46.
[6] *Ibid.,* October 1882, p. 52 ; C. J. Woodward, *op. cit.,* p. 181 ; *Census of England and Wales,* 1871, vol. ii., p. 320 *et seq.* ; 1881, vol. iii., p. 252 *et seq.*
[7] C. J. Woodward, *op. cit.,* p. 181 ; *Newspaper Cuttings* on *Birmingham Industries,* vol. ii., pp. 212-213 ; and *Report of the Chief Inspector of Factories and Workshops,* October 1880, p. 29 ; October 1880, p. 10.

glass manufacture had become almost extinct,[1] and although several glass-using industries—such as mirror manufacture—expanded, the sheet glass required for those products and for window-glazing was brought in increasing quantities from Belgium.[2] Here, again, foreign competition was ousting the British manufacturer from the cheaper lines, and was forcing him to confine his attention to high-grade commodities.

Among the other industries which Birmingham shared with the Black Country towns there were three which continued to progress in spite of the general depression, and which did not suffer severely until its second phase. The largest of these, the saddlery and harness trade, though affected by the decline in agriculture after 1875, increased the volume of its output in consequence of the growth in exports; for demand from the Colonies, South America and Russia was strong throughout the eighth decade.[3] Between 1871 and 1881 the numbers engaged in Staffordshire and Warwickshire rose from 5800 to 6300 [4]; but afterwards misfortune attacked the industry. The South African market declined and droughts in Australia brought a diminution in one of the chief sections of the export trade. Meanwhile the agricultural depression at home became more acute and trade with the United States was adversely affected by the imposition of high import duties.[5] So, in spite of the increase in exports to South America,[6] the saddlers and harness-makers during 1885-1886 were faced with a great shrinkage in demand. Values, it was declared, were then 10 per cent. less than in 1865, and whereas the export trade of 1864 had been 300 per cent. greater than that of 1849, the figure for 1885 was only 12 per cent. above that reached twenty years previously. The subsidiary leather trades, too, had changed. The manufacture of shot-belts and powder-flasks had been killed by the introduction of the breech-loader; but this loss had been

[1] C. J. Woodward, *op. cit.*, p. 203.

[2] *Newspaper Cuttings* on *Birmingham Industries*, vol. ii., pp. 206-207.

[3] C. J. Woodward, *op. cit.*, p. 351 ; W. C. Aitken, *British Manufacturing Industries* (1878), pp. 127, 134, 136 ; and *Report of the Chief Inspector of Factories and Workshops*, October 1879, p. 19.

[4] *Census of England and Wales*, 1871, vol. ii., p. 314 *et seq.* ; 1881, vol. iii., pp. 242, 250.

[5] C. J. Woodward, *op. cit.*, pp. 350-351.

[6] *Report of the Chief Inspector of Factories and Workshops*, October 1887, p. 45.

balanced by a development of the travelling-bag trade and by the introduction of cycle-saddle production.[1]

The edge-tool manufacture also remained in a prosperous condition during the seventies [2] as a result of the buoyant Colonial demands, and it was not until 1885 that the trade began to be affected adversely.[3] At the end of the period between 3000 and 4000 persons were supposed to be engaged, and, while this estimate is not much higher than that for 1865, it is probable that output had increased in a much greater degree because of the introduction of machinery during the seventies.[4]

The tinplate- and japanned-ware trade pursued a somewhat similar course. As we have seen, after a period of decline during the sixties, when its more elaborate products passed out of fashion, it had revived in the early seventies with the appearance of new types of articles, such as tin travelling trunks and gas-meters. The activity continued during the first part of the depression, partly because of the increase in the export trade and partly because of decline in the cost of production which followed the application of the power-press to certain classes of wares.[5] So, between 1871 and 1881, the number of persons engaged in the industry rose from 3400 to 4800.[6] The second period of the depression saw the beginning of competition from abroad, and the trade suffered; but throughout the period its position was far less unsatisfactory than that of most local industries. The associated manufacture, that of papier mâché, however, found its decline accentuated; but this was chiefly because its products had ceased to be fashionable.[7]

Of the minor Birmingham manufactures the pen trade not only maintained itself, but extended its output, which in 1886 was 60 per cent. greater than in 1865. " The ghost of American

[1] C. J. Woodward, op. cit., pp. 348-350.
The leather trades as a whole, including tanning and currying, saddlery, harness, whips, and other leather goods, increased their labour force from 7800 in 1871 to 8800 in 1881.
[2] Report of the Council of the Birmingham Chamber of Commerce, February 1878, p. 9.
[3] C. J. Woodward, op. cit., p. 210.
[4] Ibid., pp. 209-210.
[5] W. H. Jones, op. cit., pp. 134-137; C. J. Woodward, op. cit., pp. 207-208; and Report of the Council of the Birmingham Chamber of Commerce, February 1878, p. 9.
[6] Census of England and Wales, 1871, vol. ii., p. 315 et seq.; 1881, vol. iii., pp. 246, 254.
[7] W. H. Jones, op. cit., pp. 131-132; and C. J. Woodward, op. cit., p. 202.

competition " was laid, and there were practically no rivals on the Continent. The spread of education at home and abroad brought a steadily growing demand for pens, which was satisfied almost entirely by Birmingham. The employment in the trade rose by 70 per cent. between 1871 and 1881, and the last years of the period, 1885-1886, found the industry as prosperous as ever.[1]

About the fortunes of the wire trades it is more difficult to generalize. As far as employment was concerned there was no increase; and while some of them were progressive, others suffered eclipse. Birmingham did not share in the increase of trade which came to the actual wire-producers during the period as a result of the growth of the telephone system and the cycle industry; for wire manufacture, which once had its chief seat in the town, had come to be centred by 1880 at Warrington and Middlesbrough, while the Belgians had begun to export wire to Great Britain.[2] Many of the local wire-using trades, however, expanded, and among them were the wire-netting, wire-mattress, pin and screw manufactures.[3] But the production of hooks and eyes and other smallwares was affected by German competition,[4] which also brought about a decline in the needle trade.[5] The numbers engaged in this manufacture sank from 4300 in 1871 to 3900 at the next Census, and they had fallen still lower by 1886.[6]

Meanwhile the food and drink trades had grown, and by the end of this period cocoa manufacture was employing some 500 persons, while the breweries were increasing in size and in numbers. The rise of a subsidiary industry—viz. paper-box manufacture—was another important feature of the period; for its development affords an illustration of the new methods of packing and sale, which were beginning to appear.[7] Although many of the workers were employed in departments of the metal-smallware and pen factories, there were some specialist

[1] C. J. Woodward, *op. cit.*, pp. 205-206.
[2] *Transactions of the National Association for the Promotion of Social Science* (1884), p. 649.
[3] W. D. Curzon, *op. cit.*, p. 70 ; and C. J. Woodward, *op. cit.*, pp. 179, 211-212.
[4] *History of the Growth of Birmingham Industries* in *Birmingham Gazette and Express*, November 2, 1911, p. 2.
[5] *Newspaper Cuttings* on *Birmingham Industries*, vol. ii., p. 191.
[6] *Census of England and Wales*, 1871, vol. ii., p. 320 *et seq.*; 1881, vol. iii., pp. 246, 254.
[7] *Newspaper Cuttings* on *Birmingham Industries*, vol. ii., p. 240 ; *Report of the Chief Inspector of Factories and Workshops*, October 1879, p. 29.

P

firms, and in 1881 no less than 1400 were engaged in the trade in Warwickshire—more than twice the number returned for the previous Census.[1]

Now all the above trades were either specifically Birmingham trades or were shared between that town and the Black Country, and among them were all the industries which had suffered least from the depression. In spite of the great decline in the production of guns, buttons and glass-wares, this goes to show the truth of the statement which was made by a contemporary that, notwithstanding the general slackness of the county's trade, Birmingham not only looked busy, but was busy.[2] On the other hand, nearly every industry which was peculiar to the Black Country suffered to the full from the great slump; and, apart from the effects of the decline in iron and coal production, which will be examined in the next chapter, the result was that practically every centre in that part of our area was much more adversely affected than was Birmingham. Owing to American and German competition in the lock trade, which brought about a big decline in the output of pad-, cabinet-, and chest-locks, both Wolverhampton and Willenhall were adversely affected.[3] The earnings of the workers in that industry were 15 to 20 per cent. less in 1886 than they had been twenty years previously, and the numbers employed in it showed no increase between 1871 and 1881.[4] Other towns suffered similar misfortunes. Stourbridge, as already indicated, was injured by the fall of the flint-glass manufacture; Wednesbury and Darlaston by the extinction of the gun-lock makers; and the Dudley and Cradley district suffered from the depression in shipbuilding, which reacted on the demand for anchors and chains.[5] Although the employment in this industry did increase slightly between 1871 and 1881, a much larger proportion of the workers were women in the latter year, and the value of the output probably declined.[6]

[1] *Census of England and Wales*, 1871, vol. ii., p. 321 *et seq.*; 1881, vol. iii., p. 253.
[2] *Birmingham Gazette* (Letter), January 10, 1879.
[3] Wolverhampton suffered very severely during this period as a result of the closing down of three of the largest factories in the town—viz. Messrs Thorneycroft's Iron Works, Messrs Chubb's Lock Factory, and the Old Hall Tinplate- and Japanned-Ware Works.
[4] C. J. Woodward, *op. cit.*, p. 193; *Census of England and Wales*, 1871, vol. ii., p. 315 *et seq.*; 1881, vol. iii., p. 242.
[5] *Newspaper Cuttings* on *Birmingham Industries*, vol. ii., pp. 269-270.
[6] *Census of England and Wales*, 1871, vol. ii., p. 315 *et seq.*; 1881, vol. iii., pp. 246, 254.

But the greatest blow which the Black Country had to endure, as far as its finished manufactures were concerned, was from the precipitate decline in nail-making. The active demand between 1870 and 1875 had given a new lease of life to this failing industry, but after that period its ruin proceeded without alleviation. By 1879 wages were in most places 30 per cent. below the level of 1876. In Bromsgrove and Catshill nailers were reported to be " on starvation wages," and a man could make only six shillings by a week's labour.[1] The influx into the trade of colliers and ironworkers, after they had been turned off from their own employments, made matters worse,[2] and although a Board of Conciliation was set up to fix wages after the strike of 1879, this attempt broke down in a few months.[3] The demand from America declined, and Belgian competition began to affect sales to the Continental countries. Further, improvements in machinery enabled the production of cut nails to be cheapened; while a new type, the wire nail, also began to encroach on the market.[4] The number of workers in Staffordshire, Warwickshire and Worcestershire fell by 3000 between 1871 and 1881, and after that time the decline was accelerated. Darlaston, Pelsall, West Bromwich, Oldbury, Harborne and Wordsley were deserted by the industry, and everywhere the nailers were plunged in the utmost distress.[5] Nor was the disaster compensated for by any great advance in machine-made-nail production; for the output of this type within Birmingham and District appears to have remained stationary, and it was in other centres, such as in Leeds, that expansion took place.[6] Indeed, the only typical Black Country industry which prospered during this period was the manufacture of cast-iron hollow-ware, the output of which more than doubled during the twenty years preceding 1886.[7]

Thus, chiefly on account of the changes which occurred during the great depression, the relative importance of the various industries was very different from their position in 1860.

[1] *Report of the Chief Inspector of Factories and Workshops*, October 1879, pp. 14-15.
[2] *Ibid.*, p. 18.
[3] G. I. F. Lloyd, *op. cit.*, p. 404.
[4] C. J. Woodward, *op. cit.*, pp. 199-200.
[5] *Report of the Chief Inspector of Factories and Workshops*, October 1879, p. 18.
[6] C. J. Woodward, *op. cit.*, p. 199.
[7] *Ibid.*, pp. 181-182.

Then, in the group of finished manufactures, the great nail industry had been far ahead of any other, and had been followed by the four Birmingham staples—brass, jewellery, guns and buttons. After these came the glass, needle, saddlery and harness, lock, nut-and-bolt and screw trades; while the anchor and chain, pen, tinplate- and japanned-ware, hollow-ware, rolling-stock and wire trades were among the chief minor manufactures. By 1886, though nailing was still a leading manufacture, both the brass and jewellery trades afforded a greater volume of employment. The saddlery and harness trade came next, and ranked above glass, needles, buttons and locks, which had been stationary or declining. The tinplate- and japanned-ware, rolling-stock, hollow-ware and the anchor and chain trades had become large, and the pen, bedstead, screw, nut-and-bolt trades were of substantial importance. The wire manufacture remained small; while new trades had arisen in the food and drink and paper-box manufacture. Engineering had become vastly more important, though its size is difficult to judge, and it will concern us at a later stage.

While these adjustments had been taking place in the relative position of the various industries, changes of equal moment occurred in the methods of production, and these, too, can be associated mainly with the period of the great depression. The falling prices and the foreign competition, which became a real menace to the local hardware trades after 1875, caused the more enterprising manufacturers to seek for ways of reducing their costs. So they began to introduce machinery to perform operations previously carried on by hand, and over a wide range of industries important changes in processes occurred.[1] Some trades, it is true, failed to adjust themselves to the new conditions, and, like the glass trade, they preferred to surrender the market for the cheaper grades of ware rather than to hold it by a reorganization of their productive methods; and these trades were those which were hit particularly hard by the slump.

In the brassfoundry trade, as already shown, the change took the form of the substitution of stamping or pressing for casting, and in 1887 it was reported that in some branches the intro-

---

[1] *Reports of the Chief Inspector of Factories and Workshops*, October 1887, p. 50.

duction of machinery had effected a revolution in methods.[1] In the manufacture of cast-iron hollow-ware, machinery came to be employed for stamping and finishing the covers; and the power-press, which enabled bowls and similar articles to be made in one operation, was used more extensively in the tinplate-ware trade.[2] The process of spinning on the lathe was widely adopted in electro-plate manufacture, and the press was applied to the production of jewellery, which previously had been made by hand throughout.[3] Automatic machinery came to be employed for making umbrella ribs and the handles of edge tools.[4] Great improvements were effected in the plant of the cut-nail factories, so that by 1886 it was possible for one man to attend to five or six automatic machines.[5] During a strike in 1872, moreover, the nut-and-bolt trade " ran into machinery "[6]; while even the old gun manufacture was not unaffected. The introduction of steel barrels for sporting guns in place of the " damascened " type meant that the barrels could be drilled from a steel tube—a process which involved the use of power-machinery—instead of being welded painfully from strips of iron and steel. The plant of the rifle factories also was improved; and, to give one instance of the advance, the process of grinding the exterior of the barrels to the required size gave place to that of " stripping " on a lathe—a much less costly one.[7]

Power came to be more generally used for driving machinery[8]; and whereas in the sixties steam- or water-power alone had been available, during the seventies a new type of prime mover was introduced, which brought immense benefits to the multitude of small producers who could not afford the expensive and troublesome steam-engine. This was the gas-engine, which, by 1883, " had had a marked effect in increasing the number of factories "—i.e. places in which power-machinery was used.[9]

[1] *Annual Report of the National Society of Amalgamated Brassworkers*, 1887-1888, p. 8.
[2] C. J. Woodward, *op. cit.*, pp. 181, 206-208 ; W. H. Jones, *op. cit.*, pp. 134-136.
[3] *Ibid.*, pp. 190, 203.
[4] *Ibid.*, pp. 209, 210.
[5] *Ibid.*, p. 199.
[6] G. I. F. Lloyd, *op. cit.*, p. 404.
[7] *Private History of the Birmingham Small Arms Company, Limited.*
[8] *Report of the Chief Inspector of Factories and Workshops*, October 1887, p. 50.
[9] *Reports of the Inspectors of Factories*, October 1873, p. 46 ; October 1883, p. 52 ; *Newspaper Cuttings* on *Birmingham Industries*, vol. ii., p. 169 ; and C. J. Woodward, *op. cit.*, p. 190.

Largely because of this new motive force the system of hiring power began to decline during the seventies, and by the middle of the next decade it was dying out.[1]

The more extensive employment of power-machinery was partly responsible for the increase in the size of the typical producing units within many trades. Indeed, where an advance was made in the volume of production between 1875 and 1886, this was achieved usually by a growth in the output of the existing firms rather than by any rise in the number of separate units. So, in 1886, large factories employing upwards of 500 persons were usual, not only in the tube, rolling-stock, electro-plate and sheet-glass trades, as in 1860, but in the engineering, small-arms, lamp, pen, hollow-ware and tinplate industries also; while the typical firms in the jewellery and brassfoundry trades had increased in size. In a few industries, moreover, the movement was accelerated as a result of the assumption by factory owners of subsidiary processes, which previously had been in the hands of outworkers. Thus the depression after 1875 was said to have caused the extinction of outwork in the tube-fittings trade, which began to pass into the great factories where the tubes themselves were produced.[2] But in some industries the garret-master could still compete against the larger firms ; and this competition was even accentuated by the great depression, for discharged workers frequently set up on their own, and, having obtained materials on credit from the factor, they could, by working excessively hard, manage to undercut the factory prices. So, while there was during this period a marked advance towards large-scale production and mechanical methods, in certain industries, such as the brass and button trades, the little master seemed as prominent as ever.

Closely associated with the greater use of machinery was the change which occurred in the type of labour employed. Complaint was made by the tinplate workers and by many others that the introduction of machines had displaced skilled labour, and the more extensive application of the press to the production of jewellery and brass wares resulted in the employment of a larger proportion of female workers. The supersession of men by women was one of the most pronounced features of the

[1] *Report of the Chief Inspector of Factories and Workshops*, October 1889, pp. 30, 32.
[2] F. W. Hackwood, *Wednesbury Workshops*, p. 109.

period, and was, indeed, a part of the employers' attempt to reduce costs.[1] Even in industries which had not been affected by machinery, such as the chain trade, the proportion of female workers to the total rose considerably between 1871 and 1881.

In conclusion, it is interesting to consider the reply of the Council of the Birmingham Chamber of Commerce to the inquiries of the Royal Commission on the Depression of Trade in 1885; for the statement shows where contemporaries thought the causes of the slump were to be found, and what remedies they regarded as necessary.[2] The report declared that after a period of great and unusual activity between 1870 and 1875 there had followed a great and almost continuous depression (with one or two intervals in certain trades) since 1875, and that the slump became most severe in the year of the inquiry. The Council brought forward a multitude of explanations of the phenomenon, such as the legislative interference with the hours of work, the longer hours and lower wages of Continental workers, the activity of the trade unions, the better technical education of foreign artisans, the currency disturbances caused by the fall in the price of silver, and the agricultural depression at home and abroad; but most interesting of all was the estimate of the circumstances which had specially affected the local trades. These consisted of German and Belgian competition, the import duties imposed on British produce by foreign governments and the high cost of transport from Birmingham to the coast. Further, the proposals made by the Council for dealing with the situation show how economic distress was bringing about a change in political opinion. During the early years of the depression the Council, in spite of the increased importation of foreign goods, had declared its faithfulness to the doctrine of free trade; but in 1885, besides suggesting that railway charges should be restricted by fresh legislation, and that an international bi-metallic currency should be established, it advocated the formation of " a trading union between Great Britain and the Colonies," and the imposition of a tariff on foreign manufactured goods. It is true that as a result of the protests of a section of the Chamber a meeting was held, and, when put to the vote, the

[1] C. J. Woodward, *op. cit.*, pp. 182, 188 ; and *Annual Report of the National Society of Amalgamated Brassworkers*, 1887-1888, p. 6.
[2] G. H. Wright, *op. cit.*, pp. 307-319 ; *Newspaper Cuttings* on *Birmingham Industries*, vol. ii., p. 169.

last proposal was rejected by a small majority. But the mere fact that such a suggestion had emanated from the Council, which ten years previously had felt the position of the local industries secure against foreign competition,[1] shows the extent to which the markets of Birmingham and District were being threatened. "We are on the decline," said a Birmingham manufacturer ; "England's commercial supremacy is on the wane. We can recover only by thrift, economy, industry and a protective tariff."

[1] G. H. Wright, *op. cit.*, pp. 271, 273.

CHAPTER IV

THE END OF THE IRON AGE, 1876-1886

THE troubles of the area, though they can be attributed in some measure to the depression in the hardware trades, had their main source in the changes which came over the iron industry. The iron manufacture in the country as a whole passed through evil times between 1875 and 1886; but in this district the slump was not only more severe than elsewhere, but it marked the beginning of a permanent decline. And since the local iron trade was confined to the Black Country, where even the hardware industries had been more seriously affected than in Birmingham, the former section of our area found the period of the great depression among the most disastrous in its history.

We have already seen that the slump began earlier in the heavy trades than in the small metal manufactures, and that by the beginning of 1874 blast-furnaces, forges and mills were being shut down. Until the end of the decade the decline was practically continuous, and even the revival of 1881-1883 was of short duration and of no great magnitude. Afterwards the industry touched even lower levels, and although the majority of the local trades were beginning to recover in 1887, the iron manufacture was still found to be on the down-grade.[1] During this period some of the most famous ironworks were forced out of production. At Wolverhampton Messrs Thorneycroft & Co., an old-established firm then employing over 1000 men, came to grief in 1877.[2] Messrs J. Bagnall & Co., which had been incorporated in 1873, had to be reconstructed five years later and to write off a large proportion of its capital.[3] Of its three ironworks, which were situated at Tipton, Wednesbury and West Bromwich, the two former were permanently closed.[4] Early in the eighties the Darlaston Iron and Steel Company collapsed,[5] and Messrs J. Rigby & Sons, a large firm producing wrought-iron, axles, springs and bolts, failed in 1886.[6] Even the famous Tipton

---

[1] R. Hunt, *Mineral Statistics*, 1874-1881; *Mineral Statistics of Great Britain* (Home Office), 1882-1887.
[2] *Newspaper Cuttings* on *Birmingham Industries*, vol. ii., p. 170.
[3] *Ibid.*, vol. ii., p. 200.
[4] F. W. Hackwood, *History of Tipton* (1891), chap. xlvi.
[5] F. W. Hackwood, *History of Darlaston*, chap. xli.
[6] F. W. Hackwood, *Wednesbury Workshops*, p. 56.

concern, Messrs W. Barrows & Sons, whose B.B.H. brand of iron had possessed a world-wide reputation, was obliged to cease production in two out of its three establishments.[1] These are only a few examples of the troubles which overtook the great Staffordshire ironmasters at this time, and we have yet to mention the appearance of a tendency which later years were to confirm. This was the migration of manufacturers to iron centres on the seaboard. In 1884 it was reported that six important firms were transferring the seat of their activities from South Staffordshire to more favoured districts.[2] But statistical Tables will illustrate more clearly than any narrative the sudden and steep descent of the staple trade of the Black Country (see p. 241 *et seq.*).

After an almost continuous fall the output of South Staffordshire pig-iron in 1887 was only 40 per cent. of the production in 1871.[3] The decline relative to the country as a whole was even more spectacular. In 1860 the area had been responsible for 12·3 per cent. of the British output; in 1871 the proportion had amounted to nearly 11 per cent.; but by the end of the slump the Black Country, which then produced only 4 per cent. of the total, could no longer be considered a pig-iron centre of any importance. Over a third of the furnaces which had been in existence in 1871 had been dismantled, and only 28 were in blast.[4] In the absence of a suitable statistical measure it is more difficult to judge accurately the decline in the production of finished iron. But the number of puddling furnaces and mills in South Staffordshire had shrunk by more than half between 1871 and 1886, and though it still retained a large share of the wrought-iron trade, the fall even in this branch of the industry had been more precipitate in our area than elsewhere.[5] As the ironworks closed there was a wholesale migration of puddlers and of skilled ironworkers to Middlesbrough and the more flourishing metallurgical centres; but perhaps the best illustration of the fact that this was no normal cyclical depression, but the period of a permanent and enormous shrinkage in the industry, is to be found in the vital statistics of the leading iron-making towns. In spite of the increase in the population

[1] F. W. Hackwood, *History of Tipton*, p. 44.
[2] *Transactions of the National Association for the Promotion of Social Science,* 1884, p. 649.
[3] See Tables at end of chapter.
[4] *Mineral Statistics of the United Kingdom*, 1886, pp. 62-63.
[5] *Ibid.*, 1886, pp. 68-74.

of the area as a whole between 1871 and 1881, that of Bilston, Darlaston, Wednesbury and Sedgeley actually diminished; while in Kingswinford, Tipton, Stourbridge and Willenhall numbers were stationary.[1] It is not suggested that the migration of the ironworkers alone was responsible for this; for the decline in the hardware trades, particularly nail-making, together with the closing down of exhausted or flooded coal-mines, were contributory causes. But there can be little doubt that the explanation is to be found mainly in the fall of the iron industry.[2]

The nature of the forces which struck down that manufacture has already been suggested. The fact that the plant of South Staffordshire was old-fashioned was a great disadvantage to the district in its competition with more efficient centres during the period of falling prices; but, as far as pig-iron was concerned, the exhaustion of local supplies of raw materials undoubtedly had the greatest influence. Maintained at a fairly high level until 1878, the output of iron ore diminished rapidly after that date, and in 1885-1886 only 118,000 tons were being mined—less than a fifth of the production during the boom years.[3] By far the greater part of the ores required by the blast-furnaces, therefore, had to be brought from other centres, and the expense of transport to South Staffordshire added largely to costs. Further, coke had come to be more generally used for smelting, and in the absence of neighbouring supplies of coking coal this fuel had to be imported from Yorkshire, Derbyshire or South Wales, and mixed for smelting purposes with raw coal from the locality; while even limestone could be obtained from North Staffordshire more cheaply than it could be mined at Dudley and Wenlock.[4] Thus, depending as it did on distant sources for nearly all its raw materials, the pig-iron industry of the Black Country could not hope to rival districts in which the supplies of coking coal, ore and limestone were close at hand.

Meanwhile the local coal industry, which had responded only slightly to the boom, also entered upon a period of decline, for which the inundation of the older seams was mainly responsible. The Commissioners, set up under the Act of 1873, made attempts

---

[1] *Census of England and Wales*, 1871, vol. i., pp. 350-352 ; 1881, vol. i., pp. 347-349.
[2] G. T. Lawley, *History of Bilston* (1893), p. 262.
[3] R. Hunt, *op. cit.*, 1872, p. 85 ; 1878, p. 69 ; 1879, p. 69 ; 1885, p. 45 ; 1886, p. 51.
[4] C. J. Woodward, *op. cit.*, Appendix, p. 378 *et seq.*

to deal with the trouble. They began by improving the surface drainage, and tried to reduce the cost of raising water from the " pounds " by replacing the numerous small pumping engines by a few powerful ones.[1] But the difficulties were immense. The mine owners did not, for the most part, welcome these co-operative efforts, and the period was exceptionally unfavourable for their success. The fall in coal prices, by rendering mining operations unprofitable, led to the abandonment of private pumping in collieries which it no longer paid to work, and the difficulties of " unwatering " other mines, which were situated over the same " pounds," were thereby increased. Some owners, moreover, even went so far as to close their pits in order to avoid contributing to the expenses of co-operative drainage; and since the money available for providing pumps was raised by a levy on each ton of mineral brought to the surface, the decline in output—inevitable under any circumstances during a period of depressed prices—reduced the Commissioners' income. Nevertheless by 1886 some important results had been achieved. With their powers increased by the Acts of 1878 and 1882, which permitted them to levy higher dues, the Commissioners succeeded in bringing about a concentration of pumping power in certain districts. The owners in Oldbury, Kingswinford and, for a time, Bilston voted themselves free from the operation of the Act; but while in the two former districts pumping continued to be performed, by private enterprise, Bilston came within the Commissioners' scope again in 1881, and was amalgamated with the Tipton district. There two powerful new engines were set up to clear the mines of water, and whereas in 1875 the operations within that district had depended on no less than 80 engines, most of the work was being performed by 7 in 1886.[2] In the Old Hill district a similar concentration of power had been secured, with beneficial results. But these efforts only delayed the extinction of mining activities in the threatened areas. At Bilston, where the decline was most noticeable, while 2000 miners in 1860 had been at work, by 1893 their numbers had fallen to 200.[3] In 1890 the deep mines of Tipton produced

[1] *Report of Committee on South Staffordshire Mines Drainage*, 1920, p. 16 *et seq.*; and T. E. Lones, *op. cit.*, pp. 109-110, 118 *et seq.*
[2] *Report of Committee on South Staffordshire Mines Drainage*, 1920, pp. 15 and 20 *et seq.*
[3] G. T. Lawley, *History of Bilston* (1893), p. 253.

only half their output in 1874.[1] At Darlaston and Wednesbury numerous pits were closed, and all over the Black Country ironmasters, who had mined their own coal, abandoned their workings as their requirements decreased.

The total output of coal in South Staffordshire (vide Tables) declined to a comparatively slight extent during this period, though relative to the production in Great Britain the fall was continuous. But since the figures cover the whole of South Staffordshire, they mask the large decrease which occurred within our area. The output of the Cannock mines enormously increased, and between 1875 and 1886 amounted to one-third of the total production of South Staffordshire.[2] Thus the Black Country's tonnage fell from some 9,000,000 tons at the height of the boom to less than 6,000,000 tons in 1886. Further, the mines which had been sunk at Sandwell Park were responsible for an increasingly large quantity throughout the period, and after 1880 a new colliery company at Hamstead also began to obtain coal from under the red rocks to the east of the " visible " measures.[3] So, if the new areas are taken into account, it is evident that the older thick-coal districts suffered more severely than the above estimate of production indicates. The numbers employed by the mining industry, moreover, fell from 31,000 in 1871 to 22,000 in 1886.

While it was the exhaustion of the local supplies of raw materials which was destroying the pig-iron and the coal industries, we must look elsewhere for the cause of the decay in the wrought-iron production. To some extent, of course, this branch of manufacture was injured by the fact that larger quantities of pig had to be brought from distant sources; and the improvement in the quality of the cheaper iron of North Staffordshire, Lancashire and Cleveland was also a menace to the Black Country, with its necessarily high costs.[4] Yet a more powerful force was at work. As we have seen, during the sixties Bessemer steel had begun to supersede iron in the manufacture of railway rails; but the South Staffordshire ironmasters, who did not cater for that class of product, were not thereby seriously

---

[1] F. W. Hackwood, *History of Tipton*, p. 42.
[2] T. E. Lones, *op. cit.*, pp. 115, 121.
[3] *Ibid.*, p. 116.
[4] *Transactions of the National Association for the Promotion of Social Science*, 1884, pp. 650-653.

affected. In the seventies, however, both Bessemer and open-hearth steel was pressed into other uses, and one of the staple products of the local iron trade received a set-back. This was the manufacture of ship and boiler plates. Previously, plates of large size had been made by welding pieces of wrought-iron together. But, as the size of ships increased, this method became increasingly unsatisfactory; for not only were the iron plates likely to give at the welds, but they had to be made of great thickness. The introduction of the new steel solved these difficulties, and it became possible to make large plates of this material, which were at once stronger, thinner and less expensive than those of wrought-iron. So, during the seventies, steel began to supersede iron in shipbuilding, and a staple market of South Staffordshire was lost. About 1880, moreover, local firms began to produce large welded-steel pipes in place of iron riveted pipes, and the former proved more efficient, since they had a smoother bore and occasioned less friction. From this the next step was to employ steel in constructional engineering, and from the time of the opening of the first all-steel bridge, in 1885,[1] wrought-iron began to be driven from another large market. By the middle eighties the demand for wrought-iron was rapidly declining, and with it the fortunes of the Staffordshire iron-masters.[2]

In view of the technical advantages possessed by steel, and since it could be produced more economically than wrought-iron, it is remarkable that the period of transition was so long; for it was not until the eighties that the steel age could be said to have arrived. The conservatism of engineers was doubtless a contributory cause. The efficiency of steel had to be proved by use, while smiths and other metalworkers had to learn how to work in it before it could be extensively employed. But the chief cause of the delay is to be found by an examination of productive methods. Wrought-iron was produced on a comparatively small scale, because several of the key-processes, such as those performed by the puddler and shingler, were essentially hand-processes. Even in a large ironworks mass-production methods could not be employed, and a great output could be obtained only by duplicating processes. But steel required a

[1] This was built by a Wednesbury firm to bridge the Ganges at Benares.
[2] F. W. Harbord and E. F. Law, *op. cit.*, pp. 183-186.

large plant for economical production, and this involved a heavy
capital outlay, which necessarily impeded the transition from the
iron age.

Although Bessemer plants had been operated in South
Staffordshire since the early sixties, the steel-makers during the
seventies tended to establish themselves on the coast rather
than in the Midlands. The reasons for this have been touched
upon elsewhere. The manufacturer who was about to involve
himself in a great capital outlay would naturally turn away from
districts in which the raw materials were approaching exhaustion
and in which transport charges added to the cost of conducting
an export trade. Further, the fact that the new acid steel had
to be made from non-phosphoric ores drew producers either to
Cumberland, the site of the only British supplies, or to coastal
areas which were conveniently situated for obtaining Spanish
hæmatite. Thus, during the seventies, not only was the South
Staffordshire wrought-iron being displaced, but the steel which
was superseding it was being produced in other parts of the
country. The discovery of the basic process, however, which
enabled phosphoric ores to be used in steel-making, checked,
though only slightly, the decline of the Black Country as a centre
of ferrous-metal production. As already shown, vast deposits
of " puddlers' tap " had accumulated in the district in consequence of a century of wrought-iron production, and this, though
siliceous, contained a proportion, amounting to 50 per cent., of
iron and 2·6 to 3 per cent. of phosphorus. When mixed with
Northamptonshire, Oxfordshire and local ores, " tap cinder "
proved an excellent material from which to make basic pig for
the steel furnaces; and since in the early eighties this material
could be had for the asking in South Staffordshire, the district
had advantages for basic-steel producers which went far to
balance its deficiencies.[1] One of the first two basic Bessemer
plants in the country was established at Wednesbury in 1882.
The Staffordshire Steel and Ingot Company of Bilston erected
another a year later, and basic open-hearth steel began to be
produced in the district shortly afterwards.[2] At this time, however, basic steel was looked upon with suspicion, and was not
employed for many purposes, and the years preceding 1886

[1] F. W. Harbord and E. F. Law, *op. cit.*, p. 185.
[2] *Ibid.*, pp. 184-185; F. W. Hackwood, *Wednesbury Workshops*, p. 121;
G. T. Lawley, *op. cit.*, chap. xxv.

were significant for South Staffordshire mainly because of decline in demand for its wrought-iron in favour of acid steel produced elsewhere.[1]

The decay of the iron trade was not without influence on the organization of the heavy industries. The manufacture of wrought-iron could be conducted on a comparatively small scale, and in busy times head puddlers and shinglers often established works of their own. But there was no place for the small man in the new steel industry, and only a large capitalist could provide the expensive plant which had become necessary. Similarly, in the manufacture of pig-iron, the smaller and less economical units were forced out of production during the depression, while larger blast-furnaces were constructed; and there was, in consequence, a big increase in the average output of the Staffordshire furnaces between 1875 and 1886.[2] Thus the opportunities for the small man were reduced, and the scale of production in the heavy metallurgical trades was greatly extended.

Throughout the period, works were sold and resold many times before they finally ceased to be operated, and in some instances a curious system arose by which the owners, despairing of ever working at a profit, rented their plants to their managers or foremen, who were in a position to drive down costs to a minimum. The most obvious result of the slump, however, was the decay of the integrated firm. The ironmaster who mined his ore, coal and limestone, and who ran blast-furnaces, forges and mills, and even an engineering plant, was a common figure in the sixties and early seventies, as we have seen. But the exhaustion of the local ironstone and the flooding of the coal-mines induced most of these concerns to give up their mining activities, and they began to buy their raw materials from other districts. For many years, moreover, the finished-iron makers had been obliged to purchase a proportion of their pig from outside South Staffordshire, and during the depression the fact that supplies could be obtained from other districts more cheaply than they could

[1] The Black Country output of Bessemer-steel ingots amounted to 7200 tons in 1879 and 12,300 tons in 1882. The latter figures represented only 0·7 per cent. of the total British production (*Mineral Statistics of the United Kingdom*, 1883, p. 72).

[2] See Tables, p. 242. The typical blast-furnace had a capacity of 200-400 tons of pig-iron weekly in 1886 as compared with 100 tons thirty years previously. This was attributed partly to the general adoption of the hot blast during the period (F. W. Hackwood, *Oldbury and Round About*, p. 175).

be produced locally caused many ironmasters, who previously had made much of the pig they needed, to dismantle their blast-furnaces. Some firms gave up even their wrought-iron works and confined themselves to producing finished products. So, just when the producing unit within each stage of iron and steel manufacture was becoming larger, there was occurring in the Black Country the break-up of the great integrated concerns which had for long been representative of the iron trade; and although a few continued to exist, this form of organization was never again common in South Staffordshire. The great depression, indeed, coincided with the last years of the Malleable Iron Period, during which the Black Country had risen to fame, and henceforth its prosperity was to depend on activities other than iron production. An industrial epoch had come to an end. " After 1873 the local iron trade began to decay. . . . Steel rails and steel ships began to take the place of iron rails and ironclads. The glory of Staffordshire iron departed, notwithstanding the renown of so many of our local ironmasters and their famous brands of iron." [1]

OUTPUT OF PIG-IRON [2]

Year	South Staffordshire and Worcestershire	Proportion of South Staffordshire and Worcestershire Output of Total British Production
	Tons	Per cent.
1871 . . .	726,000	10·9
1872 . . .	673,000	10·0
1873 . . .	673,000	10·2
1874 . . .	452,000	7·6
1875 . . .	471,000	7·4
1876 . . .	466,000	7·1
1877 . . .	428,000	6·5
1878 . . .	393,000	6·2
1879 . . .	326,000	5·4
1880 . . .	385,000	5·0
1881 . . .	374,000	4·6
1882 . . .	398,000	4·7
1883 . . .	430,000	5·0
1884 . . .	357,000	4·6
1885 . . .	344,000	4·7
1886 . . .	294,000	4·0
1887 . . .	293,000	3·9

[1] F. W. Hackwood, *Wednesbury Workshops*, p. 119.
[2] The following Tables have been compiled from R. Hunt, *Mineral Statistics*, 1871-1881, and *Mineral Statistics of the United Kingdom*, 1882-1887.

Q

BLAST-FURNACES

Year			Works active	Furnaces built	Furnaces in Blast
1871	.	.	53	163	108
1875	.	.	53	155	76¼
1879	.	.	29	140	44
1880	.	.	30	137	46
1882	.	.	29	133	47½
1886	.	.	21	107	28½

				Annual Average Production per Furnace in Blast
				Tons
1871	.	.	.	6,700
1886	.	.	.	10,300

COAL OUTPUT

Year				South Staffordshire and Worcestershire (including Cannock Area)	Percentage of Total British Output
				Tons	
1871	.	.	.	10,000,000 ⎫	
1872	.	.	.	10,600,000 ⎪	
1873	.	.	.	9,500,000 ⎬	7·8
1874[1]	.	.	.	8,400,000 ⎪	
1875	.	.	.	10,300,000 ⎭	
1876	.	.	.	10,100,000 ⎫	
1877	.	.	.	9,800,000 ⎪	
1878	.	.	.	9,100,000 ⎬	7·1
1879	.	.	.	9,400,000 ⎪	
1880	.	.	.	9,700,000 ⎭	
1881	.	.	.	10,200,000 ⎫	
1882	.	.	.	10,100,000 ⎬	6·5
1883	.	.	.	10,300,000 ⎭	
1884	.	.	.	9,700,000 ⎫	
1885	.	.	.	9,900,000 ⎬	5·9
1886	.	.	.	8,700,000 ⎭	

---

[1] The output was affected by a four-months' strike during this year.

IRON-ORE OUTPUT

Year				South Staffordshire and Worcestershire	Percentage of Total British Output
1871	.	.	.	710,000	4'3
1872	.	.	.	640,000	
1873	.	.	.	580,000	
1874 [1]	.	.	.	140,000	
1875	.	.	.	720,000	
1876	.	.	.	590,000 ⎫	
1877	.	.	.	640,000 ⎪	
1878	.	.	.	590,000 ⎬	3'3
1879	.	.	.	480,000 ⎪	
1880	.	.	.	360,000 ⎭	
1881	.	.	.	310,000	1'7
1882	.	.	.	180,000 ⎫	
1883	.	.	.	150,000 ⎪	
1884	.	.	.	120,000 ⎬	0'8
1885	.	.	.	120,000 ⎪	
1886	.	.	.	120,000 ⎭	

FINISHED IRON

Year			Puddling Furnaces		Rolling Mills	
			in United Kingdom	in South Staffordshire and Worcestershire	in United Kingdom	in South Staffordshire and Worcestershire
1871	.	.	6800	2000	870	320
1875	.	.	7600	2000	910	330
1879	.	.	5100	1600	850	310
1881	.	.	5500	1600	900	320
1882	.	.	5700	1500	920	300
1885	.	.	3900	1200	800	240
1886	.	.	3400	1200	670	160

OUTPUT OF PUDDLED BARS

Year				United Kingdom	South Staffordshire and Worcestershire
1881	.	.	.	2,680,000	580,000
1882	.	.	.	2,840,000	660,000

Year				Numbers employed in and about Mines in South Staffordshire and Worcestershire [2]
1865	.	.	.	27,000
1871	.	.	.	31,000
1876	.	.	.	33,000
1878	.	.	.	25,000
1881	.	.	.	24,000
1886	.	.	.	22,000

[1] The output was affected by a four-months' strike during this year.
[2] Computations of the Inspector of Mines.

PART IV
THE NEW ERA, 1887-1914

CHAPTER I

THE FORTUNES OF THE OLDER MANUFACTURES

DURING the quarter of a century preceding the Great War the tendencies which the depression had first brought into prominence continued to exercise their influence on the industrial structure of the area. With a few exceptions, the industries which had passed the period of stress unscathed remained prosperous until 1914, and even entered upon a period of expansion after the slump was over; while most of the trades which had begun to fail between 1876 and 1886 never recovered. During the depression the chief force which had worked to modify the character of Birmingham and District, as far as its finished manufactures were concerned, had been competition from the Continent and from America. After 1886, although this still continued to exercise a strong influence, it was reinforced by two other factors. The first of these was to be found in a general change of fashion. It is perhaps dangerous to generalize about the taste of particular eras; but the Victorian age did correspond roughly to a period when fashion required ornate domestic fittings in japanned ware, brassfoundry and bedsteads, and when heavy watch-chains, securing expensive gold watches, voluminous garments requiring a multitude of buttons and heavy fastenings, and mother-of-pearl decorations, either for the person or for domestic utensils, were in demand. Even in the decoration of public buildings taste ran to elaboration, in the form of pseudo-mediæval metalwork. Now such of the old trades of Birmingham as were affected by fashion (and they were many) had grown to greatness on the wave of Victorian prosperity, and flourished by serving the taste of the period. But the great depression had begun to undermine the foundations of that extraordinary era. Germany and America were forging ahead, and, as competition became keener in the foreign markets, it was seen that the old unchallenged supremacy had gone for ever. There was a loss of complacency and a beginning of self-criticism, which naturally extended not only to economic affairs but to questions of taste as well. So, by the end of the century, the industries which were subject to the dictates of fashion were beginning to suffer. They had been created by

Victorian habits and tastes; with their supersession these industries fell. The decline of the button, gold-chain, bedstead, watch, japanned-ware, gas-fittings and " ecclesiastical " metalwork trades was, indeed, intimately associated with the end of Victorianism. They were all overwhelmed by the demand for simplicity, the consequence of a revolt against the previous ostentation, and by the necessity for cheapness in face of a more doubtful future. A more obvious and immediate influence on the development of the older trades, however, came from the impact of a group of new industries, which brought into existence a fresh demand for parts and semi-finished products.

But as these new manufactures and their subsidiaries will be studied in detail in another chapter all that will be attempted here will be an examination of the expansion or decline of the older industries (excluding iron and coal), and of their gradual transformation.

As we propose to divide the manufactures into two groups, those which prospered and those which declined, and to treat them in that order, the jewellery trade can naturally be selected as the starting-point; for its development, which had been so pronounced between 1840 and 1886, continued without serious check until 1914. The best illustration of its growth is afforded by estimates of employment, which show that the numbers in the industry increased from 14,000-16,000 in 1886 to some 30,000 on the outbreak of the war.[1] It is worth while recounting its history in some detail, since this will indicate how intimately the fortunes of the trade were bound up with changes of fashion. During the last two years of the depression the manufacture of jewellery had suffered as severely as at any time in its history; but the Jubilee Celebrations of 1887 marked the beginning of a revival, and created a big demand for medals and badges, insignia for corporations and presentation caskets for the Queen.[2] During the next five years there was great prosperity; but in 1892 the death of the Duke of Clarence reduced the demand for high-class jewellery; while the depression of 1893-1894 had serious effects on other types. Revival came in 1895, and

---

[1] The estimate of 30,000 is based on the *Annual Report of the Chief Inspector of Factories and Workshops*, 1904, p. 41 ; and on the *Supplement to the Annual Report*, 1905, p. 3. These show the employment in the Birmingham jewellery trade to have been nearly 25,000 in the early years of the century. There was certainly a considerable increase in employment before 1914.

[2] *Report of the Chief Inspector of Factories and Workshops*, October 1889, p. 32.

the trade flourished exceedingly until the end of the century and the death of the Queen. A short period of good demand, which began in 1906, came to an abrupt conclusion in 1908, when the effects of the American crisis were felt in England, and the recovery of 1909 was checked in the following year by the death of King Edward. The Coronation of 1911 led to a period of great prosperity, which lasted two years, when the trade again became depressed.[1]

But this general review of the trade does not reveal the very substantial changes which its various branches underwent during the period. In the jewellery trade proper, for instance, there was a great development of the gold branch, at the expense of the silver; for, by the nineties, silver had fallen too low in price for it to remain a fashionable metal for ornamental purposes. The silversmiths, however, found compensation in the fact that the cheapness of their metal enabled it to be extensively used for the production of small articles of toilet or table ware. The abolition of the plate duties in 1890 also helped to promote these new manufactures; and during the next twenty years a large demand grew up for silver brush-backs, cigarette-cases and picture-frames; while silver began to compete with electro-plate for table-ware. Further, the spread of organized athleticism towards the end of the century created another branch of the silversmiths' trade—viz. the production of presentation cups and shields, and brought a demand for small fancy club medals. Meanwhile, if, during the nineties, a change in men's fashions caused a decline in the gold watch-chain section, compensation was found in the rise of gold stud and link manufacture, and in the increased production of gold brooches, which accompanied a new style in women's dress; while the formation of the De Beers Combine in 1889, which steadied the price of diamonds, resulted in additional business for the stone-setters. Just before the war there was a revival of a trade which had died. This was diamond cutting and polishing. We have seen that in the early seventies this trade had been introduced into Birmingham; but it came to an early end owing to the lack of skilled labour, and it was not until 1912 that another attempt was made to bring it within the scope of the jewellers' activities.[2] The output of

[1] *United States Daily Consular and Trade Reports*, May 17, 1911, and May 20, 1913.
[2] *Newspaper Cuttings* on *Birmingham Industries* (1914-1922), pp. 73, 132, 176.

electro-plate ware, moreover, grew steadily, and in 1914 a large export trade was carried on with all parts of the world. Only the gilt- and imitation-jewellery section lagged behind, largely in consequence of the increasing keenness of foreign competition. This became serious in most branches of the jewellery trade proper during the nineties, when German goods began to oust those of Birmingham origin from foreign markets. The rise of tariff walls brought a further decrease in exports, and in some classes of goods there was active competition in the home market from foreign makers.[1] Rivalry from abroad was not, however, sufficient to hinder the expansion of the industry except in the one section mentioned.

Thus, as far as jewellery proper was concerned, the most noticeable change to record in the character of the industry was a greater concentration on high-class goods, which was due partly to a large positive increase in the gold section, and partly to a decline in the silver- and imitation-jewellery section. New branches, such as the manufacture of silver smallwares and athletic trophies, and of gold studs and links, had arisen, and the electro-plate trade had continued its progress. The increase in the size of the industry and in its range of products resulted in an extension of the jewellers " quarter "; and in 1914, as in 1860, the industry ranked among the two chief trades of Birmingham.[2] Yet, although all had gone well, a note of alarm was sounded a year before the war. The trade, it was declared, was beginning to feel the influence of a change in the direction of national expenditure. Instead of expensive jewellery, people were beginning to buy motor-cars; but, as yet, rivalry from this unexpected quarter was not serious.[3]

The brass trade was equally progressive, and in 1914, as in 1860, it ranked along with jewellery as the leading industries of the town. Employment rose from about 20,000-22,000 in 1886 to nearly 32,000 in 1911 [4]; while, in addition, there were several hundred others who were engaged in rolling nickel silver and other non-ferrous alloys, a trade which was carried on in the brass and copper mills, and should, therefore, be classed with

---

[1] J. C. Roche, *op. cit.*, chap. vii.
[2] *The Times* (Birmingham Number), October 2, 1912, p. 29.
[3] *United States Daily Consular and Trade Reports*, May, 26, 1914.
[4] *Census of England and Wales*, 1881, vol. iii., p. 246 *et seq.*; 1891, vol. iii., p. 255 ; 1911, vol. x., p. 265, 283, 297.

the brass group. The changes which occurred in these manufactures, however, were much more significant than the developments in jewellery. The first event of importance, curiously enough, coincides with the last year of the depression. In 1886 there was " a tightening up of the specifications for cartridge metal," which meant that material of a higher quality had to be produced for the manufacture of ammunition ordered by the Government.[1] The importance of this step, from a technical point of view, will receive attention in a later chapter. Here it is sufficient to state that the result was to create a division between the firms manufacturing sheet brass for cartridges and those serving the general trade; and that from this time onwards local ammunition firms all tended to embark on the production of the metal they required. The discovery of the " extruded metal " process, which enabled rods and sections of a high quality to be produced more cheaply than by rolling and drawing, also had an important influence on the industry as a whole; and after 1894 this process began to supersede the older methods of manufacture for certain classes of product.[2] Further, the rise of new industries, and the decay of others, as a result of changes of fashion, began to transform the uses to which the wire, tubes and strip metal, produced by the primary section of the trade, were put; while the branches concerned with finished goods also underwent modification. The cabinet and lighting brassfounders had depended during the mid-Victorian era on the demand for elaborate domestic fittings; but, as we have seen, taste was changing. Simpler types of ornament were coming into fashion, and the construction of houses and furniture which dispensed with much of the domestic labour previously required was destroying the market for the older products. After the beginning of the new century, moreover, the spread of electric-lighting gave an additional blow to the trade; for, instead of heavy cast gas-fittings, only a few stamped parts were now needed. Thus the cabinet and lighting branches began to suffer, and, while the stamped and pressed section benefited, the cast section as a whole declined. The fall would have been more marked if foreign taste had suffered a corresponding change; but, fortunately, it was not affected to the same extent, and, as about 30 per

---

[1] *The Non-Ferrous Metal Trades*, The Kynoch Press (1924).
[2] Brochure published by the *Delta Metal Company, Ltd.*, pp. 81-85.

cent. of the pre-war output of brassfoundry was exported, the foreign demand had an important compensatory effect. At the same time, however, although the plumbing work increased, much of the engineers' brassfoundry and of the heavy-castings trade departed to the north; the " ecclesiastical " or art branch faded into insignificance; and after 1900 the production of mounts and of brass-cased tubes for the bedstead manufacturers dwindled.

It is obvious, then, that the general increase in wealth and population, which served to explain the expansion of the brass trade up to 1886, was not the cause of its growth after that date. The explanation is to be found rather in the new demands which were growing up. The electrical industry, besides injuring the profitable gaselier manufacture, created new markets for electrical fittings, wire, tubes and sheet metal. The introduction of the turbine gave rise to a demand for brass for turbine blades; while during the first decade of the twentieth century the motor industry became an important customer. Besides requiring a multitude of brass accessories, such as lighting equipment, and so creating a new section of the brass trade, the motor firms needed copper radiator tubes and cylinder jackets; while nickel-silver wire and sheets were manufactured on a large scale, as a result of the demands of several of the new industries. Further, the producers of brass-cased tubes, whose output for the bedstead trade had declined, found a new market in supplying parts for shop-fittings, which were increasing in elaboration; and, for engineering purposes, new alloys, such as phosphor and bronze, began to be made.

So, if the brass trade during this period maintained its rate of expansion, this was not because of the growth of the markets on which it had depended before 1886. On the contrary, particularly after 1900, the manufacture of gas-fittings, of cabinet work and of most cast wares was practically stationary, and the demand for sheet and tubes from several of the older customers declined. The growth of the trade is to be attributed, indeed, solely to the fact that non-ferrous products happened to be required by the new industries, and that manufacturers were able to adapt themselves to meeting fresh demands.

Equally great developments occurred in the screw trade of Smethwick and Birmingham, and in the nut-and-bolt manufacture of Darlaston, Wednesbury and Wolverhampton. These two industries are classed in the Census Tables with the rivet trade, and the great expansion of the whole group is shown by the fact that the amount of employment afforded in the three counties rose from 5200 in 1881, and 6700 in 1891, to 12,600 in 1911.[1] From other information available concerning the trades, and from our knowledge of their localization, it is possible to distinguish fairly accurately the number found in each of the three manufactures, and so to estimate the growth of each. The Census shows, for instance, that the numbers in Worcestershire actually declined after 1891—a fact which is accounted for by the gradual diminution in the number of rivet-makers, who carried on their trade in domestic workshops. In 1911 there were 800 to 900 persons in the whole group in the Rowley Urban District, and probably most of these were domestic rivet- or staple-workers, whose trade was being drawn into the factories. The screw manufacture, on the other hand, had become a large industry, and provided employment for some 4800 persons in 1911, three-fifths of whom were women. The nut-and-bolt trade then employed 6000 to 7000 persons, mainly at Darlaston.

Both the nut-and-bolt and the screw industries, besides doubling their labour force during the period, had increased their output to an even greater degree, owing to mechanical changes. Up to 1890 the construction of Colonial railway systems had provided one of the chief markets for nuts and bolts; while the building trade at home and abroad had taken the bulk of the screws. After that date, although the Colonial and foreign orders for railway fastenings slowed down, both the Darlaston and the Smethwick trades were swept into the range of the new engineering industries, which were just beginning their great period of expansion. The electrical engineering and machine-tool trades provided fresh markets for nuts and bolts, and the cycle firms called for great quantities of " metal-thread " screws, which began to rank, as far as output was concerned, with the original products of the trade—viz. wood-screws. After 1900 the motor industry entered the field as a customer for both classes of screws, and the factories increased their range of output to include such products as tyre levers, screw hooks, and a host of other small

[1] *Census of England and Wales*, 1881, vol. iii., p. 246 *et seq.*; 1891, vol. iii., p. 255 ; 1911, vol. x., part i., pp. 265, 283, 297.

articles required by engineers. Although the greater part of these new demands was associated with developments in the home market, the export trade continued to expand,[1] and just before the war the screw manufacturers were sending abroad 50 per cent. of their output. But the nut-and-bolt makers, though the Colonies still took large quantities, had lost much of their foreign trade as a result of the tariffs.

The chain and anchor trades also continued to make great progress, and employment in them rose from 4000 in 1881 to 6600 in 1911.[2] Even here, however, there was a change in the relative importance of different types of products, and growth was limited to a few lines. It will be remembered that from very early times South Staffordshire had produced small chains for agricultural purposes, and that the introduction of the manufacture of heavy chains, cables and anchors occurred during the second quarter of the nineteenth century. Until the eighties the latter trade had increased only slowly in relative importance as compared with light-chain production; but during this period this tendency was accelerated. The great agricultural depression of the last quarter of the nineteenth century, and the rise of mechanical transport, prevented any considerable development of the older branch, and the expansion in the industry was to be attributed mainly to the greater need for heavy cables by shipbuilders, dock companies and engineers. This demand did not increase steadily; for, naturally, the industry was one which was subject to the fluctuation occasioned by the trade cycle; but the net result of the developments between 1886 and 1913 was to leave South Staffordshire with almost a monopoly of the ships'-cable trade of the world. The preservation of this position was to be attributed to the fact that, except for the makers of electric-welded chain—a trade which was growing up in the decade preceding the war—the chainsmiths still continued to find Staffordshire wrought-iron the most suitable raw material for their trade, in spite of the introduction of mild steel into many other local industries.[3]

---

[1] *The Times* (Birmingham Number), October 2, 1912, p. 39.

[2] *Census of England and Wales*, 1881, vol. iii., pp. 246, 254 ; 1911, vol. x., pp. 265, 283, 297.

[3] The workers in this industry did not share the advantage which arose from the expansion of demand. We hear repeatedly of the trade being over-supplied with labour through the drift of employees from the declining trades—viz. iron, coal and nailing—into the chain manufacture, and this kept wages

During the three years preceding the war the Cradley trade reached its zenith.[1] Even the small-chain trade was prosperous; for, while home sales had declined, a large export trade was being carried on with India and Canada. Taking the industry as a whole, about half of its annual output was exported, and there was little sign of competition in foreign markets. The only adverse tendency which was apparent was to be found in quite a different direction. As ships grew larger in size they ceased to anchor as frequently as before, preferring to tie up alongside the quay when they were in port. This was recognized as a factor likely to injure the " renewal " trade, which was an important source of demand. Otherwise the prospects of Cradley were bright and its supremacy unchallenged.

Among the older manufactures, then, the jewellery, brass, nut-and-bolt, screw, chain and anchor trades were those which were subject to a very rapid growth, and in which employment doubled during the period under review. But there were several others in which a smaller expansion occurred. Of these the steel-pen trade was typical. In 1866, 98,000 gross of steel pens had been produced weekly in Birmingham; by 1885 this output had increased to 160,000, and by 1913 to 200,000 gross weekly.[2] The Census figures likewise show a steady growth up to 1901, although there was a slight fall in the next decade :

Year	Number of Persons engaged in Steel-Pen Manufacture in Warwickshire [3]
1881 . . .	2600
1891 . . .	3100
1901 . . .	3800
1911 . . .	3700

During the eighties French pen factories had been built, and before the end of the century Germany entered the industry, while tariffs had closed the American market; yet up to 1914 the town possessed practically a monopoly of the world's steel-pen

in a chronically depressed condition (*Report of the Chief Inspector of Factories and Workshops*, October 1888, pp. 108-109).

[1] R. H. Tawney, *op. cit.*, chap. i.

[2] *Handbook for Birmingham and the Neighbourhood* (British Association Meeting, 1913), pp. 385-386.

[3] It should be remembered that the Census figures do not include certain types of workers—*e.g.* box-makers—who were employed in the pen factories. *Census of England and Wales*, 1881, p. 250 *et seq.*; 1891, vol. iii., p. 250 ; 1901, Warwickshire, p. 51 ; 1911, vol. x., part i., p. 283.

trade and exported 75 per cent. of its output. Not until just before the war, indeed, when the yellow-metal pen began to be produced in the United States, did Birmingham manufacturers suffer greatly from foreign competition.[1] The introduction of fountain pens and typewriters was a more serious matter, and it was probably the increasing use of these substitutes which was mainly responsible for the static condition of the industry during the first decade of the twentieth century.[2] Yet adverse factors were, to a large extent, counteracted by the spread of education, which provided a continual increase in Birmingham's customers, and by the change from the brush to the pen as a writing instrument in the East, especially in Japan. Meanwhile pen-makers widened the scope of their manufacture by concerning themselves to a much greater extent than previously with an allied manufacture, that of stationers' sundries, which consist of such things as pen-cases, paper-clips and drawing-pins, and the growth of this section was very rapid after 1900, on account of the appearance of more elaborate office equipment.

In the lock trade, in which 5600 persons were employed in 1911, an expansion of about the same magnitude occurred. The Census returns are not exactly comparable over the period; but it does not appear that any increase in employment occurred until the last decade, when there was a slight advance.[3] In the eighties, however, machinery had begun to be used in the trade, and after 1900 this tendency was accentuated, and led to a great increase in the proportion of female labour between 1901 and 1911. The development was associated in some degree with the replacement of the older handicraft methods by pressing and stamping; but the advent of a new type of lock was largely responsible. At the beginning of the century the locks in general use in the world fell into two main classes: the English type —which Willenhall and Wolverhampton produced for the home market, the Colonies and the Far East—and the German type, which between 1880 and 1900 had ousted those of English origin from Europe and South America. After 1900 the American cylinder lock, which had been made for some years previously

[1] *The Times* (Birmingham Number), October 2, 1912, p. 37.
[2] *Midland Captains of Industry* in *The Birmingham Gazette and Express*, September 30, 1908.
[3] *Report of the Chief Inspector of Factories and Workshops*, October 1890, p. 25; October 1892, p. 105; October 1893, p. 313; *Census of England and Wales*, 1881, vol. iii., p. 246; 1911, vol. x., part i., p. 265.

for North and South American markets, came into competition with the older types, in Europe and elsewhere, and for a time the Staffordshire producers suffered. Some years before the war, however, a few local factories took up the manufacture of this cylinder lock, which involved a highly mechanized productive process. Thus, by 1914, in addition to the older types of hand-made lock, machine-made articles of the English and the American types were also being manufactured; and the increased use of machinery, together with the replacement of wrought-iron parts and keys by malleable-iron castings, enabled a large output to be obtained, without any considerable expansion of the labour force. Willenhall still remained the centre of the trade, with about half of the total number of operatives. Wolverhampton followed, with about a quarter, and Walsall came third in importance. The localization of the industry, in fact, had not changed during our period, except for the fact that the section which had been carried on in outlying villages had disappeared. Just before the war a new branch was added to the trade; for several of the larger manufacturers took up the production of door and lock furniture. High-class articles of this kind still continued to be made by the Birmingham brassfounders; but Willenhall became an important centre for the cheaper qualities. Meanwhile the safe trade had not only expanded but had developed a new branch—viz. the manufacture of steel strong-rooms.[1] Minor Willenhall trades, such as curry-comb manufacture, had practically ceased to exist; but compensation was found in the growth of the production of stampings and light castings.[2]

The staple trade of Redditch also fell within this group of slowly expanding industries. Here, again, it was not by an increase in the labour force that the growth had been brought about; for, after declining during the eighties, the number of needle-makers remained practically stationary between 1891 and 1911, when 3400 persons were so employed.[3] The testimony of manufacturers, however, points to a steady increase of production, which lasted up to the war—an increase made possible

[1] *Midland Captains of Industry* in *Birmingham Gazette and Express*, May 16, 1908.
[2] F. W. Hackwood, *The Annals of Willenhall* (1908), pp. 165-166.
[3] *Census of England and Wales*, 1881, vol. iii., p. 250 *et seq.*; 1891, vol. iii., p. 250; 1901, Warwickshire, p. 51; Worcestershire, p. 51; 1911, vol. x., part i., pp. 283, 297.

R

by an improvement in mechanical methods and by a growth in the scale of production. Yet the rise in output cannot have been very great. The Redditch district relied on the export trade for the disposal of 80 per cent. of its products, and during this period it was finding its progress hampered, not only by the increasing use of sewing-machines, the needles for which were largely an American monopoly, but also by the competition of the Germans. The allied manufacture, that of fishhooks, which also catered mainly for foreign markets, suffered from Scandinavian rivalry, and from the American tariff wall, and grew but slowly.[1]

In this group of industries we have to note a significant change in localization, which apparently began to take place during the nineties. In 1881, 60 per cent. of the needle-makers in Warwickshire and Worcestershire lived in villages within the former county. In 1891 the proportions were the same; but twenty years later Worcestershire had become the chief centre, and had more than two-thirds of the total number. Redditch alone had about 1600 out of 3400 persons in the industry.[2] This migration is largely bound up with the changes in productive organization which have been referred to. Up to the eighties much of the trade had been conducted by outworkers in villages on the banks of the Arrow; but afterwards the factories began to absorb a larger share, and these were established, for the most part, in the centre of the industry—viz. Redditch, in Worcestershire.

There were analogies between the history of the needle trade and that of the manufacture which was carried on in many different parts of our area—viz. the edge-tool trade. Both catered largely for the foreign demand; both managed to increase their output during the period by a resort to machinery, without making any addition to their labour force; and both suffered in certain markets from German competition. To understand the edge-tool industry, however, it is necessary to refer again to the distinction between the common tool and the proprietary, or "branded," article. The large Birmingham and Wolverhampton firms, which produced the latter type, were able to take advantage of the greater need for edge tools, which accompanied the

---

[1] *Midland Captains of Industry* in *Birmingham Gazette and Express*, December 23, 1908, and *United States Daily Consular and Trade Reports*, May 17, 1911, and June 6, 1912.

[2] *Census of England and Wales*, 1911, vol. x., part i., p. 283 *et seq.*; part ii., p. 623 *et seq.*

increased demand for tropical products, like coffee, tea, sugar and rubber, towards the end of the century; for in the older and more conservative countries, such as India or the West Indies, where the natives preferred to buy articles of known quality, the high repute of " branded " tools more than offset the lower price of the Solingen products. The natives of the countries which had been more recently opened to European enterprise, on the other hand, naturally attached little value to a proprietary article, and, consequently, the merchants who handled the export trade to those parts were inclined to consider price rather than quality and repute, and to give orders to the Germans. So, while the large makers maintained a steady trade with the older markets, the firms in the " non-branded " branch had to fight hard to secure any share in the demand from the new countries.

Up to the present, little has been said of the rolling-stock industry; for its development was so gradual that a treatment of the subject could be appropriately left to this stage in our inquiry. It will be remembered that in the early sixties the local companies were concerned mainly with the manufacture of private wagons, although small quantities of passenger coaches were produced, mainly for the home railways. During the next decade the latter branch of the trade increased in importance, and the production of horse-trams became a side-line. The chief feature of the period, 1886-1914, was the change in the relative importance of the home and the foreign markets. The British railway companies were by this time in a position to satisfy their own requirements in rolling-stock; and although the home market provided orders for private wagons, for increased quantities of tramcars, and for equipment for the new London Underground services, the largest demands came during the last two decades of the century from the Colonies, India and South America, where railway construction was still going on. Further, the increasing need for luxurious travel brought numerous orders from the Continent, and distant countries, for dining- and sleeping-cars; and, consequently, by 1914 at least 75 per cent. of the total production (in value) of the local rolling-stock firms was sent abroad. The more luxurious equipment of rolling-stock had, at the same time, done much to alter the character of the industry and to render the productive process longer and more complex. In 1911 this manufacture gave employment to nearly 6100 persons, about three times as many as in 1860.[1] It was still carried on at Birmingham, Smethwick and Oldbury; while the production of railway wheels, axles, turn-tables and other railway material was still centred at Wednesbury, where one great firm had absorbed a large share of the trade.

The manufacture of welded tubes expanded only to a slight extent during the period. Although the development of gas- and water-supply systems at home and abroad brought new demands, tube industries grew up in Germany and the United States.[2] Exports to these countries, once large markets, ceased, and during the nineties international competition was experienced by British manufacturers in foreign markets which they had previously controlled. Of the 7300 persons engaged in the local tube trade in 1911 [3] probably 3500 to 4000 were found in the welded branch. The rest were concerned with weldless tubes, a manufacture which had first become important during the nineties. Its development is, however, so intimately associated with the rise of engineering that it can be more suitably discussed in a later chapter. What deserves notice here is the change which slowly took place between 1886 and 1914 in the localization of the welded section. Up to the end of the depression Wednesbury had been the chief seat of the manufacture, Walsall and Wolverhampton occupying second places. Later, however, while there was a decline in the output of the older centres, a newer firm, originally established on a small scale at Hales Owen, advanced, and by 1914 had attained a position of priority.

Between the manufactures which have already been discussed and those to which this period brought misfortune a link is provided by the hollow-ware and allied trades; for their history illustrates very clearly the process of substitution of one class of product for another that was among the most characteristic changes of the twenty-five years prior to the war—changes which resulted in a growth of some branches of this industry and a corresponding decline in others. Up to the depression the two chief sections of the hollow-ware group consisted of the

[1] *Census of England and Wales*, 1911, vol. x., part i., pp. 265, 283, 297.
[2] *Midland Captains of Industry* in *Birmingham Gazette and Express*, July 30, 1907; December 16, 1908.
[3] *Census of England and Wales*, 1911, vol. x., part i., pp. 256, 283, 297.

cast-iron and the tinplate- and japanned-ware trades, and, since both continued to develop, in spite of the great slump in other manufactures, it might be expected that their growth would have been accelerated during the next period.[1] For a time this did, indeed, occur. In the tinplate- and japanned-ware trade numbers increased from 4800 in 1881 to 6400 in 1901,[2] and, in view of improvements in mechanical methods, the rise in output must have been greater than these figures indicate. The cast-iron hollow-ware trade pursued a similar course. Exports of both classes of goods to the Colonies and to tropical countries increased, and the trades appear to have reached their zenith during the last decade of the century. Then, however, new forces, which had been gathering in strength for some years, began to overwhelm them. In the tinplate- and japanned-ware trade this was associated partly with a change in fashion. It has been shown elsewhere that the manufacture was liable to be affected by influences of this kind; but between about 1870 and 1890 fortune had been favourable. The railway companies and restaurants provided larger markets for tea-urns; travelling trunks became an important line; and cash-boxes and baths were in increased demand. But by 1900 new tendencies had become apparent. The development of the modern bathroom was injuring the market for baths and basins; tin tea- and coffee-pots were definitely superseded by china, nickel or electro-plate wares; the demand for urns fell off as it became the practice for customers in restaurants to be supplied with tea-pots; shop-keepers began to use check-tills and no longer required japanned cash-boxes; and, while tinplate travelling trunks were still needed in the tropics, fashion in England changed in favour of leather bags. Japanned coal-scuttles and decorated trays practically ceased to be produced, and, as in other trades, firms which had risen to prosperity by catering for Victorian taste disappeared,

---

[1] It was the growth of the hollow-ware trade during the seventies and eighties which mitigated the effects in Bilston of the decay in the coal and iron industries. " It was thought some years ago, on the flooding of the mines and the gradual removal of the iron trade to more favoured localities, that the industrial prosperity of Bilston was in serious peril. For a time a decrease in population actually occurred. . . . But the introduction of new trades checked the decline before much mischief could be wrought " (G. T. Lawley, *History of Bilston* (1893), p. 262).

[2] *Census of England and Wales*, 1881, vol. iii., pp. 246, 254; 1901, Warwickshire, p. 51; Worcestershire, p. 51; Staffordshire, p. 66. The figures exclude japanners.

or turned to other products, when that era and its fashions passed
into history. The papier-mâché trade, which had been slowly
dying since the middle of the century, went out of existence
altogether before 1900.

Now these changes of taste occurred first in the home market,
and the industry might have been sustained for a longer period
by the growth of foreign demands had not the section of its
manufactures which were least subject to the dictates of fashion
received another blow. With the growth of the German basic
steel industry a cheap material was provided which could be
easily manipulated under the stamp or press, and which, therefore, laid the foundations for a German enamelled stamped-
steel hollow-ware trade. So during the nineties imports of this
type of ware began to pour into England, and to displace the
saucepans, bowls and kettles previously made of tinplate. The
new manufacture was taken up by several Black Country firms,
and by 1914 some 2000 persons were engaged in it, mainly at
Wolverhampton and West Bromwich, and an export trade to
the Colonies had been worked up. Germany, however, continued to supply the larger part of the home market. The chief
effect of this innovation was to bring about a big decline after
1900 in the tinplate-ware trade. This was accentuated by the
fact that the local production of tin and black plates had dwindled
to insignificance, and that all supplies had to be brought from
Stourport or South Wales. Between 1901 and 1911 numbers
fell from 6400 to under 6000.[1] Several of the largest producers
in Birmingham and Wolverhampton went out of business during
that period, or changed over to new products, like oil-stoves and
hollow-ware made partly or wholly in copper or brass. Yet it
was not only the tinplate goods that suffered from the competition of wrought-enamelled ware. The cast section also declined
through the same cause; for its products were more expensive
than the new type of hollow-ware. Further, by the beginning
of the new century, gas-stoves were coming into general use,
and for gas-cooking the wrought-enamelled saucepan had advantages over the cast wares, because the greater strength of
the latter was no longer needed, while enamelled steel goods
were much more economical in the use of fuel. Nor was it only
from this one quarter that the older trades were menaced.

[1] *Census of England and Wales*, 1911, vol. x., part i., pp. 265, 283, 297.

During the ten years prior to the war, aluminium hollow-ware began to be used, and, although a small production grew up in Birmingham, most of the goods of this type were imported from Germany. Even if the competition of aluminium ware was not very serious, owing to its expense, in 1914, the small quantities then produced were prophetic of future developments.

Thus for two ancient trades, which had been progressive throughout most of the nineteenth century, the last years of this period brought misfortune and decline, and in their place there appeared the new wrought-enamelled and the incipient aluminium-ware manufacture. The effect on the producers of tinplate and japanned goods has been indicated. As for the hollow-ware foundries, they were obliged to occupy themselves with other castings, and many turned to the production of gas-stoves and to enamelled sanitary cast wares, for which demand was increasing rapidly. Little evidence exists concerning the numbers employed in the foundry section of the hollow-ware group, but probably the labour force in 1914 was not more than 2000 to 2500.

The galvanized hollow-ware trade remained apart from these influences, and its development continued up to 1914. It was stimulated by the demand for dustbins, which became a very important line, and for water-tanks for houses and for engineering purposes. Several firms changed over from the production of bowls, buckets and watering-cans, which can properly be called hollow-ware, into tank-makers during the period, and in the years immediately before the war the engineering demand increased more rapidly than did that of the plumbers. Meanwhile changes occurred in the localization of the manufacture. In the eighties, while part of the trade had been situated in the Black Country, Birmingham possessed the larger share. By 1914, however, most of the industry was to be found at Cradley and Lye, and the cause of the migration deserves consideration. The industry was concerned with producing cheap and common articles; the work was heavy, and much manual labour, though not of a highly skilled type, was required. Carried on as it was by many small producers, the trade was keenly competitive, and quality and prices had fallen in consequence. So, since wages constituted a large share of the total costs, and since high-grade workers were not required, manufacturers were drawn to an increasing extent to the Black Country centres, where the general wage-level was much lower than in Birmingham.

The decline in certain of the hollow-ware trades had, to some extent, been compensated for by the growth of others within the same group, and a transition from the old to the new was possible for many local firms. But in several industries, at which fashion and foreign competition had struck even harder blows, no such easy change-over was feasible. Some of these trades had been among the greatest in the district during the old era of West Midland prosperity. Among them were the ancient Birmingham staples, buttons and guns. The misfortune of the former manufacture is illustrated by the Census figures, which show it to have become positively smaller in size between 1881 and 1911. Changes of fashion and competition from abroad were the factors which were mainly responsible for this decline. The pearl-button branch, for instance, in spite of fluctuations on account of the shortage of raw materials, had remained up to the end of the depression a leading section of the trade. During the nineties, however, the butterfly-tie, which involved the use of good shirt buttons, gave place to the long tie, and so opened the way for cheaper types; while the fancy waistcoat, decorated with pearl buttons, went out of fashion. The loss of this market in the men's clothing trade was compensated for, to some extent, by the increased use of pearl buttons by women. But the change from being a trade which catered mainly for men to one which supplied both sexes equally was a great disadvantage. The men's demand had been steady from year to year; that of the women fluctuated rapidly with changes of fashion. Apart from this, men's styles of dress were set by London, and so English button-makers had a good opportunity of being first in the field when some new type was required; but women's fashions were determined at Paris, and, consequently, Continental producers tended to receive the first orders for buttons for women's dress. Thus the increase in the proportion of buttons designed for the latter market altered the balance of competitive advantage in favour of the Continent.

The export trade received a further blow about the same time. During the eighties about half the Birmingham output of pearl buttons had been sent to the United States; but the McKinley Tariff put an end to this, as to many other British exports. Nor did the evil end here. The Austrian makers also lost their market in America, and having a surplus productive capacity, and lower costs of production than the Birmingham manufacturers, they began to sell their goods in England. A little later the industry suffered even greater misfortune. Up to the nineties, mother-of-pearl had been the raw material of the industry in all countries; but during that decade a Japanese button manufacture grew up, which employed a cheaper and inferior shell, called "trocus." This type had, before the war, displaced pearl buttons for general use in England, and by 1914 the only markets left to the local industry were the high-class shirt-making trade, a part of the ladies' trade, which was of an unstable character, and a certain amount of export to countries—like Scandinavia—where the long tie was not fashionable. Thus the great pearl-button manufacture, which in the eighties had employed perhaps 2500 persons, had sunk by 1914 to a fifth of its former size.

The loss of foreign markets, as a result of tariffs and foreign competition, also brought decline to the smaller branches. The larger share of the increased demand for vegetable-ivory buttons went to Germany and Italy rather than to Birmingham [1]; while the covered- and metal-trouser-button trades were reduced to insignificance by changes of fashion. Of all the sections of the industry only the metal- and uniform-button trade continued to flourish, largely in consequence of Government orders.[2] So, although there was a slight revival during the ten years preceding the war, button-making had, by 1914, fallen to the position of a minor industry, and then employed in Birmingham only some 3400 persons, as compared with over 5000 in 1860.[3]

For the old gun trade the period brought even greater misfortune. During the depression it had lost the military trade to the factories and much of the African musket and cheap sporting-gun trade to Belgium, and the new era carried its decline even further. The colonization of Africa, the disappearance in most parts of the world of the slave trade and of tribal wars, and the prohibition by several European governments of the export of

---

[1] *United States Department of Commerce, Special Consular Reports,* No. 75 (1916), pp. 102-104.

[2] *The Times* (Birmingham Number), October 2, 1912, p. 41.

[3] For the whole area the numbers were 5600 in 1861; 5500 in 1881; and 4800 in 1911.

arms to countries which they controlled, all crippled the industry and confined its market entirely to the sporting-gun demand. Even that branch of production was injured by the long agricultural depression and the increasing urban character of the British population; and, although foreign markets continued for a time to absorb a fair quantity, by the early nineties Belgium had secured the lion's share of the world's sporting-gun trade, as far as the cheaper types were concerned. In spite of the shrinkage after 1880, moreover, the demand for guns from the United States had been one of the chief sources of the trade's activity during the ensuing decade; but in 1890 the McKinley Tariff dealt it another great blow. Its exports to America declined in value from $1,169,000 in 1882 and $349,000 in 1890 to $82,000 in 1893, and to less than $20,000 in 1905.[1] Certain types of material-makers disappeared entirely before the end of the century, and the gunsmiths relied to an increasing extent on Liège for their barrels and other semi-finished parts.[2] The manufacture of locks, previously conducted in various parts of the Black Country, had almost entirely gone by 1914; and, while the Census figures do not enable us to distinguish between the military and the sporting sections, it is evident that, at the outbreak of the war, little remained of a once great industry. It is probable that the numbers engaged in the sporting-gun trade had by then fallen to about 1500.

The fortunes of the military branch were less gloomy. Except for a firm engaged in revolver manufacture and for a Government factory acquired in 1882 from the insolvent National Arms and Ammunition Company, practically all the local military trade at the end of the previous period had fallen into the hands of one firm. In the later eighties, however, demand, which had revived in 1884, remained on the up-grade. On the adoption of the Lee-Metford magazine rifle in 1890 the trade received orders from the War Office which kept the factories busy for five years; and the introduction of the quick-firing gun provided another stimulus. New firms began to produce military arms, including the Gatling Gun Company, which acquired an old factory, previously in possession of the National Arms and Ammunition Company, for manufacturing machine guns. After

---

[1] Artifex and Opifex, *op. cit.*, pp. 228-230, 294 ; and *Report of Chief Inspector of Factories and Workshops*, October 1890, p. 26.
[2] Artifex and Opifex, *op. cit.*, pp. 23-26.

1895 the adoption of the smokeless cartridge involved an alteration of rifling, and a new pattern of magazine rifle, the Lee-Enfield, was produced in great quantities in Birmingham. When demand threatened to decline, towards the end of the decade, the outbreak of the Boer War gave it another fillip. Thus, during the first half of the new era, the military branch was prosperous; but with the coming of peace a decline occurred. For ten years magazine rifles had been produced for the services, and extensions had been made to the Government factories, which were, consequently, in a position to absorb most of the Government orders from 1901 to 1914. The establishment of the Territorials provided a small trade for the private factories, as did the introduction of new kinds of arms, such as the sporting rifle, which had first been manufactured by the Birmingham Small Arms Company in 1890, the miniature rifle, which began to be produced in 1902, and, later, the air-gun. But the output of these types was not sufficient to balance the decline in orders from other quarters. Several firms which had been established during the eighties went out of existence,[1] and in 1914 the military demand was served by one rifle and one revolver concern, besides a large ordnance factory, which was established at Coventry a few years before the war. The decline in the gun trade as a whole is indicated by the Census figures, which show a fall in the numbers of persons concerned in the industry from 5500 in 1881 to 4100 in 1911. Birmingham itself had less than 3000 gunsmiths, as compared with about 6500 fifty years previously.[2]

Meanwhile the local ammunition trade had expanded. From the time of the introduction of the breech-loader, cartridges had been made in Birmingham, and during the eighties this trade expanded. Several new factories were built for the production of solid-drawn cartridge-cases; while after 1887 shells for the quick-firing gun began to be manufactured at Birmingham and Streetly. From 1895, when cartridges loaded with smokeless powder (cordite) came into use, until the end of the South African War the ammunition - makers were very prosperous. After this there was a decline; but at the end of thirteen years of peace the trade was much larger than in 1886.

---

[1] Artifex and Opifex, *op. cit.*, pp. 26-27.
[2] *Census of England and Wales*, 1881, vol. iii., p. 241 *et seq.*; 1911, vol. x., part i., p. 283.

Year	Persons engaged in the Manu- facture of Cartridges, Explosives, Fireworks, etc. (in Warwickshire)[1]
1881	400
1891	1100
1901	2100
1911	1100

Two other trades which, like the hollow-ware manufacture, suffered no serious check during the depression, and continued to expand until the end of the century, entered upon a rapid decline during the decade preceding the war. The largest of these was the saddlery and harness trade, the expansion of which had been closely bound up with the increase in exports. For a time this growth was unaffected.[2] The Continental demand, it is true, diminished during the eighties as a result of German competition, and in the next decade the South American market began to fail; but these losses were more than balanced by the great increase in orders from South Africa. The industry reached the peak of its prosperity during the South African War, in consequence of the enormous demands of the British Government. The Census figures alone are sufficient to illustrate the rapid growth during this period:

Year	Persons engaged in the Manufacture of Saddlery, Harness and Whips (Warwickshire and Staffordshire)[3]
1881	5,900
1891	8,200
1901	10,600

With the coming of peace, however, a new era dawned. The South American and several of the Colonial markets had shown a tendency to decline for some years previously, and the interruption of British supplies during the South African War, when Walsall concentrated its activities on satisfying the military orders, led to the establishment of native industries, protected by tariffs in many of the foreign and Colonial markets; and the exports from England dwindled during the early years of the new century. Even South Africa proceeded to satisfy its own

---

[1] *Census of England and Wales,* 1881, vol. iii., p. 250 *et seq.*; 1891, vol. iii., p. 252; 1901, Warwickshire, p. 53; 1911, vol. x., part i., p. 284.

[2] *Report of the Chief Inspector of Factories and Workshops,* October 1891, p. 26.

[3] *Census of England and Wales,* 1881, vol. iii., p. 241 *et seq.*; 1891, vol. iii., p. 251 *et seq.*; 1901, Staffordshire, p. 67; Warwickshire, p. 53.

needs by establishing an industry which made use of native labour, against which the English producer could not compete, and at the same time the military demand suddenly declined. To add to the troubles of the saddlers and harness-makers came the rise of mechanical traction. The development of railways abroad during the last quarter of the nineteenth century had freed the inhabitants of distant countries from their former dependence on the horse; while in England itself trams, bicycles and motor-cars were becoming the chief means of road transport. So the trade entered upon a prolonged slump. The saddlers and harness-makers declined in numbers from 10,600 in 1901 to 8600 in 1911,[1] and these Census returns did not, of course, register the full severity of the depression. The saddlers' ironmongers, and those engaged in subsidiary trades, were likewise affected, and, although there was a slight revival in the years immediately preceding the war, it was evident that the period of progress had come to an end. Birmingham, which had long been of secondary importance, abandoned a larger proportion of its trade than Walsall, and employed less than 1300 in 1911. This tendency for chronically depressed trades to leave Birmingham more rapidly than other neighbouring centres has been commented on in an earlier chapter, and need not again be discussed.

The bedstead trade had a somewhat similar history. Escaping serious injury during the depression, the industry was reported to be developing rapidly in 1889 and to be prosperous in 1892.[2] At this time the markets which it served were world-wide, and it was usual for each firm to specialize on the particular type of bedstead required by one or two countries. The first attack on the trade's prosperity came from the McKinley Tariff of 1890, which, as we have seen, was an ominous date for a large section of local industry. The manufacturers who had concentrated on the American markets were crippled, and, later, others began to suffer. Early in the new century the imposition of higher tariffs, and the rise of foreign bedstead industries under their protection, reduced exports to Germany, the Colonies and South America; and the development of a Far Eastern and an African trade, and the increased demand for ships' berths, did little to

---

[1] *Census of England and Wales*, 1911, vol. x., part i., pp. 266, 286, 298.
[2] S. Timmins, *History of Warwickshire* (1889), p. 282, and W. J. Davis *op. cit.*, pp. 23-25.

mitigate the loss of the staple markets. At the same time a change began to affect the home demand as well. The Victorian taste for massive metal bedsteads, fitted with elaborate brass mounts, was giving place to a call for wooden bedsteads. As this new fashion spread, at the beginning of the century, the Birmingham manufacturers lost still more ground; for their workers and their plant could not easily change over to the production of this new type.[1] The Census shows that 5600 persons were still registered as bedstead and wire-mattress workers in 1911 in the three counties, and it even seems to indicate an increase after 1901.[2] But it is likely that in the earlier Census many persons employed in bedstead factories were returned as iron and brass workers; for all other authorities combine to emphasize the great fall which the industry experienced during the ten or fifteen years prior to the war. Here, again, was another instance of a manufacture which had risen on the wave of Victorian fashion and of British commercial supremacy, but which was brought low by the tastes of a new era and by the growth of production abroad.

The glass industry, even if it were afflicted by no sudden or dramatic decline, had definitely ceased to advance. In the flint-glass section, forces which had first become powerful during the depression were largely responsible for this. But, while during that period Belgian imports had been the cause of the trade's decline, between 1886 and 1914 the most serious competition was from elsewhere. During the nineties American pressed glass forced its way into the British market, and in the next decade much of the home and foreign trade was captured by Germany and Austria.[3] Firms of glass-cutters came into existence in the district who imported foreign glass in a rough state, and who performed merely the cutting, and several flint-glass makers gave up the actual manufacture of glass and confined themselves to finishing operations. At the same time the fancy-glass trade was injured by a change of fashion, and although there was a

---

[1] R. S. Smirke, *Report on the Brass Trade* (prepared in connection with the Juvenile Employment Exchange), 1913 ; *The Times* (Birmingham Number), October 2, 1912, p. 46 ; and *United States Daily Consular and Trade Reports*, May 17, 1911 ; June 6, 1912 ; May 20, 1913.

[2] *Census of England and Wales*, 1901, Staffordshire, p. 66 ; Warwickshire, p. 51 ; Worcestershire, p. 51 ; 1911, vol. x., part i., pp. 265, 283, 297.

[3] E. A. Pratt, *op. cit.*, p. 96, and *Report of the Chief Inspector of Factories and Workshops*, October 1893, p. 313.

marked revival in cut glass just before the war, when for a few years exports reached a level which they had not attained since 1873, the industry was recognized to be slowly sinking. The conservatism of masters and men in the face of improved methods of manufacture, and the lower costs of production in Germany, Belgium and America, were slowly bringing ruin to the industry. As in the gun trade and the pearl-button trade, the only market left for the English flint-glass makers was in the high-class wares. The rest had gone.[1] The decrease in Birmingham's share of the industry, as compared with that of Stourbridge, continued, and in 1911 the former town had less than 28 per cent. of the total number of workers, as compared with 35 per cent. in 1881 and 43 per cent. in 1861. The cause of the change in the relative importance of the two centres has already been explained; but an additional reason after 1886 was to be found in the increasing keenness of foreign competition in the " mounting " branch of the trade, which was situated mainly at Birmingham. Electro-platers, and others who required glass, went abroad for their supplies to an increasing extent during this period. In 1903 a Birmingham firm of " mounters " declared: " Twenty years ago we had no foreign glass account; but now 80 per cent. comes from abroad." [2]

The other branches of the trade deserve a word of notice. In the heavy section many of the earlier products had become of very little importance by 1886, and most of the home demand for sheet glass was satisfied by the Belgians. The one local firm in this branch was still responsible for a large output of spectacle glass; it manufactured chemical glass and tinted glass for fog-signals; and in 1891 it took up the production of figured glass, which was superseding the embossed variety for ornamental purposes. To an increasing extent, however, the firm concentrated its attention on rolled glass, the demand for which rose with the introduction of the modern type of factory with the glazed roof. The tendency to migrate to the coast, noticeable in other heavy trades, was not absent even here; for in 1907 the Smethwick concern established a factory at Glasgow to cater for the foreign market.[3] A year before the war a new branch of

[1] D. N. Sandilands, op. cit., chap. xii.
[2] Ibid., p. 200.
[3] A Hundred Years of British Glass Making (Chance Bros. & Co., Ltd.), p. 14.

the glass industry was introduced into Tipton, where a large factory was erected for making mould-blown illuminating ware on modern principles; while the glass-using firms, such as the mirror manufacturers, grew considerably during the period under review.[1] The bottle trade, however, remained stationary, and was of little importance in 1914. The sum-total of the developments between 1886 and 1914, indeed, was a stationary condition of the heavy-glass manufacture, a decline in the flint-glass branch and an expansion in those sections only which were new or were engaged in a finishing process. The Census reports bear out this general conclusion.

Year	Persons engaged in the Glass Industry in Warwickshire, Worcestershire and Staffordshire [2]
1881	5000
1891	5100
1901	4900
1911	5100

The classic instance of an old staple trade to which the great depression brought decline, and whose ruin was completed during the succeeding period, was the wrought-nail industry. Long in competition with the cut-nail trade, this had revived during the boom in the early seventies; but during the depression the wire nail came to the aid of the cut nail, and the great domestic industry of the Black Country fell with dramatic suddenness. In 1876 about 20,000 persons had been engaged in the whole nail trade of Staffordshire, Warwickshire and Worcestershire. By 1881 the number had fallen to 15,000, and ten years later to less than 8000. Practically the whole of this decrease occurred in the wrought branch. During the nineties the fall was even more rapid [3]; for the competition of machine-made nails was intensified as a result of the introduction of cheap basic steel. In 1895 the Nail-makers Union ceased to exist, and at that time the earnings of a man on full work amounted to no more than ten shillings a week.[4] Thus, after a long and bitterly

[1] *Midland Captains of Industry* in *Birmingham Gazette and Express*, August 20, 1907.

[2] *Census of England and Wales*, 1881, vol. iii., p. 246 *et seq.* ; 1891, vol. iii., p. 254 ; 1901, Staffordshire, p. 67 ; Warwickshire, p. 53 ; Worcestershire, p. 53 ; 1911, vol. x., part i., pp. 266, 284, 298.

[3] *Report of the Chief Inspector of Factories and Workshops*, October 1894, p. 218.

[4] G. I. F. Lloyd, *op. cit.*, p. 404.

fought struggle, the machine had overwhelmed the hand-worker. In 1907, while the total value of nails produced in Great Britain was £534,000, that of the hand-wrought type was only £51,000,[1] and seven years later only a few hundred workers still remained, in the neighbourhoods of Dudley and Bromsgrove. These survivors were engaged in making special types, such as spikes and brush nails, to which machinery had not yet been satisfactorily applied. But, as a great staple industry of the Black Country and its borderland, nailing had gone for ever.

Meanwhile the machine-made-nail industry had been transformed—to the detriment of the West Midlands. Even before 1886 Birmingham and Wolverhampton, once the chief centres of cut-nail production, had lost ground to the north. After this date, when mild steel began to displace wrought-iron, local manufacturers lost their advantage of being near to the chief source of supply of their materials. A more serious factor, however, was the encroachment of the wire nail on the markets which had previously been served by the cut nail. Introduced during the seventies, the former began to supersede the older product during the last decade of the century. Thus the cut nail, having after a long fight forced out the wrought nail, began to be replaced in turn by this new type, which was not only cheaper but which, owing to its smoothness, was more suitable for many purposes. Birmingham and District had nothing to gain from this development. During the seventies the manufacture of wire nails had been taken up by several local factories; but it never became firmly rooted in the district, and was localized chiefly at Warrington. During the nineties, moreover, Belgian wire nails began to flow into the British market in increasing quantities, and from then onwards Continental and American producers established that marked superiority in wire and wire products which they have since held.[2] By 1914, although the cut nail still maintained itself for uses where holding power was required, and although rose nails and tacks were still made by the cutting process, for building, case-making and general purposes the wire nail had become supreme. Birmingham then produced only a small quantity of both kinds. Thus the new era brought misfortune not only to the older wrought-nail industry, which had

---

[1] *Final Report of the Census of Production*, 1907, p. 118.
[2] *United States Department of Commerce, Special Consular Reports*, No. 71 (1915), p. 30.

S

long been failing, but to the cut-nail trade, which had superseded it. The following figures show how small this once pre-eminent group of manufactures had become:

Year	Persons engaged in the Manufacture of Nails in Warwickshire, Worcestershire and Staffordshire [1]
1881 . . .	14,800
1891 . . .	7,900
1911 . . .	3,200

The growing predominance of Belgium in the wire industry and the localization of the British producers at Warrington were also responsible for the stationary character of the local trades engaged in wire drawing, weaving and working. One large factory continued to exist in Birmingham for the production of wire ropes, and the wire-weaving trades maintained themselves; but between 1881 and 1901 the numbers employed in the group described above increased only from 1700 to 2000. During the early years of the new century, however, local firms were established to manufacture flexible wire cords for the motor and cycle trade, and, in consequence, the employment rose to 2500 in 1911.[2] A small and specialized branch of the wire trade, the pin manufacture, grew steadily throughout the period, and the numbers engaged, which amounted to about 400 in 1881, were almost doubled by 1914. Many of the other smallware industries, however, suffered a decline as a result of Continental competition. Of these the manufacture of hooks and eyes affords a good example; for German rivalry drove many Birmingham concerns out of the trade.[3] A somewhat larger industry decreased through the same cause. This was the production of umbrella fittings and furniture, in which employment fell from 1100 in 1881 to about 800 in 1911.[4] Other small trades became almost extinct. Rope and twine manufacture dwindled to insignificance; mediæval and artistic metalwork practically ceased; and match manufacture was completely gone by 1914. Meanwhile, at

---

[1] Census of England and Wales, 1881, vol. iii., p. 246 et seq. ; 1891, vol. iii., p. 255 ; 1911, vol. x., part i., pp. 265, 283, 297.
[2] These figures apply to Birmingham only. For the three counties the numbers were 2100 in 1881 and 4000 in 1911.
[3] The Times (Birmingham Number), October 2, 1912, p. 43 ; History of the Growth of Birmingham Industries in Birmingham Gazette and Express, November 2, 1911, p. 2.
[4] Midland Captains of Industry in Birmingham Gazette and Express, December 20, 1907.

Coventry, the watch trade, after expanding slowly until the eighties, collapsed, in consequence of, first, Swiss and then American competition. The employment, which had risen from 3400 in 1861 to 5000 in 1891, fell to 3800 in 1901 and 2300 in 1911.[1]

In conclusion, a minor manufacture, the brush and broom trade, may be briefly referred to. It was centred mainly at Birmingham and Walsall, and in the early eighties had employed nearly 1600 persons. Competition from the Continent was even then making itself felt, and it became keener in subsequent years. The production of drawn brushes by German vagrant labour, whose output was for the most part dumped in England, injured one section of the trade; while about 1895 Germany also began to turn out a sash-tool in which the bristles were fixed to the handle by a compressed metal ferrule. This, to a large extent, displaced the older type of sash-tool, and, although some local manufacturers attempted to adopt the methods of Germans, the latter permanently secured a large share of the British market. At the same time Birmingham manufacturers lost much of the trade in bone (*i.e.* tooth and nail) brushes as a result of Continental competition; the supersession of the horse by motor traction destroyed the Walsall manufacture of horse and harness brushes; and the increasing cleanliness of the streets brought a decline in the demand for bass-brooms and boot-brushes. All these adverse influences on demand were, of course, more than offset by the growth of population and of more hygienic habits; but, as much of the home market had been lost to Germany and Belgium, there was little growth in the Birmingham industry. During the thirty years preceding the war the number of brush- and broom-makers in the three counties increased from 1600 to 2100, and as machinery had been adopted to only a small extent the rise in output was in about the same proportion.[2] Only in the more expensive types did the local manufacturers retain a large share of the market.

The great expansion which occurred in the spring, chemical, paint and varnish, food and drink, and paper-box trades can be treated more conveniently in the chapter on new industries, as

[1] *Census of England and Wales*, 1891, vol. iii., p. 251; 1901, Warwickshire, p. 52; 1911, vol. x., part i., 284.

[2] *Ibid.*, 1881, vol. iii., p. 243 *et seq.*; 1911, vol. x., part i., pp. 266, 284, 298.

they were very small at the beginning of the modern period. Similarly, the growth in the production of stampings and castings, which was associated mainly with the rise of engineering, also requires examination at a later stage, and there remains merely to sum up the tendencies which we have observed at work among the older manufactures. The industries may, first of all, be classified into four main groups—the rapidly expanding, the slowly expanding, the stationary or slowly declining, and the rapidly declining trades.

MOVEMENT OF THE OLDER FINISHED MANUFACTURES, 1887-1914

Rapidly expanding Industries	Slowly expanding Industries	Stationary or slowly declining Industries	Rapidly declining Industries
1. Jewellery	1. Pen	*1. Tinplate- and japanned-ware	1. Gun
2. Brass and other non-ferrous	2. Lock	*2. Cast-iron hollow-ware	2. Button
3. Nut-and-bolt	3. Rolling-stock	*3. Saddlery and harness	3. Wrought-nail
4. Chain and anchor	4. Needle and fishhook	*4. Bedstead	4. Watch
5. Screw	5. Edge-tool	5. Glass	
6. Pin	6. Iron-tube	6. Cut-nail	
	7. Galvanized hollow-ware	7. Umbrella-fittings	
	8. Brush and broom		
	9. Ammunition		
	10. Wire products		

* Expansion up to 1890-1900, followed by a rapid decline.

In the third group a further division exists between those in which the fall was continuous after 1886 and those which grew up to the end of the century, and entered upon a downward path during the last ten or fifteen years of our period, such as the saddlery and harness, the bedstead, the tinplate- and japanned-ware and the cast-iron hollow-ware industries. The rapidly expanding trades owed their good fortune in almost every case to the fact that they were able to adapt themselves to meeting the demands of the new industries, particularly engineering, which were growing up during this period. This applies to the non-ferrous, nut-and-bolt and screw manufactures; while even in jewellery and chains there was a shifting of emphasis from older products to new ones. In no instance did any considerable growth come through the expansion of the older forms of demand. The slowing down of the rate of development in some trades and the actual decline of others were due partly, no doubt, to the increasing shortage of local supplies of raw materials; but the main influences at work were three: first, changes of fashion and the substitution of newer types of product; second, the increasing severity of foreign competition during and after the nineties, especially from Germany; and, third, the raising of tariff walls against British products, particularly by the United States. These influences affected all the industries which fall within the last three groups of the Table in a greater or lesser degree; and certain products of even the prosperous trades did not wholly escape. In all the industries the cheaper classes of goods were most seriously affected, and many producers tended to confine themselves more and more to high-grade articles or to finishing processes. This was particularly true of the gun, glass, button, brush and edge-tool trades. Finally, we have to notice the effect of foreign competition and of high tariffs on the proportion of the total output sold abroad. No statistics are available to bear out our conclusions, and we have to rely on the statement of manufacturers. But it seems evident that although in 1913 many industries, such as the chain, screw, rolling-stock, pen, edge-tool, and saddlery and harness trades, still sold the larger part of their products abroad, over the whole field of local enterprise there had been a fall in the relative importance of the export trade; while the Colonies were taking a larger proportion of the total foreign sales than they had a quarter of a century before. A complete understanding of the changes in the economic structure of the area and in the relative importance of the various manufactures will not be attained, however, until we have considered the course of events within the heavy trades and the rise of the new industries. And with these we must now deal.

CHAPTER II

COAL, IRON AND STEEL

THE great depression had brought ruin to a multitude of local ironmasters and a great shrinkage in output; while the extractive industries had failed to keep pace either with the general industrial development of the area or with the advance of the British coal trade as a whole. The ensuing years brought no recovery, and the period from 1875 to 1886, therefore, marked a turning-point in the history of South Staffordshire's heavy trades. From then onwards the basic industries, the rise of which had coincided with the first period of our area's greatness, had to reconcile themselves to occupying a position of subordinate importance in the economic life of the district.

More than this, as far as mining was concerned, after 1886 the decline was progressive; for the forces which have elsewhere been described continued to operate. The older seams were either exhausted or could not be worked in competition with more recently developed centres. Wider areas became flooded, and the increased cost of drainage pressed the more heavily on the industry as its size decreased. The activities of the Drainage Commissioners had done something, it is true, to prolong the life of certain mining districts. In the Tipton area, " the great flooded district of South Staffordshire," for instance, in addition to the drainage operations already described, semi-portable pumps were employed by the Commissioners during this period to deal with the water in the small isolated basins, or " pounds," which existed there; but, as more and more mines were abandoned, an increasingly heavy burden was laid on the Commissioners' shoulders.[1] During the nineties, although Tipton contributed less than a quarter of the dues levied on the mineral output of South Staffordshire, it absorbed over half of the expenditure; and by 1914, not only had this district's output greatly declined, but the date of complete abandonment was in sight.[2] Many mines which ceased to be worked in the strike of 1912 were never reopened; others were purchased by local factory owners and shut down in order to protect the surface;

[1] T. E. Lones, op. cit., pp. 129-130.
[2] Ibid., pp. 129-130 ; and Report of the Committee on the South Staffordshire Mines Drainage (1920), pp. 22-23.

and, as no considerable area of coal remained, such large companies as had existed went out of business, and mining was left to small men, who often employed only six or twelve workers, and who had neither the capital nor the will to apply scientific methods to the winning of the fragments of seams that remained. If Tipton was the least fortunate district, elsewhere conditions were not very different. In the Oldbury, Kingswinford and the southern section of the Old Hill districts pumping was left in private hands, and even in the northern part of the latter district the Commissioners did little. Whether the drainage operations were public or private, in every section of the old coal-field the decline was continuous, and only in the more recently opened districts, such as Sandwell Park and Hamstead, were large and profitable mines being operated in 1900. During the first decade of the new century, however, a successful sinking was made to the west of the Western Boundary Fault, and the Earl of Dudley's Baggeridge Wood Colliery, which was there established, became by 1914 one of the largest and best equipped in the country. Yielding brooch, or domestic, coal, it covered 2000 acres, and extensive use was there made of electric haulage and of hydraulic lifts.[1] But this colliery, like those at Sandwell Park and Hamstead, was beyond the limits of the visible coal-measures, and except for these three, which in 1913 employed 903, 248 and 697 men respectively, and for one or two others at Walsall and Rowley, no really large-scale mining operations were then being conducted in the South Staffordshire field south of the Great Bentley Fault.[2]

Although the published returns to the Home Office do not cover precisely the area with which we are concerned, it is possible, without much difficulty, to arrive at a fairly accurate estimate of the fall in production during this period. Between 1876 and 1886 the annual average output of the whole of South Staffordshire and Worcestershire had been about 9,500,000 tons. Of this about one-third had been mined in the district to the north of the Great Bentley Fault—i.e. in the Cannock area —and the Black Country's production had been, therefore, some 6,000,000 tons annually. During the next thirteen years the output of the whole district was practically stationary, and ranged

[1] *Birmingham Chamber of Commerce Official Guide,* 1912.
[2] *List of Mines in the United Kingdom,* 1913 (Home Office), pp. 259-276, 278-282.

between 9,000,000 and 10,000,000 tons a year [1]; but a change occurred in the relative importance of the two divisions. Cannock continued to advance, while the Black Country declined, and in 1898 the former was responsible for half of the total production.[2] So by that time the Black Country was mining only 4,500,000 tons annually. After 1900 the only figures for output which are available cover the whole of Staffordshire; but there are other means of discovering the facts we require. In 1900, when about 9,500,000 tons of coal were mined in South Staffordshire and Worcestershire, 28,600 men were employed in and about the mines. By 1913 there was an increase to nearly 30,000, of whom over two-thirds were found in the Cannock division.[3] From these data it is probably correct to infer that, while in 1913 the output of the whole of South Staffordshire and Worcestershire was about 10,000,000 tons, the Black Country was then producing only 3,000,000 tons, and was employing about 10,000 men in and about its mines. Thus, between 1887 and the outbreak of the war, the annual production of coal within our districts, in spite of the extension of the mining area beyond the eastern and western boundary faults, declined by one-half.

The fall in the output of ironstone was even more rapid. At the end of the depression about 110,000 tons were being produced annually. The output dropped to 51,000 tons by the end of the century, and between 1910 and 1913 averaged only 30,000 tons a year. It had, in fact, become negligible. The production of limestone also declined, and the only branch of the extractive industries which could boast of any degree of prosperity was that engaged in quarrying fire- and brick-clay. The Table on the opposite page will indicate the decline of the Black Country as a mining centre during the whole period covered by the survey.

[1] *Mineral Statistics of the United Kingdom*, 1887-1896 ; *Mines and Quarries Reports*, 1897-1900.
[2] T. E. Lones, *op. cit.*, p. 132.
[3] *Mines and Quarries Reports*, 1900, part i., p. 11 ; part ii., p. 56; part iii., p. 182 ; and *List of Mines in the United Kingdom*, 1913, pp. 259-276, 278-282.
[4] *Mines and Quarries Reports* (part iii.), 1900, p. 220; 1910, p. 243; 1911, p. 258 ; 1912, p. 282 ; 1913, p. 258.

MINERAL OUTPUT OF THE BLACK COUNTRY, 1865-1913

Date	Production of Coal	Production of Ironstone	Persons employed in and about the Mines
	(in million tons)	(in thousand tons)	
1865 . .	9·0	660	25,000
1872 . .	9·0	642	28,000
1887 . .	6·0	110	17,000
1900 . .	4·5	51	14,000
1913 . .	3·0	32	10,000

These figures exclude production and employment north of the Great Bentley Fault, and are estimates based on the *Reports of the Inspectors of Mines, Mineral Statistics of the United Kingdom*, 1865-1887, and *Mines and Quarries Reports*, 1900-1913.

Although reduced to insignificance as a source of raw materials, the Black Country during this period was less unfortunate as a seat of pig-iron production; for the great shrinkage in the size of the industry which took place during the depression was not accentuated during the subsequent years. It is true that the number of works in operation and of blast-furnaces built continued to fall, the former from 20 in 1887 to 12 in 1914, and the latter from 104 to 31 during the same period; and, further, while 30 furnaces were in blast in 1887, only 20 were blowing in the year before the war.[1] But the period witnessed great advances in technique, which led to economies in the use of fuel and to an increase in the capacity of the typical plant. Consequently, although the number of furnaces fell, the output did not respond in the same way. Averaging 311,000 tons a year between 1885 and 1887, the annual production of pig rose slightly, and amounted to about 350,000 tons, until the depresson of 1893, when a fall again occurred. From 1896, however, output steadily increased, and in 1907 reached 470,000 tons for the first time since 1875. During the three pre-war years, which were prosperous, the yield was 460,000 tons annually, and even the area's proportion of the total British production by that time showed a slight increase, from 4·2 per cent. between 1885 and 1887, and 4·3 per cent. between 1898 and 1900, to 4·8 per cent. between 1911 and 1913. Thus, although South Staffordshire could never

[1] *Mineral Statistics of the United Kingdom*, 1887, pp. 48-49; *Mines and Quarries Reports*, 1913, part iii., p. 268; 1914, part iii., p. 119.

hope to regain the ground which it had lost during the depression, its pig-iron industry was slowly on the up-grade during the pre-war period.[1]

The cause of this development, in view of the increasing exhaustion of the local raw materials, deserves notice. To a large extent the explanation lies in the fact that, with the growth in the number of its foundries and engineering plants, the area was becoming a larger and larger market for iron and steel. In fact the basic industries, which had originally called into being the finished-metal trades of the district, now owed their survival, not to the proximity of raw materials, but to the existence of a large local demand for metal. Besides this, the supplies of " puddlers' tap," which in the nineties cost only five shillings a ton, formed a cheap and valuable raw material for the manufacture of basic iron for the Bessemer converters. So, as the demand for forge-iron declined, many pig-iron producers took advantage of the local supplies of this material and began to cater for the basic steel works. In 1894 one-third of the Black Country's output of pig consisted of basic iron, of which the district then produced 75,000 tons out of the total British make of 279,000 tons.[2] Obviously this competitive advantage could only be temporary; for the decline in puddling meant that the accumulations of " tap-cinder," which were being drawn upon, were not replenished. By 1913 its price had risen, and one powerful factor in bringing about the recovery in the local pig-iron output was thus disappearing. Nevertheless, its influence persisted. Several great basic-steel works, which were established in the Black Country, had built blast-furnaces to supply them with molten pig, and these they had to keep in operation even when the supplies of cheap raw materials began to fail. Apart from basic-, forge- and foundry-iron production, South Staffordshire was assured a small but steady demand for another type of iron, of which it had almost a monopoly. In the rest of the country the hot blast was nearly universal; but several cold-blast furnaces continued to be operated in the Black Country, and these produced a special iron which was preferred for certain foundry purposes, particularly for the manufacture of chill rolls.[3]

[1] *Mineral Statistics of the United Kingdom*, 1887-1896 ; *Mines and Quarries Reports*, 1897-1914.
[2] *Annual Statistical Report of the British Iron Trade Association*, 1894, p. 16.
[3] F. W. Harbord and E. F. Law, *op. cit.*, p. 184.

We have seen that during this period, although a greater output was obtained, there was a diminution in the number of producing units. The result was, naturally, to reduce the area in which the industry was conducted. In 1913 blast-furnaces were no longer conspicuous features of the landscape at West Bromwich, Kingswinford, Stourbridge and Willenhall, as they had been thirty years previously, and most of the trade was confined to the district in the immediate neighbourhood of Dudley, including Netherton, Bilston, Tipton and Brierley Hill, although there were also a few furnaces at Walsall and Wednesbury.[1]

While this slight recovery was taking place in the production of pig-iron, the branch of the industry to which South Staffordshire owed its fame—viz. the manufacture of wrought-iron—continued its downward path. Statistics are not available in this field of inquiry; but the estimates of those connected with the industry are sufficient to indicate the trend. In 1893 it was affirmed that the industry had been for many years in a continual state of decay,[2] and the addresses given at the Birmingham meeting of the British Association twenty years later showed that the decline was permanent and even progressive.[3] In the early eighties the local output of puddled bar had averaged over 600,000 tons annually, and the number of puddling furnaces in operation during the later years of the depression ranged between 1200 and 1300.[4] By 1893 the number had fallen to 808, with a production of 438,000 tons of puddled bar, and by 1894 to 683, with a production of 389,000 tons. The finished-iron output was then only 365,000 tons.[5] The industry's adjustment to the new conditions of demand, however, was not yet complete; for ten years later the output was down to 338,000 tons of puddled iron, and the decline continued until 1906.[6] From that time until the outbreak of the war there appears to have been a slight improvement, and in 1913 it was estimated that there were 661 puddling furnaces in the Black Country, belonging to

[1] *Mines and Quarries Reports*, 1913, part iii., p. 268.
[2] G. T. Lawley, *op. cit.*, chap. xxv.
[3] *Handbook for Birmingham and the Neighbourhood* (British Association Meeting, 1913), p. 392 *et seq.*
[4] *Mineral Statistics of the United Kingdom*, 1882, p. 73 ; 1885, pp. 64-66 ; 1886, pp. 70-72.
[5] *Annual Statistical Report of the British Iron Trade Association*, 1894, pp. 18-20.
[6] S. Jeans, *The Iron Trade of Great Britain*, p. xii. ; *Handbook for Birmingham and the Neighbourhood* (British Association Meeting, 1913), pp. 417-418

32 firms.[1] The production of puddled iron was probably in the neighbourhood of 300,000 to 350,000 tons annually, less than one-third of the output during the early seventies. Yet South Staffordshire still retained its importance as a wrought-iron centre relative to the country as a whole, and it was responsible for about 35 per cent. of the total British output throughout this period.[2] During the early nineties, although the district's production of ship- and boiler-plates and nail rods had fallen to insignificance, it still held the lead for bar iron, rounds and squares, and turned out half the iron sheets produced in Great Britain. At that time this type of iron was still used in the manufacture of tinplates and galvanized sheets, and was a staple product of South Staffordshire. Even when the greater part of the sheet trade was taken from it, as a result of the introduction of steel, the Black Country continued to provide a large proportion of the high-grade wrought-iron still used in the country.[3]

But the coming of steel hit the industry very hard. Although the heavy first-cost of steel plants delayed the supersession of iron, more and more markets were lost to the Staffordshire mills and forges as time went on. By the nineties, steel was being used not only for railway material, constructional engineering, and for ships and boilers, but, as we have seen, it was displacing iron in the manufacture of tinplates and galvanized sheets. The cheapness of the basic open-hearth steel, which was now available, induced an increasing number of the small metal trades of the district to change over to that material, and by the end of this period the wrought hollow-ware, screw and cut-nail industries ceased to be markets for the ironmasters. Edge tools which had previously been made of wrought-iron with a face, or cutting edge, of crucible steel were now manufactured of steel throughout; the new light engineering trades were steel rather than iron users; much of the tube trade went over to the new material; while parts for locks and for many other hardware products were now pressed from steel sheets, instead of being fashioned of wrought-iron.[4] As we have already shown, the change was

---

[1] *Handbook for Birmingham and the Neighbourhood*, p. 417. All these furnaces were not, of course, in operation.

[2] *Cf.* estimates of above authorities with figures respecting the output of puddled bar given in the *Final Report of the Census of Production*, 1907, p. 171; S. Jeans, *op. cit.*, p. xii.

[3] *Annual Statistical Report of British Iron Trade Association*, 1894, pp. 19-20.

[4] *United States Department of Commerce, Special Consular Reports*, No. 71 (1915), p. 30; *The Times* (Birmingham Number), October 2, 1912, pp. 39, 43.

inevitable, not only because of the greater technical advantages of steel for most purposes, but because it was susceptible to large-scale methods of production, and could, therefore, be turned out cheaply. The only important technical advances which were made during this period in wrought-iron production, on the other hand, were connected, not with the key-processes, which remained unaltered, but with the auxiliary plant. Thus, in a few places, gas-fired furnaces were substituted for the coal-fired type; larger and faster rolling mills were constructed; and a beginning was made in the electrification of the mill engines. But these innovations involved no fundamental changes in the organization of the industry. Wrought-iron manufacture, in fact, remained a manual process; for mechanical puddling never proved successful; and the rivalry of iron and steel was of the same nature as the struggle of the domestic nailer with the factory, of the hand-weaver against the power-loom. It is true that for certain purposes the older metal held its own against the competition of cheap mild steel. For articles which were likely to suffer from corrosion, or when a reliable weld was necessary, wrought-iron was still preferred, and down to the war the manufacturers of ship's chains and cables, anchors, ship-fittings, bolts and nuts, and of certain kinds of welded tubes, still obtained their materials from the Staffordshire mills and forges.[1] But the advent of steel had transformed wrought-iron from being the staple raw material of the metal-using trades into a speciality, employed only for a few purposes.

Meanwhile, developments had occurred in the local steel industry; but they were not of far-reaching importance. We have described how a firm of blast-furnace proprietors set up one of the first basic Bessemer plants at Bilston in the early eighties, and how the Patent Shaft and Axletree Company, which had previously produced both acid and basic Bessemer, had begun to produce acid and basic open-hearth steel shortly afterwards.[2] It was not until the next decade that the great iron-master, the Earl of Dudley, entered the field. In 1893, however, a plant was constructed at Round Oak, Dudley, for making basic open-hearth steel, and this was greatly extended during the ten years prior to the war. A large steel foundry was established also

[1] *Handbook for Birmingham and Neighbourhood* (British Association Meeting, 1913), p. 418.
[2] *Mineral Statistics of the United Kingdom*, 1882, pp. 74-78; 1886, pp. 75-78.

at Wednesbury. With these few exceptions, however, none of the Staffordshire ironmasters changed over to steel production, and, owing to the greater developments which had taken place elsewhere, in 1913 the Black Country was of small importance as a steel centre. The absence of local supplies of raw materials and the great distance from the sea had drawn most of the steel-makers to the coast, and the Black Country was left with a few plants, which owed their origin to the availability of cheap "tap-cinder" during the eighties, and which continued to exist owing to the presence of a great local market. In 1904 the district produced about 200,000 tons of open-hearth steel and 100,000 tons of Bessemer,[1] and, although figures are not available for later years, it is probable that while the output may have increased slightly by 1914, certainly the Black Country did not become relatively more important.

One of the chief features of the great depression had been the decline in the number of integrated firms in South Staffordshire. This movement persisted, and except for the few firms which had changed over to steel production, and for one or two makers of wrought-iron specialities, the basic-metal trade lost what for a century had been a leading characteristic of its organization. Even the few concerns which still controlled their raw-material supplies had to obtain most of them from other parts of the country. The day when the district provided all that the integrated firms required had gone for ever. In 1913 it was stated that most of the pig- or finished-iron makers owned nothing but their own plant, and bought all their raw materials in the open market; and that, with one or two exceptions, the only integrated concerns were those engaged in steel production.[2] Thus, during a period when the tendency towards vertical combination was becoming more powerful in the metal trades of the country as a whole, those of the Black Country pursued a contrary course.

Yet, if the great integrated concern had become exceptional by 1914, the scale of production within each stage of the manufacturing process had become much greater than it had been in the heyday of the iron trade. During the seventies the comparatively small capitalist could flourish alongside the great

[1] S. Jeans, *op. cit.*, p. 38.
[2] *Handbook for Birmingham and Neighbourhood* (British Association Meeting, 1913), pp. 401-404.

firm with its thousands of employees; but during the next twenty years a fundamental change occurred. For economical production it became necessary for a master to own a large and expensive group of blast-furnaces, and now that the normal capacity of each amounted to 600 tons a week, as compared with 120 tons during the sixties, there was no place for the small man, except possibly in connection with the few remaining cold-blast furnaces. The change in the scale of pig-iron production, however, was small compared with the transformation which was effected by the advent of steel in the organization of the basic-metal trades. An engineer has put the case very clearly: " An economical unit to-day consists of one or two batteries of coke-ovens, with appliances for the recovery of bye-products, four or six blast-furnaces with gas-purifying apparatus, a row of basic-lined open-hearth furnaces, with means for charging them by machine with hot metal, scrap or ore, a slag-grinding plant, a cogging, roughing, and one or more finishing mills. . . . According to the class of ore available such a plant might be expected to turn out 3000 to 5000 tons of finished steel a week, and to cost from £1,500,000 to £2,000,000. This is a startling change from the ordinary finished-iron works of fifty years ago, turning out 200 to 250 tons a week, and costing, exclusive of blast-furnaces, only about one-hundredth part as much." [1]

The local concerns may be compared with this example of a typical modern steel plant. The Earl of Dudley's works in 1893, besides blast-furnaces, consisted of three 17 ton open-hearth basic furnaces, and a cogging and a finishing mill. Ten years later a railway was constructed to carry molten pig direct from the blast-furnaces to the steel furnaces. In 1905 a slag-grinding plant was erected to utilize the basic slag, and a 250 ton gas-heated mixer was installed for storing the molten pig between the blast-furnaces and the steelworks; while in 1907 larger and more up-to-date open-hearth furnaces were installed. At the present time the capacity of the works is between 2500 and 3000 tons of steel sections a week. To take another example. Messrs Hickman's plant consists of five blast-furnaces, two mixers of 500 and 150 tons, three 12 ton Bessemer converters, one 60 ton and three 80 ton basic open-hearth furnaces, two cogging, one

[1] J. W. Hall, op. cit., p. 24.

strip and three bar mills, and it has a capacity of 3500 tons of Siemens-Martin ingots and 3500 tons of Bessemer ingots weekly. These concerns had not reached their present size in pre-war days; but they were even then incomparably larger than the typical finished-iron works of the seventies. The effect in this district of the coming of steel, then, was not only to cause a decline in the stature of the basic trades, but to drive out the small manufacturer, and to concentrate the production of pig- and wrought-iron, and still more of steel, into a few hands. In the scale of production and in methods of organization, indeed, Bessemer and Siemens brought as great changes in the last quarter of the nineteenth century as Darby and Cort had effected in the eighteenth.

The last years of the great depression, as already described, witnessed the beginning of a tendency on the part of manu- facturers in the heavy trades to migrate to the coast. During the next twenty years the movement continued, and even in the more highly finished sheet-iron trade the district failed to hold its own. In 1898 it was declared that many sheet mills in the Midlands had shut down; while others were being opened in more advantageous districts. About the same time the Gospel Oak Company, " previously of unequalled importance in the galvanized-iron trade," ceased to operate,[1] and two great Wolverhampton firms, Messrs Lysaghts, employing over 1000 workers, and the Swan Iron Company, transferred to South Wales. A third went north to the Mersey; while a little later the Wolverhampton Corrugated Iron Company migrated also to South Wales.[2] The sheet-metal and galvanizing trade in particular was affected by these movements, because it catered mainly for foreign markets; but even when works were not closed the producers of heavy iron goods found it difficult to compete with more favourably situated concerns. The con- structional engineering firms, which turned out gas-holders, large steel pipes, bridges, iron roofs, piers and railway material, had been well placed when their materials were produced locally, and when their market was largely domestic. But after 1886 they began to suffer acutely, not only because much of their material

[1] *Wolverhampton and South Staffordshire Guide*, 1898 (Wolverhampton Library).
[2] W. H. Jones, *op. cit.*, pp. 177-178 ; *Report of Chief Inspector of Factories and Workshops*, 1902, p. 38.

had to be obtained from other districts, but because the structural requirements of Great Britain had by then been satiated, and the chief markets lay abroad. So these firms lost ground rapidly in the cruder and heavier products, and could only hold their own in branches of work which required a great deal of skilled labour. After the beginning of the new century the greater demand for structural steelwork for local factories gave them some help; but many of their old staple manufactures, such as those of gas-holders and bridges, had almost disappeared by 1914.

Another development which was associated with the decay of the iron trade must also be mentioned, since it affords a good example of a tendency which had begun to appear in several local industries. The expansion of the light finished metal and the engineering trades in Birmingham and District after the eighties created a big local demand for finished steel of various kinds; and, although most of the crude steel had to be purchased from South Wales or the North, there was an opportunity for the local manufacturer in the finishing operations. Consequently, many of the ironmasters found a new use for their mill department, now that their puddling furnaces were dismantled and their old markets had disappeared. During the nineties they began to buy steel billets and bars from other centres, occupying themselves in rolling down these to the shapes required for local consumption. This had become a very important trade by 1914. Thus, here again we find the tendency for Birmingham and District to concentrate more and more of its attention on finishing processes.

In conclusion, something must be said of the sources of the raw materials and the semi-products used in the area. Before the great depression, if much of the ore and coke had been obtained from outside, South Staffordshire produced a fair proportion of the ironstone and some of the limestone employed in its blast-furnaces; while the thick coal supplied the larger part of the fuel required for iron production and for other manufacturing purposes. In the new era, however, practically all the raw materials were from external sources. The local output of ironstone was insignificant, and supplies had to be obtained from Northamptonshire and Oxfordshire, as well as from North Staffordshire, which was also the source of supply of limestone.

T

Raw coal was no longer burned in the blast-furnaces, and, as no coking coal existed in Staffordshire, fuel for them had to be obtained from South Yorkshire, Lancashire and South Wales. For the other types of manufacturing coal, and for the household coal required in the district, Cannock was now the chief source. It might seem curious that, as the centre of the mining industry had shifted from the Black Country to Cannock, there was no migration of industries to that area. But Cannock coal was of a non-coking variety, and was therefore unsuitable both for iron production and for many other manufacturing purposes; while the fact that the transport system of the country had developed with Birmingham and District as a nodal point was more than sufficient to balance Cannock's advantage in coal supplies.

For many years the pig-iron production of the Black Country had been insufficient to meet local needs, and after 1886 by far the larger share of the district's requirements for foundry, forge or steel-making purposes were met by Derbyshire and Northamptonshire.[1] Most of the steel, too, was necessarily obtained, in the form of billets, bars or sheets, from South Wales, Yorkshire or Scotland; while some trades were beginning to use low-grade foreign steel. This last development deserves notice. The rise of the German steel industry first began to affect the British export trade during the eighties, and the Continental producers soon established a superiority in certain classes of products, such as wire.[2] It was not until the nineties that Midland manufacturers began to use foreign materials in any quantity; but from then until the war the import of German and Belgian billets by local firms of re-rollers rose steadily. The amount of Continental mild steel used by firms in the district prior to the war can have been only small compared with the quantities supplied from British sources; but the development was symptomatic of the great changes which had occurred. The area which forty years before had been a leading source of supply of ferrous metals for the whole world was now reduced to a dependence not only on other British centres but, to a small extent, on the Continent as well.

---

[1] *Handbook for Birmingham and Neighbourhood* (British Association Meeting, 1913), p. 397.
[2] Cf. *Annual Report of the British Iron Trade Association*, 1896, p. 12 *et seq.* and p. 43 ; and *United States Department of Commerce, Special Consular Reports*, No. 71 (1915), p. 30.

CHAPTER III

THE NEW INDUSTRIES

THE two preceding chapters will have shown that the great increase in the population and in the industrial importance of Birmingham and District between 1887 and 1914 cannot be attributed in any considerable degree to an expansion of the older trades. With a very few exceptions the leading manufactures of the pre-depression period declined, were stationary, or only slowly advanced during the new era, and even in the few instances in which there was rapid growth the cause was generally to be found in the appearance of a demand for new classes of product. To take one example. If the hollow-ware trade as a whole expanded, this was due, not to any increase in the demand for the older classes of goods, but entirely to the rise of new branches—viz. the enamelled stamped-steel and the aluminium hollow-ware trades. Indeed nearly all the older industries, from brassfoundry and jewellery to pen and screw manufacture, owed a continuance of their prosperity to forces other than those which maintained them in the past.

We have seen that the chief influence in bringing about a growth in the size of such of the older industries as were still progressive came from the engineering trade. This, in fact, was the source of the greater part of the fresh demands on the hardware firms, whose older markets were failing, and it is in this direction that we must look if we would discover the main cause of the growth of the entire industrial structure. Some attention has already been given to the form of the engineering industry before 1887; but it is well to review briefly the story of its development previous to that date, in order that its relative unimportance during the old era may be emphasized. A pioneer in the manufacture of the steam-engine, and a leading centre of rolling-stock production from the beginning of the railway age, Birmingham and District was, nevertheless, of small importance as a seat of machinery manufacture during the pre-depression period. There were, it is true, a few small concerns turning out stationary steam-engines, presses and machine tools, and one or two large firms with a wide range of products had grown up even before 1875; but the greater part of this output went to satisfy purely local requirements, and, for the most part, the quality of the machinery was not high, nor the volume of production large. In view of the area's high place as a metal centre some explanation of its humble place in engineering must be found. At that time the chief seats of machinery manufacture were Lancashire and Yorkshire, which had gained priority largely as a result of the great amount of mechanical equipment required by the textile industries. But in the Birmingham area the stimulus of a large local demand was lacking, because there methods of machine production had not yet been extensively applied, and in many trades no mechanical power was needed. Yet, though too far from the sea to offer advantages as a centre of marine or heavy engineering, the area possessed great potentialities as a seat of light engineering. It was then producing coal and iron on a great scale; its multitude of small metal industries were capable of supplying parts for composite products; and it had a great reserve of skilled labour of varying kinds. But as long as the engineering industry found its customers in railways, ships and textiles, Birmingham and District could hope for only a small share of the trade, and before it could achieve any prominence it had to await the birth of new types of products and the application on an extensive scale of mechanical methods to the small metal trades.

The lack of specialization exhibited by the trade before 1887 illustrates the stage of its development. Most local firms undertook to construct any kind of machine, from stationary engines to presses or lathes; and there was no attempt at standardization. Even the greater use of machinery during the seventies, and the introduction of the gas-engine into the smaller factories, resulted in no fundamental change in the engineering industry as a whole. Thus, apart from the production of rolling-stock and of structural work, down to the early eighties the local activities in engineering were limited mainly to the production of presses, lathes and prime movers for the local trades, and only one or two firms were large in size and catered for a wider area. Nearly all the more complicated and the high-grade machinery required in the district was brought from other industrial centres.

With the coming of the new era the character and size of the engineering industry entered upon a period of transformation, and by 1913 it ranked as the most important group of trades in the area. To some extent this development was a consequence of that application of mechanical methods of production to the older hardware trades which was one of the chief features of the period—a point to be discussed in the next chapter—but the main cause was the appearance of manufactures of an entirely new character—viz. the cycle and motor trades on the one hand and the production of electrical apparatus on the other. These new industries must be dealt with in some detail; for they, more than any other, are responsible for the transformation which has occurred during the last thirty-five years in the industrial character of Birmingham and District. The introduction of the bicycle trade has the first claim on our attention.

In 1863 a company had been formed to make sewing-machines at Coventry, which was then suffering severely as a result of the decline of the ribbon trade. At that time an Englishman, R. B. Turner, was connected with a firm which was conducting a riding-school and bicycle workshops in Paris. Being unable to meet the orders which were pouring in from all over Europe, Turner came in 1868 to Coventry, where his uncle was managing the Coventry Sewing Machine Company, with the suggestion that the firm should turn to bicycle manufacture. An order for 300 was given, and in 1869 the firm changed its style to the Coventry Machinists Company, and took up cycle-making in earnest, gradually abandoning the older trade. Although several small concerns had made bicycles at Birmingham and Wolverhampton for many years past, this was the first firm to execute a large order, and the occasion marked the beginning of the cycle industry in the locality.[1] Chance was not the only factor responsible for the localization; for the sewing-machine firms had plants which were particularly suitable for the new product; while the forged parts could be obtained, as indeed they were, from the Birmingham stampers. After 1870 numerous other concerns were established at Coventry, Wolverhampton and Birmingham, several of them being set up by foremen of the original Machinists Company; while great improvements were made in the construction of the bicycle. During the sixties the type of bicycle in use was the " boneshaker "—i.e. the wooden bicycle with iron rims—but the next decade saw the transition to the " high bicycle " and the tricycle, which were constructed

[1] H. O. Duncan, *The World on Wheels* (Paris, 1926), p. 297 *et seq.*

with suspension wheels, wire spokes and solid-rubber tyres. At the same time many of the features of construction which were to become integral parts of later models were invented. Adjustable ball-bearings were patented in 1873; the tangent wheel was introduced in 1874; steel tubing for frames came into use about the same time, and the chain drive and the differential gear were introduced two years later. During the later seventies, moreover, several experimental models of a rear-chain-driven safety bicycle were built; but none of these was produced in quantity.[1] The industry, indeed, was still small in size, and in 1881 it employed only 700 persons within our area, 400 of whom were at Coventry.[2] The cycle-maker still catered for the sportsman rather than for the general public, and his market was necessarily limited.

The appearance of the cycle industry as a substantial branch of the local manufactures did not take place until the end of the decade, and its rise coincided almost precisely with the opening of the new era, as we have defined it. The growth of the industry was associated with the introduction of the rear-chain-driven safety, which, first built in 1885 by J. K. Starley of Coventry, " set the fashion for the world." By 1890, in all the main features of design, the safety had assumed its present form, and the invention in 1888 of the pneumatic tyre completed the extinction of the old " high bicycle." [3]

The nineties were a period of enormous expansion. Cycles, which up to this time had been used mainly by athletes, now became an important means of transport for pleasure or business. After 1887 they were used in increasing quantities for military purposes, and eleven years later the postal and telegraph services began to provide a large and steady demand.[4] The export trade, too, rose by leaps and bounds, and cycles were sent from the Midlands to the United States and the Colonies, as well as to all the European countries. A host of local engineering and hardware firms changed over to the manufacture of cycles, including rifle, tinplate and stamping concerns, and workers flowed into the new trade from almost every metal

---

[1] H. O. Duncan, *op. cit.*, pp. 299, 303 *et seq.*
[2] *Census of England and Wales*, 1881, vol. iii., p. 242 *et seq.*
[3] H. O. Duncan, *op. cit.*, p. 585 *et seq.*
[4] A. Fox, *The Cycle Trade* (Social Study Diploma Thesis, Birmingham University Library).

industry in the district, particularly from the gun, brass and electro-plating trades. Large firms now began to be established, working with capital amounting to hundreds of thousands of pounds, and the period of great expansion culminated in the cycle boom of 1895-1897, when the prosperity of the gunmakers at the time of the American Civil War, or of the saddlers and ironmasters in 1870-1871, was equalled or surpassed. After this the industry received a set-back, partly in consequence of reckless financial proceedings during the boom period, and its exports began to meet with competition from other countries.

The adoption of the free-wheel after 1897, and the introduction of the three-speed gear in 1903, gave a further stimulus to the industry during the early years of the twentieth century, and although sales to the United States and to some other foreign countries declined, new markets were opened in Japan and elsewhere. The home demand continued to expand, and fresh customers were attracted by the big reduction of prices which occurred during the slump of 1898, when a ten-guinea machine was put on the market. During the early years of the new century the application on a large scale of the Easy Payment System to the marketing of cycles kept the industry busy, and although the rate of expansion between 1891 and 1901 was not maintained during the next decade, the industry nevertheless made a substantial advance, and, by the outbreak of the war, cycle manufacture, excluding subsidiary trades, employed more persons than any local trade, with the exception of brassfoundry and jewellery.

The great demand for cycles during the nineties carried the industry into many other parts of the country, yet in 1911 the area was still responsible for about 64 per cent. of the total employment in the manufacture, as compared with over 70 per cent. in 1891. As we shall see later, moreover, if our district maintained its position as the leading centre of cycle production, it was still more important as the source of the parts and accessories of which those vehicles were made. The explanation of this supremacy was to be found not only in the fact that much of the pioneering work had been done here, but in the character of the whole industrial structure of the West Midlands. The area was the home of a multitude of light metal trades and of a few engineering firms, all of which constituted a reservoir of the kind of skill and technical knowledge required. The cycle was a composite product, making demands on many different subsidiary industries. Tubes, forged and pressed parts, castings, metal-thread screws, wire, leather saddles, springs, and plating and enamelling work, were needed in the manufacture, and the area was the home of all these industries. From the watchmakers of Coventry to the brassfounders of Birmingham admirable recruits were available for the new factories. The tinplate- and japanned-ware firms of Wolverhampton could change without much difficulty to the production of pressed sheet-metal parts and accessories; while the rifle trade had plants which could easily be adapted to the manufacture in quantity of forged and machined parts.

As for the localization of the industry in the different sections of the area, that was subject to important changes during the pre-war period. In 1891 Coventry possessed about half of the total number of cycle-workers in our district; Birmingham and Aston came next, with a third; while Wolverhampton was the only other seat of the trade.

EMPLOYMENT IN THE CYCLE INDUSTRY, 1891 [1]

Coventry	4100
Birmingham and Aston	2600
Wolverhampton	600
Rest of District	1000
Total in Warwickshire, Staffordshire and Worcestershire	8300

The expansion during the nineties resulted in the advance of Birmingham as a producing centre, and a decline in the relative importance of Coventry—a change which was accentuated during the new century when the Coventry cycle firms began to turn their attention to motor-cars. So by 1911 Birmingham and Aston had become the chief seat of the trade, and employed some 9350 persons, or over 40 per cent. of the cycle-workers in the area; while Coventry had 5860, or 26 per cent.; Wolverhampton still occupied the third place, and at Redditch, where the trade had just taken root, about 1200 persons were employed.[2]

The forces of change which began to transform the industrial

[1] *Census of England and Wales*, 1891, vol. iii., p. 248 *et seq.*
[2] *Ibid.*, 1911, vol. x., part i., p. 412 *et seq.*, and vol. x., part ii., p. 592 *et seq.*

character of the district after the introduction of the safety bicycle were strengthened before the end of the century, as a result of the rise of the motor industry. Produced experimentally for many years, the motor-car could not become a common means of transport until the legislative restrictions on its movement on the highways were abolished. This took place in 1896, when the Light Locomotives on the Highways Act was passed; and from then onwards progress was by leaps and bounds. Development proceeded from two distinct sources. The larger concerns, which came into being about the time of the removal of the Red Flag Regulations, for a period confined their energies to the adaptation of current Continental practice; while quite distinct from these efforts was the enterprise of the engineer who evolved a new and original design, and so produced the first full-sized British petrol-motor, the Lanchester.[1]

From the first, the industry was essentially of the Midlands. The leading concerns working on Continental patents were all, in 1897, to be found in Coventry, located on various floors of an old cotton mill; and by the end of the century several other factories were established for motor-car and motor-cycle manufacture at Birmingham and Wolverhampton, as well as at Coventry. Some of these firms were newly promoted for the purpose, but in many instances they grew out of concerns engaged in other types of industry, a transition which continued to take place up to the war. At Coventry, although the earliest firms had been established for the specific purpose of motor production, the later recruits to the industry came mainly from the cycle trade, and by 1914 there were several large concerns which combined the manufacture of cars and motor-cycles with their original production of pedal-cycles, while others confined themselves to the last two types of vehicle. At Birmingham and Wolverhampton, on the other hand, the motor trade was for the most part taken up by general engineering firms, or was in the hands of men who had previously been engaged in the manufacture of gas-engines. Consequently, while at Coventry the grouping of cars, motor- and pedal-cycles was common, elsewhere there was a broad distinction between those firms producing cars and those engaged in the cycle or motor-cycle trade. The following Table illustrates the numbers engaged in

[1] H. O. Duncan, *op. cit.*, p. 865.

producing motor-car chassis and bodies and as motor mechanics in various centres in 1911.

EMPLOYMENT IN THE MOTOR INDUSTRY[1]

	Males	Females
Coventry	6,800	...
Birmingham	5,400	...
Wolverhampton	1,300	...
Rest of District	2,800	...
Total Employment in Warwickshire, Staffordshire and Worcestershire	16,300	500

Thus the two allied industries, which were practically non-existent at the beginning of the new era, together employed in 1914 nearly 40,000 persons, a larger number than any other single trade. Nor did these include all the persons affected by the new industries. As previously indicated, the cycle and, still more, the motor-car were highly composite products, which necessarily involved the co-operation of many different trades. Such local firms as could supply parts and accessories were, therefore, enormously stimulated. The non-ferrous firms were called upon for brass, copper and nickel, in the form of tubes, sheet-metal or wire; the screw manufacturers for quantities of wood-screws for car bodies and metal-thread screws for cycles and car chassis; the lock-makers for door-fastenings; the mirror manufacturers for windscreens; and the wire firms for flexible cords. A large industry, centred almost entirely in Birmingham, grew up for providing motor firms with accessories in the shape of lighting equipment, many of the old lamp manufacturers and brassfounders changing over to these new products. But perhaps the most important of all the new subsidiary trades was the manufacture of weldless steel tubes. Up to the seventies the ferrous tubes produced locally consisted mainly of the welded type for conducting gas, water and steam; but when, in the middle of that decade, the cycle industry began to employ tubular frames, a new branch was evolved, which became, during the cycle boom, of equal or of even greater importance than the older section. This was the manufacture of weldless steel tubes, which combined lightness with great strength. The productive process was quite different from that employed in the manufacture of the welded tube. Whereas the latter was made

[1] *Census of England and Wales*, 1911, vol. x., pp. 265, 283, 297.

from iron or steel strip, the former was produced by piercing a Swedish steel billet when hot, passing the short, thick tube thus secured through a series of grooved rolls, and finally drawing down the tube when cold to the required size and gauge on a draw-bench. Among other purposes the weldless tube was adopted by the Admiralty for boiler tubes to replace the non-ferrous type previously in use; but the most marked expansion of the industry was associated with the cycle boom, when several large new firms came into being, and when some of the welded-tube makers turned to this allied product. With the rise of the motor-car and motor-cycle, both of which used tubular frames, yet another market was provided, and by 1914 some 3000 persons were employed in the trade within our area. Birmingham and District had almost a monopoly of the new industry, which had been drawn there partly by the presence of the old tube trade, and partly because the greater proportion of the weldless tubes were disposed of in the locality. Besides the older firms of the Wolverhampton neighbourhood which branched into the new trade, several additional concerns were set up at Oldbury, Birmingham, Aston, and elsewhere.

The spring trade was similarly affected. Long before the appearance of these new vehicles, laminated springs and coil-springs had been produced in the locality for railway coaches, horse-drawn carriages and spring-balances; but the new de-mands swept the industry into a position of incomparably greater importance. At West Bromwich the production of both types of spring became a leading trade; while the coil-spring trade of Redditch expanded considerably in size. Even the leather trades felt the new stimulus. The tanners and curriers of Walsall, whose market among the saddlers and harness-makers was failing, turned to the production of leather for motor upholstery-work; while a number of cycle-saddle firms grew up at Birmingham, Redditch and Walsall, recruited partly from the spring-makers and partly from the leather-goods manufacturers, who found another new demand in tool-bags. Further, the coach-builders changed over to motor-body production, the coach-iron makers to axles and wheels, and almost every existing trade was in some measure affected by these new influences. Great quantities of ferrous and non-ferrous castings were required by the motor trade, and the result was not merely an expansion in the number and size of the local foundries. The introduction of the light high-speed engine also created demands for new alloys. Phosphor bronze for bearings began to be produced, and about 1900 a new industry, the manufacture of aluminium castings, was brought into the district, when a firm was established at Smethwick. Like most of the subsidiary trades, this was drawn to the locality largely because it constituted the market for most of the products; but the particular site was determined by the fact that West Bromwich and Smethwick were great centres of foundry-work, and a supply of moulders, core-makers and other types of labour was therefore at hand. In the same way the new industries brought additional orders to the firms of stampers or drop-forgers. Up to the nineties the stamping shops had been very small, and their markets were largely confined to the gun, key and general engineering trades. But cycles and motors required large numbers of standardized forged parts, and as time went on many components, such as spanners and gear-wheels, which had previously been cast, came to be made by hot stamping. So not only did the industry increase in Birmingham and the Black Country, but important concerns were established as well at Coventry, the chief seat of the new vehicle trades. Meanwhile the manufacture of chains for motor- and pedal-cycles grew up at Coventry; while the demand for pedals, cycle-carriers, lamp-brackets, gear-cases, and for a multitude of machined parts, brought more and more of the older hardware and engineering firms within the scope of the new trades.

Nor was it only the metal, leather or woodworking industries which were affected. Both the cycle and the motor industries owed their rapid development in no small measure to the invention of the pneumatic tyre, the first effect of which, indeed, was to transform cycling from the pastime of the athlete to a normal means of transport for the masses. As early as 1845 a pneumatic tyre had been invented; but it was never perfected or produced on a commercial scale, as there was no demand for it at the time. In 1888, on the other hand, when Dunlop took out his patent, the time was ripe for the new invention. The idea, the capacity for carrying it into practice, and an urgent and widespread need for the product, then happened to coincide; and the result was the inception of a great new trade. In 1889 the patent was acquired by the Dunlop Pneumatic Tyre Company, and by the following year the new cycle tyre was perfected, as a result of the invention of a valve and of Welch's patent method of attaching the tyre to the rim. On these three patents, indeed, the industry was founded; while, about the same time, the invention of the Clincher tyre created the possibility of applying the pneumatic principle to motor-vehicles as well.[1] The first Dunlop factory was established at Dublin; but, as it was inconvenient for the tyre manufacture to be situated at such a great distance from the centre of the cycle trade, an assembling factory was secured at Coventry, and later at Birmingham, and this became the main centre of the firm's activities after 1900. Other companies took up the production of tyres in other parts of the country, and though the cushion tyre had a short vogue after 1890, both this and the solid tyre were soon ousted. The figures below, which show the types of tyre fitted to cycles exhibited at the Stanley Show between 1890 and 1895, illustrate the rapidity of the change.

	Models fitted with [2]		
	Pneumatic Tyres	Cushioned Tyres	Solid Tyres
1890 . . .	20	1	1543
1891 . . .	148	511	307
1893 . . .	1066	221	42
1895 . . .	1588	7	3

In five years, indeed, the solid cycle tyre had been supplanted; while after the repeal of the Red Flag Regulations pneumatic motor tyres began to be produced. In addition, solid tyres for heavy motor-vehicles and other rubber articles were made at Birmingham, and in 1912 the production of golf balls was taken up. In 1891 the number employed in rubber manufactures in Warwickshire amounted to only a few hundreds. In 1901 the figure had risen to over 1700; in 1911 to 3350; and by 1914 some 4000 persons must have been engaged in the trade in the district.[3] Practically all of these were at Birmingham. The allied

[1] H. O. Duncan, op. cit., p. 610.
[2] Souvenir of the Pneumatic Tyre Majority Celebration (The Dunlop Rubber Co. Ltd., 1909).
[3] Census of England and Wales, 1901, Warwickshire, p. 53; 1911, vol. x., part i., p. 284.

manufacture, that of motor wheels, was taken up by firms which varied greatly from one another in origin. At Coventry the Dunlop firm had a factory for this purpose; a former hollow-ware manufacturer had taken up the trade at Bilston; while at Dudley the production of wheels, pressed steelwork, cycle parts and tanks were combined together in one establishment.

Thus, in the short space of twenty-five years, the advent of the vehicle trades had transformed the whole character of the area, which had now become the leading British centre for the manufacture of cars, motor-cycles, pedal-cycles, and their component parts. From an insignificant size in 1890 the trades had risen to engage some 40,000 persons; while several large industries, which each gave employment to several thousands of persons, such as the tyre, saddle and weldless-tube manufactures, besides a multitude of smaller ones, had arisen. Coventry, which before 1887 had pursued a course distinct from that of Birmingham, was now intimately linked with its fortunes, and was by 1914 known mainly for its connections with the new industries.

It is interesting to remark that the cycle and motor firms were largely confined to the three chief towns of the area: Birmingham, Coventry and Wolverhampton. But this does not mean that the smaller places within the Black Country were unaffected. If they did not become leading centres for the production of the completed vehicles, their resources were extensively drawn upon to provide the finished or semi-manufactured parts. The springs came from Smethwick, West Bromwich and Redditch, the weldless tubes from Wolverhampton and Oldbury, the wheels from Dudley and Bilston, the saddles and leatherwork from Walsall, and the multitude of castings, pressings and stampings from many Black Country centres. In spite of the enormous change in the prevailing type of product the distinction between the industrial life of Birmingham and that of the Black Country was, indeed, preserved. Birmingham tended to remain the seat of the finished manufactures; while the smaller places within our area still concerned themselves with the cruder products and with the parts required for the finished articles.

The new industries which sprang up during this period were all of a type which required large plants of machinery, and this, together with the fact that many of the older trades were becoming more highly mechanized, brought into being a large local demand for machine tools. Up to the eighties, as already shown, our area was not an important centre of this trade. In the country, as a whole, the two influences which had led to the greatest developments in the production of machine tools between 1840 and 1880 had been, first, the construction of railways, and, second, the rise of the interchangeable rifle. The district's machinery trades had not been greatly affected by the first influence, and, though some local firms had turned to the production of rifle- and ammunition-making machines during the late sixties, Lancashire and Yorkshire had then been the chief source of supply. It was only in the manufacture of presses —a typically Birmingham tool—that the district could claim a position of importance, as far as machine-tool production was concerned, right down to the eighties. Until then, indeed, such machine tools as were produced by local factories were the concern of the general engineering firms, and a specialized industry did not, in fact, exist, except where a few foremen, having left the larger concerns, such as Messrs Tangyes, were operating small shops in which lathes and drilling machines were made. But the cycle and the allied trades, requiring as they did a multitude of standardized machine-made parts, brought a rapid expansion in the demand for machinery, and raised the manufacture of machine tools to the position of a large and distinct Midland industry. During the nineties progress was rapid, and then the motor trade supplied a further stimulus. The electrical trades also provided a market for these products; while as the small metal industries—such as the lock, hollow-ware and brass manufactures—became more highly mechanized, local demands were still further increased. By 1914, not only was machine-tool production a trade for the specialist, but firms were tending to concentrate on particular types. It is probable that, of all the machines made, power-presses were produced in the greatest quantity; for the use of this tool, typical of Birmingham, was greatly extended after the coming of cheap mild steel. Presses were employed for a variety of purposes and trades. They were needed for the production of solid-drawn cartridge-cases, door-knobs, lock-cases, tinplate and steel hollow-ware, electric-light fittings, cabinet brassfoundry, and for a multitude of parts for the new cycle and motor industries. The manufacture of draw-benches was also increased, as a result of the growth of the weldless-tube trade; while drilling and milling machines, lathes of all kinds, chucks and vices and shearing machines, were among the other types produced in quantity within the locality, which, indeed, became famed for the lighter kinds of machine tools. Though most of them were necessarily sold within the district, there was developing in pre-war years a considerable export trade to France, Belgium, Australia and India. The largest share of this industry was in the hands of Birmingham itself, which had most of the press trade; but Coventry had also become a centre for the production of high-grade machine tools, and several Black Country towns, such as Wednesbury and Darlaston, had important factories which had grown up in connection with the local requirements in machinery. On the whole, the high-grade products were centred in Birmingham and Coventry, and the Black Country was concerned chiefly with the cruder and heavier types.

The next important industry to be added to the local activities —an industry which exercised a transforming influence over the structure of the area second only to that of the vehicle trades —was the manufacture of electrical apparatus. Electricity had been employed for many years in connection with the plating trade; arc lamps for lighthouse purposes were first constructed at West Bromwich in 1862; and incandescent electric lamps made their appearance on a large scale in the district in 1882.[1] But during the old era the production of electrical apparatus was of negligible importance, and it was not until the middle eighties that signs of growth appeared. Several firms were then established at Birmingham and Wolverhampton; the manufacture of dynamos was taken up, and the district became a leading centre of meter production.[2] The first advance of great moment, however, was made when the Birmingham Electric Supply Company was established in 1889. Previously small private installations for generating current had been in existence; but this was the first power station in the area to operate on a large scale. During the last decade of the century the industry rapidly expanded. Firms for producing dynamos, motors, pumps and other kinds of apparatus appeared, not only in the

[1] C. J. Woodward, *op. cit.*, pp. 183-184.
[2] *Ibid.*, pp. 184-186; and *Birmingham and the Neighbourhood* (British Association Handbook, Birmingham Meeting, 1913), pp. 424-434.

leading towns of the area, but in places beyond its limits, such as Rugby and Stafford, and employment in the trade rose from only 700 in 1891 to over 3500 ten years later.[1] During the rest of the period growth was at an even greater rate. The most important event was the establishment in 1901 of the General Electric Company's factory, with departments for producing a wide variety of apparatus, including switch-gear, motors, fans, steel conduits, and heating and lighting fittings. The site chosen was Witton, to the north of Birmingham, and this district, previously devoid of industrial activities, became the chief centre of the local electrical trades before 1914. Meanwhile local manufacturers were changing over from steam- or gas-engines to electrical prime movers, and the use of electric light was being greatly extended. These developments are illustrated by the published returns of the Birmingham Power Station, which was acquired by the Corporation in 1900; for they show that the number of units of current sold rose from 3,000,000 in 1901 to 63,000,000 in 1911.[2] By that year the employment afforded by this group in the three counties amounted to over 10,000, though as large firms at that time existed at Rugby and Stafford, probably not more than 7000 to 8000 were to be found within Birmingham and District.[3] The largest share of the industry was concentrated within Birmingham itself, which accounted for over 40 per cent. of the total employment. Wolverhampton came next in importance; while Coventry and Smethwick had smaller proportions of the trade.

The rapid growth of the electrical trades within the district was, as in the case of the vehicle industries, to be accounted for by the presence of subsidiary manufactures, and of the type of skilled labour required; while the fact that Birmingham had become a nodal point in the country's railway system was of great influence. Yet, if the variety of local trades proved an attraction for the new electrical manufacturers, the growth of their industry stimulated in turn many old-established concerns. When the demand for electrical apparatus first arose many manufacturers in other types of business, such as instrument-

[1] Covers the three counties. *Census of England and Wales*, 1891, vol. iii., p. 250 *et seq.*; 1901, Warwickshire, p. 52, Worcestershire, p. 52, Staffordshire, p. 66.

[2] Includes 21,000,000 units for traction. See *Birmingham and the Neighbourhood* (British Association Handbook, Birmingham Meeting, 1913), p. 222.

[3] *Census of England and Wales*, 1911, vol. x., part i., pp. 265, 283, 297.

U

makers, gas-fittings manufacturers and general engineers, changed over to the new industry, and others began to adapt themselves to the production of parts and accessories. The lighting brassfounders began to turn out electric-light fittings; general brassfounders found a new activity in the production of switches; firms in the primary branches of the non-ferrous trades began to make nickel silver and copper wire for electrical engineers; the tube-makers were stimulated by the demand for steel conduit tubes; and the stampers and the malleable-iron foundries found a new market for their products. Further, as a demand developed for high-speed engines for generating stations, local firms of engineers began to produce them. By 1914, although the area was not concerned with electric lamps and cables, practically every other section of the new industry was represented in the locality. It was, however, to industrial equipment, for which a large local market existed, that most of the attention of firms within Birmingham and District was directed, and the neighbourhood had become a leading centre for the production of motors, dynamos, pumps, switch-gear, transformers and meters.

Another specialized branch of engineering which grew from a position of small importance in the eighties to a substantial size during this period was the manufacture of weighing and measuring apparatus. The trade was not a new one in the district, having been in existence since the eighteenth century; while, as already described, one branch, the spring-balance trade, had been introduced between 1820 and 1830. Before the opening of the new era the chief types of apparatus made consisted of the spring-balance and the equal-balance scale for shops, the lever weighing-scale for coal retailers, and the heavy weighing-machine, which was not, however, largely produced in the district. The centre of the spring-balance trade was at West Bromwich, the equal-balance scale trade at Birmingham; while the heavier types were produced by the constructional engineers of the Black Country. In 1881 there were about 900 persons engaged in this group of industries.[1]

During the new era there was a very rapid development, which was associated with the changes in commercial methods, with legislative enactments and with scientific developments.

[1] *Census of England and Wales*, 1881, vol. iii., p. 241 *et seq.*

The Checkweighing Acts of 1887, 1894 and 1905, and the Weights and Measures Acts of 1899 and 1907, gave a great stimulus to the trade; there was a bigger demand for weighing-machines for handling the increasing quantities of grain which were being imported into the country; and the advance of scientific methods of production and of metallurgy brought demands for accurate testing- and weighing-machines. Further, particularly in the marketing of agricultural produce, the custom of selling articles by weight was increasing; the supersession of masonry by steel in constructional work meant that great machines had to be produced for testing bridges; while the increased demands for expensive scales accompanied the growing elaboration of retail shop-fittings. After 1895 a variety of new balances for shops were introduced, chief among which were those constructed on the " visible-weighing " principle. Consequently, during the last decade of the century, a great expansion in the industry set in, and the numbers employed increased from about 1400 in 1891 to over 3000 in 1914.[1] The spring-balance trade remained in West Bromwich; but the benefits of the expansion in demand, which had occurred mainly in the more elaborate testing- and weighing-machines, were confined largely to a great firm centred at Soho. This probably employed two-thirds of the total number engaged in the industry within Birmingham and District in 1914. Several comparatively small Birmingham firms continued to exist; but these were, for the most part, concerned with the older types of balance.

. Two minor local industries which are dealt with in this chapter because of their rapid growth during the period are the chemical and the paint-and-varnish manufacture. The former was in 1914, as in earlier years, located mainly in the Black Country, particularly at Oldbury, and it was concerned with a wide variety of chemicals for industrial, agricultural and photographic uses. Part of the acids produced found a local market in the metal trades, where they were employed for " pickling "; but the advance of the trade was to be chiefly associated with the rise of industrial chemistry towards the end of the century. It is doubtful if the Census figures include all classes of workers engaged in the industry ; they probably

[1] *Census of England and Wales*, 1891, vol. iii., p. 250 *et seq.*; 1911, vol. x., part i., pp. 265, 283, 297.

numbered over 3000 in 1914, three or four times as many as in 1887.[1]

The growth of the paint-and-varnish trade was in response to the needs of the new industries. It has been shown that from early times Birmingham and District had been the seat of a large production of black varnish and lacquer for the local hardware factories; but up to the last decade of the century the amount of paint produced was very small. The expansion of the rolling-stock industry had, nevertheless, created a demand for industrial paints, and so had laid the foundations for this section of the trade. After 1890 an important change began to occur. While several of the older markets for industrial varnishes, such as the japanned-ware, bedstead and other hardware trades, began to decline, new customers appeared. Enamels were required for the cycle, conduit-tube and the gas-fire and stove industries, and then, with the rise of the motor trade, a large local market for paint was created, which raised that section to a position of importance. During the decade preceding the war several varnish manufacturers took up the manufacture of paint, and in 1914 both branches of the industry together employed about 1000 persons. The decorating trade took a proportion of the products; but most of the paint and varnish was sold for industrial purposes. The leading producers still remained in Birmingham and Wolverhampton.

Such, then, were the fortunes of the industries which had a close association with the area's traditional concern with metal. The next group of trades to rise to a high place during this period was, however, of a very different character. Up to the end of the great depression the food and drink trades had been of small importance, and, though a few firms existed for the production of beer, vinegar, cocoa and chocolate, the total employment afforded by them cannot have been more than 2000. The new era, however, witnessed a development which for its magnitude could only be paralleled by the vehicle trades; while, since the food and drink manufactures were not associated with the traditional industries of the area, their rise was far more remarkable than that of trades which grew out of long-established forms of industrial activity. The most spectacular growth occurred in the cocoa and chocolate branch, which, in

[1] *Census of England and Wales*, 1911, vol. x., part i., pp. 266, 284, 298.

this area, was practically synonymous with the firm of Messrs Cadbury Brothers. Long situated in Birmingham, this concern remained comparatively small until its removal to Bournville, on the outskirts of the town, in 1879. From then onwards its progress was rapid. The employment afforded by the trade increased from a few hundred persons in the early eighties to some 1200 at the end of that decade, and to over 3000 at the beginning of the new century. By 1914 some 6000 persons were so engaged, a far greater total than was employed by many of the ancient staples of the area, such as buttons, guns, locks, glass and tinplate wares. During the nineties the export trade, previously small, began to expand rapidly, and by 1914 it amounted to £500,000.

This was not the only trade of the group to rise to great importance. The development of large breweries, which began in the early seventies, and which by 1887 had given Birmingham and Aston alone four big concerns, led to the creation of another staple trade. By 1914 there were a number of great breweries in Birmingham and Wolverhampton, each employing hundreds of men, and, in one case, working with a capital of over £1,000,000. In such trades as this figures of employment are but a poor guide to the magnitude of the industry, and although probably about 2000 persons were concerned, the relative importance of the breweries was much greater than that statement seems to indicate. Mineral waters were also produced in the neighbourhood, while several companies existed in Birmingham for the manufacture of sauces and vinegar, in which nearly 1000 workers were engaged. More remarkable was the rise of a large sausage-making trade, which was centred, of all unlikely places, in the heart of the old iron district, Tipton; while in Birmingham itself other concerns were engaged in sweet, cake and custard-powder production.

It is impossible to discover an accurate guide to the increase of the whole group of trades during this period, but it is probable that employment rose from some 2000 to 2500 in 1887 to about 12,000 in 1914. The development of trades of this type was not, of course, limited to Birmingham and District; for food and drink production were everywhere during this period becoming a sphere of activity for large-scale industry; but, apart from the influence which exceptionally gifted individuals may have had on the rise of certain of them, it seems clear that the reason why Birmingham secured such a large share of these trades was because of its excellence as a distributing centre for the home market. Other explanations may be found in the fact that the area, being the centre of a dense population, was itself a large market for food and drink products; while the breweries benefited by the good water which could be obtained from the local artesian wells.

Associated generally with the growing practice of employing elaborate methods of packing, and particularly with the expansion of the local food-producing firms, was the progress of the paper-bag and box-making manufacture. A small industry had existed for many years in the locality and had employed in 1881 some 1500 persons, but by 1914 the total had risen to about 4500. Many of these were not employed in factories which specialized in the above manufactures, but in departments of cocoa and chocolate, pen and other metal-smallware establishments. In addition, over 1000 persons were engaged in paper-making; while the production of stationery and envelopes was also a trade of some importance.[1]

In the opening years of the new century an allied trade made its appearance—viz. the manufacture of office equipment. The changes in business organization, which resulted in an increase in the functions of the office staff, and in the development of filing and costing systems, created an opportunity for firms which were in a position to supply, not merely the equipment required for offices in the shape of letter heads, stationery, system forms, circulars, loose-leaf ledgers and office account-books, but also the expert advice on business organization and the material forms in which that could be expressed. So, as the modern office system arose in all its elaboration, there appeared in the district, notably at Northfield, West Bromwich and Smethwick, a number of factories which were concerned with some branch or branches of these new activities. Many of them developed, naturally, from old firms of business printers, and by 1914 some 2000 persons were concerned with the trade. By that time, moreover, the area had become a centre for the manufacture of office furniture—*e.g.* desks and filing cabinets—produced not only in wood, but of metal; for many of the

[1] *Census of England and Wales*, 1911, vol. x., part i., pp. 267, 285, 299.

tinplate and sheet-metal firms turned to the production of steel furniture of this type when the demand for their older products began to fail.

At the same time an entirely new industry was growing up in connection with the local leather manufacture, which did something to compensate for the decline after 1900 in the demand for saddlery and harness. The cycle-saddle trade has already been discussed, and does not require further attention. Besides this there appeared early in the new century a large production of fancy leather goods, sports equipment and travelling bags, and many of the saddlers and harness-makers turned to these new manufactures when the older markets began to fail. From the Census returns it is possible to estimate the rapidity of this growth, though it is not possible to achieve accuracy, because, whereas in 1881 and 1911 the curriers and leather-goods makers are given separately, in the Tables of the intermediate Censuses they are grouped together. It appears, however, that in 1881 the number of makers, as distinct from dealers, of leather goods other than saddlery and harness was 500. During the next decade there was only a slight increase; but between 1891 and 1901, with the advance in fashion of leather travelling bags and in sports equipment, in addition to the influence of the new vehicle trades, numbers had risen to between 2000 and 2500. During the next period, when the failure of older branches of the leather trade was forcing manufacturers to adapt themselves to produce motor and cycle equipment and to capture the fancy leather-goods trade, much of which was in German hands, there was a rapid growth to 4700.[1] Thus, in twenty years, the industry had risen from insignificance to a position of substantial importance. As in the case of the older branch, the new sections of the leather trade were shared between Birmingham and Walsall; but whereas the latter had long held the lead in saddlery and harness, Birmingham had a slight predominance in the new branches. This was largely because of its superior powers of adaptation; but partly owing to the presence of the new vehicle trades with their demands for leather accessories in that centre.

Finally, we come to an entirely new industry which, because of its remarkably rapid progress during the present century

[1] *Census of England and Wales*, 1911, vol. x., part i., pp. 267, 285.

deserves special notice—viz. the artificial-silk trade. The most recent of all the local manufactures, artificial silk, first began to be produced on a commercial scale in this country when Messrs Courtauld established their factory at Coventry in 1905. This was the only establishment of its kind during the pre-war period; but so great was its progress that by 1914 artificial-silk manufacture could be ranked, if not among the staples of the locality, at least among the more important secondary manufactures. Employment, which amounted on the inception of the trade to only 200, rose in nine years to over 3000. The causes which led to the localization of the trade at Coventry deserve notice. The fact that the old silk trade had been located there seems the most obvious explanation; but, though this did exercise some influence on the choice of a site, actually it was a factor of little practical importance. The old silk trade did not, in fact, provide any large number of recruits for the new industry; for the productive process called for entirely different types of skill and technical knowledge. It was a combination of other factors which exercised a determining influence. Coventry had a central situation and a good water-supply. It was on a main railway line and near a coal-field. Further, the town was in fairly close proximity to Hinckley, Leicester and Nottingham, where a large proportion of the yarn was used; and finally, and perhaps most important of all, a supply of female labour was available, for which there was no great competition from other industries. In this trade, it is important to remark, while the chemical processes are performed by men, girls are required for manipulating, winding and sorting the yarn. It is necessary, moreover, for the manufacturer to be able to secure his female workers at an early age, between fourteen and sixteen, because it is very difficult to train girls who come into the business at a later age. The Courtauld promoters, partly with this point in mind, established their factory on the northern side of Coventry, in close proximity to the mining district of Bedworth, where, since the decay of the old silk-weaving trade, once carried on extensively by the wives and daughters of the miners, no suitable employment for girls existed. Consequently, there a supply of suitable labour could easily be obtained.

This, however, was not the only connection which the area made with the textile trade during the period. In 1885 a drapery

and woollen merchant of Dudley took up the production of
wholesale clothing, and the rapid development of his trade led,
by 1914, to the appearance of a large factory which gave employment to not far short of 1000 persons. Thus, in yet another
centre of the old iron industry, a manufacture which would have
seemed very incongruous to the nail-factors and ironmasters of
an earlier age took root.

So, the progress of Birmingham and District during this
period was bound up with the advance of the new industries,
and it was to trades which had been non-existent or of small
importance during the old era, or even up to 1890, that the area
looked for a prosperous future. Hardware was giving place to
engineering, and the new vehicle manufacture had become the
staple industry of the district. Few of the older industries
made any rapid advance, and even where they maintained their
prosperity they did so mainly by concerning themselves with
products which were complementary to the engineering trades.
The supersession of the hardware manufacture was, it is true,
due mainly to the rapid progress of the new industries rather
than to a positive decline in the magnitude of the old; but the
effect was to modify the whole industrial structure of the area
and to render it a centre, not so much of small metal articles,
but of finished products of a highly composite character.

CHAPTER IV

CHANGES IN MECHANICAL EQUIPMENT AND IN THE SCALE OF INDUSTRY

IF the period from 1887 to 1914 was remarkable for the changes which occurred in the relative importance of the various local industries, a transformation of equal significance was effected in the scale of production, in methods of organization and in mechanical equipment. In 1860, as we have seen, the majority of the local hardware trades were conducted in small establishments, which seldom employed more than fifty persons, while in many cases the domestic worker proper was a common figure. Only in the heavy trades of the Black Country, and in a few manufactures which had been revolutionized by machinery, was production on anything like a large scale. Further, while power-machinery was extensively used in the earlier processes of manufacture, as in the rolling mills, hand-labour, assisted by primitive machines, was still the universal method of production in the trades which produced finished products, and only here and there had machinery displaced the skilled craftsman.

From 1860, throughout the period covered by Part III., such changes as occurred were slow and by no means far-reaching. In most trades, it is true, there was a gradual increase in the size of the typical producing unit, and the introduction of the gas-engine made it possible for the small workshop owner to take advantage of mechanical methods. During the period of the depression, moreover, there was a fairly widespread movement towards a greater degree of division of labour and towards a more extensive use of machinery; but in the early eighties the large unit was still exceptional, the shop owner and the garret-master remained common figures, and there was only one important industry in which the large factory had completely displaced the small unit during the quarter of a century preceding 1887—viz. military-rifle manufacture. It is curious that the great depression, which provided such a great stimulus to the reduction of costs, should not have led to more fundamental mechanical changes than actually occurred. In the case of trades like jewellery and brassfoundry, which were concerned with products of an individual character, there was, of course, little to induce manufacturers to adopt machinery; yet there were many industries which produced articles of a standardized nature, and still clung to the older methods of manufacture. Such were the tinplate-ware, lock, edge-tool, hollow-ware and general ironmongery industries; and their conservatism needs explanation. While many forces doubtless co-operated to delay the introduction of machines, by far the most influential of these was to be found in the nature of the raw material which the bulk of the metal industries employed. Until the early eighties this consisted mainly of wrought-iron, a metal which it is very difficult to machine. Indeed, while wrought-iron continued to be the staple raw material of the metal-using trades, mechanical methods were bound to remain in a primitive condition, and the advent of machinery in hardware production had to await the introduction of the new steel, and, with it, the growth of metallurgical knowledge among manufacturers.

During the eighties these conditions were first satisfied. Bessemer and Siemens-Martin steel began to supersede wrought-iron in many of the older local trades; while the new engineering industries were steel rather than iron users. The introduction of these metals was of the utmost significance; for through them the part played by machinery was greatly extended and the factory system was, in consequence, carried into a group of trades which had remained unaffected during the earlier phases of the industrial revolution. During the twenty-five years prior to the war, moreover, the advance in metallurgical knowledge and in its application to manufacturing processes was enormous. New alloys were discovered; high-speed tool steels which permitted more rapid production and the consequent lowering of costs came to the front; and the mechanical methods of the metal-using trades were transformed. Of all the influences on practical metallurgy perhaps the most powerful of all came from the motor industry, with its demand, on the one hand, for metals suitable for a high-speed engine, and, on the other, for tool steels which would stand up to rapid production. Technical factors, however, were not the only forces at work. Over the whole field of industry, and not merely in the metal trades, manufacturers were tending to produce more standardized commodities. The simplification in the style of hardware products in general demand was associated with this development; for elaborate and massive products began to give place to lighter and cheaper articles. This tendency, as already described, was particularly evident in the brass trade, especially after electric-lighting began to spread; for the result was to create a demand for small machined parts instead of for cast ornamental gas-fittings. An opportunity was thus given to the manufacturer to produce by presses and machine tools what had previously been made in the foundry and finished by hand. At the same time the new engineering trades were bringing large demands for small standardized parts, which needed machinery for their production; while in many of the older industries the increasing severity of foreign competition during the nineties stimulated makers to cut their costs by a resort to mechanical methods. Finally, the introduction of a new type of prime mover exercised an influence over the productive methods of even the small unit. Before the end of the century, indeed, the gas- and oil-engines had made it possible for the smaller manufacturers to equip themselves with power-machinery, and had freed them from the necessity for hiring steam-power for certain processes. After this there was a great extension in the use of gas-engines, which, in fact, played a part in the history of the small metal trades analogous to that of the steam-engine during the early years of the modern industrial era. With the opening of the new century, moreover, yet another form of power came into use—viz. electricity. Firms which, owing to the nature of their business, had an inconstant load, and which, therefore, found the steam- and gas-engines expensive, because they had to be run even when their power was not required, turned to the use of electricity supplied by the local power stations. Small manufacturers, to whom both the steam- and gas-engines had proved too costly, also began to make use of electric-motors, which were easy to run and of a capacity suitable for their purposes, and so power-machinery was introduced into the smallest of establishments.

Thus, during this period, the treadle lathe passed out of use in most industries; the power-press, now increased in size, and adapted for many purposes, took the place of the hand-press; drilling machinery superseded punching; heavier steam and hydraulic stamps replaced the kick stamp; and, with the in-creased tendency towards standardized production and with the great advance of metallurgy, which made possible speedier, cheaper and more accurate machining, new and complicated machine tools made their appearance. Lathes became vastly more complex; planing, drilling, milling and boring machines became widely employed; and automatic and semi-automatic machinery of many kinds began to be a feature of the local methods of manufacture. With all these developments the new trades were intimately associated and in them the chief advances were made. Large and elaborately equipped machine-shops became a normal feature of every important motor, cycle or electrical-apparatus factory; the pneumatic-tyre manufacturers employed large plants of mixing, rolling and tube-drawing machines; while even the food and drink trades made great use of power-machinery, not only for the actual productive process, but for packing, bottling and other subsidiary operations as well.

Yet it was by no means only the new industries which passed under the sway of the machine. Before 1887 the trades which could be considered highly mechanized were the wire, tube, sheet-metal, pin, screw, cut-nail, military-rifle, ammunition and coining industries. In these no fundamental changes occurred, since development was on the lines laid down during the previous period. In cartridge manufacture, for example, the drawing presses came to be provided with a larger number of tools, so that several cartridge cases could be drawn at one operation; while automatic feeding was introduced. Again, in the production of pins, new machines were introduced for carding and packing, while in 1905 automatics were applied to the manufacture of hairpins. It is interesting to remark that improvements in wire-drawing machinery, which resulted in an increase in the size of the plant required for economical production, concentrated most of the wire manufacture, previously conducted by pin-makers, in the hands of a few large specialist firms after 1900.

Of more interest, however, is the history of the industries which were affected fundamentally. The brassfoundry trade, for instance, had its productive methods revolutionized during the period. As we have seen, demand shifted from elaborate gas-fittings and cabinet work to standardized electric-light fittings and to less ornate articles, which required little attention from skilled handicraftsmen. As the products became lighter and simpler in design it was possible to employ machinery on a much greater scale. Hot pressings and stampings superseded

castings for many purposes. The process of spinning on the
lathe advanced. Capstan lathes became widely used during the
nineties for the production of standardized gas-fittings, and
with the rise of the motor and electrical accessories' branch a
great use was made of semi-automatic machines of this character. In the cock-founding section methods were completely
changed. Up to about 1885 the various cast parts were given
out to a worker who used only a foot-lathe, and assembled and
tested the various components of the cock. After that date,
however, division of labour began to creep in. The capstan
lathe became extensively employed after 1900 for machining the
parts; while plate- or machine-moulding began to supersede the
older foundry methods. These developments were all associated
with the increase in the quantity of standardized cocks required.

Even the jewellery and gun trades, which, from the nature of
their products, could never become highly mechanized, were
not unaffected. In the former the introduction of the gas-
engine resulted in the use of power by stampers, rollers, wire-
drawers and polishers; while the electro-plate branch, which
first began to make a considerable use of power about 1880, by
1914 used power-presses and stamps for producing certain
classes of articles and machinery for burnishing and polishing.
The old gun trade remained a handicraft in the majority of its
operations; but " material-making " tended more and more to
a reliance on machines. For instance, during the seventies, while
some of the high-class gun barrels had been of steel, the majority
were " damascened "—i.e. welded by hand from iron and steel
strips. By the end of the century, however, practically all barrels
were made of steel, and this meant the extinction of the ancient
handicraft of the barrel-welder. The steel tubes from which
the new type of barrel was made were themselves produced by
machinery; while their conversion into finished barrels, which
involved drilling, boring and stripping processes, was essentially
a task for the machine tool. In the manufacture of actions also
small firms of machinists arose which began to produce them
in the rough by mechanical methods. Thus even in this typical
handicraft the earlier processes of manufacture passed from the
craftsman to the machine.

Some of the ancient trades of the Black Country remained
unaltered until the last decade of the century, when they, too,

began slowly to adopt new methods. Thus, whereas the older types of lock [1] had been made of cast-iron cases and forged- or malleable-iron parts, which had been filed and assembled by skilled workers, the cases now came to be pressed out of steel and the bolts produced from drawn sections. Milling machines took the place of the file, and what had previously been a task for the craftsman became a problem for the engineer. The coming of the cylinder lock aided this development; for that was of a type particularly suitable for mechanical production, and even the keys could be cut and differed by machinery. In the nut-and-bolt trade machinery began to replace hand-forging about 1881, and by 1914 the industry's labour force, instead of consisting mainly of skilled smiths, consisted of skilled tool-makers on the one hand, and a mass of machine operatives on the other. The hollow - ware trade also was transformed. A power-press had been in existence since 1870 for making tinplate goods, and the stamp had been employed extensively long before that time; but machinery could not be successfully applied to most of the wrought wares while iron remained the raw material of the trade. The advent of mild steel, however, gave a great stimulus to the employment of the power-press, both in the older tinplate ware and in the new enamelled-steel hollow-ware trades. In the former, moreover, folding and moulding machines for the manufacture of certain articles, such as trunks, came into use about 1900; while electric and acetylene welding was another important advance during the period. Machines also were introduced for spraying the enamel coating, and even in the cast branch several of the finishing processes, such as the polishing of the interior of vessels, came to be performed by power-machinery instead of by hand. Meanwhile the process of spinning on the lathe was largely applied to the manufacture of such wares as frying-pans; and after 1900 the galvanized hollow-ware branch, which had been conducted almost entirely by hand-processes, began to use power-presses for producing certain standardized commodities, and machines for affixing the bottoms to dustbins and other articles. Much of this trade, however, necessarily remained with the

[1] It was said of this trade in 1884: " There are . . . nearly five hundred little lock-shops in the parish, where a man and some half-a-dozen apprentices turn out an incredible quantity of locks at an incredible price " (J. T. Jeffcock, *Wolverhampton Guide*, 1884, p. 100).

hand-workers, and such things as baths owed little to machinery; while skilled smiths continued to produce the majority of the handles for the wares on the anvil. Yet even here certain kinds of standardized handles, which were required in quantity, began to be made by rolling or pressing. In the manufacture of edge tools great progress was made. Steam-hammers generally superseded tilt hammers for forging during the nineties, and just before the war the former were in turn being replaced by the pneumatic hammer. A cheaper process, moreover, was developed for certain types of tool, such as shovels. These, instead of being hammered into shape, began to be rolled or pressed; while another method, called " gobbing," or pulling out the metal— a process intermediate between rolling and forging—came into use for the cheaper tools. The employment of water-power, which had been very common in this industry in the Stour Valley, was generally abandoned, except in such places as Bellbroughton, where it was still used by the scythe-makers.

Even the brush trade was carried in the same direction. Plugging machines, for producing the type of brush in which the bristles or fibres were held in place by wire or string, had been in existence since the late sixties; but their use was not extensive until local manufacturers began to experience competition from abroad toward the end of the century. About the same time the machine-made sash-tools and whitewash brushes, in which the bristles were affixed by a compressed metal ferrule, became common, and a gradual abandonment of the older methods set in.

In the button trade the branch most seriously affected was that concerned with pearl buttons. Before 1895 this section had depended entirely on hand-labour; but in that year machinery was introduced from the United States. In consequence, though the preliminary processes, like cutting and drilling, and the finishing processes, remained unchanged, for the intermediate operations, such as turning, backing and pattern-impressing, machinery came to be employed. There were several other industries in which the advance towards mechanical methods was much slighter. Thus the wrought-chain trade, which still employed iron as its material, continued, for the most part, to pursue ancient methods; though early in the new century the production of the lighter types of wrought chain began to be influenced by the appearance, at Walsall and elsewhere, of the manufacture of electrically welded chain. Again, the finished-leather trades were not much affected; but the tanners and curriers began to make an increasing use of machinery; and power-driven rolls for removing grease, and machines for splitting the hides, became part of the ordinary equipment of the tanneries before 1914. The flint-glass trade made scarcely any change in its processes, although in the heavy-glass trade tanks began to replace pots for melting the ingredients about 1878, and the new process enabled production to be more continuous and on a greater scale.

Just as the change from the steam-engine to the gas- or oil-engine and the electric motor was common to many industries, so in a wide variety of local trades gas- and oil-fired furnaces and annealing ovens began to supersede the coke- or coal-fired type during the twenty years prior to the war. The latter was, even in 1914, still the more common, but the greater convenience of the former types, the ease with which liquid or gas fuel could be handled, the great accuracy to be obtained in temperature, were all conspiring to overthrow coke and coal from their predominant position.

Even foundry practice, moreover, was affected by the growth in the scale of production and in the demand for standardized parts for the engineering trades. Instead of the patterns being made of wood, when great quantities of the same type of casting were required metal patterns came to be employed, and mechanical methods of moulding were brought into use. The advantage of machine-moulding lay not only in the speed with which the moulds could be made but in the fact that the casting could be produced more accurately and with a smoother surface. This meant that less machining was required than in the case of the ordinary type of casting, and a great saving was, therefore, effected in the costs of the subsequent processes of production. Machine-moulding, however, was economical only when demand was for standardized articles, and the extensive application of the process had to await the growth in the market and the tendency towards standardization among manufacturers of hardware and engineering products. Another method which came to the front prior to the war was die-casting, according to which the mould itself was made of metal. For many years this process,

X

under the name of chill-casting, had been followed in the bedstead and other trades; but the rise of the new engineering industries, with their large demand for standardized castings, gave a stimulus to this branch of activity.

Just as the extension of the market called new foundry methods into existence, so the increasing demand for forged parts resulted in the rise of the drop-forging process at the expense of the skilled smith. Improvements were effected in the type of stamp used, and it became possible to produce larger and more complicated forgings in consequence. Up to the nineties the the type of stamp in use was the kick stamp or tilt hammer, which, aided by a power-driven shaft, lifted weights up to ten hundredweights. During that decade, however, a great advance was made. First, there came Brett's steam-lifter, which was followed about 1897 by the Duffield friction-belt method, by which a short steel belt, operated by a lever, was pressed to a revolving pulley when it was desired to lift the stamp. This enabled the weight of the stamp to be increased to a ton, and later to two tons, or more. Finally, in 1900, when a method, similar in principle to the band-brake, by which a wood-lined steel band gripped a revolving electric-driven steel drum, was introduced, it became possible to raise weights up to nine tons.

Thus, between 1887 and 1914, the character of the area from the standpoint of its mechanical equipment was transformed. Before that period Birmingham and District was still the home of handicraft. By 1914, partly because of the change within the older industries and of the decline of those which were essentially strongholds of manual methods, such as nail-making, and partly owing to the appearance of new machine-using trades, it could no longer be said that power - machines were mere accessories to hand-labour, as was true thirty years previously. The change had begun during the depression; but it was not until the coming of cheap steel and of the rise of the new engineering trades that the mechanical revolution became rapid, and it was, therefore, the nineties which witnessed the beginning of the new machine era.

The increased use of power-machinery in the local trades was, of course, intimately associated with the growth in the scale of production during the period. Before concerning ourselves with the details of particular industries we must briefly indicate the general forces at work. The most important influence, as already shown, was the introduction of machinery, which in turn was stimulated by the necessity for cutting costs, the consequence of competition from abroad. The smaller units in many of the old hardware trades disappeared, because they were unable to take advantage of the more economical methods which had appeared; and, sometimes as a result of natural growth and sometimes because of a series of amalgamations, production came to be concentrated in the larger units. Besides this there was another influence of a very different character. When means of urban transport were scanty, a manufacturer was then obliged to establish his factory within a comparatively small area in the centre of the towns, so that workers might be available in the vicinity. If his orders increased it might be impossible, under such circumstances, for the manufacturer to extend the scale of his operations, merely owing to the fact that no room was available within the congested factory area for fresh shops. Consequently, he would be forced to rely on outworkers for many operations, and he could not hope to render his business self-contained. Towards the end of the century, however, new means of transport began to appear. Tramway systems were extended, and the cycle provided a cheap means of locomotion to a multitude of workers; while before the war the motor-omnibus had made its appearance. Thus it was now possible for factories to be established on the outskirts of the great towns, in places where extensive sites were available, and the manufacturer could then bring all his operations under his own roof and was freed from dependence on subsidiary trades or on outworkers. In many industries, therefore, firms tended to become more self-contained, and this in itself resulted in a growth in the size of the representative unit.

The development of large factories beyond the city limits was particularly marked in the case of Birmingham, Coventry, and the other important towns in the vicinity, after the beginning of the present century. The movement was due, apart from humanitarian motives, to the desire to find sites where land was cheap and the burden of rates low; but it was rendered possible by the improvements in transport which have been indicated. Not only did manufacturers in the new trades tend to set up their businesses in places beyond the city limits, but many firms in the older trades shifted also; so that by 1914 there was a marked contrast between the large up-to-date factories of the suburbs and the small, dark shops in the older parts of Birmingham and of the other local centres.

This tendency may be dwelt on with advantage, because it illustrated very clearly the new forces which were beginning to influence the life of the Midlands, and indeed of the country as a whole. During the old industrial era the trades of Birmingham, when they migrated, had gone to the north-west—towards the coal-field. They had spread along the railways and canals towards Wolverhampton, and in this way Smethwick and West Bromwich had become closely allied to the industrial life of their greater neighbour. Instances of migrations of this kind occurred during the new era, when manufacturers sought new sites for their establishments away from the congested parts of the city. Thus the new aluminium-castings industry grew up at Smethwick; while several spring manufacturers and brass-founders moved in the same direction. But this tendency was beginning to give place to a new one, and a most significant fact was the establishment of great works to the south, east and north of Birmingham—away from the centre from which the town had drawn its raw materials and fuel in the old days. Selly Oak increased in industrial importance. To the north, Witton became the seat of the electrical industry; great factories for cycle and motor manufacture were built in the east; while to the south appeared large establishments for producing cars, cocoa and chocolate, and loose-leaf ledgers. It was no longer coal and canals that exercised a primary influence on the direction of industrial growth. Railways, it is true, were still important factors; but the development of these new industrial suburbs was part of the decentralizing tendencies which were beginning to appear. The spreading of industries beyond the boundaries originally assigned to our area—the rise of the new Coventry trades, and of the electrical industry at Rugby and Stafford—was all part of the same movement. Manufacturers were being drawn by the attraction of lower rates and rents beyond the limits of the great industrial centres, and they were beginning to seek in country districts the sites which permitted them to establish large factories.

In considering the growth in the scale of the typical Midland business we must bear in mind the change which took place in the character of the industrial structure. During the thirty years preceding 1914 several of the leading small-scale industries declined to insignificance, while others failed to maintain themselves in relative importance. On the other hand the new industries were conducted to a great extent in large factories under the control of joint-stock companies. Thus the increase in the scale of production within the area may be attributed not so much to an increase in the size of the producing unit in the older trades as to the change in the type of industry which was carried on, and, in particular, to the shifting of emphasis from hardware to engineering.

Little attention need be devoted to the trades which by the sixties had already become factory industries; for in them the changes which occurred in the scale of operations were not great. When the industry as a whole was progressive, then, as might have been expected, the size of the producing unit steadily increased up to 1914. For example, in the pen trade there was no increase in the number of producers, and the expansion in output during the half-century under consideration was made possible by an increase in the size of the ten or eleven firms which in 1914 comprised the whole industry. At that time the largest concern employed not far short of 1000 persons; while the average for the whole trade was in the neighbourhood of 450. Again, in the screw manufacture, a large proportion of the trade remained in the hands of one firm, which employed some 3000 persons, although a few small firms existed for producing screws which were not susceptible to mass-production methods. In the rolling-stock trade, always carried on in great establishments, numbers ranged from 800 to 3000 per factory. In the welded-tube manufacture the smaller producers tended to disappear, and at the end of this period the trade was concentrated in three or four firms, the largest of which gave employment to 3000 persons. The same development was to be observed in the edge-tool industry, where the small unit had become relatively less important, and by 1914 some six firms, employing from 200 to 700 persons each, monopolized the larger share of the output. As for the heavy branch of the glass trade, though numbers had fallen in the sole remaining establishment, output was probably maintained at about the same level owing to improved methods—a fact that was true of several of the stationary industries. In the cast hollow-ware trade small producers continued to exist in the production of " black " wares; but, although demand was declining, the scale of production in the enamelled branch remained large because the firms took up the manufacture of sanitary ware, stoves and electrical castings, besides, in some cases, enamelled stamped-steel goods as well. In 1914 the representative firm in the enamelled branch employed between 250 and 300 persons, and the largest had some 800. In the galvanized branch, where the outworker and shop owner had flourished throughout the nineteenth century, a few factories employing some 200 hands each began to grow up to deal with the increased demand for standardized products. On the other hand the producing units in several of the failing industries actually decreased in size, after about 1890. This applies to such manufacturers as the cut-nail, bedstead and tinplate-ware trades; but when a trade was on the decline it was usually the smaller units which were extinguished, either by a complete disappearance or by amalgamation, and production then became concentrated in a few larger firms, which could manufacture most economically.

The interest of the period lies, however, not in the industries which had for years been conducted on a large scale, but in those in which the small unit had previously been predominant and was now superseded. Of this development the lock trade affords a good example. Here, though the domestic worker and the shop owner still survived in considerable numbers, the application of machinery had resulted in the appearance of several factories at Willenhall, the largest of which employed some 300 persons in 1914. Similarly, at Darlaston, the nut-and-bolt manufacture, previously carried on in small shops, began to grow in scale after 1880, and several factories existed in pre-war days. In the button trade the garret-master had almost disappeared, and, while much of the industry was in the hands of small factory owners, with 50 to 150 employees each, there also existed a great concern, created as a result of an amalgamation early in the new century, and this employed no less than 2000 persons, about half the total number of button-workers in the area. In the needle trade, too, the outworker was fast disappearing, and the only part of the industry which was left to the workshop was the manufacture of special types. Production was, in the main, concentrated in small factories with upwards of 60 employees; while by 1914 there was, as a result of the amalgamation of several firms, one large concern which employed several hundreds of workers. Fishhooks and tackle were produced both in small specialist factories and by the larger firms engaged in needle-making.

In 1860, while much of the brass trade had been conducted in small factories, and while one very large concern had existed, the garret-man and the shop owner with only a few employees had been common to many branches. From the time of the depression till the end of the century there was a gradual increase in the size of the typical producing unit. Factories became more self-contained, and firms ceased to rely to such a large extent on outworkers and on small firms of stampers and casters; while the necessity of employing machinery in order to produce economically tended to force out the smaller men. There were some exceptions to this general development, as when the great firm which for many decades had been a predominant figure in this industry, Messrs Winfields, collapsed in the nineties. Nevertheless, over most of the industry, the scale of production was increasing, and this movement was immensely stimulated in the new century by the growth in the demand for products which were susceptible to mechanical methods, such as motor accessories and electric-light fittings. In the case of the rolling, wire and tube mills growth was particularly great; firms in the lighting and cabinet brassfoundry sections with 200 to 300 employees became common, and even in the cock-founding trade, which up to the last decade of the century had been conducted in small workshops without any power-machinery, small factories began to appear, several of which, by 1914, employed from 100 to 150 persons. Besides the units which specialized in particular branches of the trade, a few large concerns, with a wide range of non-ferrous products, from sheet and tubes to bedsteads and finished brassfoundry, had also sprung up. The garret-master was no longer an important figure in the trade, and even the shop owner was being forced out by the factory.

By the end of this period, indeed, in the majority of the older manufactures the factory was the typical producing unit, though in many instances it was still a small factory employing only about 100 persons. But in a few industries the older forms of enterprise remained. Among them were the decaying wrought-nail and gun trades. The surviving members of the former were all essentially domestic workers; and although a few small factories (none with more than 100 employees) had sprung up in the gun trade, most of the workers were still engaged as out-workers by a master gunmaker who had no factory of his own. Some of the earlier processes of manufacture, like barrel-making, stamping and action-machining, had tended to go into the factories; but the greater part of the operations were conducted on the ancient plan. The leather trades also were scarcely affected in their scale of manufacture. It is true that the tanneries had grown in size owing to the introduction of machinery; but for finished-leather products, whether saddlery and harness, or the new fancy-leather goods, little machinery could be employed, and the manufacturing process was far from complicated. So here the small unit continued to prosper, and such factories as existed were, if anything, smaller in 1914 than they had been twenty years previously, when the saddlery and harness industry was at its height. Few employed more than 100 persons. The chain trade also still pursued the older methods. In 1860, while the large ships' cables were made in factories, the small chain was the concern of domestic workers or shop owners. The decline in the demand for small chain and the rise of the electric-welded chain, which was made in factories, naturally tended to increase the proportion of the trade falling to the larger units. But, in spite of this change in the relative importance of the different classes of producer, no fundamental change had occurred in the methods and in the organization of the industry since 1860, and the domestic workers and small shop owners still survived in large numbers. Even the factories were small, the largest having about 60 and the average about 20 forges.

Finally, we come to that Birmingham trade which had once provided the best illustration of the most characteristic features of the town's industrial methods—the jewellery trade. Here new tendencies began to appear, when the introduction of the gas-engine led to the concentration of several processes under one roof. In the early years of the new century, moreover, firms proceeded to enlarge their scope of manufacture, and greater establishments began to appear. The production of chains, now conducted by automatic machines, had, even in the sixties, been carried on in small factories; but now other branches began to be affected. Yet, if the garret-master declined in relative importance, even by 1914 the large unit was exceptional in the trade. In the silver-ware branch a firm employing 150 persons was regarded as a large unit, while few in the high-class jewellery trade employed as many as 40 workers. In the manufacture of wedding rings and other articles numerous outworkers still flourished. Nor did any important change occur in the electro-plate branch. There still existed an old-established firm employing, as in 1860, some 700 to 800 persons; but this was exceptional, and numerous small makers survived. The contrast was created largely by the existence of two distinct markets. The ordinary wares, produced in small quantities and sold to the public through the retailers, could be turned out economically by very small concerns; but the demands of the steamship, railway and hotel companies, which required large quantities of standardized products, provided an opportunity for manufacture on a large scale.

When we approach the new industries we find that in all of them the large unit had, by 1914, become typical. For instance, although at the outset the bicycle was produced by small makers, and although even during the nineties certain firms supplied standardized sets of parts which were assembled in small workshops, from the time of the cycle boom the great factories began to come to the front, and were responsible for most of the output in the years immediately preceding the war. In the motor industry firms varied greatly in size, since it was possible for a comparatively small concern to flourish, because it could buy out much of the parts and accessories from specialists. Yet this was no industry for the shop owner; for the motor-car was a highly composite product, and, even though much could be obtained from subsidiary trades, a large and varied labour force was required for its production. So by 1914 the employment in the typical motor firm ranged from a few hundreds to several thousands, and there were some great companies which combined cars, cycles and motor-cycles among their products. Much of the electrical trade, too, was conducted on a large scale, one great concern employing not far short of 2000 persons. The new weldless-tube trade was in the hands of large employers;

while the production of motor and cycle accessories gave opportunities for firms of varying types. In the spring trade the small
factory was representative, and the same was true of the cycle-
saddle trade, although one firm employed over 1000 persons in
1914. The new tyre industry was on a very large scale, the leading firm having a labour force of several thousands. In the
machine-tool industry, concerns which in the late eighties had
had only 30 or 40 workers by 1914 were employing 300 or 400.
In the weighing-machine manufacture the leading company,
from employing 500 men in the early nineties, rose to the
position of a giant concern with over 2000 before the end of the
period. The sole firm in the artificial-silk trade then employed
3000 persons, about twice as many as were in the old gun trade.
The new branches of the hollow-ware industry—viz. aluminium
and enamelled stamped-steel—were both found in fairly large
factories. Many of the local breweries had an enormous output,
and the leading firm in the cocoa and chocolate trade had about
6000 workers in 1914. In the chemical industry two or three
great Oldbury concerns were responsible for a large proportion
of the output.

Yet, although most of the local industries had passed into
the factories by 1914, even in trades in which very large units
were representative, a place was found for the small man. In the
electrical industry he had a part as an electrical contractor or as
a manufacturer of accessories, and in the vehicle industries as a
motor or cycle repairer or agent. Though the lock trade was
passing into the factories, the manufacture of keys was largely
in the hands of outworkers; while in the pearl-button trade
there was a very interesting survival. In that industry numerous
outworkers continued to exist who bought pearl-shell scrap from
the manufacturers of pearl fancy goods (the button-makers
having but little scrap), and then cut out the blanks, which
they sold to the pearl-button manufacturers. This process
was essentially one for outworkers, because the use of scrap in
the factories would have complicated the manufacturing process
and would have been uneconomical.

A condition of the rise of the factory system among the older
Birmingham trades was a change in methods of management
and in internal organization, and the way in which this condition
was satisfied will be considered later in this chapter. At this

point, however, it is desirable to indicate certain changes in manufacturing policy which were common to many different industries, and which first began to show themselves during the fifteen or twenty years prior to the war; for those changes were themselves intimately associated with the new methods of production and with the growth in the size of the producing unit. One movement has already been referred to earlier in the chapter—viz. the tendency for the producing unit to become more self-contained. This, as we have seen, was rendered possible by the improvement in urban transport, which enabled factories to be moved from the more congested quarters of the towns to places where larger sites were available; but other forces were at work. Some of these were technical. The small brassfounders and many other types of manufacturer, whose operations did not warrant the maintenance of a steam-engine, had been accustomed to hire power, or to send out articles for processes which needed power-machinery to specialists. But when the gas-engine and the electric motor were available to supply them with a more convenient form of motive power they naturally began to conduct those processes in their own establishments.[1] Further, as greater attention came to be paid to the nature of the materials employed, manufacturers began to concern themselves with operations previously left to specialists, in order to ensure the quality of the finished article. The increase in the scale of manufacture also had its effect. When output reached a certain figure, then it might pay a firm to establish departments which would not have been fully occupied when the production was smaller. Thus the brassfounders, cycle manufacturers, general engineers and others found it economical to set up their own plating shops, when their output reached a certain level, instead of giving out the work. For similar reasons concerns might establish their own stamping shops and foundries; while all firms which made use of presses and machine tools would, on reaching a certain magnitude, find it desirable to have their own tool-makers and die-sinkers. The stampers, for instance, had at one time used dies which were sunk by specialists; but

---

[1] " Twenty-five years ago what polishing was required was sent out to be done by out-workmen, who hired power and worked for the trade or for several trades. But since that time the demand for polished brasswork has increased by leaps and bounds, and polishing shops have become a recognized feature in every large brass factory " (W. J. Davis, *op. cit.*, p. 40).

the larger firms now began to produce their own dies from the blue-prints supplied by their customers. In this respect change had turned a full cycle. In the eighteenth century, when dies were first used extensively by the sheet-metal trades, the craftsmen who made them were, for the most part, trained and employed by the great concerns which had adopted the new method of manufacture. As stamping and pressing spread over the whole range of small metal industries which were still mainly conducted in workshops, the die-sinker became an independent class of craftsman, working for a number of firms, none of which could keep a die-sinker fully occupied. Then, with the rise in the scale of production towards the end of the nineteenth century, the tendency was reversed, and die-sinkers again came to form part of the staff of the larger factories. Another instance of the same tendency was associated with the more elaborate method of packing goods which was growing up, and with the practice of impressing on the public by the style of the package the names of manufacturers of proprietary goods. This led to firms opening departments for printing, canister-making and box-making to serve their own needs, though such a policy was obviously practicable only for the large concerns. Indeed, although the general tendency was obvious enough, there was within each industry a great variety in the extent to which the various units could be considered self-contained. For example, in the motor industry the large firms not only produced their own engine and gear-box, and the other main components of the chassis, but in many cases they built their own bodies, and occasionally made their own castings also. The small concerns, on the other hand, obtained bodies, engine units and most of their components from specialists, and confined themselves largely to assembling operations.

The tendency towards what may be called a vertical combination of manufacturing operations may be compared with the movement, which occurred in some industries, towards broadening the basis of production; for the latter was the product of different forces. In some cases the extension of the range of output was a natural development, occasioned by the rise of new demands, to which the particular trade could adapt itself, as when a mirror manufacturer turned to produce the new type of mantelpiece which contained a mirror, or when wood-screw firms took up the production of metal-thread screws and engineers' sundries, when pin-makers turned to hairpins and sewing-cases, or when cycle firms branched into the manufacture of cars and motor-cycles. A good example of this movement is provided by a well-known Smethwick business. In its early days it produced only rolled brass and tubes. It then took up the manufacture of plumbers' brassfoundry and later of gas-fittings. In 1885 it entered the bedstead and wire-mattress trade, and, finally, in 1894 it began to manufacture electrical accessories.

Sometimes firms were induced to turn to new products largely because, having established a connection with customers who dealt in a wide range of articles, they found a market open for them. Thus the lock-makers took up the manufacture of lock-furniture — e.g. knobs and finger - plates — because they could then supply complete sets of door-fittings to builders' merchants. A similar development was when firms, which factored a wider range of goods than they produced themselves, turned to the manufacture of fresh classes of goods when demand increased sufficiently to warrant the step.

In many cases, however, the stimulus came from elsewhere than the natural development of industry. Sometimes the extension of its range of products was forced upon a firm because of the decline in the demand for goods on which it had previously specialized. So the cast-iron hollow-ware makers took up the production of sanitary wares, electrical castings and stamped-steel hollow-ware when demand for cast hollow-ware fell off; while the tinplate-ware factories for similar reasons began to produce copper and aluminium goods, besides new classes of sheet-metal products like steel office furniture or cycle gear-cases. The pen-makers turned to office sundries when the demand for pens ceased to expand early in the new century. Pearl-button manufacturers, as their original trade declined, devoted part of their attention to fancy pearl goods, thus allying themselves to the jewellers, just as, with the decline in saddlery and harness, the larger firms added fancy leather and sports' goods to their range of products.

The change in the character of industrial operations immensely strengthened the above tendency. The greater use of machinery and the growth in the size of the typical establishment raised the burden of overhead charges over a great section of the local trades. Concerns, therefore, were forced to make an attempt to secure a regular flow of work through their plant in order to minimize the effects of those charges; and, in order to keep themselves busy, they had of necessity to concern themselves with several lines of product, especially in trades in which the demand fluctuated through seasonal or other causes. When the plant was of a type which could be adapted to several classes of product, this policy was then obviously to be recommended. Thus in the great Birmingham concern which produced both rifles and cycles the manufacture of the latter had first been taken up in order to occupy the plant idle through lack of military orders. Both trades in pre-war days were highly fluctuating, the rifle demand on account of the irregularity in Government orders, the cycle trade because of seasonal changes, and the manufacturer in each trade needed some activity which might on occasion exercise a compensatory effect. More than this, the two trades were singularly well fitted to be conducted in one establishment, because in the smithy, foundry and machine shop the parts of both cycles and rifles were subject to similar operations and kept company.

While this tendency towards a wider range of product was operating in certain businesses, in others, particularly among the engineering firms, there appeared a movement in an opposite direction. Up to the eighties each engineering establishment had commonly produced a host of different types of product, from pumps and steam-engines to machine tools and presses, and nearly all the machines were built to customers' specification. Obviously such a policy was not consistent with economical methods of production; but it was necessarily followed when the quantities required of each type of article were few. When demand increased, however, firms were driven to concentrate on a narrower range, and a glance at the history of a few firms affords illuminating evidence. One which up to about 1880 produced several types of prime mover, machine tools of varying designs, hoisting tackle and pumps began to concentrate on gas- and oil-engines, pumps and hoisting tackle during the new era. Another old-established firm which at one time made all kinds of machinery, from draw-benches and lathes to coining presses and steam-engines, turned its attention towards the end of the century entirely to the manufacture of presses. The new machine-tool firms which appeared in the eighties at first undertook to make almost any type of machine ordered, but by 1914 each was beginning to specialize on a few types, such as lathes or drilling and milling machines. Similarly, several motor firms which arose from among the general engineering or tinplate firms freed themselves from their earlier activities in order to concentrate on the new demand; while there was a tendency among the motor manufacturers to concentrate on particular classes of vehicle. The edge-tool trade affords another example. Up to the nineties it was usual for the larger edge-tool firms to serve many markets and to make many types. But the growth of co-operative buying and the large orders from the great plantations, which encouraged the production of standardized types and the employment of machinery, led to specialization on the part of the various firms. So in pre-war days one was concentrating on machetes and cutlasses, another on hoes, and a third on chisels and axes. Similarly, in the cock-founding trade, the typical firm before 1900 usually produced many types of water-cock, engineers' brassfoundry, syringes and other articles. But the introduction of machinery forced firms to seek the economies of large-scale production in specialization on particular branches of the trade. One firm came to specialize on the Colonial and and South American markets, another on the Continental, and a third on the home market; while others concentrated on beer-taps, hoses and syringes. As a final example, we find that the malleable-iron foundries began to specialize in consequence of the large demands for standardized products, and of the possibility of resorting to machine-moulding. Some concentrated on cast nails and shoe protectors; others on gun parts; and others on electrical castings.

The policy of specialization and that of broadening the basis were often pursued side by side in the same industry, wherever, in fact, the advantage of one over the other was small and a matter of judgment. The large concern might be able to produce on a large scale and yet retain a wide scope of manufacture; but the small firm was forced to specialize if it wished to adopt up-to-date methods. On the whole, it can be said that specialization was most apparent in the engineering industries in which output was rapidly expanding; while the policy of broadening the basis was found, mainly, either in the very large concerns, or in industries in which the decline of the older markets had forced manufacturers to turn part of their productive capacity to serve new demands.

A natural concomitant of the new methods was the increasing standardization of products. This was an inevitable development in all trades to which machinery had been applied; but in this area it was connected particularly with the demand for standardized parts from the new engineering industries. During the nineties almost every engineering job was specially designed to the order of a customer; but as the industries passed out of the experimental stage, and as larger orders began to flow in, design at first reached a natural stability, and then definite attempts were made to limit variations from a particular range of specifications. In the foundries a higher degree of standardization was associated with the development of machine-moulding and die-casting, and in the smithies with the growth of drop-forging. In the screw trade, and in the manufacture of similar components, attempts were made to limit the sizes produced by agreement among manufacturers; while in such industries as lock manufacture the resort to machinery led to cases and parts being made in standard sizes instead of as individual products. Even brassfoundry was affected; for the reduction in the number of patterns was a condition of the growth of mechanical methods in the lighting and cock-founding branches. Yet in many sections of this industry, particularly among the cabinet brassfounders, the range of patterns kept in stock still remained enormous, and mass-production methods were out of the question. In fact, although the reduction in the varieties of each article was a condition of cheap mechanical production, it was not possible in many industries to proceed far, because customers still disliked giving up the varieties of design previously supplied to them. This was comprehensible in the case of many local trades, which produced articles of an ornamental character; but where a multiplicity of designs survived in trades making engineering components the reason was sheer conservatism. So, while the tendency was to be seen in many industries, standardization and mass production had not been carried very far in the locality except in a few manufactures, such as rifles, tyres, cycles, and certain engineering components.

From these general changes in industrial organization and

business policy we may turn to consider the transformation which took place in the administration of the typical firm. This has already been mentioned earlier in the chapter. The practices of outwork, of specialization by process, of hiring mill power, all declined in the local trades; and the traditions of the domestic system, which had continued to exercise a powerful influence over the organization of the factories and larger workshops up to the beginning of the new era, began to pass into oblivion. The transition might have been much slower than it was if the older industries had been left to adapt themselves to the demands of the new era alone; but the rise of the new large-scale industries in which the older forms of organization had never existed was of paramount importance in hastening the change; since it was those industries which more and more tended to set the example with regard to methods of organization.

Perhaps the most significant development of all was the appearance of a new system of management. During the old era the manufacturer, even if he had a large factory, usually delegated much of his authority to overhands, and had little to do with the actual productive process. He was, in truth, a factor who had gathered his dependent craftsmen into his own establishment. His relation to them had not fundamentally changed. But the new methods of production which have been described —the greater use of machinery, the division of labour, the vastly greater complication of the productive process—forced new functions upon him. In many trades the labour of large masses of semi-skilled machine operatives and labourers had to be co-ordinated with the work of the skilled tool-maker and setter-up; while the broadening of the basis of production and the inclusion of a greater number of processes within the factory meant that the activities of many different departments had to be carefully supervised, so as to ensure that no interruption in the flow of materials through them should occur. And this supervision and co-ordination was made all the more necessary as a result of the increasing burden of overhead charges attending the large units. In the establishments of an earlier day, which required no expensive plant, an interruption in the process was not a serious matter; and work had been irregular; but, inevitably, the loss occasioned by irregular work in the new factories was very great, and employers were forced to attend to the question of factory discipline.

Y

Partly for this reason, and partly owing to the reduction in hours in many trades, men began to work much more regularly, and the St Mondays and St Tuesdays of their fathers began to pass away. Further, under the old system of administration the estimate of costs was a simple matter. All that had to be taken into account was the subcontractor's price for producing certain articles and the charges of outworkers for certain processes; while certain overhead expenses, such as light, power and rent, were covered roughly by deductions from the wages paid. But the increasingly complicated character of the productive process, and the growth in overhead charges, rendered the costing of goods much more difficult, and threw much additional work on to the shoulders of the management. Further, as competition from abroad appeared, the manufacturers had to concern themselves more closely, as we shall see in the next chapter, with marketing methods. Nor were technical factors without their influence. When rule-of-thumb methods sufficed, then the overhand could be left with freedom to select his materials; but the appearance of rapid mechanical production meant that careful inspection was necessary, for defective metal might not only hold up the flow of goods, but might ruin the machine tools. Thus laboratories began to be a feature of the larger factories, and here physical and chemical tests were applied to the materials.

In this way, in most of the local trades, the functions of the employer were greatly increased, and the size of the staff, relative to the total number employed, was subject to a large expansion. The result was to detract from the responsibilities attaching to the worker, and particularly from those of the subcontractor. That characteristic figure of the old era began, indeed, to fall from his key-position in the administration of the factory. In the new industries he was practically non-existent, and even in the older trades he was being superseded by the modern foreman in the twenty years prior to the war. Yet his disappearance was not rapid. Employers, fearing to antagonize their most skilled men and to lose them to their competitors, hesitated to abolish the system, even where they realized its defects, and the overhands themselves objected to a change which would reduce their responsibilities and their gains. It was, indeed, only the under-hands who seemed anxious for the abolition of the subcontracting system. So in the ironworks, the rolling mills, the edge-tool factories, and in many others, the overhand still occupied an important position in pre-war years; and, in spite of the trade-union attacks on the system in the industry in which it was most widespread—viz. brassfoundry—it continued to survive down to the war. Yet even here important modifications in the subcontractor's position had taken place. It became usual for underhands to receive their wages, not from their subcontractor, but through the office, even where their wage-contract was with him.

In many instances, moreover, the freedom of contract between subcontractor and underhand, which placed the former in an advantageous position, was modified by the influence of the employers or by the rules of the trade unions, which were shown to be necessary to protect one group of workers against another, as well as all against their employers. For example, in the brass-foundry trade the whole position was altered by the introduction of the grading system, according to which every man in the union was placed in a class, appropriate to his skill and experience, to which agreed emoluments were attached. Thus in some trades the modern foreman, who merely supervises a department under the direction of the office, appeared; while in others the subcontractor survived in a modified form. There can be no doubt that among the most fundamental changes of the period between 1890 and 1914 was the shifting of managerial functions from the overhand to the office staff and the increasing centralization of factory control.

Another legacy of the domestic system which began to disappear during the early years of the new era was the system of charging deductions for " standings," light and power. In the new trades they had, of course, no place from the first. In the others the system changed slowly, partly, no doubt, in consequence of the Truck Acts, but mainly owing to the new conditions of industry. Plenty of isolated instances of the practice could be found in pre-war days; but it was then no longer typical of the local trades. Its decline was a tacit recognition of the fact that in the new era the provision of a workplace, machinery and materials was among the employer's normal functions. Not till then was the worker to be regarded as a man who merely sold his labour, or was the present distinction between the functions of the worker and the capitalist clearly expressed by the organization of the local industries.

The composition of the labour force was naturally affected by the changes which have been considered. The introduction of machinery and the wider functions assumed by the management resulted in the skilled craftsman becoming a much less prominent figure in most of the local trades, particularly in the brassfoundry, lock, nut-and-bolt and edge-tool manufacture, which previously required a great deal of manual skill. Certain classes of workers common to a wide variety of metal trades declined. So the extension of drop-forging and stamping brought a reduction in the number of smiths, who had worked at the anvil; the milling machine dispensed with much labour with the file; and the extended use of the power-press caused many operations for which a high degree of manual skill had been required to pass into the hands of semi-skilled workers.

The new industries varied considerably in the type of labour which they employed. The cycle manufacture had at first been a trade for the skilled; but as mass-production principles came to be applied many of these went into the motor trade, and the majority of processes passed to other classes of workers. In the motor industry, as in the other engineering trades, a large proportion of the employees were of a high grade, the fitters, turners and tool-makers forming a large body of skilled workers. In the electrical industry, too, though some scope for semi-skilled labour was afforded by such operations as winding and press-work, a large section of the employees were skilled; while in the artificial-silk, the food and drink trades, and the new branches of the hollow-ware industry, the semi-skilled worker predominated.

Yet, if in the actual production of finished articles the necessity for a great deal of skilled labour had passed away in many industries, the new methods of manufacture called into existence bodies of skilled workers for such intermediate processes as tool-making and tool-setting. Wherever the press or the machine tool superseded the old craftsmanship the need for these classes of workers increased, and, consequently, the Midland labour force of the twentieth century tended to become divided into two main groups—the skilled workers, who were engaged in making and adjusting the tools, on the one hand, and a mass of semi-skilled machine operatives on the other. In the engineering trades there grew up also the class of skilled fitters.

These developments involved a new grouping according to sex. We have seen that, in the sixties, while the respective spheres of men and women had been fairly clearly distinguished in Birmingham, in the Black Country the dividing line was much more vague, and in some trades non-existent. By 1914, however, over the whole area the respective occupations of men and of women were fairly clearly defined, partly as a result of legislative and trade-union rules, and partly because of the approximation of processes, as a result of mechanical changes, in trades which previously had little connection with one another. For example, in several very different industries, the skilled men who had made up the labour force during the old era began to be superseded by semi-skilled female machine operatives. As women's labour was particularly suitable for press-work, the advance of the power-press carried them into trades where they had previously had no part. The following Table (p. 342) shows the extent of this influx between 1861 and 1911, and the comparative figures illustrate better than any other available statistical material the great changes in productive methods which took place during the period now under discussion. Where no important mechanical changes occurred, the proportion of women then remained the same. The only exception is to be found in the chain trade, where the exceptionally weak bargaining position of the domestic workers had driven down wages and had caused men to desert the industry. In conclusion, it is important to remember that after 1890 another sphere was found for women in industry. They began to appear as warehouse hands, as typists and as clerks—a development which was associated with the new methods of management and of office routine. This was one of the most remarkable transformations in the labour force which occurred during the fifteen or twenty years prior to the war, and it must be taken into account in comparing the percentages given overleaf.

[TABLE

PERCENTAGE OF FEMALES TO TOTAL AMOUNT OF EMPLOYMENT

Industry	1861	1891	1911
Brass and other non-ferrous . .	24	22	27
Button	58	63	77
Lock and Key	...	6	18
Needle	47	48	63
Saddlery and Harness	28	28	33
Other Leather Goods	...	...	67
Chain and Anchor	6	31	32
Pen	94	92	90
Tinplate-Ware	18	22	37
Cycle	...	6	25
Electrical Apparatus	...	3	18
Jewellery (excluding electro-platers) .	28	26	35
Brush	22	49	58
Paper Bag and Box	...	95	94
Bedstead	...	26	25

THE CHANGE IN THE NATURE OF THE PRODUCING UNIT BETWEEN 1860 AND 1914

1860

Domestic Workers or Garret-Masters	Shop Owners employing under 40 Hands	Small Factories making use of Power and employing under 100 Persons	Large Factories
Jewellery	Jewellery	Brassfoundry	Pen
Gun	Brassfoundry	Heavy-Brass	Screw
Wrought-Nail	Lock	Wrought-Chain	Tinplate-, Jap-
Wrought-Chain	Button	Button	anned- and
Lock	Edge-tool	Pin	Papier-
Nut-and-Bolt	Saddlery and	Flint-glass	Mâché-ware
Button	Harness	Enamelled	Heavy-glass
Saddlery and	General	Hollow-Ware	Enamelled
Harness	Engineering	Edge-tool	Hollow-Ware
Brassfoundry	Nut-and-Bolt	Cut-nail	Welded-Tube
		Coin	Rolling-Stock
		Welded-Tube	
		Saddlery and	
		Harness	

1914

Domestic Workers or Garret-Masters	Shop Owners	Small Factories	Large Factories
Jewellery	Brassfoundry	Cycle	Cycle
Gun	Jewellery	Electrical	Motor
Saddlery and	Gun	Apparatus	Electrical
Harness	Saddlery and	Aluminium	Apparatus
Wrought-Nail	Harness	Hollow-Ware	Brewing
Wrought-Chain	Wrought-Chain	Office Equipment	Cocoa and
	Lock	Machine-tool	Chocolate
		Screw	Enamelled - steel
		Tinplate- and	Hollow-ware
		Japanned-Ware	Weldless-Tube
		Flint-glass	Welded-Tube
		Enamelled cast	Artificial-silk
		Hollow-ware	Chemical
		Edge-tool	Pen
		Cut-nail	Rolling-Stock
		Brassfoundry	Machine-tool
		Jewellery (chains,	Screw
		silver-ware and	Pin
		electro-plate)	Heavy-glass
		Saddlery and	Enamelled cast
		Harness	Hollow-ware
		Nut-and-Bolt	Edge-tool
		Needle	Brassfoundry
		General	Heavy non-
		Engineering	ferrous
		Weighing-	General
		Machine	Engineering
		Lock	Weighing-
			Machine
			Rifle

CHAPTER V

THE NEW MARKETING METHODS AND THE DECLINE IN INDUSTRIAL INDIVIDUALISM

DIRECTLY dependent on the developments which have been described in the previous chapter were the changes which occurred in the organization of the market and in the relations of the individual business units to one another. We have seen that in 1860 the figures that dominated the market were, for the home trade, the factor, and for the export trade, the merchant. Described under various names, and dealing with a small group or with many commodities, the factor had possessed two distinct though allied functions. In the first place, he was responsible for initiating production, for distributing orders, and sometimes materials, among a multitude of outworkers or small masters, for co-ordinating their activities when the product was a complicated one, and for financing manufacture, in so far as they relied on him for weekly cash payments when they delivered the products at his warehouse. The factor's second function was to market the goods; and for this purpose he had to establish connections with retailers and to employ travellers and agents to promote his sales. Throughout the earlier part of the period covered by this history the factor continued to occupy this important position and to fill these two rôles; and it was not until the last decade of the century that he began to lose ground. From then onwards, however, his decline was rapid. His first group of functions was soon lost to him, and for this the changes in industrial organization and in the scale of the typical business unit were mainly responsible. When the typical manufacturer had been a man without much capital the factor had controlled his industry because the producers were financially dependent on him. He had often provided materials and tools. He had bridged the whole period between production and sale by taking the goods at weekly intervals. And in the manufacture of articles which were complex in character, and which passed through the hands of numerous small masters in the course of production, he had normally furnished the considerable working capital which was required. But by the nineties, instead of being a domestic

344

worker or a shop owner, the representative manufacturer in many trades had become a person of sufficient capital to purchase his own materials, to assume the task of co-ordinating the various productive operations, and even to keep stocks of finished goods; while he was of sufficient standing to treat directly with the banks when he needed credit. Thus, operations previously distributed among a number of outworkers or shop owners were coming to be concentrated under one roof, and the initiative in production and the control of business policy were passing from the factor to the manufacturer. Only in the industries which clung to the older methods of organization did the factor preserve his original functions. The master gunmaker was still responsible for providing his outworkers with materials and for co-ordinating the activities of a multitude of specialized craftsmen; while the saddlers' ironmonger continued to play his part at Walsall and the nailmaster at Dudley. But these were all operating in declining industries, and the last two classes of factor had practically disappeared by 1914. In the other industries the factor had either entered the ranks of the manufacturers or been reduced to the position of a wholesale merchant. A good deal of factoring, in the old sense, still continued in all trades in which the small units survived— indeed, it was a condition of their existence—but it was usually a large manufacturer, rather than a specialized class of factor, who conducted the business.

But this was not all. Apart from his loss of the function of controlling production, the factor also began to fall from his dominating position in the market. From very early times the manufacturers in some industries had exercised a certain amount of control over the marketing of their goods. Boulton and Watt, and several of the great firms in the heavy trades, had their own agents and travellers at home and abroad during the later decades of the eighteenth century. The famous engineering concern, Messrs Tangyes, moreover, had since the sixties followed the practice of direct selling; and the founder attributed the freedom from trade fluctuations which his firm enjoyed to his system of distribution. Instead of relying on agents and merchants, he had established his own houses at Newcastle, Glasgow, Manchester and London, and he sold direct to customers from them. Part of the foreign trade was also handled in this way; for the firm had its own depots at Melbourne and Sydney. Only a very large concern with a variety of products could pursue such a policy as this, and it was recognized that a beginner must follow the Quaker's advice: " Never thou put salt water between thee and thy money." [1] Indeed, for the home as for the foreign market, any policy save that of sale through factors and merchants was impracticable for the small producers who were up to the eighties typical of most of the finished-metal trades. During the new era, however, in almost every trade, attempts were made by the manufacturers to get into closer touch with their customers. In many industries firms began to sell an increasingly larger proportion of their output to retailers; in some instances a direct trade with the public was developed; while even when most of the goods continued to pass through the hands of the factor, the typical manufacturer usually had travellers or agents to press the claim of the particular firm. The growing practice of advertisement by manufacturers and the development of a branded trade in certain wares had a similar effect. Indeed, the success of the manufacturer's attempt to get behind the intermediary to the customer might be judged in some measure by the decay of the practice, once universal, of marking the commodity with the merchant's or factor's rather than the maker's name. The change was particularly noticeable in trades in which large concerns existed. In the steel-pen industry a large trade had once been done in " special imprint " pens, which had been marked with the stationer's name only. This declined in importance, and even when pens were supplied impressed with the stationer's name it became customary for the maker's name to appear as well. The same change was noticeable in many other industries, including the edge-tool trade, where the rise of the " branded " tools led to a decline in the proportion of goods marked with the factor's or merchant's name.

The fall in the functions of the middleman was not confined to the home trade; for the methods of handling exports also began to change. In earlier days the merchant generally dealt in many commodities and in a number of markets, and he sent out his travellers with samples of goods, supplied by manufacturers with whom he had connections. He was a wholesale

[1] R. Tangye, *The Rise of a Great Industry*, p. 101.

merchant in the truest sense, and he bore the whole risk of selling the goods profitably and of developing his markets. But changes in the organization of manufacture, the growing rapidity of communication, and the spread of ordered government, of adequate systems of commercial law and of British business methods over a great part of the world, gave an opportunity to the manufacturer himself to play a part. The large firm could afford to appoint his own foreign agents and even, in a few businesses, to maintain a staff of travellers, whose functions it was to visit agents and customers abroad, and to hold stocks in his own foreign depots. He was driven to do this in many industries by the increasingly severe competition from abroad and by the fact that, unless he established personal connections with a foreign customer, a fall in the price of (say) German goods might cause him to lose all his trade, since the merchant had no incentive to continue to order from British sources. The establishment by the manufacturer of his own agencies and depots abroad was more to be recommended for the Colonies and English-speaking countries than for South America and the Far East; for in the former the customs and commercial methods of the inhabitants were similar to those of England, whereas in the latter the need for special knowledge and the greater trading risks gave an opportunity to the merchant who had specialized on those markets, and who was in a position to deal with any difficulty that arose. Thus, as far as English-speaking countries were concerned, the larger hardware and engineering firms came to depend for their orders on the work of their own foreign agents, and the merchant who dealt in those parts developed into a mere indent merchant—*i.e.* he was no longer responsible for cultivating a market for a particular product and for purchasing goods from any source which recommended itself to him; but he merely received an order in the form of a closed indent, in which the maker's name was specified. In the other chief markets for the goods of Birmingham and District, such as South America, the wholesale merchant remained, though even there he was beginning to lose ground.

It is worth noticing that the merchants themselves were affected by the specializing tendencies of the time. In earlier days many of them had served a variety of markets, but as the total volume of trade grew, and as competition for it became keener, they were forced to confine their activities to a narrower range of countries — to those, indeed, with which they had particularly good connections, or of which they had exceptional knowledge. Consequently, the exports from the district tended to go through the hands of merchants whose activities were largely confined to some particular region, such as South America, the Dominions, West Africa or the Far East.

The change in marketing methods which has just been described was intimately bound up with the increase in the size of the representative firm between 1887 and 1914. The large concerns, whether responsible for a wide range of products or for a great output of a few standardized commodities, could afford to establish their own selling organizations and to assume the functions previously left to the factor or merchant. The movement was, indeed, part of the general tendency towards the vertical combination of operations previously conducted by specialists that has already been discussed. Recent researches have shown that it may cost a firm more to sell through its own organization than through merchants; but the larger and more uniform output and the more secure market which it thus obtains may bring a reduction in manufacturing overhead charges which more than compensates for the higher selling costs. This desire on the part of manufacturers to lower their burden of overhead charges has been the chief motive which has led them towards direct selling.

But the forces which produced this change were not all from the side of the producer, for equally significant developments had occurred among the retailers. When the size of the typical retail establishment in all branches of business had been small, the manufacturer could then seldom hope to deal direct with it, and he had been forced into the hands of the factor. But with the coming of the great emporium, the multiple shop and the departmental store, which could order in quantity, there arose a possibility and an inducement to direct trading; for both sides saw their advantage in avoiding the middleman's charges. Similar factors were at work in all trades in which the consuming unit was increasing in size. For example, whereas nearly all the products of the button trade had originally passed through the hands of factors and merchants, the rise of a great wholesale clothing industry provided a type of customer who would go direct to the makers, since he required large quantities. Similarly, the growth of large plantations in tropical countries and the rise of co-operative buying in quantity enabled the edge-tool manufacturers to get into closer contact with their customers. Thus again the wheel had turned a full cycle. In mediæval times the maker with his small and highly localized market had dealt directly with his customer. The improvement in communications, leading to an extension of the market but not of the size of the producing unit, had created a gulf between maker and user, which it was the factor's function to bridge. Then, the rise in the scale not only of the producing but also of the consuming unit, together with the still greater facilities for transport towards the end of the nineteenth century, began to close the gulf and to render the intermediary superfluous. Finally, it must be noted that the change-over from hardware to engineering was not without its effect on the marketing methods typical of the locality. Whereas in many hardware trades the middleman inevitably retained important distributive functions, the finished engineering products which were purchased by other manufacturers themselves or by large consumers, such as governments or municipalities, could naturally go direct for the most part; while firms which produced parts for the engineers could often supply their customers direct, especially if they were within their own area.

The above account must not be taken to imply that in the local industries the middleman had been superseded by 1914, and that the bulk of the local goods went direct from the manufacturer to the retailer, or to the consumer. All that occurred was a reduction in the functions of the factor and the merchant, the consequent growth of the sales department within the typical manufacturing concern, and a strong tendency towards more direct trading on the part of the larger units. Yet in all industries the small firm was still dependent on a middleman, even if the latter might be himself a manufacturer; while in trades which produced small metal products, such as pins and needles, which were distributed through many channels to the public, it was impossible for the manufacturer to deal direct with the retailer, unless he had a very large store. Further, it must not be imagined that, although in the main the nature of the commodity to be sold determined the method of sale, the same general tendency was to be perceived in all the leading firms in any particular industry. Wherever the advantages of dealing direct with the retailer or through the factor were nicely balanced, there were always to be found firms who pursued diverse sales policies. Frequently, moreover, a distinction was drawn between the large and small retailer in the methods of sale which were pursued; for, while it might pay to sell direct to a great store, the small quantities required by the ordinary retailer made such methods unprofitable in dealing with him. Thus, although the factor had lost his control over the manufacturing operations, and although his functions as a middleman were declining in many industries, in his latter capacity he had still a part to play, since there were trades in which direct selling was either an impracticable policy or of doubtful advantage to the manufacturer.

The situation, as it existed in the pre-war period, may best be illustrated by a brief review of the practice of the leading industries, and attention may first be given to the hardware trades. In the distribution of hollow-ware in the home market, though the small firms were still obliged to reach the retailer through the factor, the large firms in almost every section of the industry sold direct to the big ironmongers, who were increasing in importance, and through middlemen to the small retailers. One firm in the aluminium hollow-ware trade actually ran a series of retail shops in order to cultivate a market and to bring this new type of product before the public notice. In the sale of locks, where the factor had occupied a very strong position throughout the nineteenth century, the rise of factory production led to a direct trade on the part of the few larger concerns with the ironmongers, trunk- and bag-makers, builders' merchants, or even architects, according to the class of lock supplied. The growth of more direct trading in the edge-tool trade has already been discussed, as has the influence of the the rise of the great wholesale clothing manufacture on the distribution of buttons. The largest firm in this industry, moreover, had depots in all parts of the country from which to supply its customers. In the bedstead trade the factor began to decay during the nineties, and manufacturers began to rely to an increasing extent on their own agents. As for the brass industry, although most of the finished goods passed through builders' merchants, motor-accessory factors and electrical contractors, an increasing proportion of the trade was done direct with furnishing houses, retail ironmongers and manufacturers; while most of the sheet, wire and tubes went straight to the manufacturers who used them, and such factoring as existed was on the decline. Even in the pen trade, where most of the products went through wholesalers, the tendency for the manufacturer to deal direct with the larger retail stationer had appeared. The jewellers, operating as most of them did on a very small scale, were naturally still dependent on the factor, but with the broadening of the basis of production and the rise of larger units after 1900 several of the leading firms began a direct trade with the retailer. In the electro-plate branch the orders from hotel, steamship and railway companies came direct to the only large concern, which had a number of retail agencies to cultivate its market. Finally, as the nut-and-bolt trade passed from small- to large-scale production, the products, once sold entirely through the Birmingham merchants and factors, began to pass direct to engineers and contractors.

While these examples concern the common practice in the home market, similar changes occurred in connection with the export trade. Though few firms attempted to do a direct trade with a foreign consumer, all the large ones had agents or representatives abroad to press the claims of their goods. In fact, our conclusions, with regard not only to the development of direct trading but to the causes of that change, that it came from the extension in the scale of operations of both manufacturer and retailer, are clearly borne out by the examination of almost every hardware industry.

As for the engineering industry, many of its products were used only by manufacturers, and this was an influence which favoured the direct method of sale. When the machine-tool industry was small the makers had usually received their orders from factors and merchants, but before the war all those of standing had their own agencies and travellers, at home and abroad, and dealt direct with their customers. The great Soho firm of scale and weighing-machine producers went even further; for not only were its larger weighing-machines naturally sold direct to the port or market authorities, but it established a number of retail shops all over the country for selling its other products direct to the shopkeeper. The vehicle trades fell into a different class; for they were manufacturing a complicated engineering product, which was sold to the general public in a highly competitive market.[1] Further, it was necessary, in the early days of the cycle and motor industries, to stimulate a demand for an unfamiliar type of vehicle. So exhibitions were organized, to which manufacturers sent their products; official trials and races enabled the public to judge of the performance of different types of car or cycle; agencies were established in all parts of the provinces; London showrooms were acquired by the leading firms to push their sales in that market; and travelling representatives were employed to visit the agents. By 1914 the agency system, as it existed in this industry, was already developing several features which have since become more strongly marked. In the motor industry, for example, it was customary for the manufacturer to appoint distributors (or main agents) for large areas and sub-agents for particular towns and districts; and these, on whom in the early days of the industry the maker had relied to bring his products before the public, had come to occupy a very strong bargaining position by the time the merits of the different makes of car had become well known. The agent commonly represented several manufacturers, and, as the industry was highly competitive and the public taste fickle, he was able to demand a commission which was very high in view of the functions he performed. The situation was not, in 1914, complicated by the existence of a serious " trading-in " problem, and there was then a possibility of the larger manufacturers being able to free themselves from dependence on the agent and of selling direct to the public from a chain of depots. But this attempt was not made; for the maker feared to risk a loss of his market by antagonizing the agents, and it was not in any case a step that could be taken by any save the very large producers. In the distribution of motor and cycle accessories the factor had an important share of the trade; but, though the goods destined for retailers commonly passed through

---

[1] Cf. Sir William Ashley, *Business Economics*, p. 58 : " Where the unit of sale is very costly, the market very limited and the purchaser fully equipped with technical knowledge, there is no room for an intermediary." The strong position of the agent in the motor industry may be attributed to the fact that, not only is the trade highly competitive, but, although the unit of sale is costly, the purchasers are not technical experts, as in most branches of the engineering trade, but are members of the general public.

his hands, the larger firms usually dealt direct with the manufacturer for the accessories and parts which were required by
him, though less often with the retailer. Thus the greatest firm
in the cycle-saddle industry employed its own travellers to visit
vehicle firms and retailers in the home market, while even for many
foreign markets it had its own representatives and conducted a
direct trade.

Again, in the constructional engineering trade, which catered
largely for foreign and Colonial markets, it became increasingly
necessary for manufacturers to have their own representatives,
not only because of the growing severity of foreign competition,
but because many of the leading customers, such as the Colonial
governments and foreign municipalities, made a practice of dealing with a local representative rather than through merchants or
through their own London agents.

In the electrical industry much of the industrial apparatus
was supplied on tender from the manufacturers to railway
companies or municipalities; but the ordinary domestic fittings
were usually distributed either through a wholesaler, who might
also be a manufacturer, or to an electrical contractor. The
tendency towards a combination of the functions of selling
and manufacturing, which was common to many industries, was
reversed in this branch of the trade. Before 1911 it was not
unusual for a firm both to manufacture and to undertake con-
tracting work. After the formation of the trade association in
that year, however, a clear distinction was drawn between these
two classes in the industry.

As for the other trades which rose to importance between
1887 and 1914, little need be said. In the fancy-leather trade
most of the goods passed through wholesale merchants, though
the big stores tended more and more to buy direct, even from
the small manufacturer, since they could afford to maintain the
representatives to keep in touch with him. In the paint and
varnish industry, while the decorating paints went to oil and
colour merchants, the section of the trade which expanded so
greatly during the period—viz. the industrial paint and varnish
section—was a sphere of direct trading. Much of the artificial
silk, too, went direct to hosiery manufacturers. The great firm
in which the local production of cocoa and chocolate was
centred could afford to employ its own travellers and to sell

z

much of its goods direct, though in supplying the small shop it dealt through wholesalers. The brewing industry, however, had carried the tendency much further than most others; for, with the development of the "tied house" system, the larger proportion of its output came to be sold direct to the public.

A still further development of the manufacturer's functions was to be seen in the rise of a post-sales organization in connection with the great engineering firms. Having impressed its name on the public, a concern was naturally obliged to follow up its products, if they were of a durable kind, after they had passed into use. Only in this way could the loss of reputation, which would be occasioned by any breakdown or failure of material, be avoided, and a post-sales department was obviously necessary for firms in the engineering industry, the products of which were subject to a great working strain. So in the motor, cycle and weighing-machine trades—to mention only a few— manufacturers were obliged to maintain stocks of spare parts for their various models, and to instruct their agents to supply these to customers. It was this necessity of supplying post-sales services which was one of the most potent influences in inducing makers of engineering products to conduct their own selling; since merchants could not be expected to afford satisfactory services of this nature.

Just as the new era witnessed a transformation in the scale of production and in marketing methods, so over the whole range of local industries it saw the inception of widespread attempts to limit competition among manufacturers and to build up great concerns by amalgamation. These two movements, though often coincident, are not necessarily so; for amalgamations, while they may reduce the number of competitors and lead to economies, do not necessarily result in monopoly; but they certainly create the conditions which facilitate a control over prices by the manufacturers concerned. Before giving particular instances which will illustrate these tendencies we must pay some attention both to the motives which led manufacturers to combine, and to the conditions which made the period so favourable for the movement. In the case of complete amalgamations, which, of course, often followed on the failure of price agreements, the main motive might be either to eliminate competition among the leading rivals, or to increase the efficiency of the industry and so enable it to meet the increasing competition from abroad. This last motive was present in all the vertical combinations. But whether a complete amalgamation were effected, or whether merely some form of price association came into existence, in every case the increasing burden of overhead charges provided an active stimulus. For the rise in the size of the producing unit and the concentration of manufacture in large concerns meant that competition could no longer be relied on to extinguish the less efficient units during a time of depression and to equate output and demand at profitable prices with any rapidity. The concerns with great resources could hold out for a long period; and it was in their interest to turn out goods at any price which would make some contribution to their burden of fixed charges. Thus, under the new conditions of manufacture, a long period of low prices might not succeed in reducing output sufficiently to enable profits to be made. At the same time, during the nineties, the loss of foreign markets had in certain trades made competition keener at home.

If, however, the rise in the scale of production had created this new problem, it also brought into existence the conditions which enabled it to be solved; for the greater the size of the typical firm, the smaller became the number of competitors and the easier the formation of price-fixing associations. In the heyday of the competitive era, in the few instances where those conditions existed, successful attempts had been made to control prices, and now those conditions were spreading over the whole field of industry. Further, with the growth in the size of the representative firm, there arose new methods of factory administration and of book-keeping and costing, which provided the machinery by which manufacturers could exercise a joint control over prices and output. Finally, a favourable personal element was not lacking in the Birmingham area. The strenuous individualists, who had built up their businesses during the period of great industrial expansion between 1840 and 1875, had passed away by the opening of the new era, and the inevitably less vigorous, interested or prejudiced second generation was turning the old private concerns into limited companies, which opened the way for amalgamations. This personal factor is of supreme importance, though often forgotten, in the growth both of company organization and of combines during the nineties among the older trades.

Of the two forms into which combinations are usually divided, the vertical and the horizontal, while several instances of the former took place, the integrated firm could scarcely be considered more characteristic of the local trades in 1914 than in the old era. As we have seen, throughout the first three-quarters of the nineteenth century the vertical combination had been very common in the iron and coal industries of the Black Country and had not been unknown in the brass trade of Birmingham; but the exhaustion of the local raw materials had caused a break-up of the great Staffordshire firms, and in 1914 the integrated iron or steel concern was exceptional. In other industries there were instances of vertical combinations which covered the whole country, and of which certain local firms formed part; but there were only a few amalgamations of this character which were primarily among Midland firms.

In the sphere of horizontal combinations there was a much greater contrast between the old and the new era. Before 1887, while there were many instances of the amalgamation of businesses, no general movement in this direction had occurred and very few attempts to limit competition had been made. Only in trades in which producers were few in number and of a large size had the joint control of prices been essayed; and in many of these trades it was merely the advisability of joint action in tendering for Government contracts that had led to agreements among manufacturers. In the iron industry the makers of " marked bars " had an informal association which fixed minimum prices; but the rest of the trade was purely competitive. In the military arms manufacture, from the time of the Crimean War, the leading gunsmiths had had a mutual agreement with regard to the price of guns supplied to the Government, and after the formation of the Birmingham Small Arms Company and the London Small Arms Company these two firms agreed to distribute Government orders in certain proportions between them — an arrangement to which the National Arms and Ammunition Company was admitted in 1878. Occasionally, moreover, the leading saddlery and harness-makers used to come to informal agreements regarding tenders for Government contracts. But, except in these few instances, competitive conditions prevailed over the whole field of local industry before 1887, and it was left for the last decade of the century to see general attempts made to bring to an end the old individualism and the unbridled rivalry which accompanied it. While this movement was part of a general tendency in British industry, and has already been discussed by several writers, it will nevertheless be of value to group together at this point the more important instances among the trades of Birmingham and District, and we will first of all consider the amalgamations which were effected.

The leading example of the combination movement which the area could provide was that which led to the formation of the great firm of Guest, Keen & Nettlefold. Messrs Nettlefolds of Smethwick had long been the chief manufacturers of screws in the country; during the last twenty years of the century they acquired many concerns in the Midlands and South Wales; and by 1900 they were producing steel on a large scale. In that year two South Wales companies, Guest & Company and the Dowlais Iron Company, both of which owned iron and steel works, joined with the Patent Nut and Bolt Company, which, incorporated in 1864, had factories for producing nuts, bolts and railway fastenings at Birmingham and West Bromwich, besides blast-furnaces, collieries and railway-material works at Newport. In 1902 the two groups came together as Guest, Keen & Nettlefold with an issued capital of £4,500,000.[1] Before the war several other companies in the Midlands and South Wales were also acquired, and the concern had become one of the largest in the country. Besides embracing a wide variety of finished products, this combine was also highly integrated and controlled mines, blast-furnaces, steelworks, rolling mills and engineering plants. The second most important amalgamation was of a horizontal nature. For many years the welded-tube trade had been fiercely competitive; attempts to form price associations had all broken down; and resort was had to a number of groupings which resulted in the rise of H. & J. Stewarts & Menzies of Scotland, and of Lloyd & Lloyd of Birmingham. In 1902, a momentous year in the history of the combination movement, these two firms amalgamated

[1] H. W. Macrosty, *The Trust Movement in British Industry*, pp. 37-39.

as Stewarts & Lloyds, with a capital of £1,750,000.[1] The same
year saw the formation of a great railway rolling-stock combine,
consisting of two large local carriage- and wagon-building firms,
three others outside the district, and of the famous Patent Shaft
and Axletree Company of Wednesbury.[2] Later, a local paint and
varnish concern was also absorbed. This amalgamation, which
resulted in the Metropolitan Railway Carriage, Wagon and
Finance Company, was not only horizontal in character; but,
inasmuch as it controlled firms which supplied rolling-stock
makers with axles, tyres and other steelwork, and with paint
and varnish, it was also integrated in structure. In the vehicle
trade there were several examples, of which the absorption by
the Birmingham Small Arms Company of the Edie Manufacturing Company in 1907, and of the Daimler Motor
Company of Coventry in 1910, was the chief. This great
concern before the war had an issued capital of £1,000,000.
On the opening of the new century the firm of Kynoch
possessed three factories where a variety of products, including sheet-brass, rifle ammunition, shells and gas- and oil-
engines, were manufactured. They proceeded to acquire a
works at Stirchley, which they devoted to the production of
steel shells, and in the next two years they absorbed several
other concerns, including rolled brass, tube and wire mills in
Birmingham, an explosives factory on the Thames, and paper
mills. Another combine in the non-ferrous trade led to the
emergence of Elliott's Metal Company.

One of the most important results of this movement was to
link up the Midlands with other parts of the country, notably
with South Wales and Sheffield, as far as the control and
organization of its industries were concerned. This was all part
of that great movement which was bringing a large section of
British industry under the control of firms with interests in
every part of Great Britain; and it was a particularly significant
development for a district which had long been remarkably
self-centred and isolated in its industrial life and interests.
Some instances of combines of this nature have already been
given; but the list is an extensive one. In 1901, for instance,
Messrs Vickers acquired a large motor factory at Adderley

[1] H. W. Macrosty, *The Trust Movement in British Industry*, pp. 46-47.
[2] *Ibid.*, p. 52.

Park, a local firm engaged in producing fusees and also pro-
jectiles; while Messrs Cammell of Sheffield purchased concerns
at Birmingham and Coventry, and in 1905 a great ordnance
factory was erected at Coventry, which in pre-war days employed
some 3000 men, and was owned jointly by John Brown of
Sheffield and Cammell-Laird.

Up to the present the examples of amalgamation which
have been mentioned have been confined to the engineering
and heavy-metal trades. In these the producing units were
nearly all large in size, were under the control of public companies, and were conducted according to advanced methods of
organization; so that it was to be expected that they would
soon ally themselves with this new tendency. But the movement was not by any means confined to them. In the older
hardware trades, the loss of markets and the severity of foreign
competition were forcing manufacturers to turn to more economical methods of production, and were creating a surplus
productive capacity, which reacted very unfavourably on the
profitableness of the individual concerns. So, in this group of
trades, also, there were a series of amalgamations. In the button
manufacture, for example, which was suffering from acute
depression at the beginning of the new century, three of the
leading producers amalgamated, bought up two other concerns,
and then proceeded to close down several factories and to
concentrate production on the most efficient plants. In the
bedstead trade, a long period of unprofitable prices led to two
amalgamations, one of six and the other of four businesses,
early in the century, and here the same policy was followed.

The comparatively progressive industries, moreover, were
not without instances of this movement; for they too were
affected by falling prices and of surplus capacity, often as a
result of the increasing use of machinery. So, between 1895
and 1910 several small businesses in the needle trade were
amalgamated, and a Sheffield wire plant was acquired to supply
the combine with its raw material. Several of the larger edge-
tool firms bought up the smaller businesses; while two of the
leading steel-pen firms, together with a holder and pencil firm
in Cumberland, were joined. In the umbrella-furniture trade,
a local firm first combined with its supplier of steel wire at
Sheffield, and then became linked with three other firms, two

of which were in Birmingham and one at Stroud. These examples all show a tendency not only to horizontal but to vertical combination.

The movement, which had begun during the later nineties, and reached its climax in 1902, continued to persist after that date; but there were signs of slackening in the years immediately preceding the war. The fact that amalgamations had already taken place in trades where conditions were most favourable, together with the prosperity of the years 1910 to 1913, which removed the incentive to combination, were partly responsible for this; but another influence was also at work. Through bad management or a mistaken price policy several of the combines failed to secure the advantages which their promoters had hoped, and manufacturers again tended to become sceptical of the benefits to be obtained from amalgamations. Further, the practice on the part of the great firms of buying up the smaller units tended to raise the market value of such businesses in many industries, and, by discounting the additional profits which the combine might hope to secure, automatically checked the movement.

Modern economists, reacting against the dicta of the older school, tend to exaggerate the advantages which can be secured from combinations. They point rightly to the lower financial charges and selling costs, to the possibility of large-scale production and of scientific research, and to the buying economies, which attend the larger unit, not to mention the elimination of wasteful competition. Yet, although it is outside our purpose to discuss the question in detail, there are a few other points which an examination of the history and structure of local combines brings out. It is a commonplace that the growth of the large unit, with which the combination movement is associated, leads inevitably to a shifting of control from those who have a financial interest in the business to the managerial staff. It creates, in fact, a division between the capitalist and the management. In theory, it would seem that this, by making it possible for men without capital to employ their ability in business organization, would lead to greater efficiency. In fact, however, those who occupy the position of directors or administrators are seldom chosen solely because of their ability, for such appointments as these depend largely on family

connections, on the influence of promoters, large customers or
leading shareholders. The Board of Directors and the higher
administrative staff, over whom the shareholders can exercise
but little control in a great business with varied interests in
which capital is widely distributed, draw their remuneration
in the form of salaries and fees, and not from dividends. They
are not, therefore, so intimately concerned with the success of
the business, as measured by financial standards, as in the
capitalist entrepreneur in the smaller firm. They are concerned
primarily with its continued existence; for they will continue
to draw their fees and salaries even if it is unprofitable. It is
true that an esprit de corps may develop among them, and
some check on efficiency may be kept by the shareholders; but
the results of mistaken policies or of bad management do not
fall on the heads of those responsible so immediately as in the
case of a privately owned concern. In the latter, inefficiency
is at once apparent in lowered financial returns to those
responsible. These arguments apply in some degree to all
forms of joint-stock enterprise, but particularly to the great
combine, where the organization is necessarily complex, and
where it is difficult to attach to individuals the responsibility
for ill-success.

Disadvantages such as these, however, are inevitable in all
forms of large-scale business and need not be emphasized. A
more serious objection is that the economies to which a combination lends itself are not by any means always realized in
practice. Many of the firms which were merged during this
period remained largely independent as far as their administration was concerned, and continued to be operated as separate
units. The pooling of staffs, of technical knowledge and of
plant, was often purely nominal, and thus few of the economies
of combination could be secured. Sometimes it was not to any
mistake of policy, but to the failure of the personnel to respond
to the new conditions, that the failure of a combine was due.
The staffs of old-established concerns with a long tradition of
rivalry between them sometimes proved unable to work together satisfactorily when they were amalgamated, and personal
jealousies not infrequently wrecked the best of schemes. But
perhaps the most serious danger attending the close combines,
of this as of other districts, was that of over-capitalization; for

frequently this led to a mistaken price policy being pursued, and to subsequent disaster.

When we are considering a firm which has amalgamated with its supplier of raw materials, different factors must be taken into account. While intermediate charges are reduced, and greater control over supplies and quantities can be assured, there are influences on the other side. If the parent company draws the whole of its supplies of a certain commodity from its subsidiary, then the assurance of finding a market reduces the latter's incentive towards the lowering of its costs, and this may more than balance the advantages which accrue. Where, on the other hand, the subsidiary is forced to quote prices in competition with independent concerns for goods which it supplies to the parent company, then, while the stimulus of competition remains, inefficiency may arise in another way. If such a policy is followed, the subsidiary is often obliged to quote to the parent for orders which it would not pay to touch if the former were independent. This necessarily raises the costs of the subsidiary; but, more serious than this, if, having prepared the estimate, it loses the order to some cheaper producer, then a feeling of dissatisfaction is engendered among the personnel, who feel themselves to be subject to all the disadvantages of the competitive system, together with all the defects of combination.

Troubles such as these were the inevitable accompaniment of the combination movement in its early days, when the new administrative systems were in the experimental stage, and, in spite of the unfortunate history of many of the early combines, the amalgamation movement was the necessary response of manufacturers to the new conditions of production and marketing. From the point of view of this history, however, the important fact which emerges from this examination is that during the nineties not only did free competition begin to be replaced by combines, but there was a change in the organization of business control. Up to that time, even in the large concerns, the provision of capital and the control of policy were functions which were centred in the same person. After then, while the small private firm remained common in many local trades, there began to appear, particularly in the new large-scale industries, that division between the entrepreneur and the capitalist which was to bring about fundamental changes in business policy and in the psychological atmosphere in which business was conducted.

Apart from the complete amalgamations which have been described, there occurred during the same period, in almost every branch of local industry, other attempts to control competition among producers by joint agreement. Sometimes these took the form of informal price associations, sometimes of pools, and in many instances there was a development from a loose form of price agreement to a complete amalgamation. There was, moreover, one type of association which was peculiar to this area. As many of these combines have been described elsewhere it is not necessary to do more than mention them here.

As described above, a price association had long existed among the producers of high-grade iron, which were known as the " Marked Bar " houses; but the remainder of the South Staffordshire iron industry was competitive up to 1895. Then, as it was found that during depressions the great disparity between the prices of " marked " and " unmarked " bars tended to cause the substitution of one for the other, houses concerned with both branches of the trade realized the necessity of organizing the lower-grade market. So the Unmarked Bar Association was formed. It covered Lancashire and Yorkshire, as well as the Midlands, and its object was to maintain prices in the home market, export prices being uncontrolled. This appears to have worked satisfactorily until the slump in the early years of the century, when it fell into abeyance, and, though revived in 1904, it was not afterwards very effective.[1] Another heavy trade, long associated with the Midlands, was the galvanized sheet-iron industry, and here attempts had been made to control prices by joint agreement as early as 1883. These, however, had not been successful, and after the breakdown of another price association, which was formed in 1895, the National Galvanized Sheet Association came into being. Formed in 1905, and comprising 95 per cent. of all the manufacturers in the country, the combine took the form of a pool, according to which each firm was allotted a proportion of a predetermined output for the industry, and penalties were exacted from those which exceeded the quota. Prices were raised between 1905 and 1907 from £10 to £14 a ton for sheet of a certain gauge; but during the ensuing

[1] H. W. Macrosty, *op. cit.*, p. 60 *et seq.*

depression the Association broke up.[1] In the tube trade also a number of similar attempts were made, some of which dated back to the eighties. During the next two decades there were repeated efforts to check competition; but none of these met with any success, and it was not until the great amalgamation of 1902 that much was done to prevent chronic price-cutting. After this, further attempts to cover the whole industry by agreements were made, and these culminated in the re-establishment of the British Tube Association in 1906. Other price associations, formed during the nineties, were to be found in the axle, tinned-sheet, heavy ironfoundry, hinge-making, galvanized hollow-ware, and galvanized wire-netting trades among others. Most of these, however, were informal in character, did little more than recommend selling prices to their members, and possessed no considerable authority over them.

The informal price associations which were characteristic of the nineties, having failed to secure what their proposers had hoped, gave place in many industries to the pool system. Some instances of this have already been quoted; but, besides these, the Gas Strip Association was formed in 1901, which required a deposit guaranteeing good faith from its members and which regulated the output by allotting to each firm a quota, by imposing penalties if that were exceeded, and by granting compensation if it were not attained. This was a national combine, only partly associated with this district; but it is worth noting that it fought against German competition in 1902 and forced Continental producers out of the British market.[2] A similar type of pool was formed in the cut-nail trade in 1904 and also in the bedstead trade in 1911. This Bedstead Federation will be described at a later stage. Two years before the war the heavy non-ferrous trade, which had suffered from such fierce competition among its members that both profits and quality had suffered, became organized in the Brass Wire Association and the Cold Rolled Brass and Copper Association. These were formed to fix prices and to raise the quality of the metal, and there was no attempt to establish a pool or to regulate output. About the same time the electrical industry became organized on the side both of the manufacturers and the dealers.

[1] H. W. Macrosty, *op. cit.*, p. 76; *Handbook for Birmingham and the Neighbourhood* (British Association Meeting, Birmingham, 1913), pp. 403-404.
[2] H. W. Macrosty, *op. cit.*, pp. 78-79.

Practically all the associations which have just been described were national in character and were not specifically connected with our area. But there was one type of combine which was peculiar to the district's industries—viz. the type formed under the name of the Birmingham Alliances on the initiative of E. J. Smith. The procedure according to this plan was first to determine the average cost of production in the trade by an examination of the manufacturers' books. To this figure was then added a percentage of profit, and a uniform price list was issued. Loyalty to the association was ensured by an alliance with the trade unions; for the masters bound themselves to employ only union labour, and the men agreed to work only for members of the association and to call out the employees of any master who offended against the association's rules, the men on strike being paid from a fund raised by a levy on the employers. It was agreed that a proportion of any advance in prices which was secured should go to the men in increased wages. The first alliance was formed in the bedstead trade in 1891 and spread to a host of other local industries, including the manufacture of spring mattresses, cased tubes, spun-brass mounts and ornaments, rope and twine, rolled metal, fenders, china door-furniture, china electrical fittings, ironplate-ware, coffin furniture, pins, marl, bricks, and jet and Rockingham wares. It was estimated that at one time no less than 500 masters and 20,000 workers were covered in this way.[1]

The combines were successful at first; but the higher prices attracted new firms into the industries, the number of producers in the bedstead trade, for example, increasing from forty to fifty-six between 1891 and 1899, and this led to trouble. The methods of cost determination were unsatisfactory, and the high prices which were fixed enabled the more efficient masters to make very great profits. When new firms entered the trade, and over-production ensued, these masters had then no hesitation in selling under the list prices, and the calling out of the workmen proved an ineffective sanction. Consequently, the Bedstead Alliance was dissolved early in the new century and the rest suffered the same fate. Some of these other trades were afterwards organized in price agreements of a more usual type; but

[1] H. W. Macrosty, *op. cit.*, p. 80; Sir William Ashley, *Economic Surveys*, pp. 394-398.

for many years the bedstead trade, suffering as it was from failing markets, was subject to bitter competition. An attempt in 1905-1906 to combine all the masters so as to maintain a uniform price list failed, and, except for the amalgamations and the closing of factories, to which reference has already been made, there was no check on price-cutting until 1912, when the bedstead and bedstead-fittings industry came into an association of an elaborate character. According to this, each member on entrance was assigned a percentage of a total agreed output, and was compensated for producing less and penalized for producing more than his quota. Minimum selling prices were fixed for the home and the export markets; conditions of sale were laid down; and the Federation even acted on occasions as a central buying and selling organization for its members. The position of the combine was strengthened by the practice of granting rebates to dealers who bought only from associated firms. Further, a federated workshop was established for producing tools and patterns for the trade, partly with the idea of standardizing designs and of reducing costs, and partly in order to subject the makers more closely to the association and to prepare the way for a complete merger. The fact that various classes of makers existed who produced bedsteads of different qualities proved a difficulty in this as in many other combines, but it was fairly successful up to the war and secured a 10 per cent. advance in prices before 1914.

It is evident that little success of a more than temporary character attended the majority of the price associations and pools of the pre-war period. Frequently they came to grief through a mistaken price policy. Sometimes their methods antagonized the dealers, who then gave their orders to non-associated concerns. This danger is always one of the most serious with which a combine has to contend. But usually even the most successful associations failed ultimately, because in trades in which small and large producers flourished side by side, as in so many local industries, it was impossible to combine all members of the trade, or to secure the agreement of the great manufacturer and the small master to a common policy. Even when the combine took the form of a pool it was difficult to make the penalty for disloyalty heavy enough to prevent manufacturers from selling under list prices in times of depression.

It must be noted that, besides entering the local or national combines, several Midland industries became parties to international agreements. Thus the local firm which had almost a monopoly of the English screw trade came to an agreement in 1905 with a German combine, with which it had long been in competition. According to the international syndicate so formed each of the parties refrained from sending its products to the home market of the other. A somewhat similar type of organization existed in the artificial-silk industry; for a Consortium was formed of the French, German and the local firms, according to which prices were controlled, technical knowledge was to a limited extent shared, and each member refrained from competing in the home markets of the others.

While in such a multitude of local industries the competitive régime began to pass away during this period, there were nevertheless several which remained unaffected. Among these were the gun, jewellery, lock, leather, brush and flint-glass trades. In the brassfoundry trade, while an association existed, and occasionally recommended selling prices, there was practically no control over the freedom of the manufacturer. In many other industries, too, while important amalgamations took place with the object of increasing the efficiency of the industry, or of reducing its surplus capacity, no serious attempts were made to deal with prices. The pen, button, edge-tool and needle trades, besides the new cycle, motor and machine-tool industries, were of this character. The reasons for this lack of organization are not difficult to find. In spite of the increase in the size of the producing units, in many trades (such as the manufacture of jewellery, guns and locks) the small makers were still numerous and entrance was easy, so that any movement towards combination was doomed to failure. In other industries the type of product was so varied in design and in quality that no standard list of prices could be drawn up; while a distrust of combination, inherent in the manufacturers in the older industries, was powerful enough to check any movement in that direction, except where the advantages were particularly obvious.

Yet, even in industries in which there were no efforts to limit competition, many instances occurred of attempts to regulate the conditions under which it might take place, or to form associations to deal co-operatively with problems of a technical or of a commercial character. Thus in the motor industry it had been found that the cost to manufacturers of exhibiting cars at agricultural shows and elsewhere was an excessive burden on the trade, yet it was one which had to be shouldered while complete freedom was allowed. In consequence, the Society of Motor Manufacturers and Traders was formed in 1904 with the primary object of reducing selling costs by prohibiting manufacturers from showing their cars at any save authorized exhibitions, and it was responsible for organizing the annual Motor Show at London. Associations with similar objects existed also in the cycle trade and in the machine-tool industry. In the jewellery trade, though essentially the home of the competitive small manufacturer, the severe depression of 1885-1886 enforced co-operation. Up to that time the industry had been entirely unorganized, and, except for a short-lived society formed in 1851 for mutual protection against stealing and receiving, nothing had been done to modify the individualist character of the trade. In 1887, however, an association came into being with the following objects:—

(1) to promote art and technical education;
(2) to secure uniformity of action in cases of insolvency;
(3) to watch legislation affecting the trade;
(4) to secure the prosecution of thieves and receivers;
(5) to assist in the development of foreign and colonial trade;
(6) to seek, through Parliament and other competent authorities, the removal of all restrictions on, and to support all measures for, the development of the trade.

Soon after the formation of this Jewellers' and Silversmiths' Association an attempt at price-fixing occurred, and the committee tried to induce the silver-chain makers to agree to a list of prices. This met with failure. In the exercise of its main functions, however, the Association was very successful. Its influence was brought to bear in 1906, when a committee was set up by the Government to frame a new bankruptcy law; while from 1888 arrangements existed between the Association and the Municipal School of Art for art instruction to be given to employees in the trade. In 1890 a new school, a branch of the School of Art, was opened for the exclusive use of jewellers, and in 1901 this institution gained an independent status as the

Vittoria Street School for Jewellers and Silversmiths. A similar scheme was put into operation for the training of gunsmiths by a trade which had for many years been accustomed to corporate action through the body known as the Guardians of the Proof House, who were responsible for testing the gun-barrels submitted to them.

Thus certain industries, even if they might be unsuitable fields for price-fixing experiments, found a need for trade associations, to many of which important functions were delegated. And there were few trades within the area which failed to create similar types of organizations, either for wage-bargaining, for technical purposes, or for representing the industry's interests to the Government or to public bodies. In many instances these associations, after they had been in existence for some time, made tentative efforts at price-fixing, even though they had been founded for other purposes.

PART V
WAR AND POST-WAR, 1914-1927

CHAPTER I

THE WAR AND ITS IMMEDIATE EFFECTS

It has been shown that the Birmingham district in 1914 presented a great contrast to the same area in 1860, or even in 1887. It was no longer primarily a hardware, a mining and an iron-producing centre. Such trades as the flint-glass, gun, saddlery and harness, wrought-nail, button and tinplate-ware manufacture, which were formerly among the leading activities, had fallen from prominence. Other ancient trades, like the needle, chain and anchor, edge-tool, welded-tube and pen industries, were advancing only slowly, and of the older staple manufactures the only trades which had made great progress were jewellery and brass. On the other hand, many industries of a new character had risen to substantial importance during the twenty-five or thirty years prior to the war, and the cycle, motor, tyre, electrical apparatus, artificial-silk, and cocoa and chocolate trades ranked, in 1914, among the chief activities of the area. Equally significant changes, moreover, had occurred in the method of industrial organization. The mechanical equipment of the area had greatly increased, and the outworker and the small shop owner could no longer be counted typical figures during the new era; for the new trades were nearly all conducted in large factories, and even in the older hardware manufactures the small unit had declined. The only prosperous trades of which it could still be called representative were the jewellery and chain industries, although it remained predominant in the decaying manufactures, such as guns and wrought nails.

This transformation—the change over from hardware to engineering and the rise of large-scale production—was a development which, though associated with the whole period from 1887 to 1914, was being accelerated during the immediate pre-war years. Yet in many of the older trades the changes could be observed only in a few progressive businesses; for the majority had lagged behind the more alert in the adoption of new processes or in the change over to new products. Mid-Victorian manufacturing practice survived together with the up-to-date. Everywhere there was a pointed contrast between

373

the methods of the more enterprising and those followed by the majority.

Just as more than a hundred years previously, when changes in industrial organization of a similar character were slowly taking place in the textile and in the iron industries, the Napoleonic Wars gave a stimulus to the influences at work, and immensely accelerated the process of transformation; or again, just as a coincidence of forces during the great depression struck at the already perceptible weaknesses in the Black Country's industrial structure and overwhelmed its great iron industry, so the Great War had the effect of speeding up the change in the character of our area and in the methods of organization that had been slowly taking place during the previous twenty-five years. As far as can be judged, the main permanent result of the war on the locality was of this nature. Whatever immediate reversals of existing tendencies it occasioned, whatever temporary stimuli it brought to revive dying industries, whatever dislocations it caused among the previously prosperous, the importance of the war lay, not in the liberation of fresh forces, but in strengthening those already in existence. In a consideration of the history of West Midland industries since 1914 it is obvious that a distinction must be drawn between the period of the war and of the post-war boom on the one hand, and the years which followed 1920 on the other—between, in fact, the immediate reactions of the area to the disaster and its more permanent readjustment to the economic conditions which the war left behind. The first group of phenomena, which is the subject of this chapter, will be considered only in brief outline.

The war broke out at a time when the country was just entering upon the downward phase of the trade cycle after three prosperous years. At first there was a sudden fall in output in many local industries. While certain engineering factories immediately became busy on Government orders, the interruption in the export trade, the decline in the home demand for certain classes of goods, and the general uncertainty brought a great deal of unemployment to the jewellery, sporting-gun, cocoa and chocolate, rolling-stock and other industries. By October, however, firms which were capable of adapting their plants rapidly to meet official requirements were all busy and unemployment was declining. Early in February 1915 it was reported that the adjustment of Birmingham to the needs of war was almost complete.[1]

In examining the changes which occurred during the course of the struggle we may distinguish between four classes of industry.

In the first place there were the trades which responded immediately to the new conditions—those in fact whose plant could with only small adjustments be turned to the production of munitions, and for which the war meant a greater development of their former type of business. Within this category fell not only the local firms which were already producing rifles and ammunition, but also most of the engineering concerns. These possessed plants which were already employed for, or which could easily be adapted to, the production of cars, motorcycles, cycles, shells, bombs, tanks, aeroplanes, rifles and limbers. There was an enormous demand for drop-forgings for shells and crankshafts, and this resulted not only in the extension of existing businesses, but also in the establishment by many engineering firms of smithies of their own. The need for light alloys for aeroplane engines brought a great expansion to the aluminium-castings trade, and most of the subsidiary industries which served the engineer experienced a similar growth. Apart from these trades, however, which were progressive before 1914, there were others which were rescued from a stationary or declining condition by the demands of the Government. The saddlery and harness, the sword and the bedstead manufactures were of this type; but the most marked revival of all occurred in the local iron and steel industry. Between 1913 and 1920 the annual output of pig-iron rose from 460,000 to nearly 700,000 tons. Some 370,000 tons of this consisted of basic iron, of which quantity two-thirds was sent in a molten condition to the local steelworks.

In the next class fall the industries in which the producing units, in order to keep themselves occupied, were obliged to change over to new classes of product and to modify their plant accordingly. It was mainly the hardware trades which came within this group, among them the lock, tinplate-ware, brassfoundry and needle trades, although the rolling-stock and constructional engineering firms must also be included. While

[1] *Newspaper Cuttings* on *Birmingham Industries* (1914-1922), p. 39.

these industries were still partially concerned with their normal products, the interruption of their export trade and of certain sections of their home demand gave them an excess of productive capacity, which they could devote to meet the urgent needs of war. Thus rolling-stock firms might still manufacture hospital coaches; but a large part of their plant came to be devoted to shells and limbers.

The trades in the next group were those which, although they might be largely concerned with Government orders, owed their prosperity mainly to the removal of foreign competition. Many trades which had been suffering severely from German rivalry, both at home and abroad, were of this type. Thus there was an expansion of the button trade not only because of the demand for military buttons but also because of the cessation of Continental imports. The same was true of the brush, the cut- and wire-nail, and the stamped-steel and aluminium hollow-ware industries. But the best example is provided by the glass trade. In 1914 the whole British production of optical glass was centred in one local firm, and the greater part of the country's requirements came from Germany. The outbreak of the war meant at once a cessation of imports and a greatly increased demand, and there was, in consequence, a large expansion in the size of this local trade. Similarly, the drying up of foreign supplies of chemical glass and electric bulbs brought makers in several different branches of the glass trade into the manufacture of those commodities, and finally the absence of foreign competition threw the flint-glass trade into the hands of the Stourbridge and Birmingham makers. In fact, nearly every industry which in pre-war days was losing ground to the foreigner was given a new lease of life.

The last category includes trades which remained stationary or which declined during the war because they were unaffected by the demand for munitions and were handicapped by the restrictions placed on the manufacture of commodities which were not of national importance. The cocoa and chocolate and the artificial-silk industries, for instance, found their growth retarded through these reasons; while two of the more ancient trades suffered a great decline. The chief of these was the jewellery trade. Although after 1915 there was a fair trade in patriotic jewellery and badges, the production of many of the leading lines declined, partly through the fall in demand and partly through the restrictions which were imposed on the use of the precious metals. The jewellers, moreover, could not easily adapt their businesses to the manufacture of munitions; for in many cases their plants were unsuitable for quantity production. In some branches, where machinery was employed, it was possible for firms to take up the manufacture of small parts for shells and magnetos; while others could set their skilled craftsmen to the fabrication of gauges and delicate parts. Further, one section of the industry, which had been revived just prior to the war—viz. diamond-cutting—was swelled by the establishment of a new firm, which was staffed by Belgian refugee labour. Yet, with the drift of the workers into munition factories and the services, the size of the industry diminished, and by 1916 its numbers had fallen to only 20,000. The businesses in this trade, as in many in which the small manufacturer flourished, were particularly hard hit by the war and by the enlistment of the masters. Curiously enough the other ancient industry which was most seriously injured by the war was the sporting-gun trade. In this, indeed, output became negligible; exports ceased; there was little home demand; and possessing no mechanical equipment, the gun-maker could not adapt his business to meet the needs of war. The day when he could secure any share of the military trade had long passed.

So the effects of the war varied from industry to industry. The engineering trades and all those which could adapt themselves to the demand for munitions were immensely stimulated. Some industries which had been failing through foreign competition were brought again into prominence; but others, for which there was no place in the structure of war-time industry, found their progress checked. Two important results which had a bearing on the future of the area must be emphasized. Nearly every industry had been obliged to make great extensions to its plant, and while in some cases the new machinery could serve the normal trade, many businesses were left with plants which were unbalanced from the point of view of their peace-time needs. Some departments had been swelled disproportionately as compared with the size of the factory as a whole, and this involved an expensive process of readjustment after 1918. Further, many local trades, such as the pen, needle, fishhook,

lock, screw, chain and anchor, welded-tube, constructional
engineering and the leather trades, which in pre-war times sent
a large part of their output abroad, had changed over to the
manufacture of munitions, and had all to some extent abandoned
their normal activities. It was obvious that manufacturers within
these industries, though they might be left in 1918 with larger
plants than they had had four years previously, would have a
great task before them in re-establishing their original trade and
in winning back their pre-war customers.

The difficulties, which were to be the legacy of the war, were
in some degree obscured during the first two years of peace by
the price boom and by the necessity for filling the gaps which
had been made in the supplies of all commodities save munitions.
Once the period of readjustment was over, all manufacturers
were busy. Even the trades, such as the manufacture of flint
glass, stamped-steel hollow-ware and buttons, which owed their
war-time prosperity to the cessation of imports, seemed unaffected up to 1920, and in the case of flint glass up to 1921, by
the return of the normal sources of supply to the world market.
The jewellers, left in 1918 with a greatly depleted labour force,
entered upon a period of activity, and were busy for two years
supplying demands which could be met now that precious
metals were again available. A large call for gold chains, enamelled
ware and platinum goods, together with the wrist-watch fashion,
brought renewed prosperity to the industry. The engineering
firms, which had been concerned mainly with aeroplane, motor
and shell manufacture, and which found themselves with a
greatly extended plant, looked to the motor and motor-cycle
trades to supply them with an outlet for their new productive
capacity. Many concerns of this character, however, had, as we
have seen, an unbalanced plant from the standpoint of car production—their machine shops, for instance, having frequently
far outstripped the capacity of their other departments while
they had been engaged on munitions. This was partly owing
to the fact that towards the end of the war the Government
pursued the policy of buying most of the motor vehicles it
required from the United States, so as to free the productive
resources of the motor factories for turning out aeroplanes and
shells. So here the process of readjustment was a long one; yet
the post-war demand seemed to promise a high return.

The more immediate results of this period of far-reaching change on the size of the various local industries may be judged by comparing the Census returns for 1921 with those for 1911.[1] The more fundamental effects of the war, which only became apparent after the cloud of depression had descended in 1920, will be considered in the next chapter.

[1] See Tables on pp. 460-461.

CHAPTER II

THE ADJUSTMENT OF THE AREA TO POST-WAR CONDITIONS

A PROBLEM which presented itself in 1920, when the temporary stimuli of the war and of the subsequent price boom had passed away, was whether the local industries would be likely to retain the new relative position that they had assumed one to another since 1914. Would the engineering group maintain itself in its greatly expanded condition? Would those hardware trades which had been rescued from decline by the cessation of imports during the war survive the resumption of the normal sources of supply? Would the exporting industries, which had given up their foreign markets to serve the demand for munitions, succeed in winning back their previous customers? And, finally, what would be the effect on those trades which were subject to the dictates of fashion of the changes in habits and taste which the war and the passage of six years of abnormality had inevitably caused? The history of the last eight years enables us to answer these questions with a good deal of confidence. It would be tedious to recount in detail the course of each industry through the slump, or to show how each suffered from the dislocation arising from the fall of prices at home, and the political and financial troubles abroad. All that will be attempted will be to give a broad answer to the questions imposed above, to estimate the more permanent effects of the war on local industries and to indicate their present as compared with their pre-war position.

Before embarking on this task, however, it is important to point out that, of all the great industrial areas, Birmingham and District suffered least during the post-war period. This will be seen at once if the percentage increase in the insured population of the Midland area is compared with that of northern districts, and if the proportions of unemployed workers also are taken into account.

[TABLE

INCREASE IN THE NUMBER OF INSURED PERSONS, 1923-1927

District	Number	Per cent. Increase 1927 of 1923
London	146,000	7·29
South Eastern	120,000	15·83
South Western	66,000	8·60
Midlands	101,000	6·03
North Eastern	61,000	3·09
North Western	77,000	3·73
Wales	11,000	1·81
Scotland	18,000	1·38
Northern Ireland . . .	1,200	0·47
	601,200	5·27

RATE OF UNEMPLOYMENT AMONG INSURED WORKPEOPLE (PER CENT.)

District	June 1923	June 1924	June 1925	June 1927
London	9·7	8·3	7·2	5·1
South Eastern . . .	8·4	6·2	4·7	3·7
South Western . . .	9·9	8·0	7·6	6·0
Midlands	10·2	8·3	10·9	8·3
North Eastern . . .	11·4	9·1	17·4	12·3
North Western . . .	15·1	12·4	11·5	9·6
Scotland	13·8	11·1	15·6	9·8
Wales	5·7	6·2	16·5	18·0
Northern Ireland . . .	16·6	16·5	25·4	12·1

The West Midland area could not, of course, boast as low a margin of unemployment as the East Midland counties, as the London area, or as the newer and smaller manufacturing centres of the south; yet for an old industrial district, and for one whose metal trades were subject to the great war-time expansion, Birmingham and the Black Country have been very fortunate. This is to be accounted for largely by the expansion of the new industries, particularly of the motor industry; while the very multiplicity of the local metal trades has done something to facilitate the transference of the labour from the depressed to the expanding manufactures. The older and declining trades have a close relatioñship to the rising industries, and many of them have adjusted themselves to the new conditions without difficulty—a transition which has not been possible to the more specialized areas, where the older trades do not merge so readily with the new.

The figures for particular towns within the area, however, show a considerable variation in the unemployment rate from place to place, and this would seem to indicate that there is less mobility of labour within the district than has been popularly supposed. The most prosperous town has undoubtedly been Coventry, which has had the exceptional good fortune to become not only the home of the motor trade, but a leading centre of the production of artificial silk and electrical apparatus as well. Birmingham has been almost equally well off. It is true that, while it has a large share of the expanding trades, several of the older manufactures, like jewellery and hardware, have been seriously depressed, and the process of adaptation has naturally left a margin of unemployed which is slightly higher than that of Coventry, where there have been no important industries on the decline. Nevertheless, the town has been very prosperous. Wolverhampton has suffered only a little more seriously; while Oldbury, Smethwick and Darlaston have escaped with a comparatively small margin of unemployed. The figures thus reveal that the three largest centres within the area have been the least depressed—a fact which is to be attributed partly to the localization of the new industries in those towns and partly to the mobility of labour in places which possess a great diversity of industrial pursuits. Oldbury owes its comparative prosperity to the expansion of its chemical trades and of its weldless-tube works; Darlaston to the rise of a large manufacture of motor pressings and components; and Smethwick to the advance of its engineering, rolling-stock and foundry trades. Prosperity has been, in fact, with the towns which produce the more highly finished goods and the components for the newer industries.

The places which have suffered most severely have been Wednesbury, Brierley Hill, Bilston, Tipton, Cradley and Dudley. These all have a comparatively specialized industrial life, and have been mainly concerned with the heavy iron and steel trades, which have, of course, been very depressed. Both

Cradley and Dudley have felt severely the effects of the decline in the demand for wrought chain; while West Bromwich has suffered from the depression in the iron and steel and in the cast hollow-ware industries, although its more diverse economic life and the comparative prosperity of several of its trades have prevented unemployment rising in the same degree as in the more specialized centres. Unemployment has been high in Walsall, and if this has been due in some measure to the falling off of its heavy industries, the main reason lies in the decline in the manufacture of saddlery and harness. The advancing fancy-leather goods trade employs a much higher proportion of female labour than the older Walsall manufacture, and this has resulted in the displacement of many of the skilled workmen. The unemployment figures illustrate this conclusion; for they show that whereas 16·1 per cent. of the male insured workers were unemployed in July 1927, the percentage for the female workers amounted to only 7·2. In addition to such influences as the decay of certain trades or the temporary depression of others there is another source of unemployment which must be taken into account. Since the war there has been a great increase in the mechanical equipment of many trades, and this has inevitably resulted in the displacement of certain classes of workers, and has helped to swell, temporarily at any rate, the volume of unemployment.

LOCAL UNEMPLOYMENT INDEX

These Tables show the number of unemployed persons on the registers in July 1927 and December 1927 respectively as a percentage of the insured population.

Counties	July 1927	December 1927
Warwickshire	6·6	6·1
Worcestershire . . .	8·9	9·4
Staffordshire	10·7	10·9
Cheshire	9·2	11·3
Yorkshire	9·6	9·7
Lancashire	9·8	11·4
Lanarkshire	11·3	11·5
Northumberland . .	15·4	16·7
Monmouth . . .	20·6	22·2
Durham	22·5	19·7
Glamorganshire . . .	25·6	25·9

LOCAL UNEMPLOYMENT INDEX—*continued*

Places within Birmingham and District	July 1927	December 1927
Coventry	6·7	5·5
Birmingham	6·8	6·0
Wolverhampton	7·9	7·3
Oldbury	7·9	7·2
Smethwick	8·4	7·6
Darlaston	8·6	8·9
Willenhall	9·4	9·8
Stourbridge	9·7	9·5
Redditch	10·7	9·7
West Bromwich	12·2	11·9
Dudley	12·3	13·6
Tipton	12·5	13·0
Cradley	12·6	13·1
Walsall	13·1	11·4
Bilston	13·9	12·5
Brierley Hill	14·3	12·3
Wednesbury	16·1	18·3

We may now turn to consider the subsequent history of the trades which were rescued from a stationary or declining condition by the circumstances attending the war. Most of these, as we shall see, relapsed when the demands of the Government for munitions declined, or when foreign rivals began to reassert themselves. The extractive industries, for instance, after the brief respite of the boom period, continued their downward course. The output of iron ore from South Staffordshire and Worcestershire fell even lower than its insignificant pre-war level, and it amounted to only 24,000 tons in 1920, 14,000 tons in 1921, and 12,000 tons in 1927. Practically all the ore required in the district, which reached a total of 1,700,000 tons in 1920, when the iron trade was busy, has come from Northamptonshire and Oxfordshire, besides a little from North Staffordshire.[1]

Nor was coal-mining more fortunate. During the thirty years prior to the war, in spite of all the efforts of the Drainage Commissioners, the threat of inundation was always present; and with the closing of more and more mines, and the abandonment of private pumping, an increasingly heavier task was thrust on that body. The troubles of the war period intensified its difficulties and created a burden of debt. In 1920 the complete breakdown of pumping operations in the Tipton district brought matters to a head, and a Committee was appointed by the

[1] *Mines and Quarries Reports*, 1920, vol. iii., p. 112; *Annual Reports of the Chief Inspector of Mines*, 1921, p. 95; 1927, p. 88.

Government to inquire into the whole question of mine drainage. The bulk of the report does not concern us. It is sufficient to say that the Committee recommended that the old body of Commissioners should be brought to an end, its debts settled and a new board established.[1] The most important result of the inquiry, however, was that it led to the final abandonment of pumping in the Tipton area, in which mining operations, except for surface workings, have since ceased. This was the end of an effort, which had lasted nearly seventy years, to free the Tipton mines from water. During the three months' coal stoppage in 1921, moreover, operations in the thick coal seams in the Oldbury district were abandoned and the Hawne Drainage Association, a voluntary body formed in 1894 of coalmasters in the Old Hill district, was terminated. Pumping recommenced in this area in 1923, however, and some of the mines were again set to work. In other parts of the Black Country mining continued; but a large proportion of the output has come from the mines situated beyond the exposed coal-measures. The production of the thick coal-mines has in fact become negligible, and the future of mining in that district lies not in coal but in fireclay, of which some of the most valuable deposits in the kingdom exist, and of which a large output has been obtained. Statistical information is available concerning the position of the local coal trade since 1913. In that year the mines of South Staffordshire and Worcestershire employed some 10,000 men. By January 1926 employment had fallen to 6500 [2]; while the output declined from over 3,000,000 tons in 1913 to 1,367,000 tons in the year ending June 1925.[3] Just under half of the total production was obtained from the three leading mines, each of which employed between 500 and 1000 men.[4] Thus the mining industry of the Black Country, which in 1860 had employed some 25,000 men, and had been responsible for an output of over 5,000,000 tons of coal, besides ironstone, was carried, after 1914, a stage further in its decay, and the district was obliged to rely almost entirely for its fuel on Cannock and on the new and expanding Warwickshire field.

[1] *Report of the Committee on the South Staffordshire Mines Drainage*, 1920, p. 32 *et seq.* and p. 50 *et seq.*
[2] *Report of the Coal Commission* (1925), vol. iii., p. 179.
[3] *Ibid.*, p. 196.
[4] *Ibid.*, p. 196.

2 B

There can be no doubt that the Black Country's coal industry had been brought to a premature end (for its importance is now negligible) largely by the faults in its organization. The extreme individualism which has proved so unfortunate for the British coal industry as a whole can be seen, together with its ultimate disastrous results, in the history of local mining. The lack of unanimity among the coalmasters in meeting their common difficulties, their failure to co-operate efficiently to share the burden of pumping, and the consistent opposition of a large section of them to the various Acts passed with that end in view had ruined many schemes for saving the mines. The " pernicious system of short leases," which prevailed in the district, did not conduce to harmony, since they could be terminated at short notice; and the intermittent character of much of the mining led to the destruction of great quantities of coal by crushing or by flooding.[1] The ease with which the coal could be obtained from the shallow seams in the early days had made South Staffordshire careless of the future and prodigal of its resources, and that unhappy tradition persisted too long. The great natural wealth, on which the fortunes of the whole area had been reared, was thus dissipated, and the mining industry was brought to ruin by the ineptitude and the lack of organizing capacity among those who directed it.

We have seen that the iron and steel industry received a stimulus from the war, and that in 1920 there were four more furnaces in blast than there had been in 1914. When the depression came, however, the weakness of this area, which had to draw its ore from Oxfordshire and Northamptonshire and its coke from South Wales, Lancashire and Yorkshire, became once more apparent. It was calculated in 1922 that the cost of assembling the raw material in South Staffordshire amounted to £2 per ton of pig-iron produced, and under these circumstances, in spite of the large local market, the district could not hope to hold its own.[2] Further, the pig-iron industry of this area, as of other areas, was adversely affected after the war because of the existence of great quantities of scrap metal which was available for the steel furnaces. These supplies completely upset the normal relations between the pig-iron and the steel trades. So,

[1] *Report of the Committee on the South Staffordshire Mines Drainage*, 1920, p. 53.
[2] *Manchester Guardian Commercial Supplement*, January 5, 1922.

after 1920, furnaces began to be blown out, and in 1922 there were only 4 in blast out of the 29 built in the whole of South Staffordshire.[1] Figures are not available to show the output during subsequent years for the Black Country; but it is improbable that it exceeded an annual average of 250,000 tons between 1922 and 1927—under half the production during 1914. At the present time (December 1928), except for a plant which is operated by a Bilston firm to serve its own steel furnaces and for a few cold-blast furnaces, the pig-iron industry of South Staffordshire has practically ceased to exist.

No adequate statistics exist to illustrate the course of events in the wrought-iron trade. In 1921 some 10,000 persons were employed in the puddling furnaces and iron rolling mills of the district, where half the puddlers in England and Wales were to be found.[2] After that date, however, the trade diminished. Several leading ironworks were completely closed, while others ceased to operate their puddling furnaces. To some extent this was due to the deep depression in certain of the leading wrought-iron-using trades, such as the chain and anchor manufacture; but during the last three or four years the misfortunes of the industry have been intensified by the importation of cheap Belgian iron and steel, which have displaced Staffordshire iron in such traditional uses as nut-and-bolt and small-chain manufacture. The cheaper grades of the local wrought-iron have practically ceased to be produced, and all that remains of this once great industry is the production of high-grade material by the " marked bar " houses. The figures which the Census of Production has made available illustrate the great decline during the last twenty years in the British wrought-iron trade, with which the fortunes of the Black Country have been closely linked for over a century.

OUTPUT OF VARIOUS CLASSES OF IRON IN TONS [3]
(Great Britain)

	1907	1913	1924
Puddled bars	975,000	1,207,000	309,000
Iron bars, rods, angles, shapes and sections, etc. . .	901,000	...	350,000

[1] Manchester Guardian Commercial Supplement, January 5, 1922.
[2] Census of England and Wales, 1921, Industry Tables, p. 38.
[3] Committee on Industry and Trade Survey of Metal Industries, pp. 46-47.

It seems, then, that the competition of Belgium has completed, in the last few years, what the advent of Bessemer steel began.[1] At this point it is necessary to emphasize that one of the chief features of the post-war period has been the greatly increased importation of Continental semi-manufactured steel for use by the local metal trades. A leading authority has recently stated that the bulk of the small finished bars used in the district has been imported of late years, and he has estimated that 80 per cent. of the semi-finished steel employed has been of foreign origin.[2] Before the war imports of this character came mainly from Germany, but since 1920 France and Belgium have been supplying the largest quantities. Many local trades which in the pre-war years depended entirely on British sources have been buying from abroad. As already mentioned, the nut-and-bolt and the small-chain trades, which used wrought-iron almost exclusively up to 1920, have of late years employed Belgian mild steel. The makers of galvanized tanks have purchased Continental steel sheets; the wire-nail and the pin manufacturers have used foreign steel wire; the gun-makers, who before the war used to buy solid steel tubes from Sheffield and to have the barrels made locally, have come to rely largely on Belgian barrels, except for very high-grade guns; and many other small metal industries, such as the lock trade, have been buying much of their metal abroad. The high-grade material for the engineering trade has remained in British hands, although even here the foreigner has advanced. Only in one or two instances has development been in a reverse direction; but it is worth noticing that the weldless-tube makers, who before 1914 used Swedish steel billets, since the war have purchased mainly from English sources.[3] On the whole, however, it seems that the tendency of the area to rely on other districts for raw materials and semi-

[1] The high quality of the South Staffordshire iron was in some measure to be attributed to the character of the local ores. From these a pig-iron could be produced which had " just sufficient phosphorus to allow the iron to melt well and work easily, and enough manganese to give the iron that rather subtle quality known as ' body,' while the local coals were such as prevented undue sulphur contamination." The exhaustion of South Staffordshire mines, therefore, made it more difficult for the ironmasters to maintain the high quality of their products (*High-Class Bar-Iron*; brochure published by Messrs Noah Hingley & Sons, Ltd., Netherton, p. 7).

[2] *Daily Telegraph Supplement* on *The Safeguarding of Industry*, July 31, 1928, p. 41.

[3] " The Workshops of Great Britain," Article lii., in *The British Engineers' Export Journal*, May 1925.

products has been carried further since 1920; and the Continent has come to provide a considerable proportion of local requirements. Most of the steel is imported in a crude form and is re-rolled in the district—an illustration of its increasing concern with finishing processes.[1]

The position of the local steel industry is illustrated by the following Table, though it must be remembered that the figures cover a much wider area than the Black Country. Since the slump, production within our area has been confined to three large works, excluding one firm engaged in the manufacture of steel castings. Most of the steel has been produced in the basic open-hearth furnaces; but there has been a small output of acid open-hearth steel and a fairly large production, ranging from 136,000 tons in 1923 to 28,000 tons in 1925, of basic Bessemer. The steel output, like the wrought-iron output, of the Black Country has probably reached a fairly stable level. The large market which exists among the metal trades of the locality ensures a certain quantity of demand; while the disadvantages of the area which arise from its lack of raw materials are likely to prevent any considerable expansion.

STEEL OUTPUT OF STAFFORDSHIRE, WARWICK-SHIRE, WORCESTERSHIRE AND SHROPSHIRE

Year	Output in Tons [2]
1920	806,000
1921	309,000
1922	702,000
1923	892,000
1925	826,000
1926	484,000
1927	889,000

The Black Country, during the post-war depression even more than in pre-war years, has assumed all the aspects of an ancient, but decayed, iron and steel centre. Products which were once important, but which have been superseded in the leading

[1] Much of the Belgian " iron " which has been imported into the country since the war has consisted of a mixture of iron and steel scrap, and cannot therefore be classed as puddled iron. While the Belgian product may suffice for trades which require only a low-grade metal, it is not likely to replace permanently the Staffordshire material for uses in which wrought-iron still holds an advantage over mild steel—e.g. where a reliable weld is required, where there is a serious danger of " fatigue," or where corrosion is to be feared.

[2] This output was 8·9 per cent. of the total British production in 1920; 8·4 per cent. in 1921, and 9·8 per cent. in 1927; but it will be seen that the figures cover a much wider area than that with which we are here concerned.

metallurgical districts, have made up a substantial proportion of South Staffordshire's output. For instance, while the hot blast has become almost universal elsewhere, the production of cold-blast pig has remained a feature of the local trade. The area possesses, moreover, one of the few surviving British plants for making basic Bessemer steel,[1] and it is still the chief British centre of the dwindling wrought-iron industry. South Staffordshire, indeed, is no longer in the main current of metallurgical development. The staple metals are produced elsewhere, and our area has come to be concerned largely with specialities which other centres have abandoned in favour of commodities for which there is a greater demand.

Since 1914 a course similar to that of the iron and steel industry has been pursued by several smaller local trades. The nail manufacture, for instance, benefited greatly during the war by the absence of German and Belgian competition, which previously had reduced the size of the industry. By 1920 not only was the output much larger than in pre-war years, but an export trade equal to about a quarter of the total production had been developed. Manufacturers could not, however, maintain themselves against the renewed activity of their foreign rivals, and during the last few years some 75 per cent. of the nails in use in Great Britain have come from abroad. The wire nail has even more largely superseded the cut variety, which has maintained itself only for such uses as require clenching power; and British manufacturers of wire nails cannot hold their own, since they are forced to buy imported wire, the cost of the British material being as high as a corresponding quantity of Belgian finished products. A very small number of wrought nails are still made in the Black Country and in the Bromsgrove neighbourhood, but this trade is now of negligible importance.

To the button trade the war, because of the absence of imports and of the great demand for military buttons, brought a development which it could not afterwards maintain. The employment in the local trade, which amounted to 3800 in 1921,[2] fell by several hundreds during the next seven years. But perhaps the best illustration of the course of the industry is provided by the history of the largest firm. This employed some 2000

[1] No basic Bessemer steel was actually produced in Great Britain in 1927.
[2] *Census of England and Wales*, 1921, Industry Tables, p. 137.

persons in 1914; its number rose to nearly 3000 during the post-war boom; but by 1927 it was employing only half of this number. Several other local manufacturers went out of business during the period. Though the decline may be in some measure attributed to changes of fashion in dress, the main cause was undoubtedly the competition from abroad. The Italians, who have the advantage of a dry climate, have captured most of the trade in vegetable-ivory buttons, for the manufacture of which a moist atmosphere is unsuitable. The Japanese have secured the larger part of the market for cheap pearl buttons, since the supplies of trochus shell are found mainly in the neighbourhood of their country, and only the more expensive types, which are produced from pearl shell, and for which sales are limited, can be produced in Birmingham. Except for uniform buttons, supplied to the Government, the market for metal buttons is mainly in the hands of Continental producers; and the only lines in which the local manufacturer can satisfactorily compete, and which, indeed, are said to employ some 80 per cent. of the labour in the industry, are linen and erinoid buttons. The latter have recently become important through the modern fashion in women's dress. Of the production of linen buttons Birmingham firms have almost a world monopoly.[1]

The brush and broom trade is another manufacture which has declined since 1920, chiefly through foreign competition. The introduction of mechanical methods of production has been much more rapid on the Continent than in England, and the trade lost the advantage of cheap labour when it was brought under the Trade Boards Act after the war. High-grade brushes, especially those of the older type, are still produced locally; but the cheap qualities are largely supplied by the foreigner. In addition, the growing cleanliness of the streets and the prevailing fashion in women's hair have reduced the demand for brushes, while the advance of the vacuum cleaner has not been without its effect.

The flint-glass trade, too, was unable to hold the ground it had won from the Continental producers up to 1920. Immediately after the war there was a large demand for cut glass to replace the wastage which had occurred between 1914 and 1918,

[1] *Daily Telegraph Supplement* on *The Safeguarding of Industry*, July 31, 1928, p. 42.

and attempts were made by Birmingham and Stourbridge manufacturers to capture the market in cheap wares as well as in the more expensive. Machines were obtained from the United States, productive methods were improved, and costs were in this way reduced. The trade remained busy up to 1921, but then depression seized upon it. Cheap goods again poured into Great Britain from Czecho-Slovakia, and the lines which had been developed during the war, such as electric bulbs, were lost. So, after its temporary recovery, the industry receded to a position which closely resembled that of 1913. Employment fell; many firms closed their foundries; and the practice of buying foreign glass and of performing merely the cutting operation in the district was extended.

Another example of this course of events is provided by the enamelled-steel hollow-ware trade. Before the war, while imports amounted to some 12,000 or 13,000 tons yearly, the domestic production was only 7000 tons. The closing of the home market to German competition brought a great expansion, and by 1920 imports had fallen to 3600 tons and the home output had risen to 15,000 tons, of which 22 per cent. was exported. After this date, however, foreign competition again reasserted itself, and in 1925 imports had risen to 7600 tons and in 1927 to 9800 tons. At the same time the home output fell to 9500 tons in 1925 and to 8700 tons two years later; while the total employment in the industry sank from 4500 in 1920 to under 3000 in 1928.[1] These figures, of course, cover the whole country; but, since this trade is largely localized within our area, they serve to illustrate its history. Thus the enamelled-steel hollow-ware industry has failed to maintain the progress which it made during the war, and Germany has been creeping back to her old position of predominance.

Besides these depressed industries there have been others which have declined during the post-war period, not because of competition in the home market, but because they have found it impossible to re-establish their export trade, which they lost while they were engaged on munitions. Just as certain British trades expanded during the war owing to the cessation of foreign competition, so many countries which previously were supplied

[1] *Reports of Committee on Wrought-Enamelled Hollow-ware*, 1925 and 1928, *under the Safeguarding of Industries Act.*

with certain commodities by Birmingham and District established their own industries when those supplies were interrupted. In addition, the United States and neutral countries obtained a footing in former British markets; while in many instances the difficulties of recapturing lost trade have been intensified by the imposition of tariffs to protect the new industries against renewed British competition. The duties which the British Government has recently seen fit to impose on the importation of buttons and enamelled hollow-ware are examples of the same tendency at work in this country.

It is, however, doubtful whether the war and the post-war tariffs on certain Birmingham goods have done more than accelerate an inevitable change, for nearly all the industries which have declined through these reasons since 1914 were in a stationary or only slowly expanding condition during the fifteen or twenty years preceding it. This is true, for instance, of the bedstead trade; while pen manufacture is included in the same unfortunate group. In 1913 this industry exported about 87 per cent. of its output, and practically supplied the world with steel pens. The interruption of supplies between 1914 and 1918, however, induced several countries to set up factories to supply their needs; while since the war Germany has become a keen competitor in Central and Southern Europe, and France and the United States—with its yellow-metal pen—have become more serious rivals. To the trades of the Redditch district the war dealt an equally deadly blow. Needles are commodities which are distributed through a multitude of channels over a wide area of the world, and once the connection between manufacturer and customer is lost, the difficulties of re-establishing it are immense. Further, Germany, which has the advantage of cheaper steel and a larger scale of production, has been competing successfully during the post-war era, and consequently many foreign markets have been lost. Manufacturers have branched into new products, such as hosiery needles, for which the prosperous trades of the East Midlands provide a market, and bone knitting-hooks; but these developments have been insufficient to balance the fall in the output of the staple commodities. The fishhook industry, which also produces mainly for export, has been similarly affected, although here the most serious competition has come from the Norwegians.

The changes of habit and fashion which naturally accompanied the war had a detrimental effect on a number of West Midland industries. In some the result was merely to strengthen the tendencies which could be observed long before 1914. The increasing popularity of the wooden bedstead, for example, brought a further decline in the home sales of metal bedsteads; while the economy which the post-war position enforced in domestic fittings had, as we shall see later, an important influence on certain branches of brassfoundry. But some industries which were very progressive up to 1914 suffered in the same way. Thus the simpler forms of women's dress caused a great reduction in the demand for pins from dressmakers, and the hairpin trade was injured by the bobbed and shingled hair fashion. The pin manufacture has been seriously depressed as a result of these causes, as well as of the rivalry of foreign producers, who have sent large quantities to the home market. Among the leading industries the greatest sufferer from the post-war fashions has been the jewellery trade. Crippled throughout the war, this manufacture has never recovered itself, in spite of the temporary boom from 1918 to 1920. The trade, engaged as it is in supplying luxuries, has always suffered severely during industrial depressions; but since 1920 a combination of causes has worked against it: women have turned to active and outdoor amusements, and their fashion in dress has been inconsistent with the use of jewellery; the popularity of motoring has changed the direction of national expenditure; and the improvement in taste, which is illustrated so clearly by the dress of the modern generation, has injured the trade in imitation and ostentatious jewellery. The electro-plate branch was not affected as soon or as seriously by the depression as the rest of the industry; but even that has not progressed. According to the Census of 1921 there were nearly 25,000 persons in all branches of this trade in Birmingham and District—considerably less than in 1914.[1] Since then there has been a further decline, and employment was in 1927 probably in the neighbourhood of 20,000.

Another ancient manufacture to which, as in the case of jewellery, neither the war nor the post-war period brought anything except misfortune was the gun trade. Up to 1918 it was practically closed down, and since then it has been sunk in

[1] *Census of England and Wales*, 1921, Industry Tables, pp. 83-84.

depression. The decline of the landed classes has been partly responsible for this, together with the competition of the Belgians and, during the last few years, of the local rifle factory, which has taken up the manufacture of sporting guns by machinery. Only the high-class gun and sporting-rifle trade has remained with the old workshop industry, which has been compelled since the war to look abroad to an increasing extent for its market. The employment which it afforded in 1927 was less than in 1914, and probably did not amount to much more than 1000; while the old Black Country manufacture of gun-locks has almost entirely disappeared. As was to be expected, the output of revolvers and of military rifles has been comparatively small since the war, and the only factory in the latter trade has become far more concerned with cycles, cars and other classes of product than with supplying the armed forces.

Instances have already been given of the change in their scope of production which was forced on many firms by the loss of the markets for their staple commodities after the war. Thus it has been shown that the needle-makers turned their attention to the manufacture of hosiery needles and bone knitting-hooks, and that the military-rifle factory developed a trade in sporting guns as well as in cycles and cars. Nearly every industry which was adversely affected attempted to occupy its plant in this way. This of course was not by any means a new tendency; but the circumstances of the post-war period gave it a great stimulus. The pearl-button makers turned to the production of pearl electric-light switches, links and millinery slides. The steel-pen manufacturers increased their output of stationers' sundries, and found new sources of activity in the demands for fine stampings for the aircraft, motor and electrical trades. Turning to a larger industry, the hollow-ware group, we find that an equally significant change in the type of its products occurred. The trade in this area employed in 1921 some 9000 persons— four-fifths of the total number employed in England and Wales [1]; but the distribution of the labour force between the various branches of the industry was very different from that of ten years previously. The increase in the enamelled-steel hollow-ware trade and its post-war history have already been discussed. The aluminium branch during the war made an equally great

[1] *Census of England and Wales*, 1921, Industry Tables, p. 77.

advance, and after 1920 it did not suffer to the same extent as the enamelled trade from Continental competition. Before the war, although a small production existed in Birmingham and District, most of the aluminium ware used in England came from Germany. The absence of imports after 1914, however, and the experience which the war brought in the manipulation of the metal, led to the rise of a large British trade, which in 1920 was responsible for an output of 1400 tons, and which gave employment to 3500 persons. It is true that there was a decline after 1920, owing to the renewal of Continental rivalry, and that by 1922 the industry employed only half the number of two years before; but since then there has been a revival.[1] Home production has risen, while the export trade has grown and was higher than the import in 1925. So this section, which is largely located in Birmingham, has not only increased in size, like the enamelled trade, since 1913, but it has also been more successful than the other in keeping foreign competition in check since 1920.

The advance in these new types of hollow-ware, which has accompanied the increased use of gas and electric cooking, has, however, had a disastrous effect on the older branches of the trade. The cast section, which was on the downward grade even before 1914, has still further declined. Consequently the foundries, which are still situated mainly at West Bromwich and Bilston, have carried further their pre-war tendency to engage in other classes of manufacture, and there has been a decided movement on their part to the production of motor and electrical castings and of baths and sanitary wares. Similarly the tinplate-ware trade lost ground for the same reasons, and firms in this industry have gone over to the manufacture either of other forms of hollow-ware or of pressed steelwork for the motor industry. Thus if the older hollow-ware firms have held their own, it has been because they have turned to new classes of product, and not because of the maintenance of their old markets.

Perhaps the most remarkable instance of this type of industrial transition within the more ancient trades, however, occurred in connection with the local leather manufacture. Even before the war there had existed a tendency for the saddlers and harness-makers to turn to the production of fancy-leather goods; while

[1] *Report of Committee on Aluminium Hollow-ware, 1925, under the Safeguarding of Industries Act.*

the cycle-saddle trade had already become a large and specialized branch of the industry. But in those days the productive methods employed in the manufacture of fancy-leather goods bore too close a resemblance to those pursued in the older branches to permit Walsall to compete with Germany even in the home market. The chief English centre of this section of manufacture remained at London. The war, of course, brought revival to the saddlery and harness trades; while the production of leather equipment for the forces formed another part of its activities. On the conclusion of the war great quantities of surplus stores were sold by the Government; while the marked development of motor traction carried still further the destruction of the older markets. In 1921 the number of persons employed in producing saddlery, harness and whips within Birmingham and District amounted to only 2250—less than a third of the number in 1911.[1] The once flourishing export trade practically ceased, except for the very high qualities, and although a small but steady demand for hunting saddles and for harness for delivery carts has remained, the home market has absorbed but little. Yet, to balance this decline, there has grown up a large trade in other types of leather product. Firms have changed over to the production of such fancy-leather goods as wallets and purses, of travelling bags, of leather motor accessories, of sports equipment and of leather gloves. Statistics do not exist to illustrate the extent of this development. In 1921 some 4500 persons were concerned— about the same number in pre-war days [2]; but it has been since that year that the greater part of the transformation has occurred. Unlike many of the new trades, moreover, these leather industries were not concerned mainly with supplying the home market, for about half the output has been exported during the last few years. The destinations to which these goods have gone have been in marked contrast to that of the saddlery and harness exports of earlier days. Whereas the Colonies and South America took most of the latter during the last decades of the nineteenth century, it is the United States and the Continent which have come to the front as customers for the new leather trades.

The subsidiary industries also were affected. Many of the firms which at one time produced various types of saddlers'

---

[1] *Census of England and Wales*, 1921, Industry Tables, p. 100.
[2] *Ibid.*, p. 101.

ironmongery turned to electrical castings or motor parts, while from the old buckle trade there arose a substantial brace-fittings industry. The change in the type of finished-leather goods has practically divorced the local tanners and curriers from their previously intimate connection with the rest of the industry. The hides which are dressed at Walsall consist mainly of cow-hides, which formerly were supplied to the harness-makers. But most of the fancy-leather goods are made from other classes of hide, and consequently, while the finished-goods manufacturers have had to go outside the district for much of their raw materials, the local tanners and curriers have been obliged to seek a new market for their leather. This they have found very largely in the demand for upholstery work on the part of the motor industry and of the furniture trade.

From the foregoing account it will be obvious how important have been the reactions on many and varied trades of certain of the new industries—viz. those which produce highly composite products. The expansion of these in fact has been the leading cause of the comparative prosperity, not only of the area taken as a whole, but of most of the subdivisions of it. Thus, if progress had been limited to the artificial-silk, the food and drink, or any trades which produced non-composite products, prosperity might have been confined to the few places within the area in which the chief firms in those trades were situated. If the new trades which arose had been unconnected with the main concern of the area—viz. small metal products—the labour difficulties, the capital cost and the pains of transition would have been much greater than was actually the case. As it was, the most notable expansion occurred in two industries which, of all others, required for their use a great variety of finished or semi-finished products of a type which the Midland area was peculiarly fitted to supply. Older industries which found demands for their former products languishing were able, with very little difficulty, to adapt themselves to meet these fresh needs, and so to maintain themselves under a new guise. Thus the whole area, and not merely the centres in which the new industries were found, benefited; and the pains of a slow and difficult transference of labour to unfamiliar activities and the necessity for heavy capital expenditure were avoided. In all the older industries which responded to the new demands there was a contrast between those which were dragged reluctantly along the new paths and those alert manufacturers who seized their opportunities at once. Further, there were whole industries which, though they might have no obvious advantages, seemed more able than others to break away from old habits and to turn in new directions. The leather trades provide a good example of this type. But everywhere the problem of adaptation to post-war needs was immensely facilitated for the West Midlands by the immense expansion of two of its staple industries and by the natural dependence of those industries on parts and accessories which the older local trades could turn to supply.

Before adding to the examples of these subsidiary trades let us glance at the development of the major industries themselves. The Table on page 460 shows that the employment in the manufacture of electrical apparatus (excluding electricians and electrical contractors) rose from 9100 to 25,800 between 1911 and 1921 within the three counties of Staffordshire, Warwickshire and Worcestershire. For Birmingham and District the increase was from about 6000 to 17,000 during the same period,[1] the disparity being accounted for by the fact that although Birmingham, Coventry and Wolverhampton were great seats of the trade, it was carried on to a large extent also at Stafford and Rugby as well. It is evident however that, if we consider our area alone, the industry employed nearly three times as many persons in 1921 as in 1911. The trade soon recovered from the slump and made a great advance after 1923. New firms sprang up in the area and the older ones increased in size. Coventry saw the establishment of a great factory for the manufacture of telephone equipment; the amount of industrial apparatus produced in the area rose enormously; and the production of wireless equipment was added to the scope of the activities. The figures of the Ministry of Labour for electrical engineering show that between 1923 and 1927 (July) employment increased by no less than 30·1 per cent. in the whole country. We may therefore assume that within Birmingham and District alone the numbers engaged in the industry in 1927 amounted to well over 20,000.[2]

---

[1] *Census of England and Wales*, 1921, Industry Tables, pp. 56-58.

[2] The Ministry of Labour figures show that there were 24,000 insured workers in the electrical engineering industry in July 1927 in the whole Midland area. Certain classes of workers—*e.g.* young persons under sixteen—would not be included in this total.

From the standpoint of its effects on the industrial structure of the West Midlands, the growth of the vehicle trades, which are much greater in size and in the complexity of their demands on other industries than the electrical group, is of the utmost significance. As we have already seen, the war left the motor and cycle firms with extended but unbalanced plants, which required great adaptation before they were fitted for vehicle production. Further, many general engineering firms which, since the outbreak of the war, had been engaged on the production of shells and aero-engines found themselves, in 1919, with greatly expanded mechanical equipment, much of which could be turned to the manufacture of cars. Consequently a number of firms, some of which had never before produced cars, made plans for a great output without any consideration of the possible demand. When an attempt was made in 1920 to calculate, on the basis of the income-tax figures, the number of potential car owners in Great Britain, it was estimated that the normal capacity of the works then operating was at least four times the number which could possibly be sold, even if imports were ignored, and if it were assumed that every owner bought a new car every two years.[1] Besides this there was a large influx of American cars just after the war; while the foreign markets, which in pre-war days had taken a quarter of the British output, had been captured by the United States. Finally, this trade, in common with the edge-tool, pig-iron and leather industries, were adversely affected by the quantities of war material which was available for sale. No less than 60,000 vehicles were sold at a low price by the War Disposals Department after the war, and as these were very suitable for commercial purposes, the commercial vehicle trade was temporarily killed.

For a time, therefore, the motor and allied industries suffered depression, during which great financial losses occurred. Once this period of readjustment had been passed, however, expansion set in. With the appearance after 1923 of the cheap car, manufactured on mass-production principles, there came a great increase in output. By 1925 the commercial vehicle trade also was beginning to revive; for by then the war vehicles had worn out, and it seems likely that the sale of those vehicles at

[1] D. J. Smith, *The Need for a Wider Outlook in Automobile Engineering* in the *Proceedings of the Institution of Automobile Engineers*, 1922-1923.

low prices, by accelerating the transition from horse to motor traction for commercial purposes, created a greater market for commercial cars than would otherwise have existed—at any rate within so short a time. Individual firms in all branches of the industry can point to grave vicissitudes of fortunes which are inevitable in an industry which is at once highly competitive, and of which the products are subject to the dictates of fashion; but the figures of the British output show how great has been the expansion of the trade as a whole. In 1927 the output of cars and commercial vehicles was more than twice that of 1923 and about seven times that of 1913; while the number of cars exported was more than double that of the pre-war years. Besides this, a very large export trade in chassis has grown up since 1924. Although these statements apply to the whole British motor industry, they are illustrative of the developments which have occurred in the West Midland section of it.

The motor-cycle industry has been equally progressive. This trade was still in its infancy in 1913; but it has since risen to become one of the leading activities of the area. Output has increased from 3700 in 1907 and 36,700 in 1912 to 120,400 in 1924; while exports in 1927 were three times those of 1913. The British manufacturer, indeed, has captured a large share of the international trade in motor-cycles, and about a third of the total output has been exported of late years. The pedal-cycle industry also has grown, mainly as a result of a marked increase in exports, and, from being at the beginning of the century one of the most seasonal and highly fluctuating of the local trades, it has achieved a remarkable stability and a uniform distribution of its output throughout the year. As for aero-engines and air-craft, although production has fallen since the war period, these manufactures too have become a substantial branch of the local activities.

From the Table on page 461 it will be seen that the employment in the combined group of cycle, motor and accessories manufacture within the district doubled between 1911 and 1921, and that in the latter year some 67,000 persons were engaged. The extension of the motor trade over other parts of the country, particularly the south, reduced the proportion of the total labour force which was found within our district from 36 to 33 per cent. between the two Census years; but the area

2 C

still retained a marked predominance over every other industrial region in this respect. The growth of the industry's labour force after 1923 can be estimated from the following Tables, although it must be remembered that the Ministry of Labour figures cover the aircraft as well as the cycle and motor industries, and that they apply to a wider area than that with which we are concerned. However, it is safe to assume that the rate of growth within Birmingham and District has been at least equal to that within the whole country; and we may estimate that the number employed in cycle, motor and aircraft production and repair and in body-building within the district amounted in 1927 to some 80,000.

ESTIMATED OUTPUT OF THE BRITISH MOTOR AND CYCLE INDUSTRY

(a) Census of Production

Year	Complete Motor-Cars, Commercial Vehicles and Chassis therefor Number	Motor-Cycles and Tricars Number	Bicycles and Tricycles Number
1907	10,300	3,700	613,200
1912	23,200	36,700	467,000
1924	146,600	120,400	681,600

(b) Estimate of the Society of Motor Manufacturers and Traders

Year	Private Cars	Commercial Vehicles
1919	24,000	6,000
1920	50,000	10,000
1921	32,000	8,000
1922	58,000	15,000
1923	66,000	21,000
1924	105,000	26,000
1925	121,000	32,000
1926	138,000	42,000
1927	157,000	52,000

(c) Ministry of Labour Estimated Number of Insured Persons engaged in the Production and Repair of Motor Vehicles, Cycles and Aircraft

Year	Great Britain and Northern Ireland
July 1923	192,000
„ 1924	204,000
„ 1925	214,000
„ 1926	224,000
„ 1927	233,000

	Midlands District
Feb. 1925	84,000
July 1927	94,000

EXPORT OF MOTOR VEHICLES AND CYCLES

Year	Motor-Cars and Commercial Vehicles	Chassis	Motor-Cycles	Cycles
1913 . .	7,595	1,234	16,850	147,633
1923 . .	4,232	2,022	16,002	121,817
1924 . .	12,754	2,905	37,607	200,781
1925 . .	19,315	9,735	46,642	276,468
1926 . .	16,007	16,381	48,120	280,052
1927 . .	17,877	17,819	52,805	283,358

The fortunes of the motor industry have been followed in some detail because of its vital importance to the Birmingham area, and we must now turn to the major subsidiary trades which had sprung up as a direct consequence of the appearance of the new means of transport. In the manufacture of rubber goods, which have consisted mainly of tyres, employment increased nearly fourfold between 1911 and 1921, and amounted in 1927 to some 12,000 or 13,000. Practically all this local industry was then found in the hands of one firm, which is situated at Castle Bromwich. The wheel trade was carried on in large plants at Coventry, at Bilston (where an old firm of hollow-ware makers had taken up the trade) and at Darlaston, where a constructional engineering concern had branched into the industry. This same firm, which employed in 1927 some 1200 men, had also become the largest makers of chassis frames in the country, and produced engine castings on a large scale. In the manufacture of finished cycle and motor accessories, such as lighting and starting equipment, the area was responsible in 1921 for 70 per cent. of the total employment in England and Wales, and possessed nearly 15,000 employees in this branch of industry.[1] Since then there has been a great expansion in the trade owing to the increasing elaborateness of the equipment with which cars have been supplied.

The host of smaller industries which have sprung up or have adapted themselves to meet the needs of the new vehicle trades can only be mentioned. At Smethwick, West Bromwich and Redditch the spring industries have grown into substantial manufactures. Largely owing to demands from the same source

[1] *Census of England and Wales*, 1921, Industry Tables, p. 65.

the paint and varnish trades have expanded, and the introduction of the new cellulose finish has added another branch to their activities. In 1914 the aluminium-castings industry had been insignificant; but the needs of the aeroplane designers during the war stimulated experiment in the use of light alloys and brought a rapid growth. When the war came to an end this manufacture maintained itself by seeking new customers in the motor industry, and in 1927 some 3000 persons were employed in making aluminium castings, mainly at Smethwick. At the same time the leather trades have been supplying upholstery and fittings; the screw trade both wood- and metal-thread screws; the drop-forgers, crank-shafts and connecting rods; the ironfounders, cylinders and many other cast parts; the lock trade, door fastenings; the tinplate-ware trade, pressed panels; the nut-and-bolt trade, brake connections and bright steel bolts and fastenings; the non-ferrous mills, radiator tubes and sheet metal for radiators and cylinder jackets, besides providing the accessories trade with much of its raw material; the galvanized-sheet trade has turned to petrol tanks; the weighing-machine industry to petrol pumps; and the wire industry to flexible controls. The list might, indeed, be extended indefinitely.

Besides these smaller industries several of the most important manufactures in the area were stimulated by these increasing demands from the motor and cycle trades. Thus, while there was a depression in the iron and steel tube trades after 1920, and although the welded trade has since been stationary owing to the loss of export markets, the weldless-tube manufacture, which sent most of its products to the cycle trade, has advanced since 1923. At present it probably employs some 9000 persons. The machine-tool industry, which grew considerably during the war, and which employed some 4000 persons in 1921,[1] has also grown since that date, owing to demands from the motor factories. The development of accessories manufactured on mass-production lines and of the cheap-car trade has called for an increasing quantity of mechanical equipment, much of which the local trade has been able to supply.

The non-ferrous group has been remarkably buoyant throughout the depression. Yet, if its magnitude in 1927 was greater than in 1914, this growth has only been made possible by an

[1] *Census of England and Wales*, 1921, Industry Tables, p. 54.

acceleration of a change, which was noticeable before the war, in the relative size of its different branches. The production of elaborate cast wares has declined, except for export, owing to the rise of electric-lighting and the tendency of fashion towards simpler domestic fittings. Much of the heavy engineering brass-foundry work has departed to the north, and such of the naval brassfoundry section as remains has been reduced since 1920 owing to the depression in shipbuilding. Further, the rolling, tube and wire mills have lost certain classes of customers owing to the depression of the older hardware trades, such as the bed-stead, pin and metal-smallware manufactures. Nevertheless, the non-ferrous trades as a whole have been progressive, although they have tended more and more to become complementary to the local engineering industries. As we have seen, many of the brassfoundry firms have changed over to produce motor and electrical accessories and components; while the mills have been called upon to supply wire, tubes and sheets to the new industries. Further, even if fashion has affected some of the other branches adversely, they were still assured of a steady demand for certain types of goods, merely because they supplied the sheltered industries, building and furniture-making; and the housing programmes of the municipalities after the war brought demands for locks and builders' brassfoundry.

The non-ferrous group is of interest if only because it con-stitutes the sole Birmingham staple which maintained a leading position throughout our period. The older trades of magnitude had all declined. The great depression had struck down the gun and button industries. Progressive up to the war, the jewellery trade was crippled after 1914. But the non-ferrous trades, though they could hardly boast of better organized productive units than the other industries, had grown steadily. Caused partly by the sheltered nature of its market this progressive character was due mainly to the fact that the producers were in the fortunate position of being able to adapt themselves easily to the needs of the motor and the electrical industries.

Another group of trades of a very different type had a some-what similar history. This consisted of the bolt, nut, screw and rivet industries, in which employment within our area increased from under 13,000 in 1911 to 18,000 in 1921.[1] Since then the

---

[1] *Census of England and Wales*, 1921, Industry Tables, p. 73.

trades have declined slightly through the loss of certain of their older markets. For instance, the reduction in shipbuilding and in railway development has affected the demand for certain classes of bolts, nuts, rivets and railway fastenings; while the wood-screw manufacture found at the end of the war that much of its export trade, on which it had relied for the disposal of half its output, had been largely captured by the Americans. The screw markets have not been recovered; but the nut-and-bolt makers, on the other hand, now export more than in pre-war years. It is, however, elsewhere that we must look in order to understand how the industry has managed to hold a large part of the advance which it made during the war. We find that, whereas the home demand for black forged nuts and bolts has fallen, that for bright machined nuts and bolts for engineering purposes has risen, and the Darlaston makers have turned also to such allied products as engineers' studs, motor brake-rod parts and strainers for aeroplane rigging. The screw firms, moreover, have found an increasing demand both for wood- and for metal-thread screws for the vehicle trades. Here, again, we have an example of an industry which has been saved from decay by the advance of the motor industry.

The unemployment figures on page 384 show that Willenhall has been among the prosperous towns in our area. The buoyancy of the lock trade throughout the post-war depression has been largely responsible for this. Since 1914 there has been a most marked improvement in the mechanical equipment and in the organization of this industry, and, consequently, manufacturers have not only managed to kill American competition in cylinder locks, but they have also developed a large export trade, which has recently amounted to one-third of the output. A share of the trade's prosperity may be doubtless attributed to the fact that it has supplied sheltered industries, such as furniture-making and building; while the motor trade has provided a new market, and the increased habit of travel has reacted by bringing a larger demand for locks for the travelling-bag makers. Yet the greatly improved organization of the industry is not a factor which can be left out of account.

Alone of the heavy trades the constructional engineering industry has made an advance during the post-war period. This is rather surprising, because the export trade, for which most of the pre-war output was destined, has fallen, and the tendency for the heavier work to move to the coast has persisted. The comparative prosperity of the industry is, however, to be attributed mainly to the advance in the use of steel for building purposes in Great Britain. The rolling-stock firms have also progressed.

The other trades which now rank above their pre-war position are of a very different character from those which we have examined, being unconnected with the main concern of the area —metal. The chemical industry was subject to a vast expansion during the war; new branches were established; and in one Oldbury factory alone no less than 4000 persons were employed at that time. There was, naturally, a decline after the war, and in 1921 the above figure represented the whole employment within the area. This, however, was double the pre-war number, and the industry has certainly not declined since then. A new and flourishing branch which has recently been established at Tipton is the tarmac industry, which obtains material from the local slag heaps.

The change of fashion in women's dress, which has so gravely injured the textile districts, has benefited the West Midland area by bringing about a great expansion in its artificial-silk trade. By 1927 some 5300 persons were employed in this manufacture at Coventry, besides about 3000 in a new factory at Wolverhampton. This was nearly three times the number of employees in 1914. The cocoa, chocolate and sweet trade was also much greater in 1927 than in 1914, a result which may be attributed partly to a fall in the price of cocoa, due to the cheapening of the raw material, and partly to the increasing amount of luxury expenditure on the part of the post-war generation. The whole group of food and drink trades probably employed some 16,000 to 18,000 persons in 1927.

The account of the individual trades which has been given bears out the generalization that the main effect of the war and of the post-war period was to accelerate the tendencies already discernible in the economic life of the area before 1914. The new trades which were growing during the pre-war period— both those which responded immediately to the munitions demand and those which were stationary between 1914 and 1918—have expanded. This applies to the new vehicle trades and to their subsidiaries, to the electrical-apparatus manufacture, and to the machine-tool, artificial-silk, food and drink, and

aluminium hollow-ware industries. Of these the motor, cycle
and allied industries must be singled out for special emphasis.
The number of persons employed in the production of cars,
cycles, tyres and finished components probably amounted in
1927 to about 110,000; while almost every local trade had been
swept within their influence. Forty years previously the group
had employed only a few hundreds.

On the other hand, the industries which were failing in pre-
war days, and which between 1914 and 1918 were revived through
the cessation of Continental imports, have failed to maintain
themselves against the renewal of competition from abroad.
Within this category fall the nail, glass and button industries.
Other trades which were stimulated by war demands and have
also fallen before foreign rivals are the enamelled hollow-ware
and the iron and steel trades.

To industries which depended largely on the foreign markets
—such as the needle, fishhook, nut-and-bolt, constructional
engineering, edge-tool, screw, bedstead, pen, chain and anchor
trades—the war snapped the links with distant customers. Those
trades which were in a strong position and were well organized,
like the screw trade, have managed either to recover a great part
of their lost markets or to find new outlets; but this group has
for the most part been depressed, and there is little hope of any
substantial recovery in the bedstead or chain trades within the
immediate future.

Certain changes of fashion or custom, which were obvious
long before the war, were carried much further between 1914
and 1927, and the result was to accelerate the decay of the
tinplate-ware, cast hollow-ware, bedstead and, in spite of a
temporary revival, the saddlery and harness trades. To a few
industries which had remained progressive up to 1914 a change
in fashion also brought disaster. Thus the jewellery and pin
trades were much smaller in 1927 than in the pre-war years.

Finally, we arrive at the trades which remained buoyant,
either because they supplied in some degree the sheltered industries, or because they were particularly successful in adapting
themselves to meet the needs of the new industries. The lock
and the non-ferrous industries have been considered as examples
of these types of manufacture.

The student of industrial history will find the chief interest of the period in the remarkable adaptability which was shown by certain trades, the older markets of which were subject to decay. Such of the older hardware industries as maintained themselves owed their prosperity in most cases to their ability to turn to engineering components; but perhaps the best example of adaptation has been shown by the Walsall leather trade. Apart from this characteristic, which the period brought out, the more fundamental influences of the war seem to have been the acceleration of the decline of several ancient small metal trades and the rise of the new industries which produce composite products, the speeding up of the transition from hardware to engineering. The loss by several older industries of their export markets has been balanced in some measure by the development of a foreign trade by the new industries; but the change in the destination of the district's imports has been affected. Whereas the losses have occurred in industries whose markets were world-wide, like needles or constructional engineering, the gains have occurred mainly in connection with industries like the motor trade, which sends most of the exports to the Colonies. This is another pre-war tendency which has grown in force.

It is a law of industrial development that the attack on any old-established trade by a competitor should occur first in the lower qualities of a product, and that the more ancient district should retain its market for specialities long after the manufacture of the staple products has passed to other centres. The history of a multitude of local industries bears out this truth. At one period Birmingham and District was one of the chief centres of the gun, flint-glass, saddlery and harness, iron and steel, and the nail trades; but by 1927 the district's concern with these products had come to be confined merely to the high-grade articles or to those produced by ancient methods of manufacture for a specialized and limited market. The staple products manufactured in up-to-date plants had shifted to the newer centres of industry.

This tendency was apparent, in some degree, not only in the above manufactures, but also in all the older trades which were concerned with a crude or simple type of product. During the last two decades the area has been becoming increasingly dependent on exterior sources for its coal, iron and steel, and for other raw and semi-manufactured materials. For some of these it relied not only on other British regions, but on foreign countries as well. Birmingham and District, in fact, has come to concern itself more and more with highly composite products and with finishing processes, and it has been abandoning the primary productive operations and the manufacture of the smaller and simpler finished products for which it was long famous.

TABLE I

The advance or the decline of certain Midland trades since 1923 may be illustrated by the following Tables. The figures, of course, cover the whole country; but there is no reason to suppose that the proportionate change in employment has been markedly different in the West Midlands from elsewhere.

ESTIMATED NUMBER OF INSURED PERSONS UNDER THE UNEMPLOYMENT INSURANCE ACTS

(a) INDUSTRIES WHICH HAVE ADVANCED SINCE 1923

	July 1923	*July 1927*	*Percentage Advance between 1923 and 1927*
Motor vehicle, cycle and aircraft	192,000	233,000	21·4
Electrical engineering . . .	61,000	79,000	30·1
Electrical cable, wire and lamp .	72,000	85,000	17·2
Railway carriage, wagon and tram-car	51,000	56,000	10·7
Iron and steel tube	25,000	28,000	13·3
Rubber	57,000	60,000	5·0
Constructional engineering . .	23,000	27,000	18·2
Silk (including artificial silk) . .	37,000	55,000	47·6
Stove, grate, pipe and general founding	84,000	89,000	6·0

(b) INDUSTRIES WHICH HAVE DECLINED SINCE 1923

	July 1923	*July 1927*	*Percentage Decline between 1923 and 1927*
Glass (excluding bottles and scientific glass)	28,000	26,000	8·0
Watch, clock, plate and jewellery .	49,000	45,000	8·9
Bolt, nut, screw, rivet, nail . .	30,000	26,000	13·3
Chemical	103,000	95,000	7·8
Wire, wire-netting and wire rope .	24,000	23,000	4·1

TABLE II

THE EXPORT TRADE—1913-1927

The rise or decline in the export of certain products with which Birmingham and District is concerned may be judged from the following figures. It will be observed that, with few exceptions, the increases have occurred in the products of the new industries, and the decreases in those of the older trades.

COMMODITIES OF WHICH THE EXPORT IN 1927 WAS GREATER THAN IN 1913

	1913	1924	1925	1927
Motor - cars and commercial vehicles (number) . . .	7,595	12,754	19,315	17,877
Motor-cycles (number) . .	16,850	37,607	46,642	52,805
Pedal-cycles (number) . . .	147,633	200,781	276,468	283,358
Electrical machinery (tons) .	26,860	31,429	33,216	40,878
Bolts and nuts (tons) . . .	24,600	30,700	32,900	29,100
Artificial silk, yarn and piece-goods (pounds sterling, in thousands)	..	4,360	5,412	7,610
Wrought tubes, pipes and fittings (tons)	164,400	167,800	191,900	260,200

COMMODITIES OF WHICH THE EXPORT IN 1927 WAS LESS THAN IN 1913

	1913	1924	1925	1927
Hollow-ware (tons) . . .	37,200	18,900	20,400	15,300
Bedsteads (tons)	20,800	12,600	12,900	11,600
Anchors, chain cables and chains, and grapnels (tons) . . .	34,500	16,200	15,600	15,200
Wood screws (tons) . . .	7,500	3,700	3,700	3,300
Nails, tacks, rivets and washers (tons)	23,000	17,400	17,700	18,600

TABLE III

TABLE SHOWING THE ADVANCE OR DECLINE OF CERTAIN WEST MIDLAND TRADES BETWEEN 1907 AND 1924

(a) INDUSTRIES IN WHICH EMPLOYMENT HAS INCREASED

	Number (in thousands)	
	1907	1924
Paint, colour, varnish . . .	13·8	18·7
Wrought-iron and steel tube . .	20·2	24·3
Motor and cycle	53·6	200·3
Anchor, chain, nail, bolt, nut, screw and rivet	28·0	33·6
Copper and brass, smelting, rolling and casting	21·3	25·3
Silk and artificial silk . . .	31·7	39·2
Rubber	24·0	46·6
Tool, implement	23·6	28·1
Other non-ferrous metal, rolling and casting	9·3	20·5

(b) INDUSTRIES IN WHICH EMPLOYMENT HAS DECLINED

	Number (in thousands)	
	1907	1924
Needle, etc.	13·2	12·1
Small arms	4·9	2·5
Finished brass	38·6	33·2
Jewellery, gold, silver, electro-plate	38·2	33·5
Watch and clock	5·3	4·3
Railway carriage	28·9	28·3
Saddlery, harness, leather goods .	22·6	21·4
Umbrella and stick . . .	7·6	5·5
Brush	11·1	11·0

NOTE TO TABLE III.—Certain points should be borne in mind in judging from this Table the advance or decline of the various local industries. Thus, the artificial-silk trade has been subject to a much greater development than the Table would seem to show, while the local railway rolling-stock trade has certainly not declined during the period. The figures for anchor, chain, nail, bolt, nut, screw and rivet group obscure the true development of the individual trades—the chain and anchor trades have declined, while the manufacture of bolts, nuts and screws has made a very great advance. Practically all the increase in the tube trade has been confined to the weldless-steel tube section. In the leather group, saddlery and harness has become insignificant, while the production of other leather goods has risen to importance. The extent to which the brass trade has tended to become complementary to the engineering industry is illustrated by the advance in the primary section and the decline in the finished-brass section, in which there has been a change-over to electrical- and motor-accessory production.

CHAPTER III

RECENT TENDENCIES IN INDUSTRIAL ORGANIZATION

IT has been shown that the period from 1914 to 1927 saw great changes in the structure of West Midland industry and altered completely the relative importance of the various industries. The failure of certain of the older trades to hold their own was in a large degree due to general causes which they could not control; but, since many of them were failing in the struggle with the foreigner even before the war, part of their misfortunes at any rate must be attributed to defective organization. Birmingham and District was, in fact, paying the penalty of the pioneer. In many of the ancient industries the plant was old-fashioned; the factories were cramped and badly laid out, having grown from small beginnings; while " third generation " family businesses, which were not alert to new developments, were common in them. Frequently the units were too small for economical production; and mutual suspicions, common in long-established competitive private firms, prevented co-operation either for research or to save marketing and productive expenses. To these manufactures the new trades presented a great contrast. The latter had the advantage of starting in days when greater attention was paid to lay-out and organization, and when the union between science and industry was becoming a recognized condition of success. Yet, although this contrast has persisted, it is no longer as marked to-day as it was in the pre-war period. Some of the decaying trades have changed but little their mode of production since 1914; but many other ancient industries, in which modern methods were then incipient and were confined to a few firms, can now be ranged among the well-organized trades. This change can be attributed mainly to the circumstances of the war.

A few years ago it became the fashion to describe as " the new industrial revolution " the changes which have been occurring since the war in the relative importance of the leading British industries and in their localization. But the term might with equal justification be applied to the alteration in the methods of production and to the enormous increase of mechanical equipment which have taken place in certain trades during the last twelve years. In this transformation many of the older Midland trades have had a part, and it may be said without exaggeration that, however disastrous the war may have been to the economic position of certain local industries, its effect on manufacturing technique was almost everywhere beneficial. Between 1914 and 1918, under the pressure of national demands, the mechanical equipment and the organization of the average firms tended to rise to the level of the best. The controlled factories had great sums spent on them for capital extensions; and the others found it necessary to put down new plant to meet the large orders for munitions. Under normal circumstances this increase in the mechanical equipment would have been long delayed, either through lack of capital or through doubts on the part of the manufacturers as to whether the demand for their products would make such capital expenditure worth while. There was a flow of personnel from one firm to another, and a pooling of experience and scientific knowledge. It is true that some plants became " unbalanced " through their war activities; but this was a small evil compared with the great improvements which were effected. And since 1918 the advance has not only been maintained, but has gone very much further in certain industries, as a result of the pressure of the lean years and the greater alertness of the post-war manufacturer.

It is not necessary to describe in detail the mechanical changes within each industry; so we will confine ourselves to a consideration of the main advances common to many. The progress of foundry practice has been very great. The use of oil and of gas-fired furnaces and annealing ovens has spread over a wide field. The frequent stoppages in the coal industry, together with the rise in the wages of the unskilled workers who previously handled the coal or coke, have been to some extent responsible for the adoption of gas or oil fuel; but the fact that important technical advantages can thus be secured was not without its effect. The latter types of fuel are not only easier to handle, but their use enables a more accurate control over temperatures to be obtained. Some of the larger firms have introduced into their foundries electrically driven plants, and so have greatly accelerated the rate of production. The most interesting advance since 1914, however, has been in connection with die-casting and machine-moulding, since it shows the dependence of mechanical methods on the existence of a large market for standardized products. There was a great extension of these processes during the war as a result of the munitions trade; and since 1918 the needs of the motor and electrical industries have provided the required incentive. Nor were the smithies unaffected. After 1914 there arose a large demand for drop-forged parts for aeroplanes, shells and tanks, which resulted in a great growth in the size of the forging plants. The post-war demand has not been sufficient to occupy them completely; but the motor industry has, nevertheless, taken great quantities of forged parts. There has been also an advance in technique. Many parts previously produced under the steam-hammer are now drop-forged; and larger and more complicated articles are manufactured in this way than was possible in pre-war days. If the extension of drop-forging, die-casting and machine-moulding has necessarily had to await the tendency towards mass production, it is also important to remark that parts thus produced require less machining than if made by the older methods. So the advance of these processes is notable, since they are associated with a reduction in the costs of subsequent manufacturing operations. In the rolling mills improvements have been effected so as to give faster production; while there has been a tendency for chill rolls to give place to steel rolls, which have the advantage of imparting a better surface to the metal passing through the mill. In the heavier metal trades, moreover, machine-fed annealing furnaces have become a common feature.

At the same time firms in industries which previously relied largely on hand-labour came to use machine tools for the production of munitions, and after the war these were adapted to the normal range of products. Several of the hardware industries, notably the lock trade, completely reorganized their productive methods, and elaborate machine shops and tool-rooms were set up, where previously the equipment was primitive; while the rise in the scale of production in the new engineering trades resulted in the introduction of quantities of special-purpose machines and automatics into the factories. So, during the war and the depression, there occurred a great increase in the employment of machinery within the area. Everywhere, moreover, the use of electricity for driving the plant has extended; while firms in the more up-to-date industries have resorted to an increasing extent to the method of driving their machinery from individual motors instead of from shafting. This new practice, besides being more economical, keeps the factory cleaner and gives a steadier and more easily adaptable drive to the machines than the older system does.

Equally important advances occurred in connection with the application of scientific methods to industry. Greater attention came to be paid to such problems as the quality and nature of the metals which were to be employed, and the temperatures in the furnaces and annealing ovens. Firms which previously worked by empirical methods were forced, when they came to cater for the munitions demand, to set up their own laboratories where physical and chemical tests could be applied to the metals. The increase in the use of machine tools and in the speed of production was closely associated with the application of metallurgical science to manufacture; for under such conditions frequent stoppages, through broken tools or defective materials, meant a much more serious loss than in the days of leisurely production. It was not only in the engineering trades that this progress was made; for many of the more ancient industries also were affected. Thus the demand for munition metal resulted in raising the quality of the brass throughout the trade to the level of that which had been produced before the war by only a few cartridge-making firms. There was an increase in the use of electrolytic copper by brass manufacturers which enabled a higher quality of metal to be produced; while great strides were made in the manufacture of other non-ferrous metals, especially aluminium.

All these mechanical developments were part of a general movement towards a larger scale of production, which was associated in turn with the tendency towards specialization and standardization. Specialization was not, it is true, particularly evident in trades which were badly hit by the post-war depression; for they were generally forced to broaden the basis of production so as to occupy their plants. For example, the pen-makers began to devote more time to stationers' sundries and to fine stampings for the engineers. The cast hollow-ware firms turned to other classes of hollow-ware and to general castings; the tinplate-ware manufacturers to motor panels, and the saddlery and harness makers to fancy-leather and sports' goods. But in the engineering and other trades which had made the most marked mechanical advance, specialization was the concomitant of mass production. The motor firms, particularly those which turned to cultivate the cheap-car market, have tended to specialize on a narrow range of models; while the makers of starting and lighting sets have carried this movement even further. In the electrical industry, firms which specialized on a small number of products began to rise alongside the great concerns which covered the whole field. The machine-tool industry, however, provides the best example of the tendency. During the nineteenth century machine-tool firms had usually manufactured a wide variety of products. Then, with the growth of a larger demand, each began to concentrate on a narrower range; but the difficulty inherent in this policy was that a specialized business could tender for orders for fitting up factories or arsenals in which many kinds of machine tool would be required, only if it was prepared to act as an agent for many other firms. So, in order to combine the economics of specialization with the advantages of a wide scope of production, the British Association of Machine Tool Makers was formed in 1916. This combine consisted of some eleven firms, several of which were operating within the West Midlands, and its object was to set up joint agencies in different centres at home and abroad to replace the individual representatives. Besides reducing selling costs, moreover, the Association enabled each member to specialize on one or two types of machine; for it could tender for a whole factory plant and then distribute the order among its various specialist members. Several important local firms have remained outside, or have joined merely as affiliated members, who are represented by the joint agents, but are not subject to the Association's rules. Even those firms, however, have been forced to specialize in some degree.

Along with this movement has gone a tendency towards the standardization of products. In the engineering industries, particularly in the motor and electrical trades, the British Engineering Standards Association has done much to standardize the specifications of components; but this has not gone as far as is necessary. In the brassfoundry trade, where the multitude of patterns appears overwhelming, the Masters' Association has made

2 D

attempts to reduce the number; while in the cast hollow-ware industry the number of sizes made has been reduced by joint agreement. Apart from these instances, in which standardization has been partially secured by agreement among competitive manufacturers, a similar result has often been effected merely as a natural consequence of the adoption of mechanical methods of production. An example of this is provided by the lock trade, where the variety of parts and cases has been reduced solely as a result of the supersession of skilled handicraft by the press and machine tool. It must be remembered, however, that while this movement has still far to go among the engineers, there are many local products to which the principle of standardization can never be widely applied, merely because these products are of an ornamental character and serve individual needs. Nor must standardization be confused with a reduction in the variety of finished articles. While these are often associated, they are not necessarily so; for a standardization of components may not be inconsistent with an increase in the types or patterns of a finished article, when that article is of a highly composite character.[1]

The advance of mass-production methods, which have accompanied the fore-mentioned tendencies, may be illustrated by reference to the motor industry, or to that branch of it which, since 1923, has turned to the manufacture of a cheap car. The effect on the plant and the productive process of the application of these principles is seen if the organization of the typical British engineering factory is compared with the new type. In the former there is a number of distinct departments, such as the machine shop, the body shop and the erecting shop, each of which is engaged in some specific process. In the machine shop, machines of the same type are normally found together, and are at work on the production of various articles which, on completion, are taken either to some central shop for inspection and assembly, or to a store, from which they are drawn as required. According

---

[1] The advance of simplification in the area may be illustrated by the following extract, which concerns a leading firm of edge-tool makers. " Our catalogue, ten years ago, gave over three hundred patterns. We now make regularly about seventy-five patterns only, with twenty-five patterns intermediately. . . . With our present simplified range we can set up a series of machines and run three days without a change. With the old three-hundred range we might have to change two or three times a day " (A. Spencer, " Production Methods, etc.," in *System*, February 1927, pp. 75-77).

to the principles of " flow " production, however, the articles to be manufactured move across the floor of the factory in a continuous stream, and at each stage in their progress they are subjected to some process of manufacture or assembly. Machines of the same type are not grouped together as in the older kind of engineering establishment, but they are so arranged that work can flow from operation to operation, and that inspectors can be placed at intervals. In a motor-engine factory of this type, for instance, the machine operations on the cylinder take place in a centrally situated shop, while the other parts move towards it in a stream and receive at each stage some fresh operation. This system reduces internal transport expenses and makes possible the use of special-purpose machines; but it can be applied only when great quantities of standardized products are required. In the assembly of the cheap motor-car and in certain accessory factories the " conveyor system " has come into use, by which the vehicle or component is carried mechanically from one workman to another, each of whom performs some specific operation. This system has penetrated into many trades since the war, as it has come to be realized how much may be saved by the reduction in internal transport costs, by the elimination of the finished store and by more rapid production.

It is important to notice that the application of mass-production principles to the motor industry has reacted on the trades which produce components; for the vast quantities of standardized parts required by makers of the cheap car have carried the new principles of manufacture into the subsidiary industries. Thus the extension of die-casting and machine-moulding in the foundries has been conditioned by the increased demand for standardized motor-castings; and the growth of the drop-forging industry may be similarly explained. Mass-production principles have also been applied to the manufacture of lighting and starting sets in Birmingham; but perhaps the best example of this tendency in industries subsidiary to motor manufacture is afforded by the laminated-spring trade. This industry, until the war, was carried on in very small factories and in workshops, and little use was made of machinery. The demand for standardized springs on the part of the cheap-car makers, however, has resulted in the introduction of American methods of manufacture, by which a considerable number of springs can be pressed into shape at one operation, and a large factory has been established at West Bromwich which is conducted on these mass-production principles.

In nearly all the progressive industries there has occurred, since 1914, a great expansion in the size of the typical producing unit, and the period has seen the emergence of a number of giant concerns, which have surpassed in magnitude even those great integrated firms which once flourished in the Staffordshire iron and coal trade. A few examples may be given. It is recognized, of course, that the number of employees no longer furnishes a good criterion by which size may be judged, and that it gives merely a broad indication of the magnitude of the concern in question; but no other statistical measure is available. In 1927 the leading firm in the tyre and rubber-goods industry employed about 12,000 persons in its local works; a great motor factory at Northfield had some 10,000 employees; the leading cocoa and chocolate firm about the same number; a maker of motor lighting and starting equipment, 7000; and an artificial-silk firm over 8000 in its two factories. Besides these establishments of first-rate magnitude there are a number of other large concerns which employ between 2000 and 5000 persons in the railway material and rolling-stock, motor, cycle, machine-tool, electrical engineering, weighing-machine, screw, rolled-brass and ammunition, welded-tube, aluminium-castings, boilers and general engineering trades. In the weldless-tube industry the typical firm has about 600 employees; while one has 1650. There are several great breweries, to the size of which the number of hands affords no guide. All the giant concerns and many of those in the second category are concerned with the new industries. Few were of any considerable magnitude before 1890, and many of them, indeed, can place their rise to any considerable importance within the last twenty years. It can be seen, then, that the change in the general character of the West Midland producing unit is to be associated mainly with the appearance of the new industries, which are practically all conducted in very large concerns.

But the units in the older hardware trades also have grown since 1914. In the lock manufacture, where before the war no firm employed more than 300 men, the leading concern now has over 800; while several others employ 300 or 400. These factories now serve a large proportion of the trade and very little is left with the workshop. Practically the only outwork which is now to be found in this trade, in which the domestic craftsman was once the typical figure, is in connection with the cutting of keys. In the nut-and-bolt trade, another typical small-scale industry forty years ago, the size of the firms ranges between 200 and 1400 persons. In the non-ferrous industry concerns still vary greatly in size, from the great rolled-brass firms, which employ 3000 men, to small stampers and piercers or outworking casters, who have under 20. But an increasing proportion of the trade has gone to the large firms, mainly because of the change-over to classes of product which can be economically manufactured by machinery. The greater self-containedness on the part of the more substantial concerns, moreover, has tended to eliminate the outworkers, who previously existed in great numbers for the performance of certain processes.

In the enamelled hollow-ware trade, both in the wrought and in the cast sections, the factories are large, and the leading firm employs some 800 persons; while in the new aluminium-ware manufacture the chief firm has 400. The concerns in the galvanized-ware industry are smaller, and many shop owners still survive; but in several factories some 200 persons are engaged. The production of black hollow-ware is still carried on to some extent in small Black Country foundries. In the glass trade, as in several stationary industries, there has been little variation even since 1860 in the magnitude of the producers. The sole firm in the heavy-glass branch employs no more than it did at the beginning of our period, although the output has risen. As for flint-glass manufacture, the leading concern has some 550 employees; four firms have 400 to 500; and a few others have about 100 each.

The producing units in trades which have declined since the war have been reduced in size for the most part, as there have been few attempts towards combination in them or towards the concentration of production on the most efficient plants. This applies to most of the iron and steel, pen, needle, fishhook, gun and button firms, except to such as have changed over to new types of product.

Yet by 1927, in nearly all the trades of the district, whether they fell within the engineering or hardware groups, the typical unit had become the factory, in great contrast to the position half-a-century before. In an historical account, however, there is always a danger of over-emphasizing the extent of any transformation which has taken place, and of giving the impression that a form of organization which has become typical is universal. It should be made clear, therefore, that in many industries the representative factory is still the small factory, and that opportunities for the shop owner, and even for the outworker, are still afforded by certain sections of trades in which the large factory is the rule. This applies not only to the older industries, but to the new engineering trades as well; for the inclusion of the main processes of manufacture in the large units usually creates a place for the small man in the subsidiary operations. Thus the motor industry has given rise to a large number of small firms engaged in machining and repair work; while certain electrical components may be turned out in small shops. Indeed, if the small unit has been forced out of many trades, it has appeared in increasing numbers in others. Further, several of the more ancient manufactures have never been transformed by machinery. The small units are responsible for most of the output of the leather, jewellery and chain trades. In the former a firm with over 200 hands is considered large, and ample opportunities are provided, by the fancy-leather no less than by the old saddlery and harness manufacture, for the shop owner with under 20 hands. This is due mainly to the fact that the nature of the products and the material affords little possibility of employing power-machinery. The small factory has advanced in importance in the manufacture of jewellery during the last twenty years; but the number of little masters is still very great. Only in the making of chains or of electro-plate ware, in which a few large firms have always existed, is production on anything like a large scale. The wrought-chain trade has been declining, and a good deal of the small chain has come to be imported from abroad or produced by the electro-welding process in factories; but much of the industry is still conducted by outworkers or shop owners. The sporting-gun trade is now too insignificant in size to deserve notice. The few master gunmakers who have factories of their own employ less than in pre-war days and seldom have more than 50 men; and the greater part of the industry, except for the manufacture of certain parts which is now carried on in small factories, is conducted in much the same way as it was in 1860. But these once staple manufactures of the area no longer occupy a primary place, and their organization can no longer be counted as typical of the industrial life of Birmingham and the Black Country.

The tendency towards the greater degree of self-containedness which could be observed in many industries in pre-war days has also gone further; for the increase in the output of some firms has made it profitable for them to have the subsidiary operations performed in their own factories. The desire of firms with well-known names to secure a control over the quality of their product by concerning themselves with all the stages of production has also helped towards the integration of processes. Thus many of the larger motor and electrical engineering firms have set up their own foundries since the war; while others do pressing, stamping and electro-plate work, which they previously purchased out. In every case, however, it can be understood that the attainment of a certain volume of production was an essential condition of the establishment of these subsidiary departments. Thus the growth in the size of most units proceeds, first, by an extension of operations within a certain stage, and then, once a certain level of output has been reached, by the assumption of other stages, or of subsidiary processes of manufacture. The development of motor transport carried further this process of sub-integration; for a great many firms which previously relied on the railway companies to distribute their products began after the war to deliver a proportion of their goods by means of their own fleets of motor-lorries and vans. This applies to large firms in almost every trade, but particularly to those which produce parts and accessories for the local engineering factories.

The centrifugal movement, which was forcing industries from the thickly populated areas, continued during the war and the post-war periods, because of the manufacturer's need for sites which would permit a larger scale of operations. The new giant concerns had their establishments, with few exceptions, on the outskirts of the larger towns in districts previously of a rural character. The Bushbury district, to the north of Wolverhampton, became industrialized as a result of the growth of the electrical, motor-car and engineering trades. There was a movement from Walsall, where factories had previously been confined to a very congested area, to the suburbs. Several new motor and electrical works were established on the outskirts of Coventry. In the Witton district of Birmingham the electrical and the aluminium hollow-ware industries were extended; the great Dunlop concern removed to Castle Bromwich, where the gigantic Fort Dunlop factory, begun in 1916, came into full operation in 1923. There were developments at Selly Oak, Northfield, Hunnington, and elsewhere on the outskirts of Birmingham.

Yet, while this movement was taking place in most parts of our area, the decline in certain of the older domestic industries has had a contrary effect. It has been shown that at one time large numbers of domestic workers, such as nailers, needle-makers and lock-makers, lived in villages beyond the boundaries of the area. The decline in these industries, or their concentration in factories, however, has brought an end to the industrial life of these villages; while the new means of transport, together with the increasing demand for dairy and market-garden produce from the great towns, has stimulated the agricultural activity of the district's " green borderland." Thus, whereas the leading industrialists have been carrying manufacture into areas which were previously rural, the decline in the scattered domestic industries has given rise to a tendency for some districts to revert to agriculture.

The changes in methods of management and factory control also were far-reaching. The decay of the subcontracting system was proceeding during the pre-war era, but in 1914 there were many trades which were not affected. The reforms in organiza-tion undertaken by the Ministry of Munitions, the introduction of a costing system into trades in which it was non-existent before 1914, the change in personnel, and the general destruc-tion of traditional methods in the effort towards greater efficiency, all dealt heavy blows at subcontracting. Where the system sur-vived the war it was in nearly every instance killed by the reorganization of the manufacturing process and the speeding up of production which followed in many trades on the general reduction in the normal working day in 1919 and 1920. The marked effect of a shortening of the working day on industrial organization has been noted in previous periods; but on few occasions were the results as conclusive as in 1919 and 1920. The necessity in a modern business that the management should exercise a detailed control over the progress of work through the various departments, the need for the application of scientific methods, and the increased use of machinery have all helped to drive out the subcontractor, and to throw more functions on the technical and commercial staffs. The greater attention which has come to be devoted to management—an inevitable result of the increased complexity of the productive process—has shown the advantage of removing certain duties from the foreman, such as engaging and instructing workmen, fixing piece-rates and inspecting work, and of placing them with specialist departments. In the brass-rolling mills, for example, whereas previously the overhand had run the works, now the responsibility was thrown on the works manager and the laboratory. In the paint trade, again, the trained chemist has come to stand in the place of the foreman with his empirical methods. In a whole series of industries, indeed, management became more highly centralized, and the subcontractor, instead of accepting great responsibility and using his experience for directing the performance of most of the tasks of his shop, was relegated to the position of a foreman, who acts under detailed directions from the office or the laboratory. Even in the trades in which the old system has continued, its form is much modified.

On the whole, this development meant greater efficiency, and arose inevitably from the scale and methods of production in modern industry; but, social considerations apart, the change was not unaccompanied by loss, for with a centralized system of management, responsibility is shifted from below, and the vast store of experience, inventiveness and initiative among the rank and file remains largely untapped. The introduction of " suggestion schemes " and of similar methods for interesting the worker in the problem of manufacture has thus become much more necessary in modern times than it was when a great deal of responsibility rested with the men in the shop.

A pre-war tendency which has been carried much further was that towards reducing the functions of the middleman. The rise in the size of the producing units, which enabled manufacturers to support adequate sales departments, together with the pressure of foreign competition, which emphasized the necessity of a close contact between producer and customer, were mainly responsible for the movement. It became increasingly the practice for firms to set up London showrooms, to appoint their own agents at home and abroad, to maintain staffs of travelling representatives, and to establish depots in various parts of the country from which they could distribute their goods. The greater use of advertisement to impress certain brands or names on the public notice, and so to create a more direct channel from the producer, was also a feature of the period. The old-time factor had by this time, indeed, become a mere wholesale merchant, and such factoring as existed was undertaken mainly by other manufacturers. The increasing specialization of certain trades tended, if anything, to increase the amount of factoring which makers, who had reduced their own range of products, performed.

One noticeable result of the war has been to draw manufacturers who were previously competitive closer together, for they learned from their experience during the war of the advantages of co-operation for the solution of common problems. In trades in which the units had previously preserved a jealous isolation one from another a marked advance was made. After 1919 many of them came together for the financing of joint research — a development which received in some industries Government support. On the marketing side the new spirit was evident in the formation of such bodies as the Brass and Copper Extended Uses Council, the function of which was to advertise co-operatively the uses to which the non-ferrous metals might be put. The jewellers, who had a long tradition of co-operative effort, came together during the war to finance, with the help of the Government, a shipment of samples to South America, with the object of capturing markets which previously had been held by the Germans. A very interesting example of these efforts at co-operation was provided by the gun trade. The leading master gunmakers in 1919 formed themselves into a company, called the Birmingham Registered Gunmakers' Association, the object of which was to buy gun parts co-operatively for the trade and so reduce costs. The method has resulted in considerable savings, because the purchase of parts in quantity has enabled certain manufacturers of parts to adopt mechanical methods of production, and so to supply the goods more cheaply.

In another competitive trade, the needle industry, makers have joined together for the purpose of establishing a factory to produce knitting-needles for the hosiery manufacturers.

Finally, we come to the post-war tendency to combination within the area. This, however, cannot with advantage be discussed in any detail, for it is so closely linked with national industrial tendencies that the local combination movement cannot be treated in isolation, and does not, therefore, properly fall within the scope of a history that is limiting its field to a particular district. We shall confine ourselves, therefore, to a few reflections on this subject, and shall not attempt to treat it comprehensively.

In this connection, the most obvious development since the war has been the absorption of a number of important local concerns by great national combines, and the consequent linking up of the Midland industry with that of the whole country. For example, the post-war growth of the Vickers' concern led to the acquisition of the local rolling-stock combine, together with several electrical, brassfoundry and other non-ferrous firms. Another great rolling-stock concern has passed under the control of Messrs Cammell-Laird. The tube combine, Messrs Stewarts & Lloyds, has extended its interests by acquiring the steelworks at Bilston, which is in a position to furnish raw materials to the tube factories. Practically all the largest producers of electrical apparatus have passed under the control of the General Electric Company, the English Electric Company or the British Thomson Houston Company. Messrs Guest, Keen & Nettlefold have acquired a number of other local firms, including a motor-wheel and hollow-ware factory at Bilston, and a railway-fastening works at Wolverhampton. Several drop-forging plants have passed to a large Sheffield combine. The Imperial Chemical Industries has come to include many local firms which produce ammunition, explosives, chemicals, and non-ferrous sheet, tube and wire. The great local cocoa and chocolate firm has become linked with manufacturers in other parts of the country; while the artificial-silk concern has extended its interests, not only in this country, but abroad, and has entered into agreement with Continental producers respecting markets.

The main facts which emerge from an examination of the combination movement, as far as amalgamations are concerned, is that, while instances of the movement are to be found in the majority of industries, the leading examples have been confined to the newer trades, or to those which are engaged with engineering products. In the older industries—in the jewellery, leather goods, needle, brush, pen, wrought-chain, lock, gun, button, glass and bedstead manufactures—there have been few important amalgamations, and even such price associations or pools as have been formed have proved ineffective. The brass and non-ferrous trade, in which a number of amalgamations have occurred, stands out as an exception among the older finished manufactures; but this industry, it must be remembered, has become largely subsidiary in many of its branches to the engineering and the electrical trades. Thus, while the newer local industries have yielded easily to the post-war tendency to combination, and while their control has passed to a large extent into the hands of combines with nation-wide interests, the older trades have, in the main, held themselves aloof from the prevailing tendency.

There are fairly obvious reasons for this contrast. In the first place, many of the older trades do not lend themselves to any form of price-fixing organization, because of the immense variety in the design and quality of the finished products. Under such circumstances, even when it is possible to arrive at an agreement concerning prices, it is almost impossible to enforce it or to detect disloyalty. Further, there still exists in nearly all the older trades to which reference has been made a considerable number of shop owners and little masters. These often produce articles which are different in quality from those of the larger firms, and they could not secure a market for their products unless they sold at prices lower than those charged by concerns of repute. It is, therefore, almost impossible to draw these small producers into a combine. If the larger firms agree to raise prices or to limit output in such an industry, the result would be to throw more trade into the hands of the small masters. Thus the difficulty of grading products, together with the small scale and the large number of the producing units, has maintained competitive conditions over a wide field of Midland industry. Besides this, the older trades have not presented temptations to the great national combines which have absorbed so many of the local engineering plants. Not only are these industries highly localized within our area and conducted in small units, but many of them are engaged on products which do not easily fit in with the range of articles manufactured by a great combine, and which are not complementary to its main interest. The steel firms naturally tend to absorb its customers; the electrical or the engineering concerns may take up the production of their raw materials, castings, forgings and components. But the manufacture of jewellery, leather goods, needles, locks and other metal smallwares is not likely to attract the promoter of a great amalgamation. The units of which such trades are made up are usually not suitable for the purpose; the economies which could be effected in manufacturing operations as a result of combination are generally small; the possibility of securing anything in the nature of a monopoly is remote; and, since the quantity of materials which they employ is comparatively small, such trades do not attract the large makers of raw products. Finally, it is probably fair to say that many of these industries are in the hands of private firms with a long tradition of competition behind them, and are somewhat out of touch with modern tendencies.

It has been said that the new industries have been widely affected by the post-war combination movement; but there has been one exception—viz. the motor industry. This has remained almost entirely competitive in its organization. It is true that a few instances of amalgamation have occurred and that some important firms are now included within certain great combines; but little has been done to limit competition among producers, as in the electrical or the artificial-silk industries. The various motor trade associations which exist have exercised a certain control over marketing and competitive methods, as explained in an earlier chapter; but the regulation has never extended to prices. The explanation is to be found partly in the very rapid expansion of the demand since the war—an expansion which naturally called many new producers into existence, and also rendered joint control over prices less imperative than in most other trades. But the main reason is certainly to be found in the great variety in the design and quality of motor-cars; for this has made price agreements almost impossible to effect. There seems now, however, reason to suppose that these competitive conditions are drawing to a close. The design, performance and price of cars are tending to approximate to certain standards within a comparatively small number of grades. Many small firms, moreover, have disappeared under the pressure of fierce competition, and a very large proportion of the cheap-car trade has passed into the hands of two firms. Thus an important condition of combination—*i.e.* the reduction of the producers to a small number—is being satisfied, and it seems likely that the process of amalgamation, already on foot, will ultimately destroy the competitive conditions which now prevail. At the same time the fact that many of the rival firms are under the personal control of forceful men, who were pioneers in the industry, and who may not be willing to sink their individuality in a combine, is likely to prevent this goal being rapidly attained.

TABLE SHOWING THE ADVANCE IN THE EMPLOYMENT OF POWER BY CERTAIN LOCAL INDUSTRIES, 1907-1924[1]

	H.P. (*thousands*)		H.P. *per Person employed*	
	1907	*1924*	*1907*	*1924*
Rolling, smelting and founding .	1,383·3	2,290·4	5·30	9·15
Non-ferrous rolling and casting (other than copper and brass) .	18·5	100·0	1·99	4·88
Wrought-iron and steel tube .	23·0	97·0	1·14	3·99
Wire	31·0	92·0	1·69	3·68
Copper and brass smelting, rolling and casting	43·8	92·2	2·06	3·64
Railway carriage . . .	30·4	64·8	1·05	2·29
Rubber	27·4	106·2	1·13	2·28
Engineering	327·9	1,120·9	0·72	1·91
Anchor, chain, bolt, nut, screw and rivet	23·0	50·2	0·82	1·49
Silk and artificial silk . .	18·8	53·7	0·59	1·37
Small arms	2·6	3·1	0·53	1·24
Motor and cycle . . .	15·3	194·1	0·28	0·97
Finished brass . . .	12·8	26·5	0·33	0·80
Hardware, hollow-ware and bedstead	..	57·8	..	0·80
Needle, etc.	3·3	7·4	0·25	0·61
Jewellery, etc. . . .	6·5	20·7	0·17	0·62
Brush	2·1	6·3	0·19	0·57
Umbrella and stick . . .	1·0	2·3	0·13	0·42
Saddlery, harness and leather goods	2·1	5·2	0·09	0·24

[1] Committee on Industry and Trade, *Further Factors in Industrial and Commercial Efficiency*, p. 60 *et seq.*

The greatest percentage increases of the figures of the power available per head in 1924 on those of 1907 were shown by the jewellery and plate

(265 per cent.), the iron and steel tube (250 per cent.), the motor and cycle (241 per cent.), the umbrella and stick (223 per cent.), and the brush trades (200 per cent.). The leather goods, engineering and watch trades also made a considerable advance. In the case of the jewellery, leather goods, umbrella, watch and brush trades, where the amount of mechanical power employed is still small, the period marks the beginning of the transition from handicraft to machine production. The introduction of machinery into the brush trade was largely influenced by the fixing of Trade Board rates which deprived the industry of its cheap labour. The advance in the tube trade is to be attributed partly to an improvement in welded-tube production; but mainly to the increased importance of the weldless-tube section, which requires a great amount of power-driven machinery. The change in the vehicle trades is to be attributed to the increased market which has made the adoption of mass-production methods possible. The smallest percentage advances per head occurred in such industries as rolling, smelting and founding (both ferrous and non-ferrous), which have long been highly equipped mechanically, and in the anchor, chain, screw, rivet, nut-and-bolt group. In this case, most of the chains are still hand-welded, in spite of the increase of the electro-welding process for small chains; while the screw trade has for three-quarters of a century relied on automatic machinery. The advance in this group was probably confined to the nut-and-bolt section.

CHAPTER IV

SUMMARY AND CONCLUSIONS

THE story of the rise of Birmingham and District to industrial greatness has now been outlined, and the changes in its structure during the last sixty years have been indicated in some detail. It has also been shown how the leading industries were organized at different periods with respect to production and marketing, and the broad changes in the scale of manufacture and in administrative methods have been described and explained. It now remains to summarize the main aspects of this course of development and to emphasize the chief conclusions which have been drawn from the facts presented in this survey. With these objects in view, then, let us first of all turn to the transformation which has occurred in the type of industry conducted within the area.

Although Birmingham and District had no direct share in the reorganization and the expansion of the textile trades with which the early years of the modern industrial era are mainly associated, it was during the last quarter of the eighteenth century, when those changes were taking place, that our district first achieved a position of great industrial importance. The rise of the area was, from the first, connected mainly with the growth in the size of the metal trades, and in particular with the expansion of the iron industry, which followed on the application of coal to the smelting and fining processes. It was then that the mineral resources of South Staffordshire, with its easily accessible coal, ironstone and limestone, began to exercise an attraction for the new iron industry of which the area was to remain a leading centre for nearly a century. Meanwhile the local supplies of fuel, materials and skill began to give rise to a host of metal-using trades. New industries which were to minister to the fresh needs of the period took root. Attracted to its material and human resources, trades migrated into the district from many different parts of the country. The older local manufactures expanded, or split up to form new industries, as the demands for metal products increased in extent and variety. So, by 1800, Birmingham and District was already the seat of a flourishing iron industry on one hand, and of a host of small metal trades on the other.

Throughout the first three-quarters of the nineteenth century the forces which had led to the area's rise to importance continued to operate. The steady growth in the demand for iron and for the cruder iron products meant a progressive expansion of the heavy industries. The development of canals and of railways opened up wider markets and created new industries to minister to the needs of the transport services. The great increase in the population and in the wealth of the country brought rapid expansion to the finished-metal trades and to all others which supplied articles for the household or for personal adornment; and there was a marked growth in the export trade. A few of the older manufactures were injured by changes of fashion—as in the case of the metal-button trade—or reduced in size by the discovery of new processes—as when the silver-plate industry was overwhelmed by the introduction of the electro-deposition process. But the area usually gathered to itself the new trades which rose on the ruins of the old, and only in one case, the nail trade, did substitutions of this kind have any prolonged or serious effect on prosperity. So, up to the sixties, the history of the district during the nineteenth century was that of a rapid advance along the lines laid down in an earlier period, and the result was to leave the area the hardware centre of the country and a major seat of iron production. The culminating point in this development was reached in the boom which was coincident with the Franco-German War; and this marked the concluding phase of the old industrial era.

By that time a distinction, which had been obvious more than a century previously, between the activities of Birmingham and of the Black Country had been emphasized. The former had become the home of the more highly finished products, expressed in many different metals; the Black Country was concerned mainly with the heavy industries and the cruder manufactures. There were certain trades which were fairly equally shared between the two sections, and these were for the most part the manufactures in which the advantages of the presence of highly skilled labour and of proximity to raw materials were evenly balanced. The Black Country's industrial life was based largely on iron and coal trades. It produced a third of the wrought-iron of the country and about a ninth of its pig-iron. It had become an important centre of heavy structural ironwork; while its

2 E

chief small-metal industry was still the wrought-nail trade. In addition to these widely scattered trades there were the highly localized manufactures — tubes at Wednesbury, nuts and bolts at Darlaston, flint glass at Stourbridge, hollow-ware at West Bromwich and Wolverhampton, locks at Willenhall, chains at Cradley, saddlery and harness at Walsall, tinplate and japanned wares at Wolverhampton, and springs at West Bromwich. Birmingham had a share of some of these products, such as saddlery and harness, tinplate wares, flint glass and edge tools; but its four staple industries were the brass, jewellery, gun and button trades. Other manufactures of smaller importance, but peculiar to Birmingham, were the pen, bedstead and wire-goods trades. Such was the area at the end of a century of rapid growth.

The great depression which lay on industry from 1875 to 1886, with only a short interval of comparative prosperity, stands as a watershed between two industrial eras. During this decade of bad trade, weaknesses in the competitive strength of the local manufactures were revealed, and some industries were struck down and were never to recover. When the area emerged from the depression, its character had undergone a fundamental change, and it was obvious that the direction of its future growth would be widely different from that of the past. During this period the great iron industry, to which the exhaustion of the local raw-material supplies had long been a menace, was overthrown from its high position among the local manufactures, and from being one of the leading iron centres in the country the area sank to a place of small importance in that respect. It is probable that lack of large supplies of coking coal and of ore would have brought slow decay to this industry in any case; but another cause must be sought to account for the extraordinary rapidity of the decline. This was the introduction of Bessemer and of open-hearth steel and the supersession of wrought-iron as the staple material of the metal-using trades. The production of these forms of steel necessitated the construction of new plants. These were naturally set up in coastal districts, which provided convenient sites for dealing with the export trade and for handling the foreign supplies of hæmatite required in the acid process. At the same time foreign competition first began to threaten seriously the markets of the local manufacturers; tariff walls were raised against Birmingham products, and several of the leading finished trades of the district found their growth retarded in consequence. A few of them—viz. the gun, button and flint-glass industries—declined greatly in magnitude after 1875. A further influence in bringing decay to several trades which previously depended on the manual skill of the Midland craftsmen was the introduction of mechanical methods of manufacture. This adversely affected not only the trades already mentioned as having declined, but also the larger and more widely scattered wrought-nail industry.

These tendencies to which the depression gave rise, or which it greatly accentuated, persisted after it had passed away. The heavy trades continued their migration to the coast. Other industries were forced to surrender a larger and larger part of their market to the foreigner; while many others during the quarter of a century prior to the war remained practically stationary. The advance of mechanical methods which followed the introduction of basic steel into the small metal industries was more marked on the Continent than among the local manufactures, where the weight of long traditions, of conservative employers and workmen, and of existing plant delayed the advent of new methods. Certain industries which formerly were handicrafts, such as the lock trade, were successfully reorganized, and so managed to preserve their importance; but many of the older staple manufactures were sinking to the position of minor trades in the pre-war period. The economic structure of the area, moreover, was seriously shaken by the change in habits and taste which coincided with the end of the Victorian era, and by a number of sweeping innovations which rendered obsolete the products of several important local trades. Among these were the tinplate- and japanned-ware, the saddlery and harness, the metal-bedstead and the cast-iron hollow-ware trades, which had remained prosperous until the last decade of the century, but which declined rapidly after 1900. So, by the outbreak of the war, several of the trades which counted as staples before 1875 were of small importance; while many had failed to develop in proportion to the expansion of the area's population and of its industrial activities. The only large industries of the old era which continued to advance rapidly down to 1914 were the jewellery and the brass and copper manufactures.

In spite of the decay of many once important trades the area

still increased after 1886 in population and industrial importance. Though it could no longer claim to possess any great
natural wealth—once the basis of its prosperity—the area had
built up a reserve of skilled labour and of organizing ability,
and these valuable assets attracted the newer manufactures as
the older ones fell away. The area's expansion after 1886,
indeed, was connected mainly with industries other than those
on which it had been primarily engaged during the first three-
quarters of the nineteenth century. These new industries were
concerned either with finished articles of a different character
from that hitherto associated with the area's products — *e.g.*
artificial-silk, food and drink, and rubber manufactures—or with
highly composite products, such as cycles, motor-cars, machine
tools and electrical apparatus. These engineering trades, calling
as they did for a multitude of different components, found an
area with a diverse industrial life particularly suitable for their
localization; while several of the older trades, notably the screw,
nut-and-bolt, brass and foundry industries, benefited by these
new demands. By 1914—the next great dividing-line in our
industrial history—while the coal trade was of small importance
and the iron industry no longer dominated the economic structure of the Black Country, and while many of the more ancient
finished manufactures had decayed, there had thus arisen a
number of new trades, of which the engineering group was the
largest, to preserve the area's prosperity. The district could
then indeed claim to be an engineering as much as a hardware
centre, especially as many of the older hardware trades had
changed over to the production of engineering components, and
the attention of local manufacturers had tended increasingly to
be directed towards finishing processes and towards highly
manufactured products.

Apart from its immediate effects, the main influence of the
war was to stimulate the broad changes already in progress. By
creating a surplus of productive capacity in the iron and steel
industry of this and other countries it dealt a heavy blow at all
districts in which the trade was being least profitably conducted, and South Staffordshire was one of these. Many additional furnaces were blown out after 1920. The wrought-iron
production suffered as basic steel forced its way into markets
previously served by the products of the puddling furnace and

as cheap Belgian iron invaded the country. The coal output of the Black Country dwindled to insignificance. To such of the older finished manufactures as relied on the export trade the war brought a decline, because it closed their foreign markets and so stimulated the growth of new sources of supply. By accelerating changes in taste and fashion it brought down several old industries which had been progressive up to 1914, such as the jewellery and the pin trades. In many of the hardware industries, indeed, the war and the subsequent slump played the same part as the great depression had in the history of the local iron trade. Both of these occurrences gave additional strength to new tendencies and rendered obvious economic weaknesses which had escaped notice during periods of less serious stress.

If the last fourteen years have been disastrous for many of the older manufactures, however, this is not true of all branches of the local economic life. The newer industries—the motor, cycle, electrical, artificial-silk, rubber, and the food and drink trades— which were making great progress even in pre-war days, have expanded enormously, and the comparative prosperity of the area since the war must be attributed entirely to that development. Of the older staple manufactures, only the brass trade has maintained a high position for itself; but even that trade has been far outstripped by the motor and cycle industries.

Certain aspects of this course of development have a general economic significance, and these may now be considered. First of all it is evident that the economic history of Birmingham and District during the modern industrial epoch falls into three main periods, each of which differs from the others in respect both of the rate and of the direction of progress. The first period stretches from the last quarter of the eighteenth century to about 1860, and covers, roughly, what may be known as the Malleable Iron Period. During this time, not only was the great iron trade built up, but there was also a very rapid growth in the number and in the size of the hardware and other finished-goods industries. By 1860, however, this progress was slowing down. The iron trade was then growing only gradually; several of the hardware manufactures had ceased to expand; others were making only slight advances; and the introduction of new industries by the splitting up of older manufactures in response to fresh needs had ceased. The next period covers, roughly, the twenty-five years from 1860 to the end of the great depression. In spite of the short-lived spurt at the time of the Franco-German War the area's industrial development during this period was very slight. A few trades made a considerable advance; but even their progress could not be compared with their rapid growth before 1860. And most of the manufactures were stationary or only slowly increasing, while some of the leading ones had been subject to a rapid decline. Nor did any important new industries rise to compensate for the interruption in the rate of progress of the older manufactures. British industrial supremacy gave place to an international struggle for markets; readjustments of far-reaching importance occurred in the metal trades; and the progress of Birmingham and District definitely slowed down. After 1886 we enter another epoch—an epoch of rapid development upon new lines—an epoch during which the main interests of the area shifted from hardware to engineering. The production of crude and massive articles on the one hand, and of light-metal articles on the other, gave place to the manufacture of highly finished or highly composite products, and there was a tendency towards an increasing concern with finishing processes. The progress of the area during this last period has not been so general or so uninterrupted as during the era preceding 1860; for in the course of this change-over to the new industries the district has been slowly shedding the more ancient trades. But developments of great magnitude have occurred and are still going on. So the main stages in Birmingham and District's history may be expressed as follows:

1785-1860.—The Malleable Iron Age: the period of the area's supremacy as a hardware-producing centre; an era of rapid growth in the size and variety of industries.

1860-1886.—The period of the culminating boom and of the great depression: the end of the Iron Age and the beginning of foreign competition in the finished manufactures; an era of readjustment and of only slow growth.

1886-1927.—The period of the change-over from hardware to engineering, of an increasing concern with composite products and finishing processes: an era of the rapid advance of new industries and of the slow decay of old trades.

We have seen that as the older staples surrendered to competitors in other districts at home and abroad their place was taken by manufactures of a new type, but we have still to discuss how this transformation in the district's character was so successfully effected. It remains to give an explanation of the economic recovery of the area, the industrial structure of which had been shattered by foreign competition, by the exhaustion of its raw materials, by the supersession of its products by those of new machine-using industries, and by changes in fashion. The recovery is of course the more remarkable since Birmingham and District was seriously handicapped by its distance from the sea. The problem involves a consideration of a number of separate factors, such as the character and capacity of the inhabitants, the period at which the change was effected, and the relation of the old trades to the new. It is obvious that an industrial area which is well supplied with capital equipment, enterprising manufacturers and skilled workers will have a better chance of securing a large share in any new industries that may arise than districts which are less well endowed. Further, the stimulus to adopt the new trades will be particularly keen at times when the demands for the older products of the area are failing. Now Birmingham and District was more seriously injured than any other by the changes which came over the metal trades during the seventies and early eighties; and so the local manufacturers had a much greater inducement than those of centres which remained comparatively prosperous to engage in new industries. This strong inducement rather than any special quality of superior adaptability on the part of the West Midland population was one of the leading factors in effecting the successful transition. There are countless instances of this change-over from old to new trades during the last decades of the nineteenth century. Flourishing cycle-saddle or fancy-leather goods firms rose on the ruins of the saddlery and harness business. Saddlers' ironmongery manufacturers turned to the production of brace-fittings and small motor parts. A host of manufacturers, from those producing rifles and general engineering work to tinplate-ware makers, changed to cycle, and later to motor-car, production. Cast-iron hollow-ware producers launched out as manufacturers of motor and electrical castings, sanitary fittings, motor wheels, as well as of stamped-steel hollow-ware. Constructional engineers and boiler-makers took up the trade in motor-frame pressings and wheels. Factories engaged in producing watch movements turned to the manufacture of small bolts, nuts and screws for engineering purposes. Brassfounders became concerned with lighting and starting equipment for cars, and the non-ferrous mills with tubes and strip metal for motor component factories. Others in the brass trade took up the production of electrical equipment. Pen-makers began to produce light stampings for the motor and aeroplane factories, and pearl-button manufacturers took advantage of the demand for electric-light switches. These are but a few examples of the changes which have occurred in the history of certain West Midland firms, and these illustrate the readiness and ability of manufacturers to alter the scope of their production when a strong inducement is present.

Furthermore, it is not only manufacturers in depressed industries who bring new trades to an area, for promoters from outside will naturally tend to choose, as the seat of their fresh enterprises, localities in which there is a surplus of skilled labour of the type which they require. Thus the West Midlands saw much of the labour which had been displaced from its older industries drawn into new manufactures during the last two decades of the nineteenth century. It is evident, however, that these influences on the localization of new industries have been in modern times modified by other factors; for the most depressed areas during the post-war period have failed conspicuously to attract the new and the expanding trades. Apart from the question of the relative cost of sites and the burden of rates, one reason for this has undoubtedly been the desire of manufacturers to set up their new factories in districts where organized labour is less powerful and class antagonism less bitter than it is, for example, in the coal-mining areas. In Birmingham and District, however, labour troubles have never reached serious proportions; and it must also be remembered that forty years ago, when these transitions were taking place in this area, the new engineering industries, the motor, cycle and electrical trades, required a large proportion of highly skilled labour. It was not then possible, as it has since become with the increase in the use of machinery and in the division of labour in these trades, for an employer to make use of large numbers of semi-skilled workers, whom he himself could train in his factory.

Besides this, Birmingham and District had, and still has,

special qualities which rendered it particularly adaptable. The area, as we have seen, was remarkable for its extreme versatility; and the existence within it of a multiplicity of trades meant that it came into contact with the economic life of the nation at a greater number of points than did the more specialized districts. It was in touch with a greater variety of developments. Consequently, when new industries appeared, all of which bore some relation to existing forms of enterprise, Birmingham and District could reasonably expect to attract a larger share of them than the specializing districts. This was particularly the case when the new trades were of a type which were concerned with highly composite products, for many of the local industries could without difficulty adapt themselves to the production of the components required, however varied they might be. For the motor industry, to give an example, the area could supply ferrous and non-ferrous castings, forgings, pressed steelwork, tubes in steel, brass or copper, wirework, axles and wheels, leather fittings and upholstery, copper and brass strip, electroplating work, paint and varnish, merely by drawing on the resources of existing trades. Thus it seems true to say that an area whose economic life is distinguished by the variety of its pursuits will be more adaptable and more capable of effecting rapid transitions from old to new types of industry than districts with a specialized industrial life.

The multiplicity of industries within Birmingham itself and the other larger local towns has probably helped to maintain family earnings during periods of depression at a higher level than in the more specialist centres; while the great flexibility and resilience of the area have done much to mitigate distress among the workers during times of far-reaching industrial transitions. But the mobility of labour within the district has been frequently exaggerated. The men with highly special skill could not, on the decay of their industry, hope to employ their ability to anything like its full advantage in new trades. This was particularly true of those who had been engaged in handicrafts, which were slowly overthrown with the advance of mechanical methods, and many skilled workers of that type sank inevitably to the position of semi-skilled operatives. Where the area benefited from the continually increasing variety of its industries was in the fact that the recruitment of labour soon dried up in the decaying trades, since the children of employees in the latter could easily find openings in more prosperous manufactures. This advantage, however, was not equally shared by all parts of the district. We have seen that the decay of the failing industries took place more rapidly in Birmingham, where the industrial life was exceptionally varied, than in the Black Country towns with their more specialized pursuits. In these places, indeed, there were many trades which long continued to survive merely because it was possible for employers to effect progressive reductions in the wages of workers, who had no alternative employment in their immediate neighbourhood, and whose children were forced to enter the older manufactures. So it is evident that, although the area was comparatively small, the labour force did not respond as rapidly as has been sometimes suggested to changes in the relative wage-rates in different industries. The distance of a very few miles proved a serious barrier to migrations on any considerable scale to more profitable manufactures.

The history of Birmingham and District emphasizes the fact that changes in the general price-level, which are associated with the trade cycle, are among the most potent immediate causes of industrial transformation. The weaknesses inherent in an industry may be obscured during the boom and may escape the notice of a contemporary. It is during the period of the depression, especially when this is coincident with the beginning of a long downward trend in prices due to monetary factors, that the weaknesses in the industrial structure are revealed. During the depression of the later sixties there were signs that the exhaustion of the Black Country's raw materials and the rise of other metal centres would ultimately bring decay to the great local iron trade; but in the course of the ensuing boom this staple industry rose to its zenith and was responsible for its maximum output during the century. Then in the middle seventies, when prices fell, the competitive weakness of South Staffordshire relative to newer centres was fully revealed, and its great iron industry collapsed.

Further, our history illustrates that frequently a period of exceptionally great demand is ultimately responsible not only for a subsequent temporary depression, but for permanent decay. This is especially true when the swollen demand arises from some abnormal or temporary source, as in the case of the gun-makers in the sixties and early seventies. For the result is to cause neglect of the normal markets in the anxiety of manufacturers to serve those which are temporarily more profitable; and this induces the older customers to seek for new suppliers who may be found firmly established in the older markets when the exceptional conditions have passed away. The temporary severance of connections with old customers has been, in fact, a frequent cause of decline in local industries. Examples have been quoted to show that this severance has often taken place during a boom of unusual magnitude; but the Great War, of course, provided the most numerous instances of this kind.

Illustrations of another general tendency which is associated with periods of great industrial change are given by this survey. The attack by foreign competitors on established trades occurs in connection with the lower grades of product; and it is always a very long process before the predominance of the older areas in the higher qualities has been shattered. The loss of the bulk trade is usually due to the fact that new producers are able to start with fresh plants and up-to-date methods. In this way they can manufacture more cheaply than the older producing districts, which are handicapped on the introduction of new machinery by the existence of obsolete plant and of conservative traditions. Where the whole or the most profitable part of the trade is affected by new productive methods, a stimulus to change is given to the older manufacturers, who may then successfully reorganize themselves, and may maintain their position against the attacks of foreign competitors, as in the case of the Willenhall lock trade. But where the producer is left with a choice between reorganization, so as to cater for the bulk trade, and specialization on high-grade commodities manufactured according to older methods, then the stronger inducement is for him to pursue the latter policy. The former plan involves not only heavy capital expenditure but also great risk, since the bulk trade which the manufacturer aims at preserving is a highly competitive one. On the other hand, the market in high-grade goods is usually secure; for new producing countries seldom have the skilled labour and experience which the manufacture of such commodities requires. Thus in many of the older industries of the area, such as the flint-glass and gun trades, while the main classes of product, turned out by mechanical methods, have been captured by the foreigner, the local makers have been left with the high-grade and speciality trade, for which it does not pay the mass-producer to compete.

As in the case of most of the older industrial areas, Birmingham and District for long possessed a very self-centred industrial life. Except for part of its raw materials the area was largely independent of other areas: it was concerned with many special types of product; it developed a peculiar industrial tradition; and although during the first half of the nineteenth century it drew enterprising manufacturers from all parts of the country, by 1860 this migration was dying down and the leading industries were for the most part being carried on by local families with interests confined within the limits of the district. This self-centred characteristic persisted until the rise of the new industries after the eighties. Then, although many of the rising trades grew out of existing forms of local enterprise, others were initiated by promoters who had no local interests. The extension of the joint-stock-company form of organization during the nineties accentuated this change; and then, when the combination movement began, firms began to be linked up with others in many different parts of the country, and the control of them ceased to be purely local. Thus, to a large extent, the old self-centred character of the industrial district passed away. Yet while this may be true of nearly all the newer trades, many of the older hardware industries remained under the control of families which have long been associated with the area, and held themselves apart from the great national combines which of late have become a leading feature in the industrial structure of Great Britain.

It is more difficult to construct a useful summary of the changes which occurred in the methods of industrial organization, for here the details are almost as important as the general conclusions. A few of the major developments, however, may be outlined. As far as the scale of production was concerned, we have seen that from the beginning of the great industrial era which culminated in the boom of the early seventies the producing units fell into two main groups according to the industries with which they were connected. The manufacturers of pig- and wrought-iron and of heavy articles required large plants and the association of masses of employees, and from the end of the eighteenth century firms in such industries were conducted on a large scale. These units in the heavy trades, together with those in the earlier stages of production, such as the rolling mills, made extensive use of steam-driven machinery. The finished-metal trades, on the other hand, though dependent to some extent on the great firms which turned out raw materials and semi-products, were for the most part conducted in very small establishments down to the seventies. In such trades the domestic worker, relying on a factor or large manufacturer for his working capital and his market, and the shop owner, who had assumed some of the work of co-ordinating the different processes, but who was still financially dependent on the factor, were the typical figures. This form of organization existed even for the production of complex articles which required the labour of many skilled craftsmen, and in several trades the manufacturing process was subdivided among a multitude of specialists, each with his own establishment. These methods could be followed in the finished-metal trades, because many of them were still dependent on the labour of the skilled craftsmen and made use of simple machines to which no power was applied. The existence of opportunities for hiring power for particular processes, however, enabled the small unit to persist even when mechanical methods came to be applied to certain operations. Thus the main contrast was between industries which produced massive articles and required a great deal of power-machinery, and those which turned out small products mainly by manual methods. In these small-scale industries the key position was held by the factor, whose functions varied in detail from trade to trade, but whose main responsibilities lay in initiating and financing production and in marketing the goods. Sometimes he had numbers of domestic workers dependent on him, whom he supplied with raw materials and whose work he co-ordinated. In other trades the shop owner, though dependent on the factor for marketing his products and for much of his working capital, assumed the task of co-ordination.

If most of the industries which produced finished goods were still conducted in small workshops, there were a few exceptions. The cut-nail, pin and wood-screw manufacturers, for example, had factories in the sixties; for to these products automatic machinery had long been applied, and the older methods of handicraft had passed away. In certain other trades, moreover, the large unit had appeared, not because of any mechanical developments, but because a method of production had been adopted which necessitated the splitting up of the process among a large number of semi-skilled workers whose labour required careful co-ordination. The pen trade was an instance of this type of manufacture. Finally, large units existed in many industries in which the small producer was still typical and in which the large manufacturer had no advantage, as far as the economies of production were concerned, over the small man. The existence of factories in such trades could be ascribed to the fact that certain makers had built up for themselves a reputation for superior quality and so attracted to themselves a large share of the demand. These factories usually served different classes of customer from those for which the small producer catered, and these were necessarily self-contained in character in order to ensure control over the quality of the workmanship and of the materials.

The internal organization of the larger units presented many interesting features; for we have seen that in most of them control was decentralized and delegated by the employer to subcontractors. This system grew up naturally with the rise of the factory from the older methods of industrial organization, and the relation of overhand and employer bore a strong resemblance to those of shop owner and factor. The practice of charging deductions for materials, tools and power from the wages of factory employees was another survival of the factor system carried into a later stage of development. The factory of the sixties and seventies, indeed, showed by its organization that it was even then regarded as something exceptional, and that it had not by that time shaken itself free from older systems of administration. Thus the main stages of industrial organization, as shown by the trades of the locality during the period, may be grouped as follows:

A. *Factor Stage :*
    (*a*) Domestic System Proper.
    (*b*) Shop-Owner System.
B. *Factory Stage :*
    (*a*) Subcontracting System.
    (*b*) System of Centralized Control.

The contrast between the typical producing unit in the finished-metal trades and that in the heavier industries persisted without much modification until the great depression of 1875-1886. From then onwards, however, methods of industrial organization changed profoundly. In the iron and steel trades the exhaustion of the local mines and the rise of production in more favourable localities caused a break-up of many of the older integrated firms; but the rise of the new steel industries and the growth of larger blast-furnaces caused a great increase in the size of producers in those stages of the industry, though their number in this district was few. But the most far-reaching changes occurred among the industries producing finished goods; for most of these became factory trades during the twenty-five years preceding the war. The causes of this transformation were numerous. The coming of the gas-engine, which destroyed the old system of hiring steam-power, facilitated the introduction of mechanical methods into the smaller workplaces and prepared the way for the factory. Changes of fashion, by bringing demands for simpler types of domestic fittings and ornaments, had a similar effect on certain trades, since the result was to make mechanical methods applicable to the manufacture of products which had previously been turned out by skilled craftsmen. The new demands for engineering components which lent themselves to machine production carried the tendency further in industries which were able to change over from hardware articles to these fresh classes of product. At the same time the stimulus of foreign competition compelled manufacturers in the threatened industries to reorganize their methods and forced the inefficient out of production. But probably the strongest factor was the supersession of wrought-iron as the staple material of the metal-using trades by cheap basic steel; for this lent itself readily to manipulation by presses and by machine tools.

While the scale of production was rising in the finished-metal trades, the administration of the factories was undergoing a change. Subcontracting and the associated system of deductions were tending to disappear, and the modern type of factory began to become typical of the area. This development was very gradual in the older trades; but for the area as a whole it was accelerated by the transformation in the relative importance of different manufactures, by the decay of certain ancient hardware trades, which were conservative in their organization, and by the rise of the new industries which from the first had adopted modern methods of factory administration. But in all trades in which the typical producing unit was growing in size, and becoming more self-contained, the increasing complexity of the productive processes and the necessity of careful co-ordination of the various departments brought a need for highly centralized control, and so resulted in the gradual disappearance of the sub-contracting system. The replacement of empirical by scientific methods of production in the metal trades had a like result. As this occurred there was a corresponding increase in the functions of the office and the technical staffs, the rise of costing systems, of works laboratories and of modern administrative methods. The labour force, moreover, which had at one time been made up in most trades of skilled specialists, tended over a wide range of industries to become divided into two distinct classes— the skilled tool-makers and tool-setters on one hand, and semi-skilled machine operatives on the other. There was, consequently, an approximation of the type of labour employed in a variety of metal manufactures owing to the similarity of the mechanical methods in use in many of them.

The other tendencies which appeared towards the end of the nineteenth century can be only briefly referred to. In many industries there was a movement towards the standardization and simplification of products, though this had not gone very far by 1914. In some the loss of older markets resulted in a broadening of the basis of manufacture; while in others, notably in the engineering industry, the growth in demand brought a tendency towards specialization. Further, the trades of the area which had long been in the hands of highly competitive family businesses were swept by the combination movement, and began to be linked up with manufacturing enterprises in other parts of the country. During the later nineties, when this movement first became general, the typical combine was the price association; but in the early years of the new century this form gave place to pools and consolidations. Among the various classes of combine which were formed the most interesting consisted of the Birmingham Alliances. These were peculiar to and characteristic of the West Midlands, where the relations of employers and of employed were friendly, and they

would obviously have failed to meet even with their limited
degree of success in areas in which hostile feelings existed between masters and men. With the rise in the scale of operations,
moreover, the factor lost his dominant position. The financing
and the control of manufacture passed from him, and in many
trades the producers began to make attempts to get into direct
touch with the retailer, or even the consumer. This tendency
may be attributed mainly to the growth in the burden of overhead charges in the larger businesses; for this made it more
necessary for them to ensure an even flow of orders. The increasing severity of foreign competition also had its effect; while
in the case of the engineering industries the movement was due
to the obligation of firms to supply post-sales service, for which
the merchant or factor was unfitted. The tendency was all part
of the general movement towards the development of more highly
self-contained businesses during the period.

The war stimulated all these changes. The combination
movement has extended, and the practice of the Government
of dealing with trade associations rather than with individual
manufacturers between 1914 and 1918 created a habit of co-
operation among business men which has persisted. Since 1914,
moreover, first in response to the urgent needs of the nation and
later in consequence of foreign competition, there has occurred
a rise in the general level of technical knowledge and of scientific
practice among manufacturers. Methods of administration have
been improved, and the old systems of subcontracting and of
deductions have practically died out. One of the most marked
developments during the last fourteen years has been the great
increase in the mechanical equipment of local industries, and
many trades which before the war were still largely the home
of handicraft have since come to rely on complex plants of
machinery. In all save the failing industries the scale of production has been greatly extended, and the factory system has
become typical of nearly all the leading trades. The small unit
still has a place both in the older manufactures — such as
jewellery—and in the performance of operations subsidiary to
those carried on in great factories; but the domestic worker and
the shop owner are no longer representative figures in the life
of Birmingham and District.

In conclusion, a few observations may be made concerning

2 F

the probable future development of the area. It is obviously not possible to consider this question in any detail; but the broad changes which are likely to occur, the main trend of industrial growth, may be predicted with some degree of confidence. This confidence can be justified by the fact that our conclusions are based on a careful observation of the main tendencies which have been influencing the industrial structure of the district for many years past. In the first place, it seems certain that the future of Birmingham and District lies with the newer manufactures—-with the cycle, motor, electrical, engineering, artificial-silk, rubber, and the food and drink trades. These are the industries which have shown the most marked expansion of late years, and towards their products an increasing volume of demand is likely to be directed. They are the best organized of the local trades and have, on the whole, attracted the highest grade of ability. In many of them the area has an advantage over other centres, partly because of the character of its industrial life, its labour supply and the multiplicity of subsidiary industries, and partly because of its excellent position as a distributing centre for the home market. The inland position of the area does not impose any very serious handicap on the development of an export trade in such highly manufactured commodities, of which the cost of transport to the coast is relatively low, and most of these new industries have developed a fairly large foreign trade during recent years, which has done much to balance the decline in the export of other classes of local products. These manufactures, then, are likely to mould to an increasing extent the character of the area's industrial life. The tendency for manufactures in the older trades to change over from the production of hardware to that of engineering components will probably continue. The more alert firms have already transformed themselves in this way, and the small metal trades are likely, therefore, to become in a greater degree complementary to the main concern of the district, engineering.

Yet the prospects are bright for a number of the more ancient industries, which, though they may not expand at the rate of the newer trades, may hope to maintain a degree of prosperity by adapting themselves to serve new needs and by a resort to better methods of production. The non-ferrous trades, for example, are likely to reflect the prosperity which the newer engineering trades, now their leading customer, will probably continue to enjoy; while the lock and the edge-tool industries are instances of ancient manufactures which have succeeded in warding off foreign competition by a reorganization of their productive methods. These may hope for continued success. But there are others which will never see again the days of their greatness. Some of these are handicrafts which have been destroyed by the introduction of machinery—*e.g.* the wrought-nail and the gun trades. Others have been permanently injured by changes in domestic equipment and in the manner of life of the people—*e.g.* the cast-iron hollow-ware and the tinplate-ware trades. Among the other industries which can never hope again for the steady expansion of the Victorian era are those which relied largely on foreign markets, and which have suffered from the inevitable rise of industries abroad—*e.g.* the wrought-chain, the needle and the pen trades. In certain manufactures the foreigner has established a firm hold over the home market, which was previously served by Birmingham and District, either because local manufacturers have clung to traditional methods of production, as in the flint-glass trade, or because foreigners have the advantage of cheaper raw materials, as in the steel hollow-ware and wire-nail industries, or because climatic conditions have given producers abroad advantages over those of the West Midlands, as in the case of certain classes of buttons. In these industries the area is never likely to recover any large share of its lost trade. Speculation is more dangerous concerning industries which have been adversely affected by changes of fashion, like the jewellery, metal-bedstead and pin trades. It is in the largest of these, the jewellery trade, that there is most hope of a substantial revival. As for the heavy industries, coal- and iron-mining will never be of further importance in the Black Country, and, since these raw materials are exhausted, the iron and steel industry is never likely to make a recovery. Indeed, it is probable that firms in this industry, as in the structural engineering trades, will shift the seat of their operations to the coast, as many have already done. Yet, if for many industries the decline in magnitude which they have suffered is never likely to be reversed, there will remain for most of them a certain trade in specialities and in high-grade goods, which it does not pay producers in other centres who cater for the mass trade to touch, and in the production of which this district has the advantage of skilled labour and long experience. The manufacture of expensive flint-glass ware, sporting guns and saddlery, and of high-grade wrought-iron is likely to be still retained in the area.

The increasing reliance of the area on other centres at home and abroad for raw materials and semi-products has caused alarm. Yet this development has been inevitable, and it need not be regarded as serious, since even in the hey-day of the older industrialism Birmingham and District drew the larger part of its raw materials from outside sources. Even if the large imports of foreign crude steel which have flooded the local markets of late years are unlikely to continue, the area will always have to get by far the larger proportion of its materials from other industrial centres. It will become increasingly concerned with finishing processes and with the manufacture of composite products; yet, inasmuch as both labour and organization can usually secure higher rewards in those trades than in the manufacture of cruder products, this tendency is far from being unfavourable to future prosperity.

Little need be said concerning the future scale of local industry. The size both of the typical plant and of the typical concern is likely to grow considerably in the next few years with the development of the newer trades, the mechanization of the old and the extension of the combination movement. But room is always likely to be found for a considerable number of small units. Most of these will be found in the older industries, engaged on products to which modern factory methods are not applicable; yet even the new industries are likely to provide opportunities for small men in the subsidiary processes of manufacture. The survival of the small unit is to be regarded with favour; for it gives opportunities for men without large capital to exercise the qualities of leadership in a much higher degree than is possible in the case of a salaried manager of a great concern. The existence of the small firm, indeed, is likely to preserve the qualities of flexibility and adaptability which the West Midlands has always shown, and to make it possible for the area to seize upon new industries in their initial stages. This is shown by the fact that many of the trades which were introduced into Birmingham and District during the last forty years, and which have done so much to transform its industrial character, were built up by small men who were originally concerned with other trades.

Finally, it may be suggested that our conclusions concerning the main trend of economic change within this area have an important bearing on speculations with regard to the future development of British industry as a whole. For, being an old metal centre, Birmingham and District has been the first to be affected by the forces of change, and during the last forty years it has been passing through a period of transformation which the other metallurgical districts have reached only within the last decade. As we have seen, the direction of industrial development since the great depression of the seventies and early eighties has been in this area away from the manufacture of semi-products and of the smaller and simpler articles towards highly finished and highly composite products. In certain trades the earlier manufacturing processes have passed to other centres at home and abroad, and the district has been left with only the finishing operations. Yet this transition, if it caused for a time economic dislocation and social distress, has been effected without any permanent decline in prosperity, and has, indeed, imposed no serious check on the progress of the area. The same forces which have so greatly modified the economic life of Birmingham and the Black Country have now begun to make themselves felt throughout the country, and it seems reasonable to hope that the success which has attended the transference of industrial interests in this one district may also be attained by the country as a whole. It is evident, at all events, that a shrinkage of certain of the older staple industries is not to be confused with a permanent decline in economic greatness, provided that manufacturers are alert to discover new sources of demand and do not pursue vain hopes of revival in decaying trades. The ancient centres of a great industry are inevitably caught at a disadvantage when that industry is established in other districts or in other countries, and is there organized on new and more economical lines. As the history of the local trades shows, the older centres may sometimes succeed in reorganizing their mode of manufacture and may so hold their own; but the existence of obsolete plants and of traditional productive methods imposes a serious handicap on such attempts, and in any case the older districts can never expect to regain their former position of predominance.

For them the greatest hope lies in the development of the new trades in which they have the most marked relative advantages over other centres. And the success of Birmingham and District in effecting a fundamental change in the nature of its industrial interests points to the conclusion that, for the entire country, policy should be directed towards speeding up the inevitable transformation and towards easing the process of transition, rather than towards supporting by artificial means the decaying members of the industrial structure. Only if this policy is followed is British industry as a whole likely to show, and to benefit from, that flexibility and resilience which have been the outstanding features of the economic life of Birmingham and the Black Country.

APPENDICES

APPENDIX A

STATISTICAL TABLES

TABLE I

POPULATION OF BIRMINGHAM AND DISTRICT, 1801-1861

(Estimated from the Census returns)

1801	.	.	.	.	.	.	.	.	187,000
1811	.	.	.	.	.	.	.	.	228,000
1821	.	.	.	.	.	.	.	.	281,000
1831	.	.	.	.	.	.	.	.	369,000
1841	.	.	.	.	.	.	.	.	497,000
1851	.	.	.	.	.	.	.	.	637,000
1861	.	.	.	.	.	.	.	.	819,000

PERCENTAGE INCREASE DURING EACH INTER-CENSAL PERIOD

1801-1811	.	.	.	.	.	.	.	.	21·5
1811-1821	.	.	.	.	.	.	.	.	23·4
1821-1831	.	.	.	.	.	.	.	.	31·4
1831-1841	.	.	.	.	.	.	.	.	34·6
1841-1851	.	.	.	.	.	.	.	.	28·0
1851-1861	.	.	.	.	.	.	.	.	28·7

TABLE II

POPULATION OF BIRMINGHAM AND DISTRICT IN 1861

PARISHES AND TOWNSHIPS

Parishes					
Kingswinford	.	.	.	34,257	
Sedgeley	.	.	.	36,637	
Walsall (part of)	.	.	.	37,760	
Wednesbury	.	.	.	21,968	
West Bromwich	.	.	.	41,795	
Handsworth and Soho	.	.	11,459	
Tipton	.	.	.	28,870	
Dudley	.	.	.	44,975	
Oldswinford	.	.	.	22,958	
Hales Owen	.	.	.	29,293	
Rowley Regis	.	.	.	19,785	
Harborne	.	.	.	16,996	
Darlaston	.	.	.	12,884	

Birmingham	.	.	.	212,621
Aston	.	.	.	94,995
Edgbaston	.	.	.	12,907
Sutton Coldfield	.	.	.	4,662
King's Norton	.	.	.	13,634
Northfield	.	.	.	3,130

Townships				
Wolverhampton	.	.	.	60,860
Wednesfield	.	.	.	8,553
Willenhall	.	.	.	17,256
Bilston	.	.	.	24,364
Great Barr	.	.	.	1,075
Redditch	.	.	.	5,441

819,135

TABLE III

POPULATION OF BIRMINGHAM AND DISTRICT, 1861-1921

1861	819,000
1871	948,000
1881	1,106,000
1891 (Coventry included from this year onwards) . .	1,289,000
1901	1,483,000
1911	1,640,000

1911 (with the additional population falling within the new boundaries of Birmingham)	1,698,000
1921	1,855,000

PERCENTAGE INCREASE DURING EACH INTER-CENSAL PERIOD

1861-1871	15·6
1871-1881	16·6
1881-1891	16·5
1891-1901	15·0
1901-1911	10·7

1901-1911 (with the additional population falling within the new boundaries of Birmingham included for 1911) . .	14·6
1911-1921	9·2

TABLE IV

POPULATION OF CERTAIN PARISHES AND TOWNSHIPS, 1861-1891

The object of this Table is to illustrate the effects of the great depression on the population of certain towns and districts within the area. The first group includes townships and parishes in which the population either declined or increased very slightly between 1871 and 1881. The second group consists of places the population of which increased between 1871 and 1881, but fell during the following decade.

	1861	1871	1881	1891
(1)				
Bilston (township) . . .	24,364	24,188	22,730	23,453
Sedgeley (parish)	36,637	37,355	36,574	36,860
Wednesbury (parish) . . .	21,968	25,030	24,566	25,347
Darlaston (parish) . . .	12,884	14,416	13,563	14,422
Willenhall (township) . .	17,256	18,146	18,461	19,366
Kingswinford (parish) . .	34,257	35,041	35,767	36,411
(2)				
Tipton (parish)	28,870	29,445	30,013	29,314
Dudley (parish)	44,975	43,782	46,233	45,724
Stourbridge (township) . .	8,783	9,376	9,757	9,386

TABLE V

NUMBERS ENGAGED IN CERTAIN INDUSTRIES ACCORDING TO THE CENSUS RETURNS, 1861-1911

The figures cover the employment in Warwickshire, Staffordshire and Worcestershire, except when otherwise stated.

Industry	1861	1871	1881	1891	1901	1911
Brass, copper, etc.	10,700	11,700	19,300	28,700	30,100	32,000
Small-arms	8,400	8,500	5,400	5,800	5,300	4,100
Jewellery and plate (Warwickshire only)	6,800	9,600	14,600	..	16,000	18,400
Button	5,600	5,300	5,500	4,400	3,700	4,800
Pen (Warwickshire only)	1,300	1,500	2,600	3,100	3,800	3,700
Nail	19,300	17,700	14,800	7,900	4,200	3,200
Glass	4,500	5,500	5,000	5,100	4,900	5,100
Saddlery, harness, whip	3,600	5,800	6,300	8,700	10,900	8,900
Tanning and currying	1,500	1,600	1,700	} 3,200	4,900	{ 2,100
Leather-goods (bags, etc.)	..	400	800			{ 4,700
Lock (Staffordshire only)	3,700	5,200	6,200	6,600	5,100	5,600
Needle (Warwickshire and Worcestershire)	3,500	4,300	3,900	3,300	} 3,900	4,200
Pin (Warwickshire only)	200	300	400	500		
Tinplate-ware	2,600	3,400	4,800	5,600	6,400	6,000
Screw	1,500	1,400	} 5,300	6,700	8,100	12,600
Nut, bolt, rivet	..	..				
Wire-drawing, weaving, etc.	1,500	2,000	2,100	2,300	3,000	4,000
Brush and broom	1,300	1,400	1,600	1,900	1,900	2,100
Watch and clock (Warwickshire only)	3,500	4,200	5,000	5,000	3,800	2,300
Umbrella and stick	700	600	1,100	900	900	800
Chemical	500	500	600	1,000	1,800	2,600
Paper, stationery, box-making	..	2,200	3,300	5,400	5,900	6,600
Weighing and testing machine	..	700	1,000	1,400	1,600	3,100
Railway carriage and wagon	..	..	1,300	..	3,200	6,100
Electrical-apparatus	..	..	100	700	3,500	9,100
Chain and anchor	3,100	3,800	4,000	5,400	5,800	6,600
Cycle	..	..	1,700	8,300	} 17,700	{ 22,500
Motor	..	..	..	..		{ 16,800
India-rubber and gutta-percha goods (Warwickshire only)	..	300	500	500	1,700	3,400
Cocoa and chocolate (Warwickshire and Worcestershire)	..	..	..	..	2,000	3,800

NOTE.—Conclusions concerning the development or decline of industries during the period covered by this history have been based on evidence obtained from sources other than the Census. Apart from the fact that an industry may increase or decrease in magnitude without any corresponding change being shown in the returns for that industry in successive Census reports, accurate comparisons are impossible because of differences in the methods of compilation from Census to Census. Thus, up to 1871, persons described as retired from any stated occupation were classed with that occupation, while from 1881 they were classified as unoccupied. Further, up to 1881 certain types of workers—

TABLE VI

NUMBERS ENGAGED IN CERTAIN INDUSTRIES ACCORDING TO THE CENSUS RETURNS, 1911-1921

Industry	Warwickshire, Worcestershire and Staffordshire		Birmingham and District
	1911	*1921*	*1921*
Watch and clock (Warwickshire only)	2,300 ⎫		2,500 ⎧
Jewellery and plate (Warwickshire only)	18,400 ⎭	30,100	25,600 ⎩
Brass, copper, etc.	32,000	40,100	37,700
Small-arms	4,100	3,200	3,200
Button	4,800	3,800	3,800
Nail	3,200	2,200	2,000
Chain and anchor	6,600	5,900	5,700
Glass	5,100	6,600	5,400
Tanning and currying . . .	2,100	2,200	1,400
Leather-goods (bags, etc.) . .	4,700 ⎱		4,500 ⎰
Saddlery, harness, whips . .	8,900 ⎰	7,400	2,300 ⎱
Lock (Staffordshire) . . .	5,600	6,200	6,500
Needle [1] (Warwickshire and Worcestershire)	4,200 ⎱	5,900	3,200 ⎰
Pin (Warwickshire only)	⎰		1,300 ⎱
Nut, bolt, screw and rivet . .	12,600	18,300	18,200
Wire-drawing, weaving, etc. . .	4,000	2,300	2,300
Paper, stationery, box-making .	6,600	5,800	4,100
Brush and broom	2,100	1,700	1,400
Weighing and testing machine .	3,100	5,300	4,800
Railway carriage and wagon . .	6,100	11,600	10,600
Electrical apparatus (excluding electricians)	9,100	25,800	16,400

e.g. clerks, porters and engine-drivers—had been classed with the trade with which their work was connected, but in the Census of that year and in the two succeeding Censuses they were collected under their occupational headings only. In other words, for the Censuses of 1861 and 1871 the industrial classification was more closely followed than it was between 1881 and 1901; while in 1911 figures showing the industrial classification were again available. For the local trades, however, the most serious factor which has affected comparability has consisted of changes in the definition and in the grouping of the various trades and occupations. Thus in some Censuses locksmiths have been grouped with bellhangers; in others a separate figure for the former has been given. Sometimes the figure for a certain trade has included both dealers and makers; in succeeding Census reports the makers have been shown separately. These changes have in some trades seriously reduced the value of comparison between different Censuses; and the Census figures quoted in the text and in these Tables must be regarded as affording only a general indication of alterations in the numbers engaged in each industry during our period, and as additional evidence in support of conclusions based mainly on material drawn from other sources (cf. *Census of England and Wales*, 1911, vol. x., part i., p. v. *et seq.*).

[1] Covers fishhook manufacture in 1921.

TABLE VI.—*continued*

NUMBERS ENGAGED IN CERTAIN INDUSTRIES ACCORDING TO THE CENSUS RETURNS, 1911-1921

Industry	Warwickshire, Worcestershire and Staffordshire		Birmingham and District [1]
	1911	*1921*	*1921*
Cycle	22,500⎫	67,700	64,800
Motor	16,800⎭		
Other vehicles and motor and cycle accessories	..	17,600	(*Accessories only*) 14,900
Cocoa and chocolate (Warwickshire and Worcestershire) . . .	3,800	..	8,500
Chemical	2,600	4,700	4,100
India-rubber and gutta-percha (Warwickshire)	3,400	11,500	11,500
Maltings, breweries and mineral waters	..	..	5,700
Metal bedsteads and wire mattresses	5,600	3,900	3,900
Tubes, iron and steel . . .	7,300	16,800	16,700
Cutlery and small tools . . .	..	11,200	10,400
Boilers and tanks	3,100	3,700	3,500
Stove, grate, range, fire-iron . .	3,600	2,400	2,000 [2]
Safes	..	..	1,000
Constructional engineering . .	..	4,400	4,200
Harness, furniture and cart gear .	..	..	2,900
Hollow-ware, iron and steel . .	..	9,800	9,100
Pig-iron (blast-furnaces) . . .	..	..	1,800
Puddling furnaces and iron-rolling mills	..	..	10,700
Steelworks and steel-rolling mills .	..	..	7,400
Ironworks (other branches) . .	..	..	1,200
General iron foundries . . .	..	..	14,500
Steel foundries	..	..	600
Forging (not chains and anchors) .	..	..	4,600
Machine tools	..	..	4,100
Steam locomotives and railway plant	..	..	1,400
Stationary engines and power transmission	..	..	3,700

[1] For the Census definition of Birmingham and District see page 5.
[2] Excluding fire-iron trade for 1921.

TABLE VII

MINERAL OUTPUT OF SOUTH STAFFORDSHIRE AND WORCESTERSHIRE

The figures in this Table cover the whole of South Staffordshire, including the district north of the Great Bentley Fault, and so, as far as the coal production is concerned, they differ materially from the estimates of the Black Country's output which are given on page 281.

Year			Coal Output	Iron Ore Output	Number of Miners
			(in million tons)	(in thousand tons)	
1855	.	.	7·3	..	..
1858	.	.	5·0	959	..
1860	.	.	5·3	786	..
1865	.	.	10·2	660	27,000
1870	.	.	9·4	450	29,000
1872	.	.	10·6	642	32,000
1876	.	.	10·0	590	33,000
1882	.	.	10·1	177	27,000
1884	.	.	9·7	117	24,000
1887	.	.	9·0	110	22,000
1890	.	.	9·8	53	25,000
1892	.	.	10·0	64	..
1897	.	.	9·3	42	26,000
1900	.	.	9·4	51	29,000
1913	.	.	9·5	32	30,000

TABLE VIII

PRODUCTION OF PIG-IRON IN SOUTH STAFFORDSHIRE AND WORCESTERSHIRE

Year			Output	Year			Output	Year			Output
			(in thousand tons)				(in thousand tons)				(in thousand tons)
1806	.	.	50	1873	.	.	673	1894	.	.	333
1830	.	.	213	1874	.	.	452	1895	.	.	265
1839	.	.	339	1875	.	.	471	1896	.	.	308
1854	.	.	743	1876	.	.	466	1897	.	.	400
1855	.	.	754	1877	.	.	428	1898	.	.	406
1856	.	.	777	1878	.	.	393	1899	.	.	415
1857	.	.	657	1879	.	.	326	1900	.	.	398
1858	.	.	598	1880	.	.	385	1901	.	.	341
1859	.	.	475	1881	.	.	374	1902	.	.	380
1860	.	.	470	1882	.	.	398	1903	.	.	397
1861	.	.	396	1883	.	.	430	1904	.	.	394
1862	.	.	410	1884	.	.	357	1905	.	.	430
1863	.	.	691	1885	.	.	344	1906	.	.	452
1864	.	.	629	1886	.	.	294	1907	.	.	470
1865	.	.	693	1887	.	.	293	1908	.	.	449
1866	.	.	533	1888	.	.	366	1909	.	.	482
1867	.	.	516	1889	.	.	373	1910	.	.	495
1868	.	.	532	1890	.	.	327	1911	.	.	473
1869	.	.	570	1891	.	.	350	1912	.	.	442
1870	.	.	589	1892	.	.	338	1913	.	.	467
1871	.	.	726	1893	.	.	330	1914	.	.	420
1872	.	.	673								

APPENDIX B

BIBLIOGRAPHY

THE most valuable part of the material for this book, as I have explained elsewhere, was obtained by personal inquiry from local firms or from their private histories and catalogues. A good deal of information, however, was gathered from official reports, newspaper articles, and printed records of various kinds, and the more important of these sources are included in this bibliography. The Birmingham Collection in the Birmingham Public Reference Library contains the major part of these works; others were consulted in the public libraries of Wolverhampton and Coventry; while a few were lent by local firms and by private individuals.

OFFICIAL PUBLICATIONS

Census of England and Wales Reports, 1861-1921.

Census of Production Reports, 1907 and 1921.

Commissioners of Patents' Abridgements of Specifications relating to Needles and Pins (1871).

Children's Employment Commission (1862), Reports.

Committee on Industry and Trade Survey of Metal Industries (1928), and *Further Factors in Industrial and Commercial Efficiency* (1928).

Committee on the South Staffordshire Mines Drainage, 1920, Report.

Committee appointed under the Safeguarding of Industries Act on Wrought-Enamelled Hollow-ware Reports, 1925 and 1928.

Committee appointed under the Safeguarding of Industries Act on Aluminium Hollow-ware Report, 1925.

HUNT, R., *Memoirs of the Geological Survey of Great Britain : Mineral Statistics*, 1855-1881 ; continued as *Mineral Statistics of Great Britain* (Home Office Reports), 1882-1896 ; and as *Mines and Quarries, General Report with Statistics*, 1897-1920.

Reports of Inspectors of Factories, 1865-1877 ; continued as *Reports of Chief Inspector of Factories and Workshops*, 1878-1914.

Reports of Inspectors of Mines, 1864-1914.

List of Mines in the United Kingdom (Home Office Reports), 1913.

Local Unemployment Index (Ministry of Labour), 1927-1928.

Ministry of Labour Gazette, 1923-1928.

Royal Commission on the Coal Industry, 1925, Reports.

Royal Commission on the Depression of Trade, 1885, Reports.

United States Department of Commerce Daily Consular and Trade Reports, 1911-1918 ; and *Special Consular Reports*, No 71 (1915) and No. 75 (1916).

BOOKS AND PAMPHLETS

AITKEN, W. C., *Report to the Birmingham Chamber of Commerce on the International Exhibition at Paris* (1867).

AITKEN, W. C., and LINDSEY, G., *British Manufacturing Industries*, vol. iii. (1878).

ALLEN, G. C., *The British Motor Industry* (London and Cambridge Economic Service, Special Memorandum, June 1926).

ARTIFEX and OPIFEX, *The Causes of Decay in a British Industry* (1907).

ASHTON, T. S., *Iron and Steel in the Industrial Revolution* (1924).

BELLIS and MORCOM, *A Factory of Quick-Revolution Engines* (1908).

Birmingham Official Industrial and Commercial Handbook (1919).

Birmingham Chamber of Commerce Reports of Council, 1865-1902.

Birmingham Chamber of Commerce Monthly Journal, 1903-1928.

Brass Trades Arbitration Report, 1900.

British Iron Trade Association Annual Statistical Report, 1894.

BURRITT, E., *Walks in the Black Country and its Green Borderland* (1868).

BUTTER, F. J., *Locks and Lock-making* (1926).

CADBURY BROS. LTD., *The Factory in a Garden*; *Bournville—Work and Play* (1926); and numerous other publications.

CHANCE BROS. & CO. LTD., *A Hundred Years of British Glass-making* (1924).

CURZON, W. D., *The Manufacturing Industries of Worcestershire* (1881).

DALLEY, *The Life Story of W. J. Davis* (1914).

DAVIS, W. J., *A Short History of the Brass Trade* (1892).

Delta Metal Co. Ltd. Catalogue, 11th edition.

DENT, R. K., *The Making of Birmingham* (1894).

DENT, R. K., *Old and New Birmingham* (1880).

DUNCAN, H. O., *The World on Wheels* (1926).

EDWARDS, E., *Personal Recollections of Birmingham and Birmingham Men* (1877).

FAUCHER, L., *Etudes sur l'Angleterre*, tome i. (1856).

GARDINER, A. G., *Life of George Cadbury* (1923).

GRIFFITHS, S., *Iron Trade Circular* (1862).

GRIFFITHS, S., *A Guide to the Iron Trade of Great Britain* (1873).

HACKWOOD, F. W., *Annals of Willenhall* (1908).

HACKWOOD, F. W., *History of Darlaston* (1887).

HACKWOOD, F. W., *History of Tipton* (1891).

HACKWOOD, F. W., *Oldbury and Round About* (1915).

HACKWOOD, F. W., *Sedgeley Researches* (1898).

HACKWOOD, F. W., *Wednesbury Workshops* (1889).

HALL, J. W., *The Life and Work of Joseph Hall* (reprinted from the *Proceedings of the Staffordshire Iron and Steel Institute*, 1916).

HALL, J. W., *Presidential Address on the Iron and Steel Trade* (reprinted from the *Proceedings of the Junior Institution of Engineers, Midland Section*, February 1917).

HAMILTON, H., *The English Brass and Copper Industries to 1800* (1926).

Handbook of Birmingham, British Association Meeting, 1886.

Handbook for Birmingham and the Neighbourhood, British Association Meeting, 1913.

Handbooks (Official), for Tipton (1924), Wednesbury (1924), Dudley (1924), West Bromwich (1927), Walsall (1924).

HAWKES SMITH, W., *Birmingham and South Staffordshire* (1838).

HAWKES SMITH, W., *Birmingham and its Vicinity* (1838).

HILL, S., *Present Rates of Freight to London and Liverpool from the Staffordshire Iron District* (Wolverhampton, 1865).

HINDE, A., *History of Wolverhampton* (1884).

HINGLEY, N., & SONS LTD., *High-Class Bar Iron.*

HIPKINS, W. E., *The Wire Rope and its Applications* (1896).

JAFFRAY, J., *Hints for a History of Birmingham* (1856-1857).

JEANS, S., *The Iron Trade of Great Britain* (1904).

JEFFCOCK, J. T., *The Original Wolverhampton Guide* (1884).

JONES, W. H., *The Story of Japan, Tinplate Working, Bicycle and Galvanizing Trades in Wolverhampton* (1900).

KETTLE, R., *The Ten-Yard Coal* (1864).

KIRBY, BEARD & CO. LTD., *A Short Account of the Manufacture of Pins and Needles.*

LANDER, E., *The Birmingham Gun Trade* (1869).

LAWLEY, G. T., *History of Bilston* (1868).

LAWLEY, G. T., *History of Bilston* (1893).

LELAND, *Itinerary* (ed. T. Hearne) (1711).

List of Legal Journeymen Brushmakers and Apprentices for 1874 (Wertheimer Lee & Co.).

LLOYD, G. I. F., *The Cutlery Trades* (1913).

LONES, T. E., *A History of Mining in the Black Country* (reprinted from *The Dudley Herald*, 1898).

MACROSTY, H. W., *The Trust Movement in British Industry* (1907).

NADEN, C., *Further Reliques* (1891).

National Association for the Promotion of Social Science Transactions, 1884.

National Association of Puddlers, Shinglers, etc., General Laws (c. 1870).

National Society of Amalgamated Brassworkers, Annual Reports, 1872-1890.

Observations on the Manufacture of Fire-Arms for Military Purposes (1829).

POOLE, B., *History of Coventry* (1870).

PRATT, E. A., *Trade Unionism and British Industry* (1904).

PRICE, G. A., *Treatise on Fire- and Thief-Proof Depositories* (1856).

RABONE, JOHN, & SONS, *The Carpenter's Slide Rule* (1870).

Records of the School of Mines (1853).

Review of Commerce (a description of leading firms in Birmingham), (1914.)

ROCHE, J. C., *The History, Development and Organization of the Birmingham Jewellery and Allied Trades* (supplement to *The Dial*), (1928).

SCRIVENOR, H., *History of the Iron Trade* (1841).

SHRIMPTON, W., *Notes on a Decayed Needle Land* (reprinted from *The Redditch Indicator*, 1897).

SMIRKE, R. S., *Reports on Birmingham Trades prepared in connection with the Juvenile Employment Exchange* (1913).

Steen & Blacket's Wolverhampton Guide (1871).

STRAUSS, G. L., and Others, *England's Workshops* (1864).

2 G

TANGYE, R., *The Rise of a Great Industry* (1905).

TANGYE BROS. LTD., *A Brief History of the Cornwall Works* (1926).

TAWNEY, R. H., *Minimum Rates in the Chain-making Industry* (1914).

TAYLOR, L. B., *A Brief History of the Westley Richards Firm* (1913).

The Birmingham Small Arms Co. Ltd., and its Associated Companies (Works Publication, 1924).

The Non-Ferrous Metal Trades (Kynoch Press, 1924).

TIMMINS, S., *Birmingham and the Midland Hardware District* (1866).

TIMMINS, S., *History of Warwickshire* (1889).

TURBERVILLE, T. C., *Worcestershire in the Nineteenth Century* (1852).

UNDERHILL, A., *A Popular Survey of the South Staffordshire Mines Drainage Act* (1873).

Victoria County History of Warwickshire.

Victoria County History of Worcestershire.

WALTERS, P., *The Wolverhampton Lock Trade* (1864).

WHITE, W., *History, Gazetteer and Directory of Staffordshire* (1851).

Wolverhampton and South Staffordshire Guide (1898).

WOODWARD, C. J., *Manufacturing Industries* in the *British Association Handbook*, Birmingham Meeting, 1886.

WRIGHT, G. W., *Chronicles of the Birmingham Chamber of Commerce* (1913).

WRIGHT, J., *History of Willenhall* (Wolverhampton Public Library).

UNPUBLISHED THESES (BIRMINGHAM UNIVERSITY LIBRARY)

FOX, A., *The Cycle Trade.*

HENN, K., *The Hand-made Nail Trade of Dudley and District.*

SANDILANDS, G. N., *The Midland Glass Industry.*

ARTICLES IN NEWSPAPERS AND JOURNALS

Birmingham and her Manufactures in *The Leisure Hour* (1853).

Birmingham Glass Works in *Household Words* (March 1852).

HARBORD, F. W., and LAW, E. F., *The British Iron and Steel Industry* in the *Proceedings of the Empire Mining and Metallurgical Congress* (1924).

History of the Growth of Birmingham Industry in *The Birmingham Gazette and Express* (November 2, 1911).

HOBBS, R. G., *A Midland Tour* in *The Leisure Hour* (1872).

Daily Telegraph Supplement on *The Safeguarding of Industry* (July 31, 1928).

Labour and the Poor in *The Birmingham Morning News* (1850-1851).

LAPWORTH, C., *The Geology of the Birmingham District* in the *Proceedings of the Geologists' Association* (August 1898).

Manchester Guardian Commercial Supplement (January 5, 1922).

Midland Captains of Industry in *The Birmingham Gazette and Express* (1907-1908).

MULLINS, G. W., *The Economics of the Copper, Brass and Nickel-Silver Industries* in the *Proceedings of the Empire Mining and Metallurgical Congress* (1924).

Newspaper Cuttings on *Birmingham Industries*, 2 volumes, 1863-1880 (Birmingham Reference Library).

Newspaper Cuttings on *Birmingham Industry and Commerce*, 1914-1927 (Birmingham Reference Library).

Our Industries in *Hardware, Metals and Machinery* (October and November 1875).

Pictures of the People in *The Birmingham Morning News* (1871).

SMITH, D. J., *The Need for a Wider Outlook in Automobile Engineering* in the *Proceedings of the Institution of Automobile Engineers* (1922-1923).

The Black Country in *The Edinburgh Review* (April 1863).

The Times, Birmingham Number (October 2, 1912).

Work and Wages in East Worcestershire in *The Globe* (August 12, 1880).

Workshops of Great Britain in *The British Engineering Export Journal* (May 1925).

INDEX

For Product Safety Concerns and Information please contact our EU
representative GPSR@taylorandfrancis.com Taylor & Francis Verlag GmbH,
Kaufingerstraße 24, 80331 München, Germany

Printed and bound by CPI Group (UK) Ltd, Croydon, CR0 4YY
08/05/2025
01864351-0004